Collegiate English Handbook

FIFTH EDITION

Francis L. Fennell

Chair, Department of English
Loyola University Chicago

COLLEGIATE PRESS

Collegiate Press
San Diego, California

Executive editor: Christopher Stanford
Senior editor: Steven Barta
Senior developmental editor: Jackie Estrada
Design and production: Christopher Davis
Illustrations: Rick Geary
Cover design: John Odam

Library of Congress Control Number: 2002110566
ISBN: 0-939693-59-3

Printed in the United States of America

10 9 8 7 6 5 4 3 2 1

*For Kay
and for Monica, Claire, and Mark,
all of whom love good writing*

Contents

Preface:
To the Student

This book assumes that you want to learn how to write better. Not that you are especially cheerful about it, mind you—few people like tasks that have no clearly defined beginning and end and for which progress is so hard to measure. But in my experience, most students really do recognize the need to improve their writing skills. Their attitude is usually a kind of resigned willingness.

If you have that resigned willingness, you are on solid ground. "Writing is an important skill"—you've heard the cliché countless times. And like so many clichés, it just happens to be true. When National Institute of Education researchers asked 4,000 college graduates what courses they would have taken in college if they had known what they know now in their careers, their number one response was more writing courses.

So improving your writing is an eminently practical step. The problem is that many students spend more energy yearning for it than doing it. They substitute the wish for the work.

The reason is that writing, unlike most other subjects, makes elastic requirements on your time. Twenty calculus problems may take a certain number of hours. But when you're finished, you're really finished. A writing assignment, on the other hand, is often given in terms of a word or page limit. When the 500 words are on paper, it might seem as if you are really finished here, too. But you're not—if you want to write well, that is. Those 500 words need to be gone over a second time, a third time, a fourth time—whatever it takes to make it the best writing you can produce. The difference between students who improve their writing during a com-

> *What is written without effort is in general read without pleasure.*
> —*Samuel Johnson*

position course and those who don't lies not so much in desire as in the latter group's willingness to stretch their elastic time limit—to write a third draft, or to proofread, or to revise a graded paper. If you make that second effort, your writing can and will improve.

Let's assume you have this second kind of willingness, as well as the resigned willingness that almost all students have. Here is how this book can help you:

1. Your instructor may assign the handbook as he or she would assign any other textbook. In other words, you may be asked to read certain chapters or sections of chapters. This book has been written so that it can be read continuously, one section or chapter leading into another. It is also written so that you can understand it. Exercises at the ends of the major parts of each chapter give you an important chance to test yourself on the skills you have been acquiring. Notice, by the way, that the example sentences, in the exercises and in the text itself, are taken from works by professional writers and by student writers like you.

2. Your instructor may ask you to use *The Collegiate English Handbook* as a resource. When your papers show certain weaknesses, you will be asked to consult the appropriate section of the handbook and make whatever changes are necessary. If you will be using the handbook in this way, remember that every problem covered in the text is listed in the index. Each section mentions the many possible abbreviations, symbols, or code words your instructor might use on your paper. These symbols, along with the numbered chapter sections and the list of symbols on the inside back cover of this book, should make it easy for you to find what you need. The exercises at the ends of the major parts of each chapter can help you test your knowledge.

3. You may use *The Collegiate English Handbook* as a reference book. In fact, after your composition course is over, you might be keeping the book for just this purpose. Here again the index and the list of symbols on the inside back cover will be important location aids. The sections you will probably find the most valuable are Chapter 6 on grammar, Chapters 7 and 8 on conventions such as punctuation and capitalization, Chapters 12 and 13 on research papers, and the Glossaries of Grammatical Terms and Usage.

One more thing: writing is important and practical, yes. But it need not be approached in hushed tones, as if you were conversing in an operating room during open-heart surgery. In this book, you will find a more personal style than you may be accustomed to in most textbooks. You will also find some cartoons and some apt quotations. We have an important subject, but it should never appear to be a grim one.

F.L.F.

Preface: To the Instructor

This book offers several important advantages to you as the instructor.

First, the text is a teaching handbook. Each section has been written with one question in mind: Is this explanation detailed enough so a student can understand it and use it? That is not to say that the writing is below college level. Rather, my approach has been to take into account the student's perspective and background and then to make the explanations as clear as possible. Macaulay's dictum that "nothing is so useless as a general maxim" ought to have special application to handbooks. There are no big red-letter RULES here. In their place are attempts to discuss writing, with an emphasis on understanding the process of writing—how one *does* it, not how one corrects it. If certain linguistic patterns must be changed, as at times they must, the emphasis is on understanding *why* mistakes are made—no one makes them on purpose—and what can be done about them.

Second, I have tried to give this book both a logical structure and clear transitions. Deliberately absent is the bewildering and discouraging chemistry-text appearance that handbooks so often adopt. Consequently, you can assign it to a class the way you would any other textbook—working from the first chapter to the last, for example, using the exercises to strengthen the students' mastery of each skill. Yet the chapter subsections and other signposts also allow students to use the book conveniently as a reference work, if you or they prefer. A special feature is the listing of the alternative correction symbols that might apply to a particular topic or section. Thus, if you use symbols you can continue with whatever system you find natural, without having to adopt the chart used in the back of the book unless you wish to do so.

Third, the advice this handbook offers is as up to date as possible. For example, it assumes that students are just as likely to be composing with word processors and e-mailing their papers as they are to be typing or writing longhand and that they are just as likely to be researching on the Internet as they are to be browsing library shelves. This book also distinguishes between severe faults and less grievous ones, between genuine errors and matters of taste. Whenever practical, this advice reflects recent research in stylistics and in the composing process. Guidance is desirable, but it need not be prescriptive or pontifical. *The Collegiate English Handbook* respects the diversity and flexibility of modern English, summarizing the practice of good writers rather than simply issuing orders, such as "Do not do *X*" or "A writer should never use *Z*."

Fourth, this handbook gives lengthier treatment to the problems students encounter more often. Research into student error patterns gives us the data needed for proportioning the emphasis according to the frequency or severity of the problem. Concretely, this means relatively more intensive discussions of such matters as run-on sentences, sentence fragments, subject-verb agreement, and even spelling. It means a lesser emphasis on mistakes that occur less often, such as capitalization errors or confusing *like* for *as*, although these matters are of course included for those who need them.

Fifth, the great majority of examples, exercises, and sample assignments are drawn from student and professional writing and from actual writing assignments given in a wide variety of courses (not just composition courses). They therefore have the flavor of "real" writing. Because they are words that somebody somewhere really did use, they will not be dismissed as easily as those contrived "Sue and John (is, are) going to the store" example sentences that many books provide. Furthermore, the experiences of professional writers engaged in their craft—men and women from a wide variety of cultural backgrounds—are enlisted wherever they seem appropriate.

Sixth, and perhaps most noticeably (according to users of the previous editions), the tone of this handbook is different from that in other English handbooks. The tone here is more informal, less didactic, reflecting the fact that one human being is speaking to others. Complementing the tone are numerous marginal quotes and some cartoons that provide relevant comments. They offer a respite, but more important, they remind us that writing is indeed part of a larger world "out there." They also help to restore perspective, to make us aware again of the fact that writing is after all an art, not a science. Such material is common enough elsewhere, but somehow it has been excluded from handbooks, precisely the works most in need of some leavening.

The Collegiate English Handbook will succeed or fail on the strength of its ability to teach students what they need to know in terms they can understand. If teaching does not take place in this book—real teaching, not just rule making—then it loses its reason for existence. For unless we see handbooks as more than just compendiums of rules, unless we see how they can be made to both delight and instruct, we ought not write them or publish them or ask students to buy them.

F.L.F.

Acknowledgments

I 'm grateful to the many people whose sympathetic criticism has made this book a better one. Particularly, I want to thank the student reviewers of the first edition (Raymond Bilodeau, Marla Friedman, and Virginia Krause); Harry Burke, Victoria Hughes, Laurel Meredith, Deborah Skozek, and Ellen Tritra, who provided valuable material; and Rita Lynam and Sheryl Hanson, for typing services.

For subsequent editions, special thanks to Paul Messbarger, Micael Clarke, and David Chinitz for valuable comments; to Sheryl Fallucco and Robert and Susan Bowker for making the work proceed more quickly and easily; and especially to James Denigan, whose research on the Internet and whose drafts of sections of Chapters 12 and 13 (plus the Glossary of Internet terms) have proven invaluable. Without his help, his knowledge, and his writing skills, this fifth edition would have been quite literally—impossible.

I am also grateful to Steven Barta, senior editor of Collegiate Press, for his faith in this book; to Christopher Davis for the design, and John Odam for cover design; and especially to Jackie Estrada, who as senior developmental editor carried this project to its completion and whose editorial skills have improved every page. My daughter, Monica Ann Fennell, brought her professional expertise as an editor to the preparation of the index for previous editions.

I have benefited immensely from the suggestions of colleagues at other institutions who commented on the manuscript. The consulting editors and the members of the Advisory Board provided valuable comments from students as well as themselves. Their names are listed on the following pages.

F.L.F.

Consulting Editors

Editorial Advisory Board

1
Words

When meddlesome old Polonius asks Hamlet what he is reading, Hamlet's reply is so literally true as to seem foolish: "Words, words, words." We all use words every day, and yet how difficult it is to use them with meaning, precision, and grace.

Excellent writing involves taking a very familiar item, the word—staple of our daily conversation and of all our reading and writing—and using it with uncommon skill. Excellent writing could be compared to the outstanding performance of a tennis player, a gymnast, or a dancer—someone who takes that most familiar of objects, the human body, and performs feats requiring immense control and skill. We marvel at the performance of a good athlete because we know from our own experience how difficult such feats must be. Similarly, when we see words used with skill and agility, we can appreciate the performance.

Words are the building blocks of language, whether spoken or written. Using them well takes patience and concentration, just as gymnastics or any other physical skill does. Practice over an extended period of time is indispensable.

The good news is that words *are* subject to your control; they *can* be made to do your bidding. Real improvement is possible. Some people may have a natural flair for writing, just as some people have natural athletic ability. But everyone can make noticeable progress if he or she takes sufficient care and practices. To be a great writer requires innate talent and a lifetime of dedication to the craft. Most of us, however, can be satisfied with competence, the ability to write clearly and persuasively. This goal lies quite within your range if you are willing to strive for it.

Even if you grant that such competency is attainable, you might still wonder why you should make such an effort. After all, few who watch an expert gymnast feel compelled to try the parallel bars the next morning. But the time you spend learning to write well has a practical value that should make acquiring such a skill very important to you. If you think about it for a moment, you will realize that ours is a society that more often rewards mental rather than physical attainments. A prospective employer, for example, will probably not care how strong or how swift you are. But he or she will be very interested in the strength and agility of your mind, and one of the ways a mind can be assessed is by its ability to use language skillfully.

I am not saying that everyone who succeeds always writes well. Marrying the boss's son or daughter, inheriting money from a rich aunt, being 7'2" with a devastating hook shot— all of these will do quite well. But if you lack such unusual assets, you need every other advantage you can get. Perhaps the best of these advantages is the ability to make language do what you want it to do.

So that's what this chapter is all about—words, and increasing your ability to use them well. You will learn about the most effective ways to put language to work and also about how your choice of words—or even how you spell those words—can sometimes hinder you from communicating with others.

A. EXPANDING YOUR WORD CHOICES

As a writer, you might create sentences that are absolutely error-free and still lifeless, dull. What's needed is a conscious effort to widen the word choices available to you as a writer. Good writing is vital, engaging, dramatic. Otherwise you will sound like a bureaucrat at a news conference and get just about as much attention.

"Widen the choices." Easy enough to say, but how can it be done? Isn't it difficult to proceed toward a vaguely defined goal, no matter how valuable that goal might be?

Difficulty is not the same as impossibility. There *are* things you can do to improve your writing.

Reading isn't fun; it's indispensable.
—*Woody Allen*

The first suggestion is at once the most obvious and the most difficult: Read more. There is no surer way to develop sensitivity to words. The more you read, the wider your vocabulary becomes, and therefore the easier it is for the "right" words to slip into your consciousness when you write. (Also, later on you'll score higher on the LSAT, the GRE, the GMAT, or the MCAT!)

As you read, you can take a second step: Observe carefully how the piece is written. Note good words and new words. Don't just note them mentally either. If it is at all possible, write down what you observe, maybe even copy down some phrases or sentences that catch your eye.

What should you look for? Try the following five questions. See whether the prose you are reading would justify a yes answer to each question. Then, more important, apply the questions to your own writing. The answers you get, either from your own analysis or from your instructor's, will go a long way toward telling you what kind of work you need to do. The effectiveness of any piece of writing depends on the writer's sensitivity to words.

A1. Is the Language Direct?

Good writing does not belabor the obvious, does not use six words where four will do. And no phoniness either—we like a writer who is blunt, who comes right to the point rather than talking like a witness at a Senate hearing. Here is an example from Tom Wolfe's *The Kandy-Kolored Tangerine-Flake Streamline Baby*, about the New York subway:

> In a way, of course, the subway is the living symbol of all that adds up to lack of status in New York. . . . The whole place is a gross assault on the senses. The noise of the trains stopping or rounding curves has a high-pitched harshness that is difficult to describe. People feel no qualms about pushing whenever it becomes crowded. Your tactile sense takes a crucifying you never dreamed possible. The odors become unbearable when the weather is warm. Between

> platforms . . . lunch counters serve the kind of hot dogs in which you bite through a tensile, rubbery surface and then hit a soft, oleaginous center like cottonseed meal, and the customers sit there with pastry and bread flakes caked around their mouths, belching to themselves so that their cheeks pop out flatulently now and then.

Not a wasted word. The writing is crisp, lively, frank—just like good conversation—and we appreciate Wolfe's directness.

For another example, here is a student paper. The writer recalls the first time he met his scuba-diving instructor and the instructor's girlfriend:

> Mike was about 24 years old, had blond hair, and wore white swim trunks to accentuate his rich tan. He originally came from Indiana. After graduating from a West Coast diving school, he decided to come here, to the Virgin Islands, to teach. Felicia had a picture-book body—I couldn't make up my mind whether to watch Mike's daredevil driving or her belly button. She looked like a California blonde: straight waves of hair bleached by the sun, falling gently on her bronzed shoulders, turquoise eyes surrounded by long jet black lashes, moist lips hiding her shell white teeth until she smiled. Surf spray beaded her long slender legs, giving her a clean, wet look. When she rested her head on Mike's shoulder, while he was trying to drive, and gently caressed his arm, I would have given anything to trade places with him.

Again we appreciate the writer's directness, the confidence we feel that he is making every word count, holding nothing back.

What can happen when a writer is not direct? A lot of things, but unfortunately few of them are good.

Take this example:

> Just as there are many different types of illegal drugs, so there are also many different types of alcohol, all of which are harmful to an individual in one way or another. These can range from beer or wine coolers having the lowest alcohol proof to Everclear which has the highest alcohol proof.

> Although this harm from alcohol is not quite as severe as it is with other drugs, there is still a great risk involved in drinking alcohol. These risks can include violence, accidents, and blackouts or personality changes which can occur when one is in the drunken state.

That was written by a student in a composition class. After some work she was able to shorten it to half its original length—51 words instead of 100—and improve it in the process:

> Alcohol, like illegal drugs, comes in many different types, ranging from beer and wine coolers with the lowest alcohol proof to Everclear with the highest. Although the immediate harm may not be quite as great compared to other drugs, alcohol still involves risks, including violent behavior, accidents, blackouts, and personality changes.

Check some of your own writing. Does every word carry its own weight? Go over what you have written sentence by sentence. What words or phrases or even whole sentences can you cut without diminishing your meaning? It's like pruning a shrub—the more you trim it back, assuming you don't harm an essential part, the better and more luxuriantly it will grow. Be a word ecologist; don't waste a single one. And you needn't worry that your writing will look skimpy or bare, because in a later section we will be discussing how the addition of more details will make your prose still more effective. Cut now so you can add later: It's like tightening your belt at lunchtime so you can enjoy a big dinner.

Another type of wordiness is needless repetition. Here are two examples:

> Even though *the idea* of paddling the kayak scared me, I was still fascinated by *the idea*.

> The decision *that we* shouldn't go was one *that we all* agreed had to be made.

Such repetitions are annoying and lessen the impact of sentences. This is true even when the repetition involves the use of different words:

The frantic pace of life *today* is characteristic of the *modern world.*

It is better to ease such repetitions out of your writing:

Even though the idea of paddling a kayak scared me, I was still fascinated.

The decision not to go was one that we all agreed had to be made.

A frantic pace of life is characteristic of the modern world.

The problem of **wordiness** does not always manifest itself so obviously. Many writers are so addicted to wordiness that they fail to realize its grip on them. They don't just *decide,* they *arrive at a decision.* They don't *try,* they *make an attempt.* Richard Altick has drawn up a list of some of his favorite examples, together with their simpler alternatives; here are some of them:

Wordy	Concise
in an efficient manner	efficiently
in the matter of (in respect to)	about
in many instances	often
avail oneself of	use
is in the process of being	is being
inform us of the reason	tell us why

There are many others: *subject matter* rather than *subject, prior to* rather than *before, undertake* rather than *do.*

The cause of this wordiness disease is unknown. I suspect it comes from the natural desire to impress the reader. *Make an attempt* somehow sounds more impressive than *try.* But it won't fool thoughtful readers—in fact, it will only annoy them. And remember that whatever annoys a good reader interferes with communication, simply by calling attention to itself rather than to the message.

This same cause might be responsible for another debilitating disorder: the **big-word syndrome.** Many writers can't resist the temptation to offer a two-bit word when a nickel one will do. I had a friend in high school who spent ten minutes every day ransacking the dictionary, laying rough hands on whatever big words he could find and then using them indiscriminately in everything he said or

> *I am a Bear of Very Little Brain, and Long words bother me.*
> —*Winnie-the- Pooh*

wrote. Thus, every old lady became a *dowager*, every place a *locality*, every statement a *pronunciamento*. It didn't matter to him if he had the wrong context or the wrong connotation—the fun was in using the biggest words in the humblest places.

This fondness for the big word is becoming all-pervasive in our society. If I look around the city where I live, for example, I find that where once we had dogcatchers, now we have *canine control officers;* where once you could hire a gardener, now you must *contract with a landscape service;* where once trash was picked up by a garbage collector, now you can call a firm that bills itself as *solid state ecologists* (it's true, honest!). Or take the university where I work. The night watchman has been replaced by a *security officer,* the maintenance people have become *facilities management staff,* and the lunchroom is now a *food service court.* Even my own English department is not immune, now that the freshman English director has become

the *Director of Instruction in Writing* and the tutoring office has been renamed *The Clinical Assistance Program in English.*

The reason for this galloping word inflation? Often just harmless vanity. You feel better about yourself if you can say you are a *building superintendent* rather than a janitor or if you work in a *health care delivery facility* rather than a clinic. But good writers are aware of these evasions and shun them, because they deaden the impact of the message. Good writers are properly fearful that while bathing their egos in the warm waters of their own words, they risk drowning their suffering readers.

Allied with the big-word syndrome is another ailment, **jargon.** Because language is so powerful, it often seems to be at cross-purposes with the needs of scientists and others who use the language to convey the results of scholarly investigations. Those who study a subject scientifically find that emotions and value judgments often interfere with arriving at truth. They must strive to be precise and dispassionate both in their investigations and in their statements of results. Yet simple, everyday words are often words with strong connotations. Therefore, some writers have gotten into the habit of dealing with this fact by replacing simple words with complicated but neutral words known only to other people working in a certain field. The outcome is often jargon, as in paragraphs such as the following:

> Obligation was induced in two-man work groups by arranging for one member to contribute more to a common task which resulted in a higher joint reward. Friends responded to such obligation by deferring to their benefactors in a second interaction session while strangers who were obligated repaid through greater effort and the assumption of leadership. Self-esteem was positively related to deference.

That's from a sociology journal. Almost impossible to understand, right? But if you cut out the jargon terms such as *interaction session* and *positively related to,* and if you cure the big-word syndrome, this is what it says in simple English:

> Suppose two people are working together on a project and both are given equal rewards even though one contributed more than the other. In such cases we found that if the two workers were friends, the lesser contributor was likely to let his or her friend be the leader in any future work sessions; but if the two were strangers, the lesser contributor

would "repay" by assuming leadership and doing extra work. In either case, if co-workers deferred to each other, it made them feel good about themselves.

We need not pick only on sociologists. Jargon is in the vocabulary of nearly all professions, from police officers (*the suspects were apprehended leaving the premises*) to sportscasters (*looks like this new pitcher has a real hummer*). Anywhere a specific group develops its own specialized vocabulary, it will include jargon. When you are speaking, you have immediate clues about whether your listener is following you, so jargon is usually harmless. But you should keep it out of your writing.

Analogous to jargon is the euphemism. Some words seem too painful or too emotionally loaded, so the writer substitutes other words for them to disguise or hide the true meaning of what is being said. The disguising words are called **euphemisms.** For example, our society does not like to face death, so we have devised numerous euphemisms to wall ourselves off from that experience. Some are harmless, gentle euphemisms, such as *pass away, enter into rest,* or *go to one's eternal reward,* whose principal purpose is to comfort the bereaved. Others are humorous, such as *croak* or *kick the bucket,* which allow a comfortable emotional distancing to those not immediately involved. Sometimes people use euphemisms out of politeness, when what they say may be unpleasant to some readers. An example is the school board that instructs teachers to describe children's behavior to parents with such phrases as "resorts to physical means of winning his point" (i.e., hits other kids) and "shows difficulty in distinguishing between imaginative and factual material" (i.e., lies). Maybe the parents are mollified, but they probably get the message eventually anyway, and it is probably no more palatable later than earlier. Despite the good motives that prompt them, euphemisms ought to be avoided. Put it to your reader straight, using words to communicate rather than evade.

So what does it mean to be *direct* in your writing? In summary, it means making sure that your words are not too many, too big, too specialized, or too evasive. That's just another way of saying you must avoid wordiness, the big-word syndrome, jargon, and euphemisms.

A2. Is the Language Fresh?

If one of your primary duties as a writer is to fasten the attention of your readers on what you say, make sure that what you say is new to them. Even when the subject is familiar, you have to jolt them into new ways of seeing or feeling. Readers must sense that your writing is original, the product of a mind dealing actively and intelligently with the world around it, rather than "just more of the same old stuff." Your choice of words will show whether you have kept out of the well-worn grooves of the familiar.

Take this brief passage in which L. Rust Hills describes an ice cream cone:

> It is a huge, irregular mass of ice cream, faintly domed at the top from the metal scoop, which has first produced it and then insecurely balanced it on the uneven top edge of a hollow inverted cone made out of the most brittle and fragile of materials. Clumps of ice cream hang over the side, very loosely attached to the main body. There is always much more ice cream than the cone could hold, even if the ice cream were tamped down.

Hills describes a most familiar object, yet his choice of words lets us see it in a new way. He achieves this effect with such words as *mass, domed, hollow, inverted, brittle, fragile, clumps,* and *tamped.* None of these are unusual words, the kinds of big words I was cautioning you about earlier. But how many of us would have thought to use them when describing an ice cream cone? We would probably have settled for easy choices, such as *cold* or *smooth.* Hills's willingness to seek out better, fresher words gives his writing an edge and makes us want to read more.

I will be frank: There is no simple way to cure the language blahs. If your prose is often lifeless because the words are

I would sooner read a timetable or a catalogue than nothing at all.
—W. Somerset Maugham

too easy, too familiar, the problem is usually one of vocabulary. You may know a great number of words but actively use a much smaller number. To enlarge both the number of words you know and the number you use, the best long-range program is the one I mentioned before—reading.

In the meantime, however, there is one very important step you can take, and that is to examine your writing carefully to see whether you have unintentionally fallen victim to **triteness** or **clichés.** These are phrases or expressions that are worn out from overuse. They should be discarded not because they are "wrong" but because their very familiarity allows readers to tune out momentarily when they encounter them. The reader whose attention is periodically disengaged quickly stops being a reader at all. Holding readers is like landing a battling swordfish—you must keep them hooked at all times while reeling them in, because once lost, they may be gone forever.

Why does a reader tune out momentarily when he or she encounters a cliché? Put simply, the problem is that the reader knows in advance what the next few words will be and subconsciously skips over them. For example, if a friend moans to you about her chemistry midterm tomorrow and starts to say that she is going to have to "pull an . . . ," you know that "allnighter" is coming next. The phrase is a cliché. Here are some others:

hotter than a firecracker	met the acid test
the long and short of it	last but not least
it goes without saying	keeping up with the Joneses
till hell freezes over	Don't rock the boat.
All's well that ends well.	Look before you leap.

Although such phrases may be harmless in conversation, readers have every right to slide over clichés like these. The writer obviously did not think them up, and if the words do not represent the writer's own thinking, why should the reader give serious attention to them?

Of course, the matter of triteness is more subtle than the above list would suggest. Those phrases are obvious; we all recognize them, and for that reason we are not so often tempted to use them. The more serious temptations are the little two- or three-word combinations that recur frequently but just do not have the status of being a cliché or a stock phrase.

Consider this paragraph from a student's paper:

> *Well now* Anna is dead. She died slowly and painfully, but *for the first time in months* Anna *knows peace.* When I saw her lying on the bed *breathing her last,* I *couldn't help but think that* I had helped *put her through this.* If we would have *let nature take its course,* Anna would have *been at peace* much sooner. But we didn't and *nature took her revenge.*

The paragraph is as dead as its subject because almost all of it seems overused. The most obviously well-worn parts are in italics. We feel that the writer has put words down like a computer: Push a button for dying and out comes some variant of *knows peace,* automatically. Only a few of the italicized phrases are genuine, four-star clichés (*let nature take its course,* for example). But a concern for fresh language makes us realize that the whole paragraph needs to be thought through again and then rewritten. Compare the original with this possible revision:

> Anna is dead now. She died slowly and painfully, but at last her months of torment are over. When I saw her lying in that grim hospital bed, her lungs straining for the few last breaths that remained for her, I was stricken with the realization that I was partly responsible for her agony. If we had not interfered, nature would have given her body rest long before now. But we didn't, or couldn't, and the revenge of an outraged nature had been terrible to see.

I think you will agree that this version is fresher.

This last point about the dangers of habitual two- or three-word combinations cannot be emphasized too strongly. Dead writing rarely has more than a few scattered clichés, but it always has lots of these simple plug-in phrases. To make sure you understand what I mean, underline the tired language in the following student paragraph:

Christmas shopping has always been a highlight of the year for me. It's always a great challenge to find that certain gift for that special person. A lot of people couldn't be bothered or simply don't care to do all the legwork; instead they take the easy way out and give money. When I'm ready to go shopping, I always drive to a big shopping center. Here there is every store imaginable, readily waiting at your fingertips. Of course this doesn't mean you won't have to fight your way through the crowds.

What words did you underline? Let's compare lists. There is always some room for disagreement in matters of this sort, but your list ought to include at least several of the following overused phrases:

a highlight of the (year)	do all the legwork
it's a great challenge	take the easy way out
that certain gift	every (thing) imaginable
that special person	waiting at your fingertips
can't be bothered	fight your way through the crowds

Tired language, all of it. Puts readers to sleep very quickly.

So, for an apprentice writer, the simplest rule of thumb (another cliché) is this: If the phrase or expression is familiar to you, don't use it, unless you can establish an excellent reason for doing so.

A3. Is the Language Concrete?

Concrete words refer to objects we can touch or see. *Egg* qualifies. So do *lawn, book, peach, giraffe,* and *submarine.* These words are often contrasted with **abstract words,** such as *democracy, experience,* and *bountiful,* that name concepts or qualities (*democracy* and *experience* are concepts, while *bountiful* is a quality).

Now, the usual advice is to use as many concrete words as possible rather than abstract ones. Good advice it is, too. The difficulty is that such a recommendation runs counter to a central fact about human beings: that mental growth can be defined as an increase in the ability to understand

> There is one stylistic development which most people seldom notice in themselves or others, but which should be watched. As we grow older, we use more and more abstract nouns and adjectives: we move up the semantic ladder. The man who at 25 would have said "tough nut to crack" will when he is 55 say: "Conceivably that might be a problem which admits no solution."
> —Gilbert Highet

and use abstractions. In other words, the more your intellect matures, the more you will want to generalize, to abstract (in the sense of thinking about universals rather than the particular examples that give rise to the universals). Writers quite naturally will find themselves using words to represent this kind of abstract thinking. Unconsciously they may even seek out abstract words as a way of showing that they have arrived at full intellectual maturity.

Fight that tendency. The abstract thought is good, but present it as concretely as possible. Thinking may be a generalizing process, but perception—and perceiving is what readers do—begins with the real world. Don't write:

> Experience teaches us to exercise care when driving an automobile.

Instead write:

> Two dented fenders and a cracked front grille have taught me that you don't argue the right-of-way with a gravel truck.

Both sentences may have originated from the same collision, but dented fenders and cracked grilles are concrete objects, while experience is an abstraction. The second of those two sentences is far more graphic and therefore less likely to slip by the reader unnoticed.

Another way to make language concrete besides replacing abstract words with concrete ones is to be specific. Replace highly abstract words with words that while technically still abstract, exist on a much lower level of abstraction. *Colorful*, for example, is an abstract word describing a quality; *vermilion* still describes a quality but is much more specific than merely being *colorful*. So if you cannot use concrete words, be as specific as possible in your choice of abstract words.

Of course you cannot avoid abstractions. If you want to talk about *socialism* or *existentialism*, you probably must use those words. If you say that a friend of yours is *talkative* or *sensible* or *fractious*, you are assigning qualities. The point is that you ought to be as concrete as the context allows.

A4. Is the Language Colorful?

We human beings are sensuous creatures, no doubt about it. From our very first moments we live by responding to what our senses tell us. And we often enjoy most of those pleasures that gratify as many of our five senses as possible. If you need confirmation of this fact, think about the way a successful rock group appeals to sight, touch, and smell as well as sound. Or think of an auto race: the shattering roar of the unmuffled engines, the odor of gasoline and burning rubber, the kaleidoscopic colors, the palpable tension in the pit of your stomach. We enjoy more delicate pleasures, too, but the senses always play a dominant role.

Good writing, especially good narrative and descriptive writing, is often like Nirvana or the Daytona 500—it draws on your senses. Such writing is dramatic, detailed, colorful. Here is an example of what I mean. Norman Mailer describes Chicago:

> A great city, a strong city with faces tough as leather hide and pavement, it was also a city where the faces took on the broad beastiness of ears which were dull enough to ignore the bleatings of the doomed, noses battered enough to smell no more the stench of every unhappy end, mouths—fat mouths or slit mouths—ready to taste the gravies which were the reward of every massacre.

It's all there in that one sentence: sight ("faces tough as leather hide"), sound ("bleatings of the doomed"), smell ("the stench of every unhappy end"), taste ("gravies"). That's what real color, real sensory appeal, means.

Memorable sentences are memorable on account of some single irradiating word.
—Alexander Smith

Student writing can have the same appeal. Consider this student's description of a high school classmate eating lunch:

> Her favorite method of eating her eggs was to split them apart by sticking her thumbs through the unshelled surface—and then tearing them in two. The yolk was still quite fluid and would trickle down her fingers. She licked her fingers, moaning as she tried to catch each drop with her tongue. An odor of eggs, mingled with whatever chemical we had been using in the lab the period before, impregnated the air as she stuffed the speckled mass into her mouth.

You can see the "speckled mass," hear the moan, smell the chemicals, feel the yolk trickling down the fingers.

We often object to clothes that are pale, drab, uninviting. The same applies to what we read, even if we are not so conscious of what it is we don't like. When you describe or narrate, try to give pictures that can evoke sensory responses in your readers. And capture these pictures in color, not black and white.

A5. Is the Language Figurative?

You will recall my saying earlier that a writer must choose words as precisely as possible in order to convey meaning accurately. Finding the right word, the best possible word, is one way of reaching that goal. Another good way is to use comparisons. Of course, you use comparisons quite often when you talk: You might describe a building as *taller than the Holiday Inn;* you might identify your friend Jody as *the one with the short blond hair cut sort of like Ellen's;* you might say your new car is *faster than my old Sentra.* But somehow comparisons get forgotten when you write. To neglect them is to pass up one of the simplest ways of clarifying your meaning.

Using comparisons in writing is called **figurative language.** Here are some good comparisons from student writing:

> Jeanie always ripped her food apart with a twisting motion of her wrists, as if she was wringing a chicken's neck.

I looked up in awe, like a country boy from Peoria looks up at the Sears Tower.

Breathing under water was like trying to suck a McDonald's milkshake through a thin straw.

> *The metaphor is probably the most fertile power possessed by man.*
> *—José Ortego y Gasset*

Everyone got out of the way when Carl bulldozed his way onto the dance floor.

I tried to swallow, but my mouth was burlap dry.

The first three are more explicit as comparisons. They use *as if* or *like* to draw attention to the comparison, and because of their explicitness they are called **similes.** The last two are more implicit and can be termed **metaphors.** Even though there is no *as* or *like*, the comparing process—of aggressiveness to a bulldozer, of dryness to burlap—is still quite evident.

Sometimes an apprentice writer can give us too much of a good thing. Comparisons are good. But comparisons that are too extravagant begin to try the reader's patience, especially when combined (as they often are) with the big-word syndrome. The result is **flowery writing,** a term that is itself a comparison. Here, for example, is a student-written sentence with enough floweriness to make us choke on the sweetness:

> After years of self-love worthy of the immortal Narcissus, now the swelling tides of devotion, the swirling waves of loyalty, and the infinitely deep fathoms of love bring Tom to a realization of the majestic current which is Maggie's soul.

Floweriness is not found only in student writing. Advertising prose is often fertile ground for such blossoms:

> The light falls differently now. Behind the scent of woodsmoke there's a hint of snow. How will you dress for the new season? Wouldn't it be lovely to put on these new colors of Highland heathers, blued, greyed, softened with hints of autumn's mists? Singularly "Ultima II" [lipstick].

Two added points about figurative language. The first is to avoid **mixed metaphors:** writing that begins with one comparison and then adds another, incongruous to the first. The student who wrote that she was going to be "tackling two sides of the same coin" mixed metaphors from football and money. In a sentence such as *He put his nose to the grindstone and dug into the subject,* it is hard to imagine someone digging very well with his nose in such an awkward position. The surest way to avoid mixed metaphors is to avoid clichés, as the writer of our example sentence would have discovered had he eliminated the two cliché phrases *put his nose to the grindstone* and *dug into.* But even if you have not used clichés, it is still a good idea to check your metaphors to make sure they are consistent.

The second point is that you should stay clear of comparisons that are too far-fetched to be convincing or illuminating—this sentence, for example:

> She could often be heard serenading herself in the halls and bathrooms, her distorted echoes leading me to compare her mouth to the Grand Canyon.

We grant that the girl is a poor singer. But comparing her mouth to the Grand Canyon is too extravagant. It just does not do the job that a comparison should, which is to tell us something about the quality of her voice or the size of her mouth (we're not sure which). Compare her voice to a screechy phonograph, maybe, or her mouth to a guitar amplifier, but keep the comparison credible.

A6. Is the Language Richly Connotative?

Your paper has come back with a word or phrase underlined, and your instructor says the problem is with your word choice. You know the word has an acceptable usage, so at first you are puzzled. But when you look the word up in the dictionary, you discover that it has the wrong **connotation** (implied meaning) when used in the way you have used it.

Connotation has to be understood in comparison with its companion term, denotation. **Denotation** is the kernel of meaning that remains when a word is stripped of any emotional associations we might bring to it. Denotation is the technical meaning, the clinical meaning. Some words carry no emotional freight at all and have only a denotative value. Take a word

Without knowing the force of words, it is impossible to know men. —*Confucius*

like *farad*, for example. It is defined as "the unit of capacitance equal to the capacitance of a capacitor between whose plates there appears a potential of one volt when it is charged by one coulomb of electricity." No, I don't understand it either. The point is simply that *farad* is a technical term. It does not have emotional significance to us, even if we know something about electricity. It remains, and should remain, neutral.

But other words, while they do possess a core of denotative meaning, can never be used successfully without an awareness of their connotation, their power to suggest or imply. These words stimulate emotional reactions. We don't just understand, we respond. And most of the time we don't need a dictionary to tell us the connotation of a word either. If someone calls you an "idiot," you will not assume that he or she has measured your IQ and determined that your mental age is less than three years, a condition to which psychologists assign the technical term *idiocy*. You will ignore the denotation and respond directly to the connotation, which is that you are silly and foolish.

However, there are other words for which the connotations are more subtle, less readily apparent. Consider the word *opportunist*. In the strict sense it might seem to mean any person who takes advantage of his or her opportunities. But in actuality the word has negative connotations: Opportunists are disreputable, they care more for success than for principle, and people do not trust them. To call someone an opportunist is usually not a compliment, except maybe in sports. A good dictionary will make you aware of this connotative value. *Funk and Wagnalls Standard College Dictionary*, for example, defines an opportunist as one "who uses every opportunity to contribute to the achievement of some end, and who is relatively uninfluenced by moral principles or sentiment."

Definitions are not the only means for becoming aware of connotation. Check on a word's synonyms, because they often provide clues. So if your instructor indicated you have used a word improperly, check the dictionary to make sure you did not use the word in such a way as to allow its connotation to obstruct your intended meaning. You might use *opportunist* and intend it as a compliment. But your reader can hardly be blamed for not taking it that way.

Some words, by the way, have both good and bad connotations, and only the context provides clues as to whether they convey what they should. Other words have connotations known only to a certain group, or maybe only to a certain person. These words may have rich emotional associations for only the select few.

Finally, the fantastic richness of association that clings to some words gives them their special power. Only by reading more can you begin to appreciate that wealth and to understand how connotation, far from being something to avoid, is one of the chief glories of our language.

EXERCISES

1. Eliminate all unnecessary words in the following passages and then write your own tightened versions.

   A. Most people detest storms but there's a lot to be said for a good storm once in a while. Besides the fact that it's good for the environment and helps the grass grow, it serves another purpose. Right now, in the study room of the library, I can hear the rain falling on the roof. At first one notices it, like when I entered the room, but after a while it becomes inaudible and fades into the background. All this sort of creates a peaceful and tranquil atmosphere around here. The upper half of the room is dark like that of a cathedral. The dark, wooden tables and chairs are lined up like pews, each side separated by a large aisle. Along with all this there is a strange silence broken only by a cough or a squeak of a chair. Suddenly the mood of the whole place changes. There is a great crash of thunder, and streaks of lightning illuminate the room through the now-bright stained glass windows. The lake can be heard dashing against the shoreline. Outside it is not yet dark, but a black line of clouds hovers above the horizon. The lake too is black and violent. Between the clashing waves and the dormant clouds is this sort of gray mist. The whole picture seems to depict that second before the judgment day when the world will end. . . .

B. The mechanical workings of the car are extremely interesting. Those all-important air shocks are of little or no good, and after riding in the crazy car, you're not quite sure all of your body is still with you or if it got bounced off and fell out the window somewhere. The brake linings are so worn that you literally come to a screeching halt. The linkage is such that when you try to shift gears you are stopped halfway in between gears and are forced to coast until you lift up the guard plate on the shifter and manipulate the rods with a screwdriver, which can really shock someone who has never seen the process before. Sometimes that doesn't work, so all you have to do is talk to it a little and give the shifter a good swift kick and off you go. It's really a fantastic little automobile, after you get used to it.

2. Reduce the following to a single word or a shorter phrase:

meet with the approbation of	resembling in nature
a long period of time	it is the belief of
making a judgment	each and every one of us
subject matter	as of right now
subsequent to	thunderstorm activity
	prior to

3. Do you know what the following jargon terms mean? Can you think of other simpler ways to explain or define them?

From education:

accountability	compensatory education
language arts	heterogeneous grouping
individualized instruction	

From football:

bump and run	blitz
crossing pattern	bomb
get burned	

From management:

bottom-line consciousness	systems capabilities
growth potential	product development
impact study	

From computers:

the net	down time
surfing	hard drive
boot up	

4. What are some common euphemisms or slang words for the following?

sleep	love (*verb*)
get drunk	get angry
drive a car	tired
kill	hate (*verb*)
crazy	old person
policeman	movie

5. What is the meaning and function of these euphemisms?

antiperspirant	stonewall (*verb*)
backburner (*verb*)	politically marginalized
ex-offender	join your forefathers
mentally incompetent	rip off (*verb*)

6. Create a metaphor or simile using each of the following:

wet	ached
mansion	shrub
dark green	old
laughing	horror-stricken

7. The following statement was issued by a school administrator. Examine the use of language in the statement. Where do you find unnecessary words? Jargon? The big-word syndrome? Leaving aside these cumbersome uses of language, what—if anything—is this "statement" really saying?

PRINCIPAL'S PROGRAM DESCRIPTION
FOR MIDDLE SCHOOL

The program will be governed by district policies and general procedures. It will strive toward the realization of the districtwide goals derived from the Board of Education policy statement. We believe that children are most helped toward the achievement of success in a school atmosphere in which teachers work constructively together. We believe in the concept "Middle School." We believe that humanness makes all human beings equal. We believe that each individual is unique. We believe that we help all pupils develop positive self-concepts. We believe in meeting the individual needs of each pupil. We believe in helping pupils experience success. We believe in the long-range goal of individualization through flexibility within a heterogeneous setting.

8. Write a short (one- or two-paragraph) essay on how Flannery O'Connor uses language in the following passage, from the book *Three by Flannery O'Connor.* Pay special attention to the use of concrete words, fresh and colorful words, and figurative language (metaphors and similes).

Ruby came in the front door of the apartment building and lowered the paper sack with the four cans of number three beans in it onto the hall table. She was too tired to take her arms from around it or to straighten up and she hung there collapsed from the hips, her head balanced like a big florid vegetable at the top of the sack. She gazed with stony unrecognition at the face that confronted her in the dark yellow-spotted mirror over the table. Against her right cheek was a gritty collard leaf that had been stuck there half the way home. She gave it a vicious swipe with her arm and straightened up, muttering, "Collards, collards," in a voice of sultry subdued wrath. Standing up straight, she was a short woman, shaped nearly like a funeral urn. She had mulberry-colored hair stacked in sausage rolls around her head but some of these had come loose with the heat and the long walk from the grocery store and pointed frantically in various directions. "Collard greens!"

she said, spitting the word from her mouth this time as if it were a poisonous seed.

9. Many public figures in this country are known for their fascination with words: comedians such as George Carlin ("the seven words you can't say on television"), educators such as Richard Mitchell (*Less Than Words Can Say*), authors such as Edwin Newman, and newspaper columnists such as William Safire. Choose one of these figures, investigate his or her interest in and use of language, then write a brief description of what you have discovered.

10. Write a short essay that builds on this statement by novelist Joseph Conrad: "There must be a wonderful soothing power in mere words since so many men have used them for self-communion." Use your own experiences in the essay wherever possible.

11. Take your two most recent papers. Underline the following:

Metaphors and other examples of figurative language
Words that are either unusually formal or unusually informal
Words that are unusually concrete or abstract
Vivid details
Phrases or passages that are needlessly wordy
Examples of jargon, euphemism, or the "big-word" syndrome
Clichés or trite expressions

Then, after examining the words and passages you have underlined, write a short one- or two-paragraph summary of what you have learned. Of course, as you frame your conclusions you must bear in mind the nature of the writing assignment that gave rise to this written response: Some kinds of words are more appropriate for one kind of assignment than for another. Also, be sure to concentrate just as much or more on the positive side of your conclusions, on the things that you did well or that you can augment in the future; don't let your paragraphs degenerate into a list of "here's what I did wrong."

B. SPELLING

Now for another important word about words: spelling. No matter how successful you are in choosing the best possible words for saying what you want to say, you can blow the whole game by misspelling them. Actually, spelling is more a matter of convention than anything else—we could consider it in Chapter 8 just as easily. But in most people's minds, spelling a word properly is intimately connected with using it properly. So you cannot afford to overlook another strategy for ensuring that your words have the best possible impact on your reader, and that strategy is to make sure your spelling is as good as it can be.

If you already spell with reasonable accuracy, you probably don't need any special work. Perhaps you should not even read any further in this section. The most you have to remember are the two rules that apply to any writer: (1) when in doubt, check, and (2) when not in doubt but later proven wrong (e.g., your paper comes back with a spelling error circled), memorize the corrected spelling. That would suffice.

However, if you are among the large group of people who do have trouble—sometimes small trouble, sometimes big—with spelling, the rest of this section is designed to help you. (Want a quick way to know whether you are? In a typical passage of 500 words, if you misspell more than two or three, I'd say you have at least a small problem. If you miss more than five or six, call it a big problem.)

The first question you should ask yourself is also perhaps the most important: Are you ready to make the sacrifices of time and energy necessary for improving your spelling?

After all, there are some plausible arguments for *not* working much on spelling. Here are a few of them:

1. Spelling is only a convention, an agreement for the sake of convenience. Alternative spellings usually do not affect meaning. If you were to see the sentence *I went*

> *"Students to Site Grievances at National Conference"* the press release was headed, thereby suggesting that the students in the National Students Lobby might be wise to lobby for courses in spelling, if, as appears, it is not part of their curriculums.
> —*Edwin Newman*

to there house today, you would know that *there* is a possessive pronoun even though it is not spelled *t-h-e-i-r.* What is most important in any piece of writing is content—what the words say rather than how they are spelled.

2. Spelling in the past was very flexible. The great Elizabethan writers, including Shakespeare, often spelled a word in whatever way seemed best at the time. There were no dictionaries or other authorities around to contradict them.

3. Even in our current, less flexible times, variant spellings exist for many words. We know that the British have *labour* to our *labor, centre* to our *center.* We know, too, that we can *surprise* or *surprize* someone, that we can accept or ignore *judgments (judgements),* even when made by *archaeologists (archeologists).* There are numerous other examples.

4. Some great writers are horrible spellers. F. Scott Fitzgerald wrote the following three sentences in a letter to his editor Max Perkins. I have taken the liberty of marking them up as if they had appeared in a freshman paper.

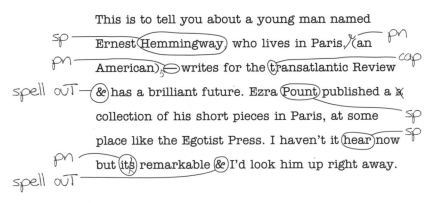

This is to tell you about a young man named Ernest Hemmingway who lives in Paris. (an American), writes for the transatlantic Review & has a brilliant future. Ezra Pount published a collection of his short pieces in Paris, at some place like the Egotist Press. I haven't it hear now but its remarkable & I'd look him up right away.

The punctuation problems are bad enough, but there is no excuse for the three spelling errors that mar this passage. Fitzgerald knew Hemingway and Pound personally, and surely he ought not to have been so careless as to confuse *h-e-a-r* and *h-e-r-e*. Yet he did, and he made similar mistakes quite often. If one of the greatest twentieth-century American novelists can misspell so easily, why should *we* be fussy?

5. Spelling in the English language is often illogical, quirky, even downright ridiculous. Why we have *neighbors* rather than *naybors* we find hard to understand. Ditto for *lieutenant* (*lootenent?*), *scheme* (*skeem?*), and *foreign* (*forin?*). If spelling is so difficult, if it *requires* (*rekwires?*) *knowledge* (*nollidge?*) of so many *exceptions* (*eksepshuns?*), why *should* (*shood?*) we be so *conscious* (*conshus?*) of it?

6. Many personal computers now come equipped with software programs that check spelling, so writers can "let the computer take care of it" rather than worrying about it themselves.

Yes, you could make these arguments. They would be true, every one of them. Also, I'm afraid, totally irrelevant. The fact is that most people expect a writer to spell with reasonable accuracy. The person who dismisses your job application by saying, "Why doesn't she learn to spell?" might be blind to historical process and contemporary vagaries, might not agree with you about the primacy of content over convention. No matter—your application is just as dead. Correct spelling is taken as one of the marks of an educated person. This opinion is probably based on a *non sequitur:* Good spellers are often good writers; therefore, bad spellers are bad writers. But the belief is a prevalent one, even—especially?—among college teachers, and you cannot wish it away.

So spelling is important. That brings us back to the original question: Are you willing to sacrifice time and energy to improve yours? Be-

> *They spell it Vinci and pronounce it Vinchy; foreigners always spell better than they pronounce.*
> *—Mark Twain*

cause that's what it takes—your effort and your determination. With those qualities you are ready to make significant improvement. No one misspells on purpose. The task is to find out why and where you usually make mistakes—in other words, to discover the patterns in your errors and then to systematically begin the work of curing them. To improve your spelling, I recommend a three-stage process. These stages are in an order of decreasing severity, and you enter the process at the stage most appropriate for you. Thus, if you have a severe spelling problem, follow all four steps, beginning with the first. If your problem is less severe, you can begin with the second or perhaps even third, and then follow through to the end.

Oh, and what about those computer spellcheckers? Well, for one thing, since they're not portable, they won't do you much good in the countless writing situations—writing essay exams, filling out job applications—where computers are not involved and where spelling is still important. Second, this software can do a lot of things, but there's much that it can't do, such as distinguish between homonyms (*here*, *hear*) or improperly spelled proper names *Hemmingway*, *Pount*. In fact, not a single of the errors in the F. Scott Fitzgerald letter would have been caught by a computer!

B1. Spelling Patterns and Problem Situations

No one can memorize the spelling for every one of the thousands of words used in everyday speaking and writing. Fortunately, most spelling is systematic, although there are exceptions to every pattern. It is one of the conventions of our language, for example, to spell the plural of most nouns by adding -*s* on the end: *boat, boats.*

Learning to spell is really just a matter of learning the conventions used in English and then memorizing the few balky words that do not fit conveniently. Learning spelling patterns is a large task, too large to cover in detail here. But if you are a "terable speler," there is no other way. Get yourself a good short guide to English spelling. (One is *50,000 Words Divided and Spelled* by Harry Sharp, published by New Win Publishers, Hampton, New Jersey.) Then work right through the book, cover to cover. Allot maybe fifteen minutes a day to it, for about three months. At the end of that time you ought to be a much improved speller.

Experience shows us that six problem areas are involved in a disproportionate share of spelling errors. The reason these six are special plagues is that in many cases the pronunciation gives no clue as to proper spelling. In other words, the proper spelling and the most common improper one can both be pronounced the same way. Therefore, you have to rely on knowledge of the system, as both spelling versions are often going to "sound right" and perhaps even "look right."

Here are the six areas:

1. *Doubling a final consonant before adding a suffix (ending).* Why is it that with simple verbs such as *saunter* and *prefer,* the past-tense forms are spelled differently— *sauntered* (*r* not doubled) in the first case but *preferred* (*r* doubled) in the second? After all, these words are quite similar—verbs of two syllables ending in *-er.* If you are going to put an ending on such words, how do you know whether to double the final consonant before adding the ending?

The secret is to concentrate not on similarities in the words but rather on differences. In our two words used as examples, notice that in *saunter* the accent is on the first syllable, while in *prefer* it falls on the second. On the basis of such distinctions, a system has been devised that provides guidance for what to do with words that end in a single consonant.

The system works like this. When adding an ending to such words, you do *not* double the final consonant except in those cases that meet *all three* of the following criteria: (1) the base word must end in a single consonant preceded by a single vowel, (2) the base word must be one syllable or must be accented on the last syllable, and (3) the suffix must begin with a vowel. In these cases, and in these cases only, the final consonant of the base word is doubled.

Examples of words that meet all three criteria include the following:

refe*rr*ed	permi*tt*ing
submi*tt*ed	ru*nn*ing
fa*tt*est	sa*dd*er
sle*dd*ing	qui*pp*ed

Using *referred* as a particular instance of this rule, note that the base word *(refer)* ends with a consonant (*r*) preceded by a vowel (*e*), that the base word is accented on the last syllable, and that the suffix (*-ed*) begins with a vowel. If the base word ends with two consonants, such as *hard*, its final consonant is not doubled: *harder, hardest*. If the accent falls on any syllable but the last, as in the word *saunter* mentioned earlier, the final consonant is not doubled: *sauntered, sauntering.* If the suffix begins with a consonant rather than a vowel, such as *-ness*, again the final consonant is not doubled: *tenderness, resourcefulness.* (Incidentally, *quipped* makes the preceding list because the *ui* combination counts as only one vowel.)

Of course, such a system cannot cover the many words for which confusion about doubling the consonant does not involve the final consonant. If you spell *apologize* as *appologize*, there is no simple rule to tell you why you have erred. The problem here is with the base word itself, and if a larger amount of reading does not help you "intuit" the correct spelling for such words, the only other remedy is simply to look them up when you are in doubt or when you unintentionally misspell them. Although the system just described applies only to final consonants, it is still quite useful, as final consonants are a common source of spelling errors.

2. *Adding a prefix.* In adding a prefix such as *mis-* or *un-* to a base word that begins with a consonant, do not double the last consonant of the prefix: *misdirect* (not *missdirect*), *undoing* (not *unndoing*). A possible confusion arises, however, when the consonant that ends the prefix and the consonant that begins the base word are the same: *misspell, unnatural.* It *seems* as if you are doubling the last conso-

nant of the prefix and the word looks "wrong" because you are so familiar with the procedure of not doubling these conso-nants. Therefore, many writers are sorely tempted to use *mispell* or *unatural*, to go with *ireconcilable* instead of *irreconcilable*,

People do not realize that spelling misteaks are easily made.
—student paper

nonuclear instead of *nonnuclear.* This temptation must be resisted. The system is always uniform: prefix plus base word; never any doubling, and never any reduction to a single consonant either.

3. *Silent e.* Here is another one of those seemingly myste-rious contrasts: When a suffix beginning with a vowel, for example *-able*, is added to base words that end in a silent *e*, sometimes the silent *e* is dropped, but sometimes it is not. Thus *resolve* becomes *resolvable* but *replace* becomes *re-placeable.* What gives here?

The answer this time is rooted in how the words are pro-nounced (how would you say *resolveable? replacable?*). We need not go into the intricacies of it. All you must do is keep one principle in mind: If the suffix begins with a vowel, drop the silent *e* at the end of the base word unless (1) the silent *e* follows a *c* and the suffix is *-able*, or (2) the silent *e* follows a *g* and the suffix is *-able, -ance,* or *-ous.* Many words have the silent *e* dropped in this way:

dare	⟶ daring	dance	⟶ dancing
type	⟶ typical	pale	⟶ palest
move	⟶ moving	resolve	⟶ resolvable

Examples of the two exceptions include words such as *displaceable*, where the silent *e* follows a *c* and the ending is *-able*, and *knowledgeable* and *outrageous*, where the base words end in *g* and a silent *e* and the suffixes are *-able* and *-ous*, respectively. Of course, if the suffix begins with a con-sonant, the silent *e* always remains, as in *careful* or *niceness*.

4. *ei or ie?* Every writer has experienced the woes caused by *i*'s going before *e*'s when it should be the other way around—or vice versa, *e*'s before *i*'s.

My sainted fourth-grade teacher used to give the first rule for solving these dilemmas: "Children, it's *i* before *e* except

after *c*." Of course we would then ask her about *weigh* and she would glower. Still, she was on the right track: *i* does go before *e*, as long as the *ie* combination is pronounced like a long *e* (the vowel sound in a word such as *she*). Thus, *i* precedes *e* in words such as p*ie*ce, *believe,* or *chief.*

What my teacher's formula could not cover was the occasions when the *ei/ie* combination is not pronounced as a long *e* but rather as a long *a* (the *a* sound of words like *male*). That's where *weigh* comes in. Also *neighborhood, veins,* and other words in which the *e* comes before the *i* because the pronunciation is a long *a*.

(That puts us one step up on my fourth-grade teacher, right? Then how come we spell *weird* the way we do, or *either?* It turns out she was pretty shrewd after all, because she had another bit of advice that covers these words, and a few others like them, perfectly: "Children, there are exceptions to every rule.")

5. *A final y becomes i.* If you are adding a suffix to a base word that ends in *y*, and if the letter that comes before the *y* is a consonant, change *y* to *i*. Otherwise, don't. So we have *silly, silliness* and *hoary, hoariest,* because in these and similar cases the letter that comes before the *y* (*l* and *r* here) is a consonant. This rule is true for any suffix, by the way, even a simple -*s*, as when the verb *dry* becomes *dries* or the noun *gully* becomes *gullies.* An example of a word where the *y* is preceded by a vowel and therefore does not change would be *delay*—thus *delays, delaying.*

So how come *dry* doesn't become *driness* instead of *dryness;* why doesn't *say* become *sayed* instead of *said?* "Children, there are exceptions to every rule."

6. *Noun plurals.* Most noun plurals are formed by adding an *-s* to the singular: *pencil, pencils; theme, themes.* If the noun ends in *s, z, ch, sh,* or *x,* however, *-es* is added:

boss, bosses	church, churches
lass, lasses	ash, ashes
buzz, buzzes	ax, axes
arch, arches	tax, taxes

Some words that end in *f* or *fe* have plurals ending in *-ves:*

wife, wives	leaf, leaves
wharf, wharves	thief, thieves

But: *chief, chiefs; roof, roofs; belief, beliefs.*

A final *y* preceded by a consonant must be changed to *i* before an *-es* is added to form the plural:

lady, ladies	reply, replies
tragedy, tragedies	berry, berries

However, according to the principles noted in item 5, words ending in a *y* preceded by a vowel are made plural by just adding *-s:*

journey, journeys	ray, rays
attorney, attorneys	boy, boys

Some plurals are formed irregularly (*mouse, mice*), and some have foreign plurals (*alumnus, alumni; curriculum, curricula*). If you are not sure how to form the plural of a noun, check your dictionary.

B2. Problem Words

If your spelling problems are minor but annoying, you might be able to cover most of them by studying the following list of 100 most frequently misspelled words, from *The University Spelling Book* by Thomas Clark Pollock and William D. Baker. Check your papers to see whether a good proportion of your problem words appear on this list. If they do, close attention to the list might be all you need to cure most of what ails you. Underline the ones that you don't "know you know," then memorize them.

accommodate	height	profession
achievement	interest	prominent
acquire	its, it's	pursue
all right	led	quiet
among	lose	receive
apparent	losing	receiving
argument	marriage	recommend
arguing	mere	referring
belief	necessary	repetition
believe	occasion	rhythm
beneficial	occurred	sense
benefited	occurring	separate
category	occurrence	separation
coming	opinion	shining
comparative	opportunity	similar
conscious	paid	studying
controversy	particular	succeed
controversial	performance	succession
definitely	personal	surprise
definition	personnel	technique
define	possession	than
describe	possible	then
description	practical	their
disastrous	precede	there
effect	prejudice	they're
embarrass	prepare	thorough
environment	prevalent	to, too, two
exaggerate	principal	transferred
existence	privilege	unnecessary
existent	probably	villain
experience	proceed	woman
explanation	procedure	write
fascinate	professor	writing

Actually the preceding list "cheats" because it gives separate listings for words that are often confused—for example, *their / there / they're.* So just to play square I will add some

other favorites, words that in my experience seem to cause
students unusual hardship:

absence	cloths, clothes	nickel
accept, except	complement,	none, no one
acquaintance	compliment	parallel
actually	condemn	precede, proceed
adolescent	conscience	right, rite, write
advice, advise	desirable	roommate
affect, effect	dessert,	sergeant
already, all	desert	sincerely
ready	dining	skiing
altogether, all	grammar	sponsor
together	guarantee	susceptible
attendance	hypocrisy	therefore
breath,	irresistible	truly
breathe	judgment	unusually
capital,	knowledge	visible
capitol	later, latter	weather, whether
challenge	maneuver	yield
cite, site, sight	moral, morale	

B3. A Reminder

I'm sorry if this sounds anticlimactic, but we must end with
something that applies to all writers in all places:

1. If you are in doubt about how to spell a word, use your
   dictionary or your spellcheck software—that's partly
   what they are for. Before you begin a writing assignment,
   for example, make sure the dictionary is nearby. Most
   people don't have the fortitude to go down three flights
   of stairs to consult it, but they will look up a word if the
   means for doing so is right at hand.
2. If you are not in doubt about how to spell a word on an
   assignment yet discover that you misspelled it after all
   (perhaps when your spellchecker highlights it for you),
   take note of the word and look up its proper spelling as
   soon as possible. Concentrate especially hard on such a
   word, because you have to erase from your mind your
   previous impression of the correct spelling.

This advice applies to all writers, good spellers and bad. Practically no one can do without it. Take this very chapter you are reading now. I'm a fairly good speller, but as I wrote I found myself unsure of the spelling of several words. I checked them, using both a dictionary and (later) the computer, and most of the time my initial impression was right. But three times that impression was wrong: *colloquial* (I had *colloqial*), *misspelling* (I had *mispelling*), and *anticlimactic* (*anticlimatic*). I did my penance, and thus you are able to read them in their proper form. What's sauce for this gander . . .

EXERCISES

1. Study the following list of irregular words. As you do, you might circle the letter or letters that are most likely to cause misspellings. The list is from William Drake's *The Way to Spell: A Guide for the Hesitant Speller.*

hoarse	avalanche	aviary
gruesome	vanquish	municipal
biscuit	soliloquy	argument
eager	jewelry	fluorine
speak	dilapidated	verbatim
speech	exorbitant	medieval
view	affidavit	moccasin
aerial	derogatory	piety
superfluous	menagerie	assassin
intravenous	demagogue	traceable
nuisance	dungeon	initiative
poignant	diagnostician	ingredient
innuendo	flagrant	miniature
accessory	demerit	parliament
insipid	vigil	differential
linen	tacit	quotient
denim	material	peculiar
ancient	maniacal	erratic
enervate	esteem	appetite
auxiliary	curiosity	ricochet
prosaic	vineyard	amethyst

carburetor	hiatus	lecherous
trauma	cocoa	jeopardy
essential	punctual	reconnoiter
anxious	wondrous	repugnant
conscious	covet	vagrant
conscience	scoundrel	embarrass
fascinate	quantity	frightening
separate	definite	lightning
amateur	except	familiar
similar	suppress	existence
meant	discoveries	forward
roommate	influential	marriage
colossal	acknowledge	initiate

2. Find the spelling error in each of the sentences below:

A. Now that charter fairs are lower, a lot more people are traveling to Europe.

B. It was all ready after midnight and Deb still hadn't shown up.

C. These thunderstorms should not affect our plans for leaving tommorrow morning.

D. People use to meet at church socials; now they go to singles' bars.

E. The judge illuded to the story of King Solomon.

F. The affects of nuclear testing have not been completely determined.

G. We haven't seen one another since we were altogether at Christmas.

H. The Swansons lived in a motel until there new home was ready.

I. The kidnappers alluded police for nearly three days.

J. Economists say that to much government control is worse than to little.

K. I was led to believe that the accident occured yesterday.

3. Combine the base words and suffixes or prefixes:

Examples:

ir / responsible ——▶ **irresponsible**

debate / able ——▶ **debatable**

A. courage / ous   I. permit / ed
B. notice / able   J. stare / ing
C. lovely / ness   K. sad / est
D. un / natural   L. stubborn / ness
E. funny / er   M. occur / ing
F. change / able   N. dip / ed
G. ski / ing   O. replace / able
H. mis / state

4. Choose the correct word(s) to complete each sentence:

   A. What were they (referring/refering) to?
   B. What an (embarassing/embarrassing) situation!
   C. Despite our arguments, they remain (unyeilding/ unyielding).
   D. I can't (accept/except) your point of view, nor can I follow your (advise/advice).
   E. Has the building (site/sight) been chosen (all ready/ already)?
   F. The (preceding/preceeding) message was brought to you by General Motors.
   G. It's (unbelieveable/unbelievable) that the problem of nuclear power generation should not be (resolvable/ resolveable).
   H. Follow this general (principal/principle) and you will always (sucede/succeed) in business.

5. Give the plurals of the following nouns:

   A. balcony   E. alloy
   B. thief   F. chief
   C. fox   G. speech
   D. penny   H. journey

2

Good Sentences

People communicate in many different ways. Words are only part of that process. Hand gestures, for example, convey a rich assortment of meanings depending on the culture. In Jordan a street vendor might ball up his fist and thrust it upward in the general direction of a customer. He means that the offer he has just received is much too low and the customer can go to blazes for all he cares. In Vietnam if you beckon a child toward you with your palm upward, as we might do, you will be insulting the child, because only animals are summoned that way. Of course, we are more familiar with our own system of gestures: thumbs-up to show that everything's okay, for example, or a shrug of the shoulders to convey indifference.

We communicate with our bodies in other ways besides gestures. Posture can speak volumes, from the folded arms that tell of authority to the careless slouch that means defiance of that authority. Eyes speak, too, such as the familiar wink that suggests intimacy.

We even structure the space around us to send messages to others. For most Americans the proper conversational distance is about three feet. Other cultures define space differently. Latin Americans prefer standing much closer, even for ordinary conversation; proximity need not mean aggressiveness, as it would to a North American. In America, we show our interest in others by looking directly at them. In Asian cultures people express interest and respect by lowering their eyes, not by looking at someone squarely; Asians interpret directness as boldness.

When speech is added to movement and gesture, communication becomes still more complex. Yet even here we do not rely solely on words. Grunts, "hmm" noises, signs—these and dozens of other sounds punctuate every conversation, and we complement them with countless pauses and repetitions. Furthermore, we quite often do not organize our speech into neat, clear, and coherent sentences, precisely because we can make use of these other devices for conveying meaning. Instead we spill out our words in an untidy, imprecise, confusing rush.

So words are only part of our communication in everyday life, and words often are not ordered into complete sentences. Then why are complete sentences such an important part of writing? The answer has perhaps occurred to you already. Precisely because writing does not offer the props we rely on during conversation, we must give it a special order and clarity. Only then can it be understood by someone distant from us in both space and time. Sentences impose this order.

Using sentences effectively is therefore just as essential as using words effectively. Reading the work of a writer who has poor sentence structure is like listening to a tape rather than participating in the conversation: Everything comes out half-garbled.

This chapter examines ways to make your writing more cohesive by closely examining the structure of your sentences. If your papers come back to you marked with such symbols as *frag, shift, awk, confus, f s,* or *coh,* this chapter should be an important resource for you.

A. SENTENCE STRUCTURE

Can you recall hearing a young child recite one of his or her first poems? Usually it goes something like this:

> My mom loves tea
> My mom loves me
> And sometimes she gets a little too picky.

Good poems they are, too—direct, warm, and candid. When we think of them as *poetry,* however, they jar. Like the example above, such poems have too many syllables in some of the lines, or they change rhythmic patterns, or the rhymes don't quite rhyme. In short, these poems strike us as a little "off."

So, too, with sentences. Sometimes, without the writer's intending so, the arrangement of words in a sentence makes

> Who errs and mends,/To God himself commends.
> —Cervantes

it sound "off." The result is confusion for readers. Remember, they rely solely on the structure of the sentence to give order to the writer's ideas and help them make sense of what they read. When confusion occurs in some part of a paper you have written for one of your classes, the paper is likely to come back with a sentence or sentences marked for revision, perhaps by means of such symbols as *frag, coh, shift,* and *awk.* This section can help you interpret these symbols. Its purpose is to explain how to find out what is wrong with a sentence and what kind of changes you should make to correct the problem.

We begin by discovering what a sentence is.

Al. What Is a Sentence?

Of course everybody knows what a sentence is. Of course. Then how about a quick definition? Suddenly we all pause, hem and haw a bit, offer one or two possibilities, and then retract them. If we define a sentence as something made up of a subject and a verb, for example, where is the subject in a sentence like *Stop it!*? If we define it more generally as the basic unit of communication, what makes sentences more basic than words? Even if we separate speech from writing, don't we recognize that there are obvious connections between how we organize at least some of our speech and how we organize writing as sentences?

In other words, just about every formal definition we might construct would be open to one or more exceptions. The perfect definition would be harder to achieve than the perfect cup of coffee. It is not important that you have a definition. But what *is* important is knowing the *signs* or *clues* that signal the presence of a sentence:

- In speech, the signal is usually a falling pitch at the end of a group of words (you might say we "hear the period").

- In writing, the signals are capitalization at the beginning, a punctuation mark at the end, and the presence of both a subject (even if only understood) and a complete verb.

Let's be a little more specific. The first description, the one based on speech, relies on the verbal clues people give each other when they talk. Read aloud the following three lines:

You are coming home now.

Are you coming home now?

If you are coming home now . . .

The words used are almost identical in each case. Yet when you read them aloud, another person could recognize the first line as a complete declarative sentence, the second as a complete question, and the third as only part of a sentence. He or she would be able to make this distinction easily because of the way you let the pitch of your voice rise or fall to show the completion of a sentence unit. When we do use sentences, listeners know how to interpret these changes in pitch as markers for sentence units.

In writing, we can rely on capitalization of the first word and on some kind of end punctuation (period, question mark, exclamation point) as the easiest clues to sentences. However, while each sentence must have these signals, the converse is not true—that is, the mere presence of such clues does not guarantee a sentence. A proper name, for example, is always capitalized, and a midsentence interjection might be followed by an exclamation point *(but oh! what a difference)*. Neither of these would be sentences by themselves.

What *does* guarantee a complete sentence is the presence of a subject, even if it is only an understood subject, and a complete verb. Each of these two elements deserves a closer examination.

The word *subject* has two relevant meanings. The most familiar one is as a word occupying a certain place in a sentence. Consider the word *woman* in this sentence:

The woman behind me in the train spoke to the conductor.

Woman fills the subject place. To find the word filling the subject place in this or any sentence, perform a simple test: locate the verb, then ask *who?* or *what?* Here the verb is *spoke.* Who or what "spoke"? Clearly, "woman spoke." So *woman* fills the subject place.

But subject can also mean not just one word but rather a whole group of words, in fact all the words in a sentence that are not part of the predicate. (The *predicate* includes the verb and the words associated with or modifying the verb—more on this in a moment.) In our sample sentence, the full subject includes *woman* and all the words that explain it. Thus *The woman behind me in the train* is the full subject.

To keep these two meanings of *subject* distinct, and to make clear which meaning I intend each time I use the word, I will use the term **simple subject** to mean a word filling the subject place, such as *woman* in our example sentence. I will use the term **complete subject** to mean the whole group of words, everything in the sentence that is not the predicate.

I said earlier that sentences must have a complete verb (what is sometimes called a *finite verb*). You must identify the verb before you can tell whether it is complete. To find the verb, locate the word or words in the sentence that would change if the time of the sentence changed. For example, suppose a sentence refers to the present time:

I show my true feelings only to my family and close friends.

Change it to the past or future:

I showed my true feelings only to my family and close friends.

I will show my true feelings only to my family and close friends.

Clearly, *show* is the verb in the original sentence because it is the only word that changes when the time changes (*showed, will show*). Every sentence has a word (such as *show, shows, showed*) or a group of words (such as *was showing, are showing, will have been shown*) that changes to indicate time.

Remember that a key word in this description is *changes*. Some words do show time but are not verbs—*yesterday*, for example, or *today, tomorrow, then,* or *now.* None of these words can be verbs because none changes its form to show a change in time.

This test will locate the verbs in a sentence. However, you also need to determine whether the verb you have identified is the complete verb the sentence needs. That means keeping in mind two other principles:

1. A verb with an *-ing* attached to it cannot be the complete verb unless accompanied by another word that shows time.
2. A verb preceded by a pronoun such as *who, which,* or *that* or by a conjunction such as *if, although,* or *since* cannot be the complete verb. (Unless the sentence is cast as a question, such as "Who are you?")

Let me explain how the first principle works. Verbs with an *-ing* ending—that is, with a suffix added to a complete verb (*seeing, ringing, being*)—must be accompanied by other words that can change as the time changes in order to constitute a complete verb. Thus:

My hands were trembling as I removed the cap from the bottle.

The organ is playing quietly but sonorously.

Trembling and *playing* need *were* and *is* to complete them, because *were* and *is* can change to show a change in time (*are trembling, will be playing*). By themselves these verbs cannot form sentences:

My hands trembling as I removed the cap from the bottle. [not a sentence]

The organ playing quietly but sonorously. [not a sentence]

These -*ing* words can appear by themselves in sentences, but when they do there will always be a complete verb somewhere else in the sentence. For example:

The crackling of some twigs gave away my presence.

Crackling we know cannot be the verb because it is not accompanied by another verb that changes to show time changes. So we look elsewhere, and sure enough we come across *gave*. *Gave* can change (*gives*, *will give*) and is therefore the complete verb for the sentence.

Now for the second principle: A verb preceded by a pronoun such as *who*, *which*, or *that* or by a conjunction such as *if*, *although*, or *since* cannot be a complete verb. Look at the following example:

I do not know what I said to him when he came to my room that night. *James Baldwin*

When you read this sentence you encounter three verbs that might be the complete verb. *Do (not) know, said*, and *came* are all verbs that can change as the time changes (for example, *will know, says, comes*). But *said* is ineligible because it is preceded by the pronoun *what*. *Came* is ineligible because it is preceded by the conjunction *when*. So *do (not) know* remains the only verb that can be the complete verb for the sentence. The other two are the verbs for the dependent clauses in the sentence. (We will take up dependent clauses in Chapter 3.)

A complete verb is essential for a sentence. But a verb, just like a simple subject, can be accompanied by a large number of words that modify or explain it. These other words together with the verb itself can be termed collectively the **predicate.** The example sentence we used before was this one:

The woman behind me in the train spoke to the conductor.

We agreed that *woman* is the simple subject and that *The woman behind me in the train* forms the complete subject. So now *spoke* is the complete verb and *spoke to the conductor* forms the complete predicate, because these last words help describe to whom the woman spoke.

By now you should understand what a sentence is, whether or not you can offer a quick definition. To summarize:

- You should be able to find subjects—simple and complete (simple subject plus any explanatory words).
- You should be able to find complete verbs and complete predicates (complete verbs plus any explanatory words).
- You should further understand that sentences consist of at least a simple subject and a complete verb, and usually of a complete subject and a complete predicate.

A2. Sentence Fragments

The sentence fragment is perhaps the most obvious and is certainly one of the most frequent sources of confusion for readers. A problem sentence may distract your readers because what you have written is not really a sentence after all but rather a fragment (often abbreviated by the symbol *frag*). A sentence fragment, as its name implies, is only a part of a full sentence, lacking the subject and/or verb. Take this student-written example:

FRAGMENT: What agnosticism means to those who profess it.

REVISION: I wonder what agnosticism means to those who profess it.

In some cases the form of the verb is not the complete form necessary for a sentence, as in this example from a student paper:

FRAGMENT: Idealism giving way to pragmatism in today's world.

REVISION: Idealism is giving [gives, will give] way to pragmatism in today's world.

In student writing, fragments most commonly occur with sentences beginning with subordinating conjunctions such as *since, because, whereas,* and *although.* These conjunctions signal the beginning of a subordinate (i.e., dependent) clause, one that cannot stand by itself. The reader therefore expects this dependent clause to be followed by a complete, *independent* one, since each sentence must have at least one independent clause. If no independent clause is present, the result is a sentence fragment, as in this example from a student paper:

FRAGMENT: Since self-confidence begins with self-respect.
REVISION: Since self-confidence begins with self-respect, we must value our own achievements.

Now I must emphasize to you right away that sentence fragments are not always wrong. Everyday speech abounds in them: *Ready to go? Sure.* So when you record that speech on paper in the form of dialogue, naturally you will use fragments often. Fragments are also common in much of modern advertising copy:

Élan. Spirit. Dash. Animation. Characteristic of this Blazer as of all Christian Dior clothing. Styled to project the personality of the individual . . . to make you feel like no one else . . . to underscore your own *élan.*

Furthermore, good writers often use fragments to achieve special effects:

Rain all night until dawn. No sleep. Christ, here we go, a nightmare of mud and madness. *Hunter S. Thompson*

Finally, we are accustomed to fragments used as transitions: *Now for my last point.*

If fragments are so common, so much a part of what we read every day, and if their use can be perfectly appropriate, you might begin to wonder, "What's the problem?" Perhaps your paper has one or more sentences your instructor has labeled *frag* or *fragment*, and you're not sure why you can't do once or twice what professional writers do all the time.

The answer is that fragments are exceptions to normal sentence structure. Like all exceptions, they can be used only with good reason. Two good reasons stand out as justifications for fragments. The first is to provide emphasis or realism in certain special circumstances such as dialogue, transitions, and advertisements. However, I would be willing to bet that what your instructor circled on your paper was not dialogue, a transitional device, or advertising copy. The second good reason is the creation of a special effect, as long as the reader has no trouble filling in the missing parts of the sentence. By noting the fragment on your paper, your instructor is probably saying that he or she does not see how you have created any special effect or that the missing parts of your sentence cannot be reconstructed easily. If neither of these two "good reasons" applies to your sentence, it would be better if you had not made an exception to the normal pattern.

If you are still in doubt about whether you have made legitimate use of a fragment, a good test is to ask yourself whether you knew you were using a fragment at the time you wrote it. If you did, and your use of it was deliberate, maybe you have a case. But nineteen fragments out of twenty are used unconsciously. If your problem sentences were written this way, you should probably read through this section very carefully.

Also, there are degrees of permissibility among sentence fragments. Fragments in recorded dialogue, for example, are hardly ever wrong. At the other extreme, fragments that result from using an improper verb form are hardly ever right. Between these extremes are countless fragments, each of which must be judged on its own merits. Regarding this gray area, remember that professional writers have made these decisions

The privileges of a few do not make common law.
—St. Jerome

hundreds of times. Because of their wide reading and their experience, they can usually make tactful choices. You have less experience in such matters, so you are better off playing the percentages. A complete sentence is never wrong; a fragment might be. If there is any doubt, be safe for now and avoid the fragment. Then, as you gain more experience in writing, you will find yourself making occasional use of fragments, but you will do so with the self-assurance born of long practice.

Let's review again some examples of common sentence fragments. Try to clarify in your own mind what fragments are and what should be done about them. The most common type of sentence fragment is the dependent clause that stands alone. Here is a passage from a student journal, a sentence followed by a sentence fragment:

> I worry about whether I will get a job. Although I am convinced that new opportunities will open up before the end of spring.

The reason this kind of fragment is encountered so often is that it looks deceptively like a complete sentence. It has a subject (*I*) and a complete verb form (*am convinced*), and it is readily understandable to the reader. The only reason it needs to be revised is that it is a dependent clause, since it begins with a subordinating conjunction (*Although*) and cannot stand by itself without an independent clause. (See Chapter 3 if you need to review what independent and dependent clauses are.) One good solution is to attach it to—or make it depend on—the preceding sentence:

> I worry about whether I will get a job, although I am convinced that new opportunities will open up before the end of spring.

Alternatively, the fragment can be expanded into a complete sentence by adding a new independent clause:

> I worry about whether I will get a job. Although I am convinced that new opportunities will open up before the end of spring, I still can't help being anxious about my prospects.

Either way, the dependent clause is now attached to an independent clause and the fragment is eliminated. (The meaning of the two revisions is of course different.)

The second type of fragment occurs when the writer uses a phrase rather than an independent clause—in other words, when he or she omits the subject or the predicate, as in this example from a student journal (a sentence plus a fragment):

> In physical appearance I look like many other teenagers.
> With my eyes brown, my hair black.

This type of fragment is a little easier to identify than the first because it does not resemble a complete sentence so closely. Here the fragment has no verb and perhaps not even a subject (we are not sure of the function of *eyes* or *hair*). The remedies for this type of fragment are also similar, such as including the phrase in a preceding sentence or attaching it to a newly created subject and verb:

> In physical appearance, with my brown eyes and black hair,
> I look like many other teenagers.

> In physical appearance I look like many other teenagers. I
> have brown eyes and black hair.

A third type of fragment results from using an inappropriate verb form, thereby leaving the sentence without a complete predicate. Here is another example of a sentence followed by a fragment, from a newspaper letter:

> Politicians fear newspapers. Knowing the power of the written word.

Knowing is inappropriate because verb forms with the *-ing* ending do not by themselves constitute complete verbs. In other words, they cannot form predicates on their own. For example, *know, knew,* and *will know* are complete verb forms; in the revision, the complete verb form *know* should be chosen because it is in the present tense and therefore corresponds to the tense of the earlier sentence. Also, the subject (*politicians*) should be represented by a pronoun (*they*):

Politicians fear newspapers. They know the power of the
written word.

If this kind of fragment occurs frequently in your writing,
and especially if the nature of this type of error is not immediately clear to you, the chances are that the real difficulty
is not the fragment, even though your paper might be marked
that way. Instead the problem is most likely a weak grasp of
verb forms. Because verb forms are important to understand,
I'd suggest you review the section on them in Chapter 6.

A final type of fragment usually results from the writer's
momentary confusion, as in this example from a student
journal:

Terry, who claims that he really worries about passing calculus, nevertheless playing bridge in the union rather than
getting ready for the midterm.

Here the writer identified his subject (*Terry*), then got going on a perfectly good dependent clause. When the time
came to return to the main clause, he forgot that he had
not yet provided a complete predicate and went on to compose a phrase (*playing bridge in the union*). One way to
solve the problem would be to add a complete verb form
for the predicate:

Terry, who claims that he really worries about passing
calculus, nevertheless wastes several hours each day playing bridge in the union rather than getting ready for the
midterm.

Alternatively, the phrase could be revised so that it contains
a complete verb and contributes to forming an independent
clause:

Terry, who claims that he really worries about passing calculus, nevertheless plays bridge in the union rather than
getting ready for the midterm.

Haste and inadequate proofreading are normally the causes
of the kind of sentence fragment we've been discussing. A
simple practical solution is to ignore all dependent clauses

and other extraneous elements as you reread each of your sentences; check just the subject-predicate "heart" of the main clause and see whether it is capable of standing by itself as a complete sentence. Had the writer of the previous example followed this procedure, he would have seen this: *Terry . . . playing bridge in the union.* Immediately the difficulty would have been apparent.

Sentence fragments are quite common in student writing. If you need help in this area, be assured you are far from alone. Let me provide a six-stage "cure":

1. Reread the preceding paragraphs on fragments.
2. Examine the four common types of improper sentence fragments described and make sure you know why each example needs to be changed.
3. When you do not understand why a change is necessary, consult the other cross-referenced entries in this handbook that give background information.
4. Study the sentence fragments your instructor has identified in your papers, noting which of the four types they seem to resemble.
5. Rewrite your own sentence fragments as complete sentences.
6. For further practice, do the exercises given on pages 58–59.

Your prose should be healthy in no time. If your fragments do not fit one of the four types discussed here, or if you are still not sure about some points, ask your instructor for additional suggestions.

A3. Fused Sentences

If your instructor has noted that your paper has a "fused sentence," sometimes abbreviated as *fus* or *f s*, you have probably written a sentence that in its structure looks like this one:

> The lovers will meet in a turret on the ruins of an ancient city the time chosen for the poem is the moment just before they catch sight of each other.

Actually the term *fused sentence* (singular) is misleading, as there are really two sentences here rather than one. After all, there are two noun subjects (*lovers* and *time*), two verbs (*will meet* and *is*), as well as the other components that would be necessary for two separate, independent sentences. The problem is that there is no punctuation mark or transitional word between the two clauses (i.e., between *city* and *the*), as there must be if these are to be two independent units.

To eliminate a fused sentence, you can use a period and capitalization to preserve the idea of two separate sentences:

> The lovers will meet in a turret on the ruins of an ancient city. The time chosen for the poem is the moment just before they catch sight of each other.

A semicolon would keep them as a single sentence and still allow the two units to be separate:

> The lovers will meet in a turret on the ruins of an ancient city; the time chosen for the poem is the moment just before they catch sight of each other.

Still a third possibility is to combine the two units:

> The lovers will meet in the turret on the ruins of an ancient city, with the poem beginning just at the moment before they catch sight of each other.

The last alternative, because it involves the creation of a sentence modifier (see page 203), is not the easiest choice, but under some circumstances it might be the best.

Of course you may understand all of this perfectly well, and the fused sentence on your paper might be the result of simple carelessness. If so, you know the remedy as well as I do. But if you made the mistake in all innocence, and especially if you are not sure even now exactly what is wrong, the problem may be more serious. Perhaps you are not yet familiar with the structure of a complete sentence. Under this circumstance I would urge you to reread pages 44–48 on sentence structure, review pages 249–252 on punctuating the end of sentences, and check out pages 123–127 on transition words.

EXERCISES

1. Convert the following student-written sentence fragments into complete sentences. Let your imagination supply any missing information:

   A. Each of the children impatiently waiting for their turn to pin the tail on the donkey.
   B. Separate experiences, beyond those forced upon them by the fact that the husband goes to his office, while the wife remains home to clean and shop.
   C. Because his arrogance will not allow him to admit he is wrong.
   D. The carnies shouting tempting statements to their prospective patrons, promising quick and sure rewards.
   E. When all of a sudden I heard a voice yell, "Watch out!"
   F. Which certainly will not endear her to the voters.
   G. We had decided on the chicken kiev until the waiter, frowning as if it was somehow our fault, muttering that they were all out of that item.
   H. A funny feeling in my throat and I broke out in a cold sweat.

2. Here is an example of the deliberate use of sentence fragments by a professional writer, Thomas Merton. What reasons might he have had for using them?

   Our famous course in Contemporary Civilization had involved me, one winter afternoon, in a visit to the Bellevue Morgue, where I had seen rows and rows of iceboxes containing the blue, swollen corpses of drowned men along with all the other human refuse of the big, evil city: The dead that had been picked up in the streets, ruined by raw alcohol. The dead that had been found starved and frozen lying where they had tried to sleep in a pile of old newspapers. The pauper dead from Randalls Island. The dope-fiend dead. The murdered dead. The run-over. The suicides. The dead Negroes and Chinese. The dead of venereal disease. The dead from unknown causes. The dead killed by gangsters. They would all be shipped for burial up the East River in a barge to one of those islands where they also burned garbage.

3. Find three or four other examples of sentence fragments used by professional writers. What justifications might the writers offer for these fragments?

B. CONFUSING SENTENCES

Structural difficulties caused by incomplete and "over-complete" sentences (fragments and fused sentences, respectively) are not the only possibilities. Writers can unwittingly confuse their readers in one or more of the following ways.

B1. Shifts

Sentences in both idea and form are expected to have a certain logic to them, to be consistent from one part to another. But sometimes that consistency is lacking, because the writer has used one grammatical form in the first part of the sentence and then without good reason has shifted to another grammatical form later in the sentence. We need to examine five kinds of such shifts: shifts of tense, voice, and mood, which have to do with verbs, and shifts of person and number, which have to do with pronouns.

A **shift of tense,** often abbreviated on papers by *t*, *tense*, *tnse*, and *shift*, occurs when a sentence has two or more verb forms that logically ought to be consistent with one another but are not. Consider this example from a student paper:

> We were just coming out of the drugstore when suddenly he is standing there right in front of me, staring at me.

The first verb, *were coming*, describes a continuing action in the past. The verb of the second clause, *is standing*, describes an action that happened at the same time—the *coming* and the *standing* occur simultaneously. Yet the tense of the second clause has shifted. Instead of describing a continuing past action, as *were coming* does, it describes a continuing present action, *is standing*. So the unintended shift must be eliminated by making the tenses of the two verbs the same, either both in the past or both in the present:

> We were just coming out of the drugstore when suddenly he was standing there right in front of me, staring at me.

> We are just coming out of the drugstore when suddenly he is standing there right in front of me, staring at me.

Please notice two important cautions about shifts in tense:

1. A simple change in tense is not wrong. Many sentences change tenses quite properly, as in this example:

> I have known many young people who, particularly in late adolescence, come to a belief in magic, to compensate for their having been deprived of it prematurely in childhood. *Bruno Bettelheim*

In this case our sense of time has not been violated. The verb of each clause has the tense appropriate to express the time of the action described in the clause.

2. Keeping the tenses the same throughout a sentence does not guarantee the sentence will be consistent. Can you see what is wrong with this example?

> I was thoroughly exhausted after supper because I worked hard all afternoon.

Was and *worked* are the same tense—and therein lies the problem, because clearly the working took place *before* the state of exhaustion, and in fact had caused the state of exhaustion. We can correct this unintended shift by putting the second clause further back in time:

> I was thoroughly exhausted after supper because I had worked hard all afternoon.

So keep aware of the *time logic* of your sentences. Make sure that the tense of any verb is the logical tense for that verb in relation to the tense of other verbs. Be especially careful about sentences that shift from the past tense to the present, as in the first example above. Here is another example to help you clinch your understanding of this point:

> I dropped my quarters into the machine but nothing comes out.

Because these two events happened at the same time, there is no reason to shift from past tense to present. Therefore *comes* should be *came:*

> I dropped my quarters into the machine but nothing came out.

Alternatively, *dropped* should be *drop:*

> I drop my quarters into the machine but nothing comes out.

Shifts in voice or mood occur less frequently. **Shifts in voice** happen when part of a sentence is in the active voice and part is in the passive (see active and passive voice, pages 105–106):

> Although we formed a committee to study the problem, the observation was made by all of us that such a committee would not provide any easy solutions.

Technically, this sentence is grammatically correct. But there is no good reason for shifting from the active voice (*formed*) to the passive (*was made*). Because it is generally better to avoid the passive, as discussed on page 105, putting the verbs in the active voice improves the sentence and makes the two parts of the sentence parallel:

> Although we formed a committee to study the problem, we all observed that such a committee would not provide any easy solutions.

A **shift in mood** arises when a sentence begins in one mood, such as declarative (a statement), and then changes to another, such as interrogative (a question). Here is an example from a newspaper letter:

> The government intends to discourage gas-guzzling SUVs by taxing them heavily, and what is this going to accomplish?

The first half of this sentence, up to the comma, is declarative: It makes a statement. The second half is interrogative: It asks a question. But changes in mood should occur only between sentences, not within the same sentence. The writer should make these two halves into separate sentences:

> The government intends to discourage gas-guzzling SUVs by taxing them heavily. What is this going to accomplish?

Pronouns can cause trouble, too. (Abbreviations for pronoun errors can include *shift, pro* or *pron, ref, number, person.*) In fact, the most frequent shift of all for most writers involves pronouns, and that is the unintended **shift in number.** In such cases one part of a sentence will refer to a singular person or thing, while a different part of the sentence will refer to the same person or thing in the plural. For example:

> Sometimes a customer will barge right to the front of the line, and then they demand immediate service, as if they had been waiting all day.

Customer (singular) is the subject, but the plural pronoun *they* is used to refer to it. The increasing frequency of this kind of shift probably comes from the fact that writers are trying to avoid sexist language (see Chapter 8). Knowing that a customer can be either male or female, they use the plural pronoun to avoid making a gender-specific reference. However, such a shift from one number to the other within the same sentence should be removed. Like this:

> Sometimes customers will barge right to the front of the line, and then they demand immediate service, as if they had been waiting all day.

Alternatively, of course, *customer* could be kept singular and the pronouns could be made singular as well (*as if he or she had been waiting*).

Because this kind of shift is so frequently made in the papers of beginning writers, we should look at another student-written example:

> The adoptee would know not only more about his genealogy but also more about themselves and how they function.

Do you see that the writer of this sentence first considered *adoptee* in the singular (*adoptee, his*) but then shifted the pronoun number to the plural (*themselves, they*)?

By now you can probably guess that a **shift in person** means an unnecessary change in the person of a pronoun from one part of a sentence to another. Here is an example from a magazine article:

> A good hiker puts in maybe thirty miles a day, and by then you really know the meaning of the word *tired*.

The first independent clause describes hikers in the third person, but the second independent clause, in referring to those same hikers, uses the second-person pronoun *you*. Again either of two revisions is possible, as long as the writer is consistent:

> A good hiker puts in maybe thirty miles a day, and by then he or she really knows the meaning of the word *tired*.

> On a good day's hike you put in maybe thirty miles, and by then you really know the meaning of the word *tired*.

The important thing to remember about all these kinds of shifts is the ultimate goal: consistency. If you can become aware of the need for this consistency—if you can see, for example, how logic demands that verb tenses be related to one another according to the times when various events have taken place—then you will help the reader by making such distinctions clear. In the meantime, while you are developing this awareness, correct those shifts that instructors or other readers call to your attention.

B2. Mixed Constructions

Shifts are not the only source of illogic in sentences; sometimes confusion arises when a writer begins a sentence with

All good writing is like swimming under water and holding your breath.
—F. Scott Fitzgerald

one kind of construction and then later uses another kind incompatible with the first. The result is called a mixed construction, often abbreviated *mis, mixed,* or *coh[erence]*. An example would be a sentence like the following one from a student paper:

> By the look in his eye and the way he twisted his hands provided evidence enough of his guilt.

The problem here is that the sentence opens with a phrase and then proceeds directly to the verb, *provided.* Because the phrase is a long one and because it includes a clause, the writer forgot that after all it was still just a phrase and that no proper subject had yet been stated. The sentence must be revised so that the phrase has a subject it can modify; in this case the subject becomes the pronoun *we:*

> By the look in his eye and the way he twisted his hands we had evidence enough of his guilt.

Perhaps a better alternative is to convert the phrase itself into a proper subject:

> The look in his eye and the way he twisted his hands provided evidence enough of his guilt.

Just as a dependent phrase cannot be a subject by itself, neither can a dependent clause:

> Because your vitamin intake decreases makes dieting a danger to your health.

Again the writer could provide a subject that the dependent clause can modify:

> Because your vitamin intake decreases, dieting can be a danger to your health.

Or, the clause can be made into a noun plus a phrase:

> The decrease in your vitamin intake makes dieting a danger to your health.

Forms of the verb *to be* cause their own special set of difficulties. The verb *to be* is a linking verb. Therefore, it

sets up an equation: The subject is said to be in some way
the same as the complement (the noun or adjective that follows the linking verb). Occasionally the subject is mistakenly linked not to a complement that can be equivalent to
the subject but rather to an adverb clause. This is particularly true of adverb clauses introduced by *where* or *when*,
as in these two student-written examples:

> Revenge is where you make another person suffer for what
> he has done to you.

> The highest honor this country can bestow is when the presi-
> dent awards the Medal of Freedom.

Such sentences need revision because the adverb clauses
do not modify the verb *is* but instead try to serve as complements. So a legitimate complement—a noun or an adjective—must be used in place of the clause:

> Revenge is the act of making another person suffer for what
> he has done to you.

> The highest honor this country can bestow is the Medal of
> Freedom awarded by the president.

The necessary equations have now been established: *Revenge = act; honor = Medal.*

 The *is where* and *is when* constructions have a close relative, *the reason is because*, found in sentences such as the
following from a newspaper article:

> The reason many people file their income tax forms too late
> is because they fail to plan far enough ahead.

Reason needs a genuine complement after the linking verb
is:

> The reason many people file their income tax forms too late
> is their failure to plan far enough ahead.

Reason = failure and the equation is restored.
 Alternatively, one could use a *that* clause:

> The reason many people file their income tax forms too late
> is that they fail to plan far enough ahead.

B3. Omitted Words

Sometimes necessary words are left out of a sentence through simple neglect. Perhaps you are writing swiftly and your mind is flying ahead of your fingers, so that you think the word but your pen or keyboard fails to record it. Or perhaps as you type up the final copy of a handwritten draft you skip past a word in the draft. The result might be a sentence that is clear to the reader even though a word has been omitted:

> The president's economic advisers, no matter what their plans, must face the inevitability congressional revision.

Immediately we recognize that the word *of* has been inadvertently left out of its proper position before *congressional* and must be restored.

In other sentences, however, the omitted word may not be so obvious, and the meaning of the sentence will then be unclear. This, for example:

> Some of the amendment's feel that its prospects this year are very shaky indeed.

We know that a plural noun has been left out after *amendment's*. But what noun? Perhaps the word is *supporters*, *defenders*, or *proponents;* then again it might be *opponents* or *enemies*.

The only solution for such mistakes is careful proofreading. But another category of omitted words is even more troublesome and probably would not be eliminated in the proofreading stage. This category usually illustrates Alexander Pope's statement that "a little learning is a dangerous thing." For example, a writer may know that the following sentence is quite proper even when the bracketed words *who have* are removed:

> Volunteers who have given more than five hours of their time or [who have] contributed more than $50 are entitled to go to the annual banquet.

The reason the second *who have* combination can be dropped is that its presence is understood—in other words, the reader sees the paired verbs *given* and *contributed* and knows that *who have* applies to them both.

Occasionally, however, the tense of paired verbs might change. When the tense changes, both verbs must be written out in their entirety. Should part of one be omitted, as *who have* was omitted above, the result is a sentence like this one:

> Medicine has and always will attract people concerned just with making money.

The student writer of this sentence assumed that, since a form of *attract* is the verb in both cases, one can be left out as understood. But it can't, because the change in tense from past (*has*) to future (*will*) means that the form of the verb *attract* must also change—*has attracted* for the past, *will attract* for the future. The sentence should read like this:

> Medicine has always attracted and will always attract people concerned just with making money.

Prepositions can cause similar difficulties. It is quite all right to eliminate one of two prepositions used with a compound verb or with two adjectives, *if* the preposition would be the same in both cases:

> I am astounded [by] and even outraged by Young's offhandedness.

Because *by* goes with both adjectives—*astounded* and *outraged*—the first *by* is unnecessary. But verbs and adjectives often have specific prepositions associated with them. For example, we are charmed *by* people, but we can also be interested *in,* attracted *to,* or angry *with* them. If a writer uses two verbs or two adjectives, and if the appropriate prepositions are different in each case, then both prepositions must be written. If one is omitted, the result is this kind of sentence:

> Flat-tax groups are dedicated and working for the overthrow of our entire taxation system.

The preposition *for* goes with *working* all right, but not with *dedicated*. The preposition *to* must be used with *dedicated*, so the sentence should read:

> Flat-tax groups are dedicated to and working for the overthrow of our entire taxation system.

One final type: Can you see what has been mistakenly omitted from these two student-written comparisons?

> Tuition here costs no less than any other private university.

> American small cars like the Focus are now as economical if not more economical than the imports.

These comparisons are not as precisely worded as they should be. The first sentence, if taken literally, says that tuition costs less than any university, which does not make sense. In the second sentence, *than* goes quite well with *more economical*, but it cannot also be appropriate for *as economical* (*as economical than*?). Yet the absence of any other word after *as economical* implies that *than* is understood. When the omitted words are inserted, the comparisons become exact:

> Tuition here costs no less than it does at any other university.

> American small cars like the Focus are now as economical as, if not more economical than, the imports.

B4. Lack of Parallel Structure

Parts of a sentence that are in a series or are joined by a coordinating conjunction (see page 91) need to have the same grammatical structure. In other words, they have to be *parallel*. Consider this student-written sentence:

> My philosophy is rooted in the idea of equality and realizing that each person has his or her own strengths and weaknesses.

If you examine this sentence carefully you will see that the words *idea* and *realizing* serve the same function. Both are objects of *is rooted in*—in other words, *is rooted in the idea* and *is rooted in realizing.* But *idea* and *realizing* are not parallel in structure, because the former is a noun and the latter is an *-ing* word, or gerund (see page 489). While each by itself would be a perfectly appropriate form, when used jointly they must be parallel. Therefore, the sentence needs to be changed. The best choice is to make *realizing* into its noun form *realization,* so that *is rooted in* has two nouns as its objects:

> My philosophy is rooted in the idea of equality and the realization that each person has his or her own strengths and weaknesses.

Another possibility is to use two *-ing* words as the objects and then to make both clauses similar in form:

> My philosophy is rooted in believing that all people are equal and realizing that each person has his or her own strengths and weaknesses.

Be especially careful of the need for parallelism when you use *-ing* words, infinitives (see page 490 for a definition of *infinitive*), and adjectives. The following three sentences illustrate the proper use of parallelism in such cases:

> Older people *walking* city streets or *taking* public transportation are particularly vulnerable to this type of crime.

> Male movie stars are no longer always *handsome, virile,* and *diffident.*

> *To* die, *to* sleep—perchance *to* dream. *William Shakespeare*

Most writers experience their greatest temptation in those sentences like our first example, where the form of any one of the nonparallel parts would be satisfactory if used alone. Here is another student example:

> In tennis, I like volleying and to hit the big serve.

Both of the following sentences are acceptable:

> In tennis, I like volleying.

> In tennis, I like to hit the big serve.

The trick is in seeing that when they are used together the resulting sentence has parallel construction:

> In tennis, I like volleying and hitting the big serve.

> In tennis, I like to volley and to hit the big serve.

Two final examples from student papers may clinch the point:

NOT PARALLEL: The advantages of capital punishment are twofold: (1) those who are truly beyond help will not be allowed back out to commit more crimes; (2) so people will think of the consequences before committing a serious crime.

REVISION: The advantages of capital punishment are twofold: (1) those who are truly beyond help will not be allowed back out to commit more crimes; (2) people will think of the consequences before committing a serious crime.

In the revision, the dependent clause *so people will think* . . . is changed to an independent clause, *people will think* . . . ; thus both advantages are stated as independent clauses.

NOT PARALLEL: The foreman was curt, irritable, and a man to be feared.

REVISION: The foreman was curt, irritable, and fear inspiring.

Remember that there is no single "right" way to revise nonparallel sentence structures. In the last example, for instance, you could avoid the awkwardness of creating an adjective out of the phrase *a man to be feared* by making it function differently:

> The foreman was curt and irritable, altogether a man to be feared.

The point is simply that like function always requires like structure.

B5. Awkward or Confusing Sentences

This final category of sentence problems is the hardest to define. Thus far we have dealt mainly with sentences that might have been understandable to the reader but that contained some errors in structure. In this case we are talking about sentences for which the reader's reaction can be summed up in just one word: *Huh?* Your instructor might signal his or her own *Huh?* by using such symbols as *awk* or *awkward, conf[using], coh, illog,* or maybe just a plain question mark.

When the meaning of a sentence is not clear, one of the reasons, as we saw in Chapter 1, might be the choice of words. But sometimes the sentence itself may be at fault. Consider this example from a student's paper:

> Some scientists claim marijuana causes nausea and dizziness, but the user of marijuana comes nowhere near resembling these effects.

At first reading, the sentence is illogical. How can a user resemble an effect? After a moment's thought we can see what happened. Two possible ways of expressing her meaning occurred to the writer:

> . . . but the user of marijuana does not experience these effects.

> . . . but the real effects of marijuana come nowhere near resembling the effects described by scientists.

Because the two possibilities probably came to her simultaneously, they were combined into one hybrid sentence. Either of the original possibilities by itself would be fine. But a combination of them confuses us.

A similar confusion can also result from undue haste in determining what structure a sentence should have. Here is one example:

> Another question about the Chappaquiddick party is why the men who were married were their wives not there.

The writer evidently plunged into the sentence without giving sufficient thought to the possible complications. Her ideas are all there, but they need to be sorted out. As it stands now, the last clause says literally that the men were their wives, which of course is absurd. A little reordering of the sentence allows the meaning to emerge clearly:

> Another question about the Chappaquiddick party is why the wives of the married men were not there.

A sentence can also be confusing if it is *ambiguous*, having more than one possible meaning. An ambiguous sentence can be understood in at least one other way besides the one the author intends. Consider this example:

> Pound wrote to Eliot many times while he was editor of *Poetry* magazine in Chicago.

It's not clear from this sentence that it was Pound, not Eliot, who was the editor. Here is another example of ambiguity:

> The essay was described as the best ever written by the English instructor.

Who wrote the essay? The English instructor or a student? Take care not to confuse the reader with sentences like these that have more than one possible interpretation. Here are alternative wordings:

> The student's essay was described as the best the English instructor had ever read.

> The essay was described as the best one the English instructor had ever written.

A sentence can also be technically correct but so awkwardly constructed that the reader loses his or her bearings. Try to read this monster from a student paper:

> If three-quarters of the state legislatures (that is, thirty-eight states in total) ratify an amendment within seven years (every proposed constitutional amendment, once approved by Congress, has a time limit of seven years to be ratified by the states—if the legislatures do not approve by then, the amendment becomes extinct), it will become the law of the land.

By the time readers have untangled this
knot of parentheses, clauses, and commas
to arrive at the true subject—the pronoun
it—they will have long since forgotten
what *it* means. The problem here is like

*Backward ran sentences
until reeled the mind.
—Wolcott Gibbs*

one we will see in Chapter 4, where too great a separation
between pronoun and antecedent overtaxes readers' memories and confuses them. Here the abundance of intervening
phrases and clauses breaks up the continuity of the sentence and strains the reader's patience and concentration.
It is better to eliminate the awkwardness by separating the
material and putting like ideas together:

> Every proposed amendment, once approved by Congress,
> must be ratified within seven years or it becomes extinct; if
> three-quarters of the state legislatures—or thirty-eight states
> in all—ratify the amendment within the time limit, it will
> become the law of the land.

That sentence is much less troublesome to a reader.

The causes for confusing, illogical, or awkward sentences
are many. Sometimes haste (by the author) makes waste
(for the reader). Sometimes writers cannot see how the
possible implications of a sentence could puzzle their audience. Sometimes words are left out because the ideas they
represent seem clear to the writer, even though they are not
necessarily clear to a reader. In short, the hobgoblin is usually a variation on that ancient lament, "But I know what I
mean!" The reader would then have to reply, "You may know
what you mean, but all I have to rely on is what you *write*,
and I don't understand what you write."

If your experience is at all like mine, you often are vaguely
aware that a sentence you have just written might be confusing or awkward. You have an uneasy feeling that it's "not
quite right." Probably you can't say what, if anything, is
wrong with it or how it should be reworded, and besides,
you are already busy on the next sentence. What I do in
such cases is simply put a question mark next to a printout
of the sentence and then keep right on going. The question
mark just means the sentence ought to be looked at again.

Later, during the revision process, I reexamine these sentences, weighing them more carefully this time. Reading them now, from a fresher and more objective viewpoint, do I see problems with any of them? If so, which ones? In each case, what is the source of the problem, and how can I go about making the meaning clear to my reader?

EXERCISES

1. The following sentences have been written by students. Identify the problem in each case and rewrite the sentence to eliminate it.

   A. First of all because the researchers into TV violence are biased.
   B. Kay likes walking to work rather than to take the car.
   C. The sun came out and was beating down on our heads I was the last one to leave the beach.
   D. I hated to enlist but nevertheless I knew it will be the best choice for me.
   E. Even though, in the past ten years, there have been two federal laws passed that challenge sex-based discrimination on the job.
   F. On any typical weeknight you can see people beaten, car accidents, and people murdered all in your own living room.
   G. Love is where you give more than you take.
   H. Women want equality to lie within the laws of society.
   I. And didn't even find out until the next morning.
   J. Which is a necessary thing to do if you want to solve our economic difficulties.
   K. Ms. Wilkes has it all: money, looks, being well liked.
   L. To ensure a fair distribution of parts throughout the class.
   M. People sometimes have been very generous to me, but just because he gives me something I don't have to like him.
   N. Going home for Christmas vacation, which I have looked forward to for several weeks.
   O. The bus came toward us and stops right next to the curb.
   P. By "equal" a woman means in terms of legality.
   Q. The city has failed to provide the city employee with the basic necessities of life they are searching for.

R. Because you can't promise the customer a good deal and then not deliver the goods.

S. Often my mother is puzzled and even angry with me.

2. Take the last three papers you have written. Do any of the five sentence faults listed in Part B occur more than once in those papers? If so, carefully study the relevant section(s) of Part B, and rewrite the faulty sentences.

3. The following sentences can give you explicit practice with shifts and faulty parallelism. Rewrite the sentences.

   A. A very good place to change your tire is on a leveled spot and try to avoid sloping areas such as a hill.

   B. Different messages pass our conscious mind and work its way into the subconscious.

   C. Depressants have some unusual effects on the body such as a lack of interest in the surroundings, inability to move or talk, pulse and respiratory rate slows, depression deepens.

   D. We were led out to the back lot and I find myself staring at the shiny, smiling grilles of brand new Chevy trucks.

   E. I wear glasses and I choose black frames because it didn't make me look too old.

   F. He spent two hours hunting, trapping, and finally he captured the turtle.

   G. Mr. Fugueroa gave us confidence and writes words of encouragement on our homework and tests.

   H. I could see she was as delighted giving the earrings as I was to receive them.

   I. Governments change quite frequently in Italy and it lasts only about six months on the average.

4. The following sentences are for one reason or another confused, illogical, mixed up. Decide—as well as you can—what the author *intended* to say: Rewrite each sentence so that it conveys the meaning you have discovered.

   A. The two people with vows of love and desire to spend the rest of their lives together making each other happy.

   B. The dress will be done to your specifications and a sense of personal achievement when the garment is finished.

C. Studies have shown women who drink like animals.

D. Clocks are currently for the most part universal in appearance.

E. In conclusion, there is not one single word to describe myself.

F. Man repeatedly establishes himself as possessor of integrity and goodness, far outweighing the collective sum of his negative qualities.

G. Natural parents will be allowed to reunite with the adults they gave up as children.

H. The mind is truly a wondrous organ bursting with feelings.

5. Rewrite the following student paragraphs, correcting whatever sentence faults you encounter.

A. Sometimes I really get fed up with the way people act. So much hatred. It's really sickening to hate so many things and people. Realizing you have these prejudices too. I feel rotten trying not to act opinionated. But I find it hard not to cut people up, to say what I really think, and letting my true feelings come to the surface.

B. War has a historical base point. The histories of man are filled with stories of fighting between one group and another and it tells of neverending struggle. The Greeks fought, the Romans fought, the English fought, and then there is the war in Kosovo or Afghanistan for us. Man endowed his children with tales of combat and gives them weapons of destruction from the time he first walks. Because man does not truly wish peace, despite what he says to the contrary. Warrior classes have always had the greatest respect. This is still true today. Evidence can be found in anything from our habit of electing presidents only from those who have a military background, to on the other hand military prestige associated with "the uniform," and is this sensible? I believe man is not a rational creature. If you haven't guessed.

3

Better Sentences

The playwright Ben Jonson once claimed that a writer's "reason [cannot] be in frame whose sentence is preposterous." Jonson was putting it a bit strongly, perhaps. But surely he was right in finding a close relationship between the structure of a writer's sentences and the clear statement of the writer's ideas. Now that we have analyzed ways to make sure your sentences are structurally *sound*, we move on to discuss how to make them structurally *mature*. This chapter explains the various ways you can improve your sentences, thus helping you achieve a clearer and more effective writing style.

A. SENTENCE VARIETY

Variety in the types and lengths of sentences you use is an important goal, because it is an index of the maturity of your writing style.

A1. Variety of Sentence Types

Sentences can be categorized according to the number and types of clauses they contain. A **clause** is any group of words that has a subject and a predicate. If a clause has a complete verb, it can form a sentence by itself, as we saw in Chapter 2. It is therefore called an **independent** or **main clause.** On the other hand, if a clause is introduced by a pronoun such as *who, which,* or *that* or by a conjunction such as *if, although,* or *since,* it cannot form a sentence by itself and is called a **dependent** or **subordinate clause.** (Again, the exception is if the clause is in the form of a question beginning with *who* or *which.*)

When a sentence has only one independent clause, and therefore only one subject-predicate combination, it is called a **simple sentence:**

Procrastination can endanger your academic health.

The first word is the subject; the remaining group of words is the predicate. Note that it is quite possible to have two simple subject words and still have a simple sentence:

Procrastination and *inattention* can endanger your academic health.

The two italicized words are both examples of simple subjects. Together, however, they form only one complete subject, and this is the crucial test. Two or more simple subject words, by the way, form what is called a *compound subject.* Similarly, the predicate can contain two verbs (thus being termed a *compound predicate*) and still make only a simple sentence:

Procrastination *can endanger* your academic health and *destroy* your peace of mind.

Now that you know that two simple subject words together make a compound subject, and two complete verbs make a compound predicate, you can probably deduce what a **compound sentence** might be. If there are two or more independent clauses in a sentence—in other words, two or more clauses that by themselves can form separate sentences—and if the clauses are connected by a semicolon or by *and, but, or,* or *nor,* the result is called a compound sentence:

> Unions must represent all hourly employees in labor nego-
> tiations, and therefore they resent and lobby against right-
> to-work laws.

If you replace the comma in this sentence with a period and
capitalize the first letter of the *and* that follows, the two
independent clauses would then become two simple sentences. Because they are joined by the comma and the *and*
conjunction, the clauses form not two separate sentences
but rather one compound sentence. Observe, too, that this
particular compound sentence has a compound verb (*re-
sent* and *lobby*) in the second of its two independent clauses.

Every sentence has either one independent clause
(simple) or more than one (compound). In addition, many
sentences contain a dependent clause, one that has a subject and a predicate but cannot form a sentence on its own.
When one or more of these dependent clauses are present,
the sentence is said to be a **complex sentence.** Consider
this example:

> Few people realize the horrendous odds against them when
> they play the state lottery.

The clause *when they play the state lottery* is a dependent
clause because it begins with the conjunction *when* and therefore cannot stand alone as a sentence. The inclusion of this
clause allows us to term the example a complex sentence.

Furthermore if a sentence has two or more independent
clauses (thus compound), and one or more dependent
clauses (thus complex), the resulting hybrid can be termed
a **compound-complex sentence.** Here is one:

> Artists have rarely been well paid for their labors, and now
> if the NEA is eliminated their future looks even bleaker.

Two independent clauses are joined by the conjunction *and*,
forming a compound sentence. The second independent
clause includes the dependent clause *if the NEA is eliminated*, so the full sentence becomes compound-complex.

To clarify these differences in your mind, refer to this
diagram summarizing types of sentences:

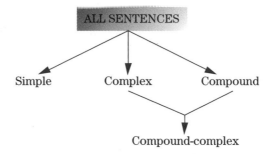

Simple enough? Complex enough?

The importance of knowing how to categorize sentences is simply this: You now have a good way of finding out why and how your sentences might be too monotonous.

Consider this example paragraph:

> It took a good deal of courage when I registered for class on June 11. But I am pleased that I decided to take the step. On that day I purchased all the textbooks that I would need for this class. I wanted to be sure that I would have all the material I needed. Then I got my bill, both for this course and for the textbooks. I realized I'd better get serious about returning to school if I was going to spend my hard-earned money. I also realized that I was going to have to start saying no to social invitations. It is going to be very hard, but I am determined to do well.

The paragraph is made up of eight sentences. Notice the sources of monotony:

1. Almost every sentence—six of eight—is a complex sentence following the formula of main clause + dependent clause. Only one sentence (the fifth) is simple; only one (the last) is compound; none is compound-complex.
2. Almost every sentence—again six of the eight—has *I* as the subject; the other two have *it*.
3. Every sentence begins with the same pattern of simple subject + verb, with perhaps at most a conjunction or brief phrase intervening. Compare them:

   It took . . .
   But I am pleased . . .

On that day I purchased . . .
I wanted . . .
Then I got . . .
I realized . . .
I also realized . . .
It is going to be . . .

*The world's a scene of
changes, and to be
Constant, in Nature
were inconstancy.
—Abraham Cowley*

In other words, this paragraph shows almost no variety in sentence type or in choice of simple subject. And within the one type of sentence that does predominate (complex), the same pattern is used over and over, main clause + dependent clause, main clause + dependent clause, clakety-clack, clakety-clack, like the railroad cars of a fast passenger train. It's as if the writer has one formula for making sentences and cannot think of breaking free of it.

Suppose the paragraph were rewritten to use a greater variety of sentence patterns. It might read like this:

> Although it took courage to register for class on June 11, I'm pleased I decided to take the step. On that day I also purchased all the textbooks I would need for class, so that I would have the necessary material. But when I got my bills, both for the course and for the books, I suddenly realized that if I was going to spend my hard-earned money, I had better get serious about school and start saying no to social invitations. It's going to be hard—but I'm determined to do well.

Eight sentences have been pared to four, monotonous patterns have been broken up, and some ideas have been emphasized more than others. The paragraph still needs work, especially on word choice and level of detail, but at least a first step has been taken.

Here is a paragraph that illustrates the variety of sentence structures a good writer can produce. The novelist Eudora Welty is describing for us a scene in a Ross MacDonald detective novel; the sentences are numbered so that they can be discussed in the paragraph that follows. The excerpt is from a review of *The Underground Man*.

> (1) Fairy tale and living reality alternate on one current to pulse together in this remarkable scene. (2) The woman

is a pivotal character, and Archer has caught up with her;
they are face to face, and there comes a moment's embrace.
(3) Of the many brilliant ways Mr. MacDonald has put his
motif to use, I believe this is the touch that delighted me
most. (4) For of course Archer, this middle-aging Califor-
nian who has seen everything in a career of going into impossible trouble with his eyes open, who has always been
the protector of the weak and the rescuer of the helpless, is
a born romantic. (5) Here he meets his introverted and ail-
ing counterpart—this lady is the chatelaine of the roman-
tic-gone-wrong. (6) He is not by nature immune, especially
to what is lovely or was lovely once. (7) At a given moment,
they may brush close—as Archer, the only one with insight
into himself, is aware.

Notice the immense variety in the structure of the seven
sentences that make up the paragraph. We could sum up
our observations on them like this:

(1) simple sentence
(2) two compound sentences, joined by a semicolon (four
    simple clauses in all)
(3) complex sentence; dependent clause + main clause +
    dependent clause
(4) complex sentence; subject + two dependent clauses +
    verb and complement
(5) compound sentence; two independent clauses
(6) complex sentence; main clause + dependent clause
(7) complex sentence; main clause + dependent clause

How do you learn to write sentences with the variety of
Eudora Welty's rather than the monotony of our first
writer's? The first step is to increase your awareness of sentence patterns. Notice what sentence patterns you habitu-
ally use. Use terms such as *complex* or *compound* to characterize your own writing. Take a few paragraphs from something you have written recently and analyze them the way
we have just analyzed Ms. Welty's paragraph.

Then, having determined the patterns you use most often, ask yourself some questions. Begin with something you
have already written, trying to revise a couple of paragraphs

according to the answers you receive. Then start a new writing project—perhaps an English paper—and ask the questions *while you write,* incorporating the answers as you go along. Here are the questions:

1. Do your sentences begin the same way too often? For example, do they almost all begin with a noun subject, with a conjunction such as *but,* with a personal pronoun such as *I,* or with the indefinite *there* (*There is . . .*)? If so, try sometimes to begin with a phrase or a dependent clause. And vary your simple subject, especially if that subject is too often a personal pronoun or the indefinite *there.*

2. Do you almost always use the same subject-verb-object (S-V-O) pattern in your sentences? Remember that occasionally it is permissible to invert the usual word order, either by a question or—every once in a great while—by putting the subject last (O-V-S) or perhaps even in the middle (O-S-V), thus throwing special emphasis on the words that stand in the subject's usual place. Here is an example:

> Glorious islets, too, I have seen rise out of the haze.
> *Thomas Carlyle*

The O (*islets*)-S (*I*)-V (*have seen*) pattern focuses the reader's attention on *islets.*

3. Do you almost always use simple sentences? compound sentences? complex sentences of a certain predictable pattern? If so, try to find ways to break out of those confining patterns. Perhaps you also need to examine more carefully the relationships among your ideas, so that you can learn to subordinate some ideas to others (in other words, put some ideas into phrases or dependent clauses rather than leaving them as independent clauses). Effective subordination enables you to clarify your meaning by showing which ideas are more important and which less, which ideas are conditional on others and which are not. We'll discuss this further in the next section.

A2. Variety in Sentence Length
Each time I teach a writing course I run a little experiment near the beginning of each semester. When the first batch of papers is about to be turned in, I ask the writers to do

The joy of life is variety.
—Samuel Johnson

some counting. First I pick a paragraph, quite arbitrarily—let's say the third paragraph. Then I have them count the number of words in their third paragraph and divide by the number of sentences. The result is the average number of words per sentence. Having secured this figure from each writer, I can go on to establish an average number of words per sentence for the entire class. I write that average on the board, along with the shortest sentence written by anyone in the class and also the longest. The results for a three-year period are as follows:

Year	Average Words per Sentence	Shortest	Longest
1	14.8	7 words	26 words
2	14.5	8 words	31 words
3	15.2	7 words	28 words

While my experiment can hardly be called scientific, the pattern is always consistent, as these statistics show. Most of these beginning college students write sentences averaging about fifteen words in length and showing little variation from that average. Never has a writer averaged fewer than ten words or more than eighteen. The shortest sentences are never less than five words and the longest rarely exceed thirty.

Compare these figures with those for professional writers. Although there may be considerable variation from author to author, most professionals average twenty to twenty-five words per sentence. Furthermore, they show greater extremes, from the really short two- or three-word sentence to the long fifty-word unit. My favorite example is a paragraph written by Norman Mailer that averages thirty-nine words per sentence, the shortest being three words and the longest, one hundred and three!

What happens if your sentences don't vary in length? Let's go back to the example paragraph we used earlier. Its original version went like this:

It took a good deal of courage when I registered for class on June 11. But I am pleased that I decided to take the step.

On that day I purchased all the textbooks that I would need for this class. I wanted to be sure that I would have all the material I needed. Then I got my bill, both for this course and for the textbooks. I realized I'd better get serious about returning to school if I was going to spend my hard-earned money. I also realized that I was going to have to start saying no to social invitations. It is going to be very hard, but I am determined to do well.

We agreed this is a pretty dull paragraph, despite the fact that each sentence is technically "correct." Part of the dullness comes from monotony in sentence length. The shortest sentence here is ten words, the longest nineteen, the average fourteen. Again we are reminded of the clakety-clack of the train wheels. After a few pages of such a monotonous pattern, the reader is fighting off sleep.

Suppose we agree that variation in sentence length is desirable—what then? You can't just go out and stitch a few sentences together, or chop off a few words here and add a few there. After all, the length of a sentence must relate to, and in fact is determined by, its meaning.

The process of achieving greater variety in sentence length is a gradual one that, again, depends on *increased awareness*. As long as you keep yourself aware of the goal, you can make progress toward it. A good yoga teacher or physical therapist would tell you that, if you cannot do a particular exercise at first, you should be content with picturing the exercise in your mind, going through it in your imagination; in time the muscles will relax and stretch and attune themselves to the new demands you wish to make on them. So, too, with writing.

Besides keeping the general goal in mind, it may also be helpful to remember a few principles:

1. A series of short sentences often gives the effect of speed and is therefore appropriate for describing tense or dramatic moments in a story. Otherwise such a series might make your prose seem choppy, almost childish.
2. A single short sentence is a valuable way to give emphasis. It allows you to offer a pithy summation of the pre-

ceding sentences, especially if it comes at the end of the
paragraph.
3. Longer sentences are often appropriate for detailed description and for more leisurely explanations and arguments. But they are always achieved by adding new, more
precise details or by pushing the ideas to a still deeper
and more thoughtful level. They should not be created
by yoking two separate sentences (unless they are closely
related in meaning) or by padding with filler words.

To get a better grasp of the importance of variety in sentence length, compare the student paragraph on page 86 with
the following paragraph by Lewis Thomas, from *Lives of a
Cell: Notes of a Biology Watcher.* Dr. Thomas describes his
reaction to the idea that humans might have a temporary
but important role to play in the drama of evolution:

> I would much prefer this useful role, if I had any say, to
> the essentially unearthly creature we seem otherwise on the
> way to becoming. It would mean making some quite fun-
> damental changes in our attitudes toward each other, if we
> were really to think of ourselves as indispensable elements
> of nature. We would surely become the environment to
> worry about the most. We would discover, in ourselves, the
> sources of wonderment and delight that we have discerned
> in all other manifestations of nature. Who knows, we might
> even acknowledge the fragility and vulnerability that always
> accompany high specialization in biology, and movements
> might start up for the protection of ourselves as a valuable,
> endangered species. We couldn't lose.

Notice how Thomas exemplifies the principles we have
been discussing. His sentences range from three words to
thirty-two, with an average of twenty—six more than our
typical freshman writer. The longer sentences result from
his elaboration of an idea—for example, the idea that we
are an endangered species, which he develops in the fifth
sentence. Yet his longest sentence is juxtaposed against the
shortest, sentence six; the sharp, colloquial, emphatic *We
couldn't lose* summarizes his reaction and makes for a dramatic conclusion.

Some other practical hints:

1. Analyze a representative sample of your own prose to see how it compares to the statistics reported earlier.
2. Remember that the goal is greater *variety* in length, which means shorter as well as longer sentences.
3. Coordinate this section with the preceding pages on greater variety of sentence *types*.
4. Do the following exercises.

EXERCISES

1. Identify the following student-written sentences as simple, compound, complex, or compound-complex. Also, identify any that are cumulative or periodic.

   A. Two ex-convicts brutally slaughtered an innocent family of four.
   B. I always thought that life was too precious to waste on work.
   C. I'm settled into my room now: clothes hung up, refrigerator plugged in, plants and posters all in place.
   D. Freezing is one of the least-damaging food processing methods, and many items could be free of additives if they were frozen.
   E. I really intend, now that this case is over and my workload has lightened, to take my first extended vacation.
   F. For four years I had to wear a coat and tie, and if a teacher saw me with my coat off he could give me demerits.
   G. Their very number makes it difficult to identify potentially dangerous criminals.
   H. Each area of the hospital establishes its own visiting hours within the general guidelines.
   I. I found out that I was capable, that I had the knowledge and the confidence necessary for this job, despite what my boss thought.
   J. Multiple-choice questions usually offer four possible answers.

2. Study the following paragraph by E. B. White closely. Observe especially its variety in sentence length and in

> *Practice is the best of all instructors*
> *—Publius*

sentence type. Prepare a summary of your observations.
The paragraph is from an essay called "A Slight Sound
at Evening."

There is also a woodchuck here, living forty feet away
under the wharf. When the wind is right, he can smell my
house; and when the wind is contrary, I can smell his. We
both use the wharf for sunning, taking turns, each adjusting his schedule to the other's convenience. Thoreau once
ate a woodchuck. I think he felt he owed it to his readers,
and that it was little enough, considering the indignities
they were suffering at his hands and the dressing-down they
were taking. (Parts of *Walden* are pure scold.) Or perhaps
he ate the woodchuck because he believed every man
should acquire strict business habits, and the woodchuck
was destroying his market beans. I do not know. Thoreau
had a strong experimental streak in him. It is probably no
harder to eat a woodchuck than to construct a sentence
that lasts a hundred years. At any rate, Thoreau is the only
writer I know who prepared himself for his great ordeal by
eating a woodchuck; also the only one who got a hangover
from drinking too much water. (He was drunk the whole
time, though he seldom touched wine or coffee or tea.)

3. Rewrite the following paragraphs to give them more variety in sentence structure. Make any other improvements you can.

A. All my life people have called me by some name other than
my own. I was called "Pat" by my first grade teacher. She
confused me with my sister Pat. I had to endure this mixup
all through grammar school and high school. Even at times
people I went to school with called me "Pat." I don't see
why they would confuse us, because we look nothing alike.
Even now in my new job this still happens to me. I have
been working at the same place for over eight months. You
would think the other employees would know me by now.
I am called "Linda," or "Cheryl," but never Nancy. You would
think they could remember who I am, because I don't look
at all like Linda or Cheryl. I guess I should start wearing a
name tag.

B. I am an incurable junk collector. The best example of this is my bedroom. On every available space are statues, bottles, stuffed animals, and assorted knickknacks. Relatives or friends mention something they gave me ten or more years ago. I go into my room and find it, much to their amazement. People ask me if my room gets too crowded or if I lose anything. I say no, it is only the dusting I find difficult.

C. Values play a major role in our society. People use these values to make certain decisions in their lives. Values can be stated as a person's view of right and wrong. Courage is an extension of a person's values. Courage takes a person's values and puts them into the person's life. How people use their courage is completely up to them. This courage could be physical or mental. Anyone can make a courageous act. It is only the ones who follow through on their intentions by actions who are truly courageous.

4. Review the most recent paper you have turned in, as suggested on pages 84–85. Do you find that your paper reflects the observations on page 86 about lack of variety in sentence length and sentence type? If so, rewrite one page of the paper, incorporating the suggestions for variety contained in this section.

B. IMPROVING SENTENCES

Other ways to improve your sentences do not depend on variety in type or length but still reward those who study and practice them.

B1. Coordination and Subordination of Clauses

Coordination means linking independent clauses together with coordinating conjunctions, such as *but, and, nor, or, yet, for,* and *so.* When these conjunctions are used, they give equal status to each of the clauses they join. In other words, like any good *coordinator* they simply bring individuals together—in this case individual clauses—without asserting the superiority of one to another.

Look, for example, at this short passage:

> We are in a world of facts, *and* we use them, for there is
> nothing else to use. We do not quarrel with them, *but* we
> take them as they are, *and* we avail ourselves of what they
> can do for us. *J. H. Newman*

The three italicized coordinating conjunctions link the separate-but-equal clauses that make up this passage.

Subordination, by contrast, does just what its name implies: It subordinates one clause to another. For one clause
to be subordinate to another, it must depend on the other.
So subordination means making a clause dependent and
therefore of lesser importance both grammatically and logically. Writing that is rich in subordination is therefore rich
in dependent clauses and in complex sentences.

Subordination is usually achieved in one of two ways.
The first is by using a subordinating conjunction, such as:

if, as if	after	while
that, so that	as long as	because
although	until	unless
since	when, whenever	how
before	where, wherever	whether

Here are some examples:

> We may all be transcendental yet, *whether we like it or not.*
> *E. B. White*

> The main answer, I suppose, is *that I was born that way.*
> *F. L. Lucas*

The italicized dependent clauses are introduced by the subordinating conjunctions *whether* and *that,* respectively.

The second way to subordinate is to use relative pronouns
such as *who, whoever, whose, that, which, what,* and
whatever:

> There exists a group of men and women who are reluctant
> to acknowledge the role played by competition in their lives.
> *Jennifer Ring*

Dependent clauses act as replacements for three and only
three kinds of words: nouns, adjectives, and adverbs. One

reason we use clauses is quite simple: The alternative (using nouns, adjectives, or adverbs alone) would be infinitely more cumbersome. Instead of saying *an old man who walks slowly and with great dignity*, for example, we would have to say *a slow-and-greatly-dignified-walking old man*. In addition, as we shall see more clearly in a moment, clauses can allow the writer to show how some ideas are more important than others.

Naturally enough, when clauses replace nouns they are termed *noun clauses* and do a noun's work. For example, they can act as:

1. a subject

   What she wanted was not help but confirmation. *A. Alvarez*

2. the object of a verb

   Many think *that seeds improve with age*. *H. D. Thoreau*

3. a complement (a word or words that complete the predicate, often following a form of the verb *to be*)

   The trouble is, in general, *that there is nobody at home*. *C. H. Cooley*

Noun clauses most often begin with *that, what, whatever, whether, who, why, when,* and *where.*

When a clause modifies a noun or pronoun like an adjective does, it is called an **adjective clause:**

Doctors *who charge $70 for a ten-minute office visit* cannot expect much sympathy from their patients.

Here the italicized clause modifies the noun *doctors*. Such clauses are usually introduced by relative pronouns, especially *who, which,* and *that,* but *when, where,* and *why* sometimes appear. Quite often the relative pronoun is understood, or omitted:

The car *(that) I would most like to have is* a Mazda MR-6.

Adverb clauses can modify:

1. a verb

> We undoubtedly scavenged *whatever we could.* *Robert Ardrey*

2. an adjective

> He was as tired *as he had been those nights on the grave-yard shift.*

3. an adverb

> Darkness arrived more quickly *than we thought possible.*

4. a main clause

> *If the scheme of things is purposeless and meaningless,* then the life of man is purposeless and meaningless too. *W. T. Stace*

Several conjunctions can introduce adverb clauses. Among the most common ones are *after, although, as, because, before, if, since, so, than, though, unless, until, when, whenever, where,* and *while.*

Why should you be aware of these types of dependent clauses and their possible uses? The sole purpose is to help you practice effective subordination. And effective subordination in turn is helpful for two reasons.

First, subordination enables you to make your reader aware of the relative importance of your various ideas. Depending on the focus of a paragraph, some ideas deserve greater emphasis than others. Those of lesser importance should be made subordinate to—dependent on—the main ideas, as a signal to the reader of the proper weights to assign to them. If you do not subordinate, you imply that all ideas have equal importance, which in most cases is not true. Consider this sentence:

> Samuelson's theory simply cannot be accepted, but Samuelson's theory is persuasive in many ways.

This sentence is poor because it implies equality between these two ideas. Consider two possible revisions:

Samuelson's theory, *although persuasive in many ways,* simply cannot be accepted.

Samuelson's theory, *although it cannot be accepted,* is persuasive in many ways.

The two revisions obviously differ in meaning. The first, by subordinating the favorable comment, makes what is basically a negative judgment of Samuelson's theory. The second, on the other hand, subordinates the negative comment and thus offers a more favorable judgment. As these examples indicate, the use of dependent clauses allows you to distinguish major ideas from minor ones. It is up to you as the writer, of course, to decide which ideas are major and which minor.

Second, effective subordination enables you to be more exact in expressing your meaning, because you can show the precise relationship between major and minor ideas. Did the minor idea occur before or after the major one? Is the minor idea a cause or an effect of the major one? Does the dependent clause define or give emphasis to a noun in the main clause?

As an example of precise subordination, examine this sentence by the noted columnist Walter Lippmann:

And so, if we truly wish to understand why freedom is necessary in a civilized society, we must begin by realizing that, because freedom of discussion improves our own opinions, the liberties of other men are our own vital necessity.

This sentence contains four dependent clauses:

if we truly wish to understand

why freedom is necessary in a civilized society

that . . . the liberties of other men are our own vital necessity

because freedom of discussion improves our own opinions

The third clause is structurally the most important because it is an indispensable part of the main, independent clause. Without the third clause the sentence would be incomplete. This structural importance mirrors the fact that the idea that it offers is also the most important. The first clause is introduced by *if* and therefore expresses *condition*, the condition under which the main clause can be realized. The second and fourth clauses, also of lesser importance, raise the question of reasons (*why . . . because . . .*). Together these four clauses express a complex idea, but Lippmann is able to be clear in expressing it because he has mastered the art of effective subordination.

What practical steps can you take to improve your use of subordination? I would make three suggestions.

The first is to check your recent papers to see how often and in what ways you have been using dependent clauses. Do you find them to be comparatively scarce—say, an average of fewer than one per two or three sentences? Do you find any sentences where the relative importance of various ideas could be emphasized by subordinating some ideas to others? Locate the conjunctions that begin your dependent clauses. Are they the right conjunctions to express your meaning? As an example of what to look for, read this paragraph from a student paper:

> The Food Additives Amendment to the Food, Drug, and Cosmetic Act was passed in 1958. This act gave the FDA the authority to regulate the use of all food additives. The agency made up a list of all additives and circulated it among food technologists, biochemists, nutritionists, and medical people. Each one was asked for his or her evaluation of the safety of these substances. Some additives were considered harmful. These were tested at once and the bad ones were prohibited. Those additives to which the experts did not object were placed on an official roster, the Generally Recognized As Safe (GRAS) list. Such additives had not been proven safe. Since 1958 some substances have been removed from the GRAS list and others have been restricted to specific foods or specific quantities. These additives caused problems.

The paragraph is not a bad one. But if you examine it closely, you will see that it has almost no subordinate clauses. Consequently, the author has missed several opportunities to make her meaning more precise by subordinating some ideas to others. Notice how both the relative importance and the precise relationship of her ideas is made clear in this revised version:

The scientist shows his intelligence, if any, by his ability to discriminate between the important and the negligible.
—*Hans Zinsser*

> The Food Additives Amendment to the Food, Drug, and Cosmetic Act, passed in 1958, gave the FDA the authority to regulate the use of all food additives. The agency made up a list of additives and circulated it among food technologists, biochemists, nutritionists, and medical people. Each was asked for his or her evaluation of the safety of these substances. Those that were considered harmful were tested at once and then prohibited if necessary. Those additives to which the experts did not object were placed on an official roster, the Generally Recognized As Safe (GRAS) list, although they had never been proven safe. Since 1958 some substances have been removed from the GRAS list or restricted to specific foods or specific quantities because they were found to cause problems.

Notice how ten sentences have been cut to six, how ideas of lesser importance have been subordinated, how one idea has been contrasted to another (*although* . . .), how one idea has been identified as the reason for another (*because* . . .). This is the kind of analysis and the kind of revision you need to apply to your own completed papers.

My second suggestion is to evaluate each paragraph *before* you write it, trying to sort out in your own mind what the focus is and which ideas are more important. Consider also how your ideas relate to one another and how those relationships can be expressed by the right conjunctions. Above all, try to be aware of the need to make subordinate clauses an integral part of your style. On the average, a professional writer uses a subordinate clause about once every two sentences. Please note this is an average figure and says nothing about whether any particular sentence should have dependent clauses. But how close to this average do you come?

The third practical step is to learn to recognize the two most common pitfalls writers might encounter when using subordinate clauses. One is the temptation to be so concerned with using dependent clauses that you unintentionally confuse your reader. If dependent clauses are put together in a close series, especially if they begin with similar conjunctions, the result can be a sentence like this one:

> The test which a child is given that determines if he has any learning disabilities which need attention is one that is quite easy to administer.

By the time the reader sorts out all the *which's* and *that's*, he or she is hopelessly lost. Better to simplify the construction:

> It is quite easy to administer the test that determines whether a child has significant learning disabilities.

The other pitfall is the inexact or overfrequent use of *and* and *as*. *And* is a conjunction that gives equal status to two words or ideas, expressing no meaning of its own. Whenever possible, replace it with more definite subordinating words such as *because, when,* or *where:*

> WEAK: I like Dr. Silverman very much and calculus is now one of my favorite courses.
> REVISION: Because I like Dr. Silverman very much, calculus is now one of my favorite courses.

Note that the revision is more precise, because it shows cause and effect. A writer needs to be alert to such cause-effect relationships.

Another overused construction is the adverb clause beginning with *as*, when a more precise word would be better:

> WEAK: As I had not come home by the time he went to bed, Dad left the porch light on.
> REVISION: Because I had not come home by the time he went to bed, Dad left the porch light on.

B2. Cumulative and Periodic Sentences

The terms *cumulative* and *periodic* describe, or categorize, sentences and also the process of writing sentences. The

cumulative sentence begins with the independent clause, which marks the grammatical heart of the sentence. Then, once the essentials of the independent (main) clause have been stated, the writer adds details in much the same way a painter might add details to an initial sketch. These details can be considered further refinements of the main idea. They are provided in numerous ways, principally by adding phrases and dependent clauses. Consider these two examples from student writing:

> Her hands were always moving, pushing her glasses back up her slim nose, patting her hair into place, tapping a non-existent ash off the end of her cigarette.

> I lied, which was probably a foolish thing to do, especially since I knew the truth could not be hidden much longer.

The first sentence shows the cumulative process by having its independent clause—*Her hands were always moving*—followed by three phrases. The second sentence also begins with the main clause *(I lied)*, followed by two dependent clauses.

The process of writing a **periodic sentence** is different because some or all of the independent clause is held back until the end of the sentence. While both cumulative and periodic sentences contain descriptive phrases and dependent clauses, a cumulative sentence can be cut short after the main clause and still be grammatically complete, whereas a periodic sentence cannot, since part of its main clause is at the end. Here are two student-written examples of periodic sentences:

> When my father had been wheeled into the recovery room, and the heart monitor and the glucose tubes had been disconnected, I finally relaxed.

> At last she had found, in a small insignificant-looking pamphlet, a pamphlet that seemed to promise nothing very special, the real answer.

> *I attribute such success as I have had to the periodic sentence.*
> *—Edmund Wilson*

In the first example, dependent clauses precede the main clause that ends the sentence *(1 finally relaxed)*. In the second, a portion of the main clause begins the sentence, but an essential part—the object of the verb—is postponed until the end, after the completion of a phrase and a clause.

Periodic sentences are less common, although it is good to know what they are and to be able to use them. Cumulative sentences are not rare at all; in fact, some people contend that cumulative sentences are the typical sentences of modern writing, especially of narrative and descriptive writing. Practice in creating effective cumulative sentences can be important in developing your writing skills by allowing you to elaborate on your ideas.

Here are some good examples of cumulative sentences:

> Billy's native arrogance might well have been a gift of miffed genes, then coming to splendid definition through the tests to which a street like Broadway puts a man on the make: tests designed to refine a breed, enforce the code, exclude all simps and gumps, and deliver into the city's life a man worthy of functioning in this age of nocturnal supremacy. *William Kennedy*

> January 11, 1965, was a bright warm day in Southern California, the kind of day when Catalina floats on the Pacific horizon and the air smells of orange blossoms and it is a long way from the bleak and difficult East, a long way from the cold, a long way from the past. *Joan Didion*

> Suddenly the briefcase fell open, spilling out not a sheaf of papers but rather a bottle of aftershave, a shoebrush, deodorant, and two pairs of sky-blue underwear. *student writer*

Perhaps a question might occur to you: How is writing a cumulative sentence different from the subordinating process discussed in the previous section? You would be correct in observing some overlap, because a cumulative sentence often involves adding dependent clauses. One difference, however, is that the cumulative process can also involve single words or phrases as well as clauses. A second difference is that the cumulative process always means having the main clause at or near the beginning and then adding modifiers to it, while the subordinating process is not limited to this form.

You can understand more about the process of writing cumulative sentences by looking at this example:

> We walked on toward the prison, coming as near as we could, for the crowd was enormous and in the dim light silent, almost motionless, like crowds seen in a dream. *Katherine Anne Porter*

The independent clause can be stated easily: *We walked on toward the prison.* The next clause adds details about that walk. It could therefore be said to be at a lower level of generality, because it modifies the main clause and makes it more specific. The second clause in turn is modified by still another clause: *for [because] the crowd was enormous and . . . silent, almost motionless.* This third clause explains why they could not come nearer and works on a still lower level of generality. Another detail about the crowd itself is added by the phrase *in the dim light,* which therefore works on the fourth, lowest level of generality, as does the remaining descriptive phrase *like crowds seen in a dream.*

So we could schematize the whole sentence by printing it this way:

(1) We walked on toward the prison,
  (2) coming as near as we could,
    (3) for the crowd was enormous and . . . silent,
       almost motionless,
    (4) in the dim light
    (4) like crowds seen in a dream.

Do you see how this rewriting of the sentence shows us the way Porter began with the main idea and then sharpened her description by adding phrases and clauses that supplied more details? In other words, do you see how the phrases numbered (4) give details about clause (3), how clause (3) gives details about clause (2), and how clause (2) gives details about the independent clause (1)?

Apply this way of looking at sentences to some passages from professional writing and from your own writing. Such

> *Practice and thought might gradually forge many an art.*
> —*Virgil*

analyses will probably teach you an important truth: Less- experienced writers do not use as many cumulative sentences as professionals, and when they do use them, their sentences usually do not go beyond two or at the most three levels of generality.

Having learned this truth, the next obvious step is practice. That means writing several kinds of cumulative sentences, following as many patterns as possible—independent clause, then adjective phrase, or noun or verb phrase, or any one of several types of clauses. Sometimes a phrase or a clause might precede the main clause, with one or more clauses then following it. Try first to perfect writing on two levels of generality, then work on three or more. You might ask your instructor for further assistance.

One more word about the terms used in this chapter. Notice that *all* sentences must fall into one of the first four categories—simple, compound, complex, or compound-complex. But not all sentences can be categorized as coordinate or subordinate, cumulative or periodic. A simple sentence, for example, might be neither coordinate nor subordinate, neither cumulative nor periodic. These last four terms refer instead to *options* that writers can use to achieve greater variety in their sentences and to better express what they want to say.

B3. Repetition and Emphasis

While needless repetition has no place in good prose (as discussed in Chapter 1), some circumstances invite repetition and make it fruitful. Consider the following paragraph by Loren Eiseley, from *The Immense Journey*. It describes a dramatic moment in a forest glade. A group of sparrows has just watched helplessly as a young sparrow was eaten by a raven:

> The sighing died. It was then I saw the judgment. It was the judgment of life against death. I will never see it again so forcefully presented. I will never hear it again in notes so

tragically prolonged. For in the midst of protest, they forgot the violence. There, in that clearing, the crystal note of a song sparrow lifted hesitantly in the hush. And finally, after painful fluttering, another took the song, and then another, the song passing from one bird to another, doubtfully at first, as though some evil thing were being slowly forgotten. Till suddenly they took heart and sang from many throats joyously together as birds are known to sing. They sang because life is sweet and sunlight beautiful. They sang under the brooding shadow of the raven. In simple truth they had forgotten the raven, for they were the singers of life, and not of death.

The number of repetitions here is remarkable. In case you missed some, these are the most obvious ones:

It was then I saw the judgment. It was the judgment . . .

I will never see it again . . . I will never hear it again . . .

so forcefully presented . . . so tragically prolonged . . .

another took the song . . . and then another . . .

they took heart and sang . . . They sang . . . They sang . . .

the singers of life . . . and not of death.

Here repetition plays a valuable role. It heightens the drama of what was for Eiseley a very important moment, and it gives special emphasis to this climactic paragraph of a section of his book.

Be alert for ways in which you can use repetition as effectively as Eiseley. Here, for example, are two student sentences that drive home their message through artful repetition:

Every day my environment grows colder: the weather grows colder, this room grows colder, the people grow colder, I even grow colder toward myself.

Life allows for countless rich experiences if you are open to them, if you retain your youthful optimism, if you keep a light heart and never forget the potential brilliance of the present moment.

Do you see how these sentences are made more memorable, more insistent because of their repetition? See whether your own sentences can profit from this technique. (But bear in mind a corollary: Repetition must be used sparingly, lest it call too much attention to itself.)

There are other patterns a good writer uses for emphasis besides repetition of words or phrases. One pattern is based on speech rhythms. It tries to provide repetition not of words or phrases but of *units of sound,* much like poetry does. Consider this sentence by John Ruskin in which he describes the onset of a rainstorm in an Alpine valley:

And then you will hear the sudden rush of the awakened wind, and you will see those watchtowers of vapor swept away from their foundations, and waving curtains of opaque rain let down to the valleys, swinging from the burdened clouds in black bending fringes, or pacing in pale columns along the lake level, grazing its surface into foam as they go.

There is one small use of word repetition here (*you will hear . . .and you will see*), but for the most part this sentence relies for its effectiveness on the rhythm that undergirds it and becomes apparent when you read it aloud. The nearly equal length of each of the separate units making up the sentence (twelve, thirteen, eleven, nine, nine, and eight words, respectively) suggest the rush of the storm as it sweeps through the valleys in great gusts of wind. This rhythm of sound is even augmented by other devices borrowed from poetry, devices such as *alliteration* (using the same first consonant, as in *pacing . . . pale, lake level*).

Closer to home, here is a sentence in which a student writer describes her Grandpa's singing as she recalled it from her childhood:

> I would sit there listening to Grandma's sobs from the kitchen, and watch the tears of pain flow down Grandpa's cheeks, but his strong voice never faltered and his courage never failed.

Can you feel the rhythm of *his strong voice never faltered and his courage never failed*?

Achieving such rhythm is admittedly difficult, in part because it depends so much on "feel." But it is a goal worth keeping in mind.

A second pattern is more easily accomplished. Quite often in sentences we list *items in a series*, especially when using parallelism or repetition. In these circumstances it is important to arrange the items in a precise order, usually from least important to most important because that is how readers have come to expect them. Here is a student-written example:

> My brother is petty, devious, sometimes even cruel.

The brother's three vices are arranged in ascending order, from least to most important. If you doubt the need for such an arrangement, consider an alternative version of the sentence:

> My brother is devious, cruel, sometimes even petty.

As you can see, the effect of the sentence is destroyed because the emphasis does not fall where the reader expects it to. When you list items, make sure to order them for proper emphasis.

Speaking of emphasis, remember to *put your sentences in the active voice* whenever possible. Don't write a sentence like this one:

> The effects of his addiction are described by De Quincey in *The Confessions of an English Opium Eater.*

Instead write:

> De Quincey describes the effects of his addiction in *The Confessions of an English Opium Eater.*

It is not that the active voice is so good, but rather that the passive voice can dissipate the power of a sentence. The reason is that the subject of a passive-voice sentence is acted upon rather than doing the acting. In the sentence above, the subject (*effects*) is acted upon (*are described*) and must "passively" accept whatever the verb requires of it. But in the active-voice version, the subject (*De Quincey*) does the acting. Only in situations where what has resulted from an action seems more important than the actor would the passive voice be preferable:

> McDonald's restaurants have now been opened in more than thirty countries, including Russia.

Here what has resulted (the opening of all those restaurants) carries more importance than who opened them—in fact, who opened them is never even specified.

So sometimes the passive voice may be useful or desirable. I had a history teacher in high school who thought that the passive voice was more "refined" than the active. Consequently, his lectures to us would contain sentences like, "It will be learned by you for tomorrow what were the causes of the Punic Wars" or "Today the rise of the nation-state will be discussed by me." Take care that such weak, unemphatic sentences are avoided by you.

This chapter may seem to have been based on a paradox. On the one hand I have said that you need to achieve variety in your sentences, variety in both length and type. On the other hand I have also encouraged you to use certain repeated patterns, in words, rhythms, and word order, to give your prose a better emphasis. Paradoxes, however contradictory they may at first appear, do after all state a truth: In this case, the truth that writing better sentences means using both variety and pattern simultaneously.

This ability to live cheerfully with apparent contradiction is a sign of intellectual maturity. Our example drawn from writing is like a happy tension described by the Zen master Yao-shan. A young monk asked him, "What does one think about while meditating?"

"About nonthinking," Yao-shan replied.

"How does one think about nonthinking?" puzzled the monk.

"Through superthinking."

EXERCISES

1. Combine each of the following pairs of sentences into one by converting one of the sentences into a dependent clause and including it in the other sentence, the one that emphasizes what you believe to be the more important idea. Use appropriate subordinating pronouns or conjunctions for the new dependent clause.

   A. According to the "big bang" theory, the universe was formed by an explosion 10–20 billion years ago. This theory is now accepted by the scientific establishment.

   B. Older people need contact with younger people. This is especially true when older people are confined to nursing homes.

   C. Soon I was escorted to the back to meet "Mr. Raymond." "Mr. Raymond" was to cut my hair.

   D. In South America there are many superstitions similar to those in North America. There are others that are different: spilling wine is good luck, leaving a broom upside down in a corner will get rid of unwanted guests, rain on a wedding day is good luck.

   E. The reason TV viewers get frustrated watching sports events is not the failure of their favorite team. The reason is that their advice is not being followed by the coaches.

   F. The province of Quebec is French-speaking. The province of Quebec is where there is talk of separating from the rest of Canada.

   G. The school sent a nasty letter to your parents. This happened when you had "earned" more than twenty demerits.

   H. Juan Carlos de Borbón was appointed chief of state by the Spanish dictator Francisco Franco. Juan Carlos is now king of Spain.

2. Convert the following clauses into cumulative sentences by adding words, phrases, and dependent clauses. You can use the three sentences on page 100 as models.

EXAMPLE: the wind blew harder (clause)

Suddenly the wind blew harder, pushing the tree limbs against the windowpanes, whining through the many cracks that I should have puttied the previous fall (cumulative sentence—adds phrases and clause)

A. the rain fell heavily
B. it was a typical Saturday night
C. the cigarette burned slowly in the ashtray
D. some TV commercials are really bizarre
E. he looks like a 1930s gangster
F. everybody has a secret ambition
G. movies have offered many unintended lessons
H. she smiled
I. most politicians love the sight of a large crowd
J. the pain was unbearable
K. every family has at least one colorful ancestor
L. this election has but one important issue
M. dark clouds began to drift in
N. Russian military power has declined
O. calculus can terrify the unprepared student

3. The following passages are monotonous, dull. Rewrite them. Use coordination and subordination to show the connections between ideas.

   A. My most important vacation memory is of my cousin Bud. Bud was tall, dark-haired. He grabbed me in his huge hands. He lifted me high into the air. He planted a kiss on my cheek. The kiss was itchy. His mustache was prickly. This was at the time we first met. My heart was his from that moment on. In the next few days he took my sister and me shopping. He took us to the movies. He took us to the country fair. My father said I was too young for pierced ears. My mother insisted growing girls had to eat their beets. Bud stuck up for me in those quarrels. That vacation lasted only five days. Bud is the only memory left. The reason is the way he seemed larger than life. I was a highly impressionable ten-year-old.
   B. In high school I was a jock. I didn't like the image. I especially didn't like being considered dumb. I tried to fight

the image. It was hard. After all I still played football. Events have a way of tripping you up. During one game I was playing offensive guard. This was in my junior year. On a certain play the guard is supposed to "pull." He is supposed to block the defensive tackle on the other side of the ball. Meanwhile the other guard is supposed to block the nose-man. The nose-man is the defensive player opposite the center. I got confused. I pulled to block the tackle. I should have stayed to block the nose-man. The other guard did his job correctly. This of course made him run straight into me. THUNK! Down I went. My teammates were groaning. The coaches were screaming. Two thousand spectators were roaring with laughter. Suppose I wanted to find a good way of showing how stupid jocks were. I could not have found a better way than this.

4. Study the use of repetition in the following paragraph by Joan Didion, from *Slouching Towards Bethlehem*. Prepare a short summary of what you observe.

This is a story about love and death in the golden land, and begins with the country. The San Bernardino Valley lies only an hour east of Los Angeles by the San Bernardino Freeway but is in certain ways an alien place: not the coastal California of the subtropical twilights and the soft westerlies off the Pacific but a harsher California, haunted by the Mojave just beyond the mountains, devastated by the hot dry Santa Ana wind that comes down through the passes at 100 miles an hour and whines through the eucalyptus windbreaks and works on the nerves. October is the bad month for the wind, the month when breathing is difficult and the hills blaze up spontaneously. There has been no rain since April. Every voice seems a scream. It is the season of suicide and divorce and prickly dread, wherever the wind blows.

5. Revise the following sentences for greater emphasis.

A. As the storm grew more violent, the wheel was gripped tightly by his sweaty hands.

B. With a fury stemming from both pain and rage, "Damn you!" she screamed.

C. Some messages are being sent by the subconscious to the conscious mind and the subconscious represses other messages.

D. "Say it now!" was the one overriding thought I had in mind.

E. Chuckles, outright laughter, and smiles greeted the opening sentence of his campaign speech.

F. That the government would continue the same policy was promised by the foreign minister in his U.N. speech yesterday.

G. The differences are many; in some instances they are fundamental.

H. Forster uses, to deal with important issues, a light, comic touch.

I. I shouted, hoping he would hear and then respond immediately, "Throw!"

6. Discuss the use of emphasis, repetition, and rhythm in the following passage by L. E. Sissman, from "'Into the Air, Junior Birdmen!'"

Detroit, summer, 1938. A spun-gold Sunday morning. In my small, north-facing bedroom, I wake slowly to the Sunday sounds. Big yellow Detroit Street Railway trolleys trundle infrequently by, a high, electric hum above the fierce metallic screech of the wheels upon the rails. A few early cars shift and start off from the Warren Avenue lights. Over on the polyglot East Side, a hundred various Catholic churches, Slavic churches, Scandinavian churches flung up by homesick immigrants begin their solemn monody of calling the faithful—and the habituated—to Mass or service. And then, faint but clear above the choirs of bells, comes the unignorable whine of a single-engine airplane. I slip out of bed, whip on my spectacles, and, after some drawing and quartering of the sky, descry a plane high over the Hotel Palmetto, Residential Rates. It is a Stinson monoplane, and the pilot, perhaps purely for his pleasure, is executing a series of shallow, lazy dives and zooms.

7. Study the following three passages closely. Observe how the authors achieve variety through coordination and

subordination, periodic and cumulative sentences, repetition, and emphasis. Write one-paragraph summaries of what you observe about each passage.

A. I watched a television reenactment one night of an execution by lethal injection. It was well done; it was horrible. The methodical approach, people standing around the gurney waiting, made it more awful. One moment there was a man in a prone position; the next moment that man was gone. On another night I watched a television movie about a little boy named Adam Walsh, who disappeared from a shopping center in Florida. There was a reenactment of Adam's parents coming to New York, where they appeared on morning talk shows begging for their son's return, and in their hotel room, where they received a call from the police saying that Adam had been found: not all of Adam, actually, just his severed head, discovered in the waters of a Florida canal. There is nothing anyone could do that is bad enough for an adult who took a six-year-old boy away from his parents, perhaps tortured, then murdered, him and cut off his head. Nothing at all. Lethal injection? The electric chair? Bah. *Anna Quindlen*

B. There is no suggestion, however, that he draws the gun reluctantly. The Westerner could not fulfill himself if the moment did not finally come when he can shoot his enemy down. But because that moment is so thoroughly the expression of his being, it must be kept pure. He will not violate the accepted forms of combat though by doing so he could save a city. And he can wait. "When you call me that—smile!"—the villain smiles weakly, soon he is laughing with horrible joviality, and the crisis is past. But it is allowed to pass because it must come again: sooner or later Trampas will "make his play," and the Virginian will be ready for him. *Robert Warshow, "The Westerner"*

C. Whenever anything alarming happened to the landward side—or sometimes just because it was getting so hot—she [primeval woman] would go back into the water, up to her waist, or even up to her neck. This meant, of course, that she had to walk upright on her two hind legs. It was slow and ungainly, especially at first, but it was absolutely essential if she wanted to keep her head above water. She isn't the only creature who has ever had to learn to do it. Although, as we have seen, she is almost unique in having learned to walk upright all the time, there is another mammal who does it for part of the time, and probably for the same reason. The beaver, whose ancestors also spent a good deal of time in shallow water, whenever she is transporting building materials or carrying her baby around, has the habit of getting up on her hind legs and proceeding by means of a perfectly serviceable bipedal gait. *Elaine Morgan,* The Descent of Woman

Paragraph Unity

The human mind, in order to digest a large amount of data, must break these data into patterns. Otherwise the circuits overload and then work less efficiently or even short out. For example, if you want to memorize a series of eight digits, such as 83197245, psychologists can show that the mind will work best when it arranges the numbers into two groups of three followed by one group of two: 831-972-45. Other patterns the mind can impose, such as grouping by fours (8319-7245) or by twos (83-19-72-45), won't serve as well. But any pattern is better than no pattern at all, as would be the case if you tried to memorize all eight at once. Try to memorize a student identification number or a credit card number and you'll see what these psychologists mean.

This truth about the mind's need for grouping patterns has an important application to writing. When you break up an essay into paragraphs, sentences, and words, you do so in part to make it easier for your readers to digest what you say. Readers have to grapple with myriad impressions as they read, and you increase your chance of communication if you order your writing in such a way that the mind can process it conveniently. After all, you could still write as the scribes did back in the Middle Ages, when parchment was so expensive that often no spaces were left between paragraphs, sentences, or even words. Peoplecouldstillunderstandwhattheyread,asthisshows. But the process would be much more painful.

Paragraphs, therefore, like the sentences we considered in the previous chapter, are a way of giving order to what we say. Paragraphs simply work on the next level up: Just as words are grouped into sentences, so sentences are grouped into paragraphs. This chapter discusses ways to improve your use of this important ordering pattern.

When you begin a paragraph, what must you keep in mind? Two things: The paragraph must be *unified,* and the paragraph must be fully *developed.* Weak paragraphs will almost always be characterized by a failure in one or both of these important features. This chapter explains paragraph unity; the next explains paragraph development.

A. PARAGRAPH FOCUS

In Chapter 2 we said that writers do not have to be able to define a sentence, but they must know the function of a sentence and the signs and clues that signal its presence. The same holds true for the paragraph. Dictionary definitions are misleading at best; how can you tell what a "point" is when a paragraph is defined as dealing "with one point only"? The important test is whether you understand what paragraphs do and can use them effectively.

An important function of paragraphs is to help us give order to what we write. But "order" is not a very precise description either. How do we know what ordering devices, what patterns to use? How do we know when a new para-

graph should begin? If one of your paragraphs has been returned with marginal notations like ¶ *unity,* ¶ *con[tinuity]*, ¶ *focus,* or *coh[erence]*, how do you give the paragraph the order it needs?

Again there is a parallel with sentence structure. Just as you intuitively "know" which sentences are grammatical and which not and have used grammatical sentences since early childhood, so, too, you usually "know" what makes up successfully ordered paragraphs. To prove to yourself that you have this ability, please read the following passage by Ralph Raphael, from his book *Edges*. In its original form the passage consists of two paragraphs, and I would ask you to mark where you think the second paragraph begins:

> The salesmen are all professionals who follow the country-fair circuit. The pen vendor, aged forty-three, has been a drummer ever since he was eighteen years old. His sales pitch, repeated verbatim every hour or so, seems to have a will of its own which has little or nothing to do with the stone-faced man who delivers it. It's just a job like any other job, although it demands that he have no home other than the camper in which he travels. Like the barkers and peddlers of years past, the people of the fair are creatures of the road who remain forever on the outskirts of the communities they serve. But the salesmen are not alone. The "carnies," as the amusement-park folks call themselves, have transformed the country-fair circuit into a way of life. Traveling together in one continuous party, they wear "carny power" insignia on the back of their Levi's jackets and like to hang together when the local toughs start hankering for a fight. They are proud to belong to a select group of "gypsies, tramps, and thieves," self-appointed outcasts from the small-town societies in which they set up shop. Like the salesmen who travel beside them, they live off the suckers who come to the fair to blow a few bucks and catch a passing glimpse of bright lights and fancy things.

You probably recognized that the second paragraph begins with the sixth sentence, "But the salesmen are not alone." You were not the writer of these paragraphs; nevertheless, you knew how they should be organized.

The question is, *how* did you know? What clues, what signals, did you use to arrive at your decision? I would bet that, without even realizing it, you used one or more of the following three signals: change of topic, transition word or phrase, or a sense for modern paragraph length.

In this section we will examine the first two of these three signals in more detail, because they show how to recognize unified paragraphs, and, more important, they help explain how to construct them. (The third signal will be analyzed in the next chapter.) We will also consider other ways to reinforce the order given to a paragraph.

A1. Clarity of Focus

Although the statement that a paragraph "deals with one point only" is not a very workable one, it touches an important truth. Part of our understanding of what makes a paragraph comes when we realize that a writer is considering a new aspect of a topic. Strictly speaking it would not be right to say that when an author begins a new paragraph he or she "switches topics," because to switch topics completely would be to start a new essay. But we can say that each paragraph should take up a new *aspect* of a topic, or a new subdivision of it, or a new extension of it.

Consider the Ralph Raphael passage you just read. It starts with the topic of salesmen at county fairs. The author provides an example, the pen vendor, and devotes four sentences to him and others like him. Then he takes up the subject of the "carnies." Immediately we recognize that a new aspect of his general topic (county fairs) has been introduced. And sure enough the sentences that follow all say something about this new group of people. These sentences form a coherent, distinct unit and therefore can be marked off as a separate paragraph.

So we do have a sense for how new aspects of a topic need to be set off as separate paragraphs, to help the reader organize the material mentally, but how do we distinguish between a new aspect of a topic and a continuation of the topic? The question is one of *focus*. A good analogy would be to think of looking at a subject through a pair of binoculars. When you look through binoculars, you must adjust the focus dial until your subject can be seen clearly. In the process, you dial out all that does not belong to the subject, and you zero in on one particular focal point. In writing a paragraph, you do the same thing—you focus on one particular subject and make it clear for the reader.

Here is an example of a paragraph that is "out of focus," that does not concentrate on a single subject:

> Gus, a twenty-eight-year-old jock, has to be the most egotistical person I have ever had the misfortune of meeting. From the moment he walked in the clinic I could tell he thought himself superior to everyone else. I had gotten this job at the clinic through a friend of my mother's. Although physical therapy was not my intended career, I thought I would get valuable experience in dealing with the public. Anyway, Gus came into the waiting room and introduced himself to the receptionist by telling her what a great lover he was. After boasting about his car and his ability as a skydiver, Gus excused himself to comb his hair and preen before the mirror. Then, as luck would have it, I found he had been assigned to me for his therapy.

Most of the paragraph deals with its subject—detestable Gus. But two sentences, the third and fourth, are devoted to a different matter altogether: how the author got her job. Yet, we can't just begin a new paragraph with the third sentence, because sentences five, six, and seven belong with the first two as part of the introduction to Gus. The only solution is to remove sentences three and four from the paragraph entirely. If the subject of how the author got her job is an important one, it can be treated in a separate paragraph somewhere else in the paper. If the subject has no special value, it should be left out.

A bit more complicated is the paragraph that entertains so many topics that the focus is lost entirely, leaving only a murky fog:

> Murder is a serious crime. Every day you can look in a paper and read about someone being murdered. I think that failure to apply the death penalty is a major factor in the increase of deaths. A person can now murder someone and be pretty certain he will not be executed. I think that if a person kills someone he deserves to die except in time of

> So quick bright things
> come to confusion.
> —William Shakespeare

war or accidental death. After all, the person he murdered didn't want to die. With proper enforcement of the death penalty there would be fewer murders. A person would be less likely to commit murder if he knows he can be executed for his crime. If the death penalty is not enforced there is but one choice: carry a gun. That way if your life is threatened you get to kill him before he gets to kill you. The law works two ways: if he kills you he goes to jail, and if you kill him you get off on self-defense. There would be fewer murders if everyone carried a gun. Not many people would try to kill you when they know you carry a gun.

The writer begins the paragraph as if he will focus on a fact: the prevalence of the crime of murder. By the third sentence, however, he is trying to analyze what he believes to be the *cause* of this fact—namely, failure to enforce the death penalty. By the fifth sentence he is off on still another issue, the *desirability* of the death penalty. Yet in the seventh sentence he is back to the determination of cause and effect—what would be the *effect* of enforcing the death penalty? Finally the ninth sentence, by urging people to carry guns, hoists the fifth and last flag under which this paragraph is made to sail.

In short, the writer of this paragraph has little sense of what focus means. At least five topics are introduced, each of which deserves one or more paragraphs of its own. The most that can be said of the paragraph is that it has something to do with murder, guns, and the death penalty. We get a rough idea of how the writer feels (very angry), but the haphazard way he spills out his ideas makes it impossible for him to be clear or convincing.

So it is important to test each of your paragraphs with the question, "Does it have a clear focus?" Unless you can answer yes, the paragraph ought to be rewritten. If the paragraph in its original form deals with two topics, one after the other, a simple division at the point where the second topic begins is all that will be required. Sometimes, however, as in the case of the murder–guns–death penalty paragraph, no such easy solution is available. In these cases the best course is to take each of the separate topics and make it the focus of a completely new paragraph.

A2. Topic Sentences

One device that is often helpful in keeping a paragraph focused is the **topic sentence.** Such a sentence often appears first in the paragraph, and it summarizes the subject the rest of the paragraph will develop.

Some people offer as a rule the idea that "all paragraphs must begin with a topic sentence." Such advice is well intentioned because it is directed to the problem of focus. But the advice can also be misleading, because as a statement about all writing it is simply not true. Professional writers, for example, use explicit topic sentences in only about 55 percent of their paragraphs and position those sentences in many places besides the first. Often the topic will be implied rather than stated, or else it must be deduced from the other sentences. The important issue is whether the paragraph has a single unified focus, not whether that focus is summed up in an initial topic sentence.

But even though a paragraph need not have a topic sentence, such sentences are often very useful. They enable readers to steer their way more easily by following topic sentences as signposts the writer has set out. Observe how the italicized topic sentences clarify the focus in each of the following student-written paragraphs:

> *Another reason we should abandon pass-fail grading is that society no longer is able to determine which students have the ability to go on to medical school, law school, or graduate school.* With the pass-fail system as it is now used you can have a potential doctor with an A average and a potential doctor with a D average, and you lack any means for telling the difference between them. Thus, academically inferior people become eligible for important positions in our society. I believe that the people who are going to guard my health, take care of my legal matters, and teach my college-age children should be above average in academic ability.

> *The strangest character I ever met was a fellow called Pete Karmanlis.* His old, tattered clothes and drooping mustache gave him the appearance of a 1960s hippie. His black eyes flashed as he talked, and he accompanied his wild words with even wilder gestures. But this appearance was in sharp contrast to his personality. Pete's father was an old-country Greek and Pete had been brought up as a "gentleman." His manners were excellent, and he delighted in bowing the continental way and kissing my hand ("with your permission, of course").

In the first example, the entire paragraph develops one of the author's reasons for opposing pass-fail grading, and that reason is stated clearly in the opening sentence. In the second example, the remainder of the paragraph (following the topic sentence) tells us more about why Pete Karmanlis was "the strangest character I ever met."

In these two example paragraphs, the topic sentence appeared at the beginning. Topic sentences can, however, appear at other places in the paragraph, especially at the end, as in this example from professional writer Mary Lefkowitz:

> When Pythagoras's wife Theano was asked how she could ever become as renowned as her husband, she replied, quoting the *Iliad*, "by plying the loom and sharing his bed." In the *Iliad* these words are spoken by Chryseis, the young woman captive who became Agamemnon's favorite concubine. *The ancients, in short, seem not to have thought it surprising that the wife of a famous philosopher in the relatively settled world of the sixth century B.C. demanded of life little more than a woman captured in war might expect.*

The position of this topic sentence is not as important as its function of advancing and making clear the focal point of the paragraph.

While it is not true that all paragraphs have explicit topic sentences, the statistic quoted earlier reminds us that 55 percent of all paragraphs *do* have such sentences. Check your own writing, and if recognizable topic sentences do not occur quite frequently, you are probably neglecting one of the best ways to give your paragraphs the unity readers need.

A3. Using Transitions

You may have identified the beginning point of the second Raphael paragraph (page 117) by the change to the topic of "carnies." It is also possible that you used the second of our clues: transition words. When you saw the word *But* at the start of the sixth sentence, perhaps you recognized it as a member of that group of words that often marks the beginning of a new topic and therefore a new paragraph. Perhaps you recognized the fact that the entire sixth sentence acts as a transition, a bridge, between the topic of pen vendors and the topic of carnies.

A transition in your life is the passage from one stage to another. Similarly, transition words signal a passage from one stage of the discussion of a topic to another stage. At the same time transition words can show the relationship between the first stage and the second.

Transition words do not just tie paragraph to paragraph. They also connect the idea of one sentence to the idea of another sentence within the same paragraph (I've italicized the transitions):

> No one wanted to be stuck forever with an impossible partner. *But*, for all that, they knew pretty much what they wanted from one another. *Allan Bloom*

And they connect clause to clause within a sentence:

> The cynicism of both Mohsen and his eulogizers disgusted me, *but* my encounter with this late-lamented guerrilla leader was an important lesson about Beirut. *Thomas Friedman*

Transition words are extremely important. They enable you to build bridges from one statement to another, to connect what is to come with what has gone before. Thus, you as a writer can use transitions to give coherence to your paragraphs and guide the reader through your subject. In this section we are discussing transition words as they apply to paragraphs, but you should realize that in most cases this material applies equally to transitions between sentences and clauses.

Transition words or phrases show a *relationship*, as noted earlier. Using transitions requires careful study of how the ideas in one paragraph relate to the ideas in another. Sometimes the relationship is one of **contrast,** and it will be shown by words or phrases like these:

however	nevertheless
but	in spite of
by contrast	on the other hand
although	despite
regardless	even though

Sometimes the relationship is one of **similarity;** the new aspect of the topic is an addition to the other aspects that have already been considered. Words or phrases that show this include:

again	once more
moreover	second (or third, etc.)
also	in addition
furthermore	besides
and	next
another	likewise
similarly	in the same way

In narration or description a writer might have occasion to use transition words that establish a **time or place relationship:**

later	farther on
soon	nearby
adjacent to	below
beyond	opposite to
afterward	now
presently	shortly
immediately	simultaneously
meanwhile	here
earlier	there
next	last

Then, too, the new paragraph might show the **consequence** of the previous paragraph or else an **example** of it. Words or phrases such as the following might be used:

so	hence
as a result	for example
therefore	as an illustration
consequently	another example
thus	for instance
because	accordingly

Finally, the transition words might show a special relationship between the new paragraph and a whole group of paragraphs that have preceded it. The new paragraph might be either a **repetition** or a **summation**:

as a result	therefore
in other words	in summary
as I have said	in short
to repeat	in brief
in conclusion	as we have seen

Most transitions between paragraphs are accomplished by single words, usually conjunctions (*but, and, therefore*) or stock phrases (*for example, on the other hand*). These words or phrases appear at or near the beginning of the new paragraph. Sometimes, if one of these common words or phrases does not express the relationship precisely enough, an entire sentence might be needed for a transition:

How should we proceed?

The third case is curiously unlike the first two.

Let us move on to the next issue.

The introductory sentence to the "carnies" paragraph could also serve as an example.

This use of complete sentences as transitional devices points up the one important difference between transitions for sentences and transitions for paragraphs: Obviously a sentence could not be a transition for a sentence!

I must emphasize strongly the importance of transitions for paragraphs. They signal to readers how they should read the upcoming paragraph: what aspect of the topic it will consider, what approach to the topic it will take, how it relates to what has gone before. Readers could perhaps determine these matters for themselves, but the transition words act like rails, keeping them right on course. Readers who have been helped this way will reward you with increased attention to your message.

In this book, for example, I have tried to make frequent use of transition words to ease your way through the text. Just as an arbitrary example, consider the last six paragraphs of section A2 of Chapter 1 (pages 13–15). All five paragraphs begin with either a transition word (*Although*, *So*), a transition phrase (*Of course*), or a transition sentence (*This last point . . . cannot be emphasized too strongly*). Even this very paragraph you are now reading uses the transition phrase *for example*.

Transition words *within* a paragraph, in other words between sentences and clauses, are also important as a way of emphasizing the focus of the paragraph. Such words give readers valuable signposts as they proceed through the paragraph, thus allowing readers to understand the underlying unity of the paragraph. Observe the italicized words and phrases in the following paragraph from "What Is Style?" by F. L. Lucas:

> *Why* and *how* did I become interested in style? *The main answer*, I suppose, is that I was born that way. *Then* I was, till ten, an only child running loose in a house packed with books, and in a world (thank goodness) still undistracted by radio and television. *So* at three I groaned to my mother, "Oh, I wish I could read," and at four I read. *Now* travel among books is the best travel of all, and the easiest, and the cheapest. (*Not* that I belittle ordinary travel—which I regard as one of the three main pleasures in life.) One learns to write by reading good books, as one learns to talk by hearing good talkers. *And* if I have learned anything of writing, it is largely from writers like Montaigne, Dorothy Osborne, Horace Walpole, Johnson, Goldsmith, Montesquieu, Voltaire, Flaubert, and Anatole France. *Again*, I was reared on Greek

and Latin, and one can learn much from translating Homer or the Greek Anthology, Horace or Tacitus, if one is thrilled by the original, and tries, however vainly, to recapture some of that thrill in English.

> *Only connect! That is the whole of the sermon.*
> *—E. M. Forster*

Lucas uses transitions to guide us, first posing the topic question (*Why and how . . . ?*), then showing his response (*The main answer*), the origin of that response (*Then . . . So . . . Now . . .*), its limitations (*Not . . .*), and its corollaries (*And . . ., Again . . .*). Here a successful writer uses transition words to ease us through his subject and keep his paragraph unified. Take Lucas's paragraph as a model for how you might use transition words yourself.

Much college writing is weakened by its poor or limited use of transition words. Check some of your own recent papers. How often did you begin a sentence or a paragraph with a transition? When you did, were you using only the most common transitions such as *but, and,* and *however?* If you find that transition words are scarce and limited to a few choices, you are missing out on one of the easiest ways to guide your reader's attention. Study the list of transitions on the previous pages, and see how they and others like them might be helpful in making your writing clearer to your reader.

A4. Special Types of Paragraphs

In Section A3 I noted how certain paragraphs can be single-sentence transitions from one part of a discussion to another. In fact, paragraphs can have any number of special functions in an extended piece of writing.

Opening paragraphs have the important role of engaging the reader in the subject of the essay. But the fact of the matter is that some opening paragraphs are good, some mediocre, and some downright terrible. A weak introduction gives readers a poor disposition before they read what you have to say. Either they will put the paper aside and never finish it at all, or else—perhaps because they are obligated to do so—they will continue reading but without much enthusiasm or goodwill.

Fortunately, good opening paragraphs for papers often fall into recognizable categories. Here are some categories you might find useful:

1. *An anecdote.* Open with a brief story that illustrates or introduces your topic. Usually this story can be drawn from your personal experience or from the experience of someone you know. For example, Martin Luther King opened one chapter of his account of the civil rights struggle in the South with a description of Mrs. Rosa Parks refusing to give up her seat and thus launching the Montgomery bus boycott. Just be sure the story you tell relates to your subject and that its relevance is clear to your reader.

2. *A quotation.* A succinct quotation can serve the same purpose as a story. Here is the opening paragraph of an essay by Mayme Logsdon that discusses why one should learn mathematics:

> A pupil of Euclid, when he had learned a proposition, inquired: "What advantage shall I get by learning these things?" Euclid called a slave and said, "Give him sixpence, since he must needs gain by what he learns."

But don't quote the dictionary, even to start a definition paper. Essays that begin, "According to Webster's dictionary . . ." are following a pattern so hackneyed that readers will groan.

3. *A question.* A good question or two can hook your reader's interest. Barbara Lawrence, for example, poses the following questions:

> Why should any words be called obscene? Don't they all describe natural human functions?

Notice I said a *good* question. Nothing can deter a reader more than a silly or obvious question. "Have you ever wondered why I chose to come to this university?" (No, I haven't.) "Is it easy to become a veterinarian?" (Of course you are going to say it isn't.) Ask genuine questions, ones for which the answer isn't obvious, ones in which your reader might really be interested.

4. *An expression of strong emotion.* To stir your reader's curiosity, make a strong statement, such as this one by L. E. Sissman:

> I've grown damn sick and tired of having the youth culture, whatever that is, rammed down my throat by members of my own generation.

Don't fake it, however. Be angry only when you really are angry. If you simply playact, the rest of your essay will give you away, and your reader will feel deceived.

5. *Figurative language.* In Chapter 1 I talked about metaphor and its ability to clarify your meaning. Metaphors can even help clarify the purpose of an entire essay. When Ashley Montagu wanted to write about the American character, he began his essay this way:

> There is an electric spark in the air. Americans may not be consciously aware of it; nevertheless, they behave as if they were affected by it: they are jumpy, alert, excited, hopping about all over the place like jack-in-the-boxes.

If you open your essay with figurative language, just be sure your choice is a fresh one. Beware of clichés or tired metaphors: "They say you should look before you leap." Use them only if you can give them an unusual twist: "To look before you leap is good advice for most folks, but all it ever teaches me is how far I will fall."

6. *A surprise.* Mildred Cavanaugh:

> Some feminists shout for equal pay for equal work, others want abortion on demand. All I am asking is that women be treated like men on the obituary page.

A surprising opening signals to readers that your mind is awake and active. They will anticipate hearing what you have to say.

7. *An introduction.* An introduction to the topic is acceptable as long as it is kept brief and lively:

> The theory of mutation is a concept as exalted as that of time or death.

In that one-sentence paragraph Robert Ardrey names his topic (the theory of mutation), stresses its importance, and shows the approach he expects to take.

The danger to avoid is the kind of opening paragraph that one writer has called "throat clearing." In such paragraphs all the author really says is "ahem" once or twice, settling into the topic like an old hounddog flopping down on a favorite rug. Here is an example:

> It is quite difficult to pinpoint one event in my lifetime that could honestly be called a turning point. More than one event has an influence on you. But I will try to describe one important occasion, even though there are many other factors that could be considered.

That paragraph doesn't engage readers, it doesn't carry them forward, it doesn't really *say* anything.

Single-sentence **transition paragraphs** are not the only kind. Here is an example of a longer transition paragraph by the professional writer Susan Noakes, one that makes clear just how the next part of the essay will proceed:

> . . . If it were, the broadly cultural consequences of such recognition would be considerable.
>
> Before describing at least a few of these consequences, I must make clear that my emphasis on the need for widespread understanding of the reading process as essentially semiotic in character should not be taken to imply that semiotic theory alone can provide the foundation for an adequate theoretical model of reading. Several other movements in twentieth-century reader-oriented theory bear centrally and directly on the problems that have been treated in this book.
>
> The first is deconstruction . . .

The transition paragraph acknowledges what has gone just before ("consequences") and explains what will come next ("movements").

Still another special kind is the **dialogue paragraph,** whether in fiction or nonfiction. The basic principle is this: Be sure to start a new paragraph each time a new speaker speaks. In the following example, Laura Bohannan describes how, when she summarized the plot of *Hamlet* for an African chief, he wanted to know how many other wives Hamlet's father had had:

> "He had no other wives," I told him.
> "But a chief must have many wives! How else can he brew beer and prepare food for all his guests?"
> I said firmly that in our country even the chiefs had only one wife, that they had servants to do their work, and that they paid them from tax money.

Notice that a new paragraph begins when the chief speaks, again when Ms. Bohannan speaks, and again when she resumes her discussion of cultural differences.

Finally, essays need good **concluding** or **ending paragraphs.** Your last paragraph should be more than a quick dash over the same ground. Particularly deadly is the "conclusion" paragraph like this one:

> In this paper I have explained how hobbyists can detect and control diseases in their fish. Tropical fish hobbyists will be able to enjoy their pets to a greater extent knowing they are in control of fish disease.

Instead, look for a way to send your reader away still thinking. Rather than "wrapping it all up," let the reader do some of his or her own packaging. Here are some suggestions for possible good endings:

1. Let your final paragraph pick up on a story, quotation, or theme used at the beginning of the paper.

2. Propose a question that will prod the reader into thinking further on the subject.

3. Speculate about the future—where might this subject lead us next year? Twenty years from now?

4. Offer a concluding story, or perhaps an appropriate quotation from another writer.

5. Surprise your reader. A good one-sentence paragraph can have special impact if it comes last. When Mary McCarthy closed a review of a book by J. D. Salinger, she posed a series of questions for the author. Then she added one more sentence, the final paragraph; the question it asked showed her true opinion of Salinger:

> Or [did Seymour kill himself] because he had been lying, his author had been lying, and it was all terrible, and he was a fake?

Suddenly, surprisingly, we realize the extent of Ms. McCarthy's contempt for the author she is reviewing.

EXERCISES

1. Into how many paragraphs would you divide each of the following passages? Where would your divisions occur? Why?

A. So self-contradictory, indeed, has love become that some of those studying family life have concluded that "love" is simply the name for the way more powerful members of the family control other members. Love, Ronald Laing maintains, is a cover for violence. The same can be said about will. We inherited from our Victorian forefathers the belief that the only real problem in life was to decide rationally *what* to do—and then *will* would stand ready as the "faculty" for making us do it. Now it is no longer a matter of deciding what to do, but of *deciding how to decide*. The very basis of will itself is thrown into question. *Rollo May,* Love and Will

B. I live on northern Puget Sound, in Washington State, alone. I have a gold cat, who sleeps on my legs, named Small. In the morning I joke to her blank face, Do you remember last night? Do you remember? I throw her out before breakfast, so I can eat. There is a spider, too, in the bathroom, with whom I keep a sort of company. Her little outfit reminds me of a certain moth I helped to kill. The spider herself is of uncertain lineage, bulbous at the abdomen and drab. Her six-inch mess of a web works, works somehow, works miraculously, to keep her alive and me amazed. The web itself is in a corner behind the toilet, connecting tile wall to tile wall and floor, in a place where there is, I would have thought, scant traffic. Yet under the web are sixteen or so corpses she has tossed to the floor. The corpses appear to be mostly sow bugs, those little armadillo creatures who live to travel flat out in houses, and die round. There is also a new shred of earwig, three old spider skins crinkled and clenched, and two moth bodies, wingless and huge and empty, moth bodies I drop to my knees to see. *Annie Dillard*, Holy the Firm

2. Examine the following student-written paragraph, printed exactly as it was written. Ideally the paragraph ought to be broken into smaller paragraph units; where would you make the divisions and why? Would you have any other suggestions to make to the author, based on what you have learned in previous chapters?

An egghead is anyone who seems so absorbed in the pursuit of knowledge that she hardly sees the obvious pleasures of life. An egghead would never dream of lazily watching three soap operas in a row on a midsummer afternoon or of getting wasted on a Saturday night, and having to think of an alibi for her parents for staggering in at three in the morning when curfew was at twelve sharp. Instead of living and having fun, an egghead thinks. Starla (not her real name) was one person I knew in high school who fits perfectly into the category of the type of person I have just described. Starla never dated guys, never watched television, never went to dances, and never listened to any together music. Whenever I saw Starla in the halls, her head was bent, her feet shuffled lethargically, and her back twisted into a question mark above the twelve books under her right arm. Her appearance unequivocally suggested lofty contemplation. At noontime, while everyone else gossiped and giggled, Starla sat silently in a corner thumbing through pages of a massive philosophy text. She would always respond to our invitations to come join our conversations with a simple, "No thank you."

3. The phrases and clauses below are all statements about America. If you were to write a clearly focused paragraph on the topic "cultural uniformity in America," which statements would you use and which would you exclude? Using only what you think are the relevant statements, write the paragraph.

    A. The system of education, from grade school through college, is similar in every state.
    B. McDonald's are everywhere.
    C. America is still a haven for immigrants and their diverse cultures.
    D. The same television programs are seen in every city in America.
    E. Social issues like abortion cause tension and division in America.
    F. Regional dialects are disappearing in favor of a standardized American English.

4. Below you will find three student-written paragraphs that are not clearly focused. State the reason(s) for this lack of clear focus and suggest the changes that would be necessary to restore proper focus. Then rewrite the paragraphs.

    A. Even though their civil rights are now guaranteed by law, blacks are being exploited in the job market. They are still the last hired and the first fired. Teenage unemployment is higher for blacks than for whites. When employers do hire blacks the reason is often pressure for "affirmative action," so employees know they were hired not because of their ability but because of their skin color. Housing is another problem. Integrated communities are not yet too common; therefore certain areas are still almost exclusively inhabited by blacks or whites. Lending institutions often discriminate against the black home buyer, either by redlining or by charging higher interest rates on mortgages.

B. What type of person does it take to commit murder? Can a normal person take a life for no apparent reason other than the lust to kill? Such a bizarre act cannot be committed unless the person is mentally deranged. The point is, can we take the lives of such people? This brings up the matter of capital punishment. I feel that a person who kills is not responsible for his acts. Capital punishment is an eye-for-an-eye punishment. The person being punished does not realize what he did. There must be a better solution, a more humane one.

C. [Charmaine's grandmother] would immediately get onto the topic of Dina, her future granddaughter. She lovingly referred to her as the woodpecker who was after her grandson's money. She would relate some of her experiences with the woodpecker. "That city woman stares at me like a woodpecker. I asked her, vat you looking at, do I owe you money or something?" Charmaine's grandmother was sick for a long time, but she refused to see a doctor. She said, "Dat son-of-a-bitch will kill me when I sleep." She thought all doctors were vampires, out to suck both blood and money.

5. Below you will find six topic sentences. Choose any three, and then write well-focused paragraphs using these topic sentences as the starting points.

A. Modern advertising is designed to create "needs" that do not exist.

B. Somehow examinations always show up more of what I don't know than of what I do.

C. People much prefer gossip to talking about ideas.

D. The most important effect of September 11 on American attitudes is . . .

E. Some people seem to believe that natural resources in this country are unlimited.

F. Everyone has at least one phobia—one irrational fear—like fear of heights or electric appliances or elevators or car washes.

G. When I was a child, my favorite TV program (book, toy, amusement) was . . .

6. Here are the beginnings of several paragraphs. Underline the transitional words, phrases, or sentences. What relationship between this new paragraph and the paragraph that went before is being established by each word, phrase, or sentence you have underlined? For example, will this new paragraph contrast with the old one? Add to it? Offer an example of it?

A. Nor is it just a literary gift; it is, I repeat, characteristically human. Almost everything we do . . . *Jacob Bronowski*

B. Let us look first at the spurious sexual models conjured up for our anxious society by the sorcerers of the mass media and the advertising guild. Like all pagan deities . . . *Harvey Cox*

C. Consider our welfare system. Surely unadmitted fear . . . *George Eliott*

D. In summary, with the onset of the child-centered nuclear family, an institution became necessary . . . *Shulamith Firestone*

E. There is, for example, the whispering campaign, the circulation of anonymous rumors by men who cannot be compelled to prove what they say. They put the utmost strain on our tolerance . . . *Walter Lippmann*

F. Let us make an altogether new start here. Let us look at scientific man in his dealings with animals . . . *Erik Erikson*

G. History also suggests, however, some reasons for the difficulties encountered on the road. In the absence of a paradigm . . . *Thomas Kuhn*

7. Comment on the use of transitions in the following paragraph:

Then, too, the whole system is less than democratic, because it is biased toward the large adoption units—the large adoption states and the big-city school districts—and particularly biased toward the ones that make a narrow selection of books. For example, the recommendation of a social studies book by the Texas State Textbook Committee can make a difference of hundreds of thousands of dollars to a publisher. Consequently, that committee has traditionally had a strong influence on the content of texts. In certain periods, the committee has made it worthwhile for publishers to print a special Lone Star edition of American

> *Whatever you make habitual, practice it; and if you would not make a thing habitual, do not practice it, but accustom yourself to something else.*
> —*Epictetus*

history, for use in Texas alone. Much more important, it has from time to time exercised veto power over the content of texts used nationwide. For example, in 1961 a right-wing fringe group called Texans for America intimidated the committee, and it pressed several publishers to make substantial changes in their American history and geography texts. Macmillan, for one, deleted a passage saying that the Second World War might have been averted if the United States had joined the League of Nations. . . . Various publishers deleted references to Pete Seeger, Langston Hughes, and several other offenders against the sensibilities of Texans for America. *Frances FitzGerald*

8. Below you will find five pairs of sentences. In each pair, assume that the first sentence is the concluding sentence of one paragraph and the second sentence is the opening sentence of a new paragraph. Based on the relationship that you see between the two sentences, what seem to be the most appropriate transition words or transition phrases to introduce the second sentence?

A. . . . We were made to feel very much at home.

_____ it came as quite a shock when they told us abruptly the next morning that we would have to leave.

B. . . . So Sunday afternoons are usually pretty quiet in Pine Plains.

_____, take this last Sunday.

C. . . . So the fourth reason for my not joining was the discriminatory nature of the club's membership.

_____, I can recapitulate the reasons for my decision in one simple sentence.

D. ... She danced on and on, oblivious of the noise, the smoke, the smell of cigarettes and beer.

_____, on the other side of the dance floor, Phil was watching her and doing a slow burn.

E. ... My inexperience really showed.

_____, there was another factor in my nervousness besides inexperience.

9. Consider the following five opening paragraphs. What makes them particularly effective?

A. Does the yeti, or "abominable snowman," really exist? Or is it just a myth without practical foundation? For the last four months our Himalayan mountaineering and scientific expedition has been trying to find out—and we think we know the answer. *Sir Edmund Hilary*

B. Love! Attar of libido in the air! It is 8:45 A.M. Thursday morning in the IRT subway station at 50th Street and Broadway and already two kids are hung up in a kind of herringbone weave of arms and legs, which proves, one has to admit, that love is not *confined* to Sunday in New York. Still, the odds! All the faces come popping in clots out of the Seventh Avenue local, past the King Size Ice Cream machine, and the turnstiles start whacking away as if the world were breaking up on the reefs. Four steps past the turnstiles everybody is already backed up haunch to paunch for the climb up the ramp and the stairs to the surface, a great funnel of flesh, wool, felt, leather, rubber and steaming alumicron, with the blood squeezing through everybody's old sclerotic arteries in hopped-up spurts from too much coffee and the effort of surfacing from the subway at the rush hour. Yet there on the landing are a boy and a girl, both about eighteen, in one of those utter, My Sin, backbreaking embraces. *Tom Wolfe*

C. In Greenwich Village a dreamy young beggar in a tattered Ivy League summer suit and a button-down collar with both buttons missing turns on an uptown couple to ask, "Gimme a quarter for a Cadillac, hey?" *Herbert Gold*

Beauty from order springs.
—William King

D. Strange, the things that suddenly become fashionable. Take backpacking, for instance. *Patrick McManus*

E. November fourteenth has been good for humanity: it has given the world such people as the inventor Robert Fulton in 1765, artist Claude Monet in 1840, Prime Minister Jawaharlal Nehru of India in 1889, and Prince Charles of England in 1948. But its primary significance for me lies in the fact that on this day in 1970 1 made my own quiet entrance. *student paper*

10. Go over some recent papers you have written, checking the introductory paragraphs and the concluding paragraphs. Are there any cases where you fell victim to "throat clearing" or tired "in conclusion..." paragraphs? Do you see any ways in which the suggestions made in Part A4 of this chapter would have been helpful?

B. LOGICAL ORDER

Even if your paragraph has a clear focus and helpful transitions, it can still be weakened by haphazard, illogical organization. Confused or jumbled paragraphs puzzle the reader unnecessarily. This section offers advice on how to ensure that your paragraph is well ordered.

You should know from the start what a paragraph is going to do. Perhaps it will tell a story or continue a story already begun. Perhaps it will describe an object or a place. Perhaps it will list something—reasons, or ideas, or a series of items. Your task is to make sure that the order of the sentences in your paragraph is the logical order, given the implied promise you have made to your reader at the start.

B1. Chronological Order

Suppose the paragraph will tell or continue a story, for example. Most probably you will need to use **chronological order.** In other words, you will describe the events of the story in the order in which they occurred, from earliest to latest. Here is an example paragraph by Larry McMurtry from his book *The Last Picture Show*, in which he describes part of a basketball game:

> This time it happened to Sonny, and in the very first minutes of play. Leroy Malone managed to trip the gangly Paducah center and while the center was sprawled on the floor Sonny ran right along his back, in pursuit of the ball. Just as he was about to grab it somebody tripped *him* and he hit the wall head first. The next thing he knew he was stretched out beside the bench and one of the freshmen players was squeezing a wet washrag on his forehead. Sonny tried to keep his eyes closed as long as he could—he knew Coach Popper would send him back into the game as soon as he regained consciousness. He feigned deep coma for about five minutes, but unfortunately the coach was experienced in such matters. He came over and lifted one of Sonny's eyelids and saw that he was awake.

Each event follows the other in chronological order, from Leroy's foul to Coach Popper's lifting the eyelid.

Sounds obvious, you say. Of course earlier events go first, later events come after. But you would be surprised how often this simple principle is ignored. Consider this example:

> My habits have not changed when making the transition from high school to college. In my first semester last year I almost set a school record by being late nineteen times for my first-period class. They almost kicked me out. When I came here I told myself I was going to turn over a new leaf. That pledge lasted about three days, and now I am almost always late for political science at 8:30. In high school the cause was usually the fact that I turned off my clock radio and went back to sleep. I wonder if I can cure myself next semester.

If you arranged the events described in this paragraph in their chronological order, obviously the failures so far this semester precede the wish for better luck next semester, and the failures in high school precede the failures so far this semester. The order of sentences in the paragraph in its current form is unnecessarily confusing, because the sixth sentence (about the clock radio) is out of its proper position.

B2. Spatial Order

Suppose a paragraph describes a place, even a building or a room. Then you need to give it **spatial order,** in which you describe the space from a single, consistent vantage point, as in this paragraph by Joan Didion, from *Slouching Towards Bethlehem:*

> And then, just past that moment when the desert has become the only reality, Route 15 hits the coast and there is Guaymas, a lunar thrust of volcanic hills and islands with the warm Gulf of California lapping idly all around, lapping even at the cactus, the water glassy as a mirage, the ships in the harbor whistling unsettlingly, moaning, ghost schooners, landlocked, lost. That is Guaymas. As far as the town goes, Graham Greene might have written it: a shadowy square with a filigree pergola for the Sunday band, a racket of birds, a cathedral in bad repair with a robin's-egg-blue tile dome, a turkey buzzard on the cross. The wharves are piled with bales of Sonoran cotton and mounds of dark copper concentrates; out on the freighters with the Panamanian and Liberian flags the Greek and German boys stand in the hot twilight and stare sullenly at the grotesque and claustrophobic hills, at the still town, a curious limbo at which to call.

Notice how this description of Guaymas begins with the approach from the north on Highway 15, proceeds through the center of town with its square and cathedral, and ends with the wharf and the harbor beyond—exactly the spatial order appropriate for someone whose first encounter with the town is from an automobile.

Again the order of this example paragraph might have seemed easy to arrange. Examine the following student paragraph, however. See how it begins with a general view of the Florida Keys, narrows to the white sand beach, then suddenly turns back to the more general view:

> Last August we took our yearly vacation in the Florida Keys. Siesta Key is located about seventeen miles from the mainland. Its two most impressive features are its warm Gulf breezes and its clear, aqua-colored water. I especially liked one section of beach. The sand was white and warm to the touch. I could skin-dive or snorkel, and when I wasn't busy there were interesting beach people I could talk to. The Florida Keys are also noted for their exciting opportunities for fishermen.

The order of this paragraph lacks the consistency we found in the earlier paragraph on Guaymas, and therefore it confuses and annoys the reader.

When you are planning a descriptive paragraph, the usual order for the paragraph is the order of place. In other words, you might start at one side of an object and work your way to the other side, or you might start at the top and work down, or you might start at the near side and work to the far side (as in Joan Didion's paragraph). Another possibility is to select the most important feature of the person, object, or scene you are describing—the feature that has the most meaning—and then include the details that help to build this dominant impression.

B3. Emphatic Order

When your paragraph is to offer a list, a little forethought can pay dividends. If the list is of reasons, for example, the reasons could be arranged in the order of ascending importance—that is, from least to most important. Just as logically the paragraph could begin with the most important and work down to the least important. Either way is possible: The point is that there must be some principle that governs the order of appearance, so the list will not be haphazard. Here is a student-written paragraph that illustrates the benefit of paying careful attention to what we might call **logical** or **emphatic order:**

> *Order is a lovely thing;*
> *On disarray it lays its wing,*
> *Teaching simplicity to sing.*
> *—Anna Branch*

> This proposed law [censoring certain movies] is irresponsible. First of all, we already have a rating system that requires theaters to prohibit young people from seeing X-rated or NC-17–rated films, so a new censoring board would only duplicate an existing procedure. If the present procedure isn't always followed, let's just make sure it *is* followed. Second, this law would raise an even more important question: Will we or will we not observe the Constitution, which guarantees freedom of speech? And the constitutional issue leads me to what I think is the most overriding concern of all, and that is the blindness of the mayor toward the real cause of violence among young people. You can never cure violence by restricting people's rights. Instead you have to recognize that violence comes from poverty, a poor education, a broken home, drugs, alcohol—in other words from the *environment* in which these young people live.

The paragraph develops three reasons and lists them in order of ascending importance. We sense that this writer knew what she was doing, that she was writing in a clear and orderly fashion. This impression helps in a subtle way to make her argument more persuasive.

Mastering the names for these ways of achieving order is not important. Moreover, there are other ways besides the ones just mentioned, and you might get some additional help by studying the common paragraph patterns described on pages 151–161. The vital point is that some appropriate order must be evident in your paragraphs if you want them to be readable.

If your paragraphs have been criticized for lacking order, planning the paragraphs might help. Sometimes the planning can be done in your head; sometimes it is better to plan on paper with a few short notes about how the paragraph will be organized. Consider first the focus your paragraph will have and then decide on the logical order for the kind of paragraph you will write. (Exercises 3 and 5 of Part A should be useful if you need experience in planning paragraphs.)

If this kind of foresight is not possible, at least give your paragraphs some *afterthought.* In other words, check each paragraph during the revision process, making sure it has a clear and logical order. Such an effort will pay great dividends in terms of your reader's attention. It's not so much that a reader will notice how well ordered your paragraphs are. Rather, it is a matter of silently preventing the confusion (and exasperation) that a poorly ordered paragraph must cause.

EXERCISES

1. What logical ordering pattern is at work in each of the following paragraphs? Explain your answers.

   A. But I go back. There are four beliefs that I know more about from having lived with poetry. One is the personal belief, which is a knowledge that you don't want to tell other people about because you cannot prove that you know. You are saying nothing about it but you see. The love belief, just the same, has that same shyness; it knows it cannot tell; only the outcome can tell. And the national belief we enter into socially with each other, all together, party of the first part, party of the second part, we enter into that to bring about the future of the country. We cannot tell some people what it is to believe, partly because they are too stupid to understand and partly because we are too proudly vague to explain. And anyway it has got to be fulfilled, and we are not talking until we know more, until we have something to show. And then the literary one in every work of art, not of cunning and craft, mind you, but of real art; that believes the thing into existence, saying as you go more than you even hoped you were going to be able to say, and coming with surprise to an end that you foreknew only with some sort of emotion. And then finally the relationship we enter into with God to believe the future in—to believe the hereafter in. *Robert Frost, "Education by Poetry"*

B. Mr. Newton rose early, as usual, just before the sun came up, dressed himself as best he could despite his arthritis, and hurried down to the main floor of the nursing home via the elevator. His white shirt, yellowed by age, pressed nicely, ornamented by a purple and gray striped tie, was tucked neatly into his baggy, gray suit pants. He shifted himself impatiently on the large metallic walker which he used to support his unsteady body. As soon as the elevator door opened he hurried—at a turtle's pace—out of the elevator, getting caught twice in the elevator door, and then headed for the glass door directly ahead. Walking at a pace of one step every fifteen seconds, he finally made it. *student writer*

C. The kitchen held our lives together. My mother worked in it all day long, we ate in it almost all meals except the Passover *seder*, I did my homework and first writing at the kitchen table, and in winter I often had a bed made up for me on three kitchen chairs near the stove. On the wall just over the table hung a long horizontal mirror that sloped to a ship's prow at each end and was lined in cherrywood. It took up the whole wall, and drew every object in the kitchen to itself. . . . A large electric bulb hung down in the center of the kitchen at the end of a chain that had been hooked into the ceiling; the old gas ring and key still jutted out of the wall like antlers. In the corner next to the toilet was the sink at which we washed, and the square tub in which my mother did our clothes. Above it, tacked to the shelf on which were pleasantly ranged square, blue-bordered white sugar and spice jars, hung calendars from the Public National Bank on Pitkin Avenue and the Minsker Progressive Branch of the Workman's Circle; receipts for the payment of insurance premiums and household bills on a spindle: two little boxes engraved with Hebrew letters. One of these was for the poor, the other to

buy back the Land of Israel. *Alfred Kazin*, A Walker in
the City

2. Below you will find four lists of items. Choose two of
   the lists; then include all of the items on each list in paragraphs on the topics indicated. In both cases you will
   have to decide on a *plan* for the paragraphs. Then, depending on your plan—several plans are possible—you
   will have to rearrange the order of the items on the list
   so that your paragraph has a coherent order.

   A. modern supermarkets

checkout counters	household products
frozen food	customer service desk
meat department	dairy case
shopping carts	deli
produce	

   B. causes of traffic jams

traffic accidents	inadequate roads
poor weather	special events
rush hour	drivers

   C. a sports event

excitement	cheers (boos)
spectators	tickets
teams (competitors)	tension
Coca-Cola (popcorn,	celebration
hot dogs, frozen yogurt)	

   D. causes of trend to reject urban living for suburban life

crowded conditions in cities	high urban crime rates
	hectic pace of city life
lack of trees and gardens in cities	pollution problems in cities

Paragraph
Development

When you divided the passage by Ralph Raphael in Chapter 4 (page 117) into two paragraphs, you might have used a third clue to paragraph division: your sense for the approximate length of the modern paragraph. This clue is usually the one that readers are least aware of. Yet it might be the most important of all, because your awareness of it can help develop your paragraphs more effectively.

Even if you have never cracked a book that was not assigned in school, you still have read literally thousands of pages of prose. Inevitably you have picked up a sense for the typical length of a paragraph in modern writing. You know—even though you are probably not aware you know—the fact that *typically* the modern paragraph is between 50 and 150 words long. Of course many paragraphs are shorter and many are longer. But when you read the Raphael passage in its undivided form, you may have sensed that it was longer than usual (it contained 224 words), and you may have begun looking for ways to break it into units more typical in size. Sure enough, the two original paragraphs, with 111 and 113 words, respectively, fall within the range we have termed average (just as this one, at 137 words, does!).

It has not always been thus. If the undivided Raphael passage had been shown to a college student a hundred years ago, he or she probably would have seen nothing amiss. Until our own century the typical paragraph was much longer. Paragraphs of a page or two in length were not uncommon a century ago and earlier. Paragraph size is not an absolute. Just as we might find earlier paragraphs inordinately long, so the Victorian reader would find our shorter units equally strange. (It follows that our shorter paragraphs must be more tightly focused than a Victorian writer would have felt necessary.)

While the trend is now toward shorter paragraphs, we must still recognize that 50–150 words usually means three well-developed sentences *at least*, and probably more. (The Raphael paragraphs are five sentences each.) In fact, my own experience as a teacher tells me that students are more likely to write paragraphs that are too short rather than too long. Just as we saw in Chapter 2 that the typical student sentence might average 15 words rather than the 20–25 words common among professional writers, so, too, the typical student paragraph averages only two or three sentences and perhaps some 40 or 50 words. Rare indeed is the paragraph that approaches the 150-word end of the scale. Check a group of your own papers and see whether what I have just said holds true for you.

Why are student-written paragraphs shorter than the typical paragraphs of professional writers? Part of the answer may be that without knowing it, student writers are influenced by the short paragraphs in newspaper and magazine writing. Journalistic practice should not be confused with ordinary paragraphing.

Perhaps, having seen short paragraphs in newspapers or magazines, you have been influenced by these examples. But there is another and even likelier cause for shorter paragraphs: Student paragraphs often are not developed enough.

Undeveloped paragraphs are paragraphs that do not elaborate. These paragraphs need additional reasons, comments, examples. If your instructor has called attention to this weakness in your writing, perhaps through such symbols as *dev*[elopment], ¶ *dev*, or *det*[ail], most probably this is what he or she means. And even if your instructor has not remarked on this point—after all, it is a weakness, not an error—chances are you could still profit from the suggestions that follow. Fuller paragraph development can make the difference between a mediocre writer and a really good one. It's that important.

When you begin a paragraph, you make a commitment to the reader. (Often that commitment is implied in the topic sentence.) This commitment is your promise of what the paragraph will be about. Every unified paragraph will have only one such commitment. The good writer, however, knows that he or she must elaborate on that opening promise. Good writers build on the opening statement by offering additional reasons, additional comments, additional examples. Sometimes these additions will be of only one type (e.g., examples); sometimes the paragraph will combine several types.

Usually a writer does not think, "Now I am going to use Method 3 for the development of good paragraphs." The process is ordinarily not a conscious one. But if you need to develop your paragraphs further, it helps to *make* the process a conscious one. The following section offers some practical methods for increasing your awareness of how paragraphs can be developed.

A. PARAGRAPH PATTERNS

Suppose for a moment you are the author of the following paragraph, copied verbatim from a student paper:

> I enjoy listening to music no matter what I am doing. Music makes me feel relaxed and brightens my mood.

Let's further suppose that this paragraph has been returned to you with a symbol like ¶ *dev* next to it, or perhaps a comment like, "This idea needs more development" or "Don't just generalize, give some examples." What can you do to improve the paragraph?

One possibility is to think about whether you can use one of the traditional paragraph patterns. Many paragraphs—not all, but about half—follow certain familiar patterns, certain familiar methods of naming and then developing a subject. These patterns are not familiar by accident. On the contrary, we know them well because many writers have used them. By acquainting yourself with these patterns and then reviewing them in your mind when you are at a loss for a good means of developing a subject, you may be able to elaborate on your topic more successfully.

This section of the chapter will describe some of the most common paragraph patterns. To learn them, and to see whether you can use them (perhaps on a subject such as the "I like music" paragraph), you can ask yourself a series of questions.

A1. Example(s)

The first question you should ask is, can you develop your paragraph by means of **example?** This pattern is the most frequently used. Paragraphs that use this pattern often begin with a general statement, just like the original paragraph about music. But they are never content to stop there. Instead they go on to illustrate the generalization through one or more detailed examples. In fact, they can be reduced to a simple, almost algebraic formula:

generalization + illustration(s)

(The parantheses around the pluralizing *s* show that there can be one example or several.)

Here is a typical example paragraph by M. F. Fasteau from *The Male Machine:*

> What is particularly difficult for men is seeking or accepting help from friends. I, for one, learned early that dependence was unacceptable. When I was eight, I went to a summer camp I disliked. My parents visited me in the middle of the summer and, when it was time for them to leave, I wanted to go with them. They refused, and I yelled and screamed and was miserably unhappy for the rest of the day. That evening an older camper comforted me, sitting by my bed

as I cried, patting me on the back soothingly and saying whatever it is that one says at times like that. He was in some way clumsy or funny-looking, and a few days later

> *Example is the school of mankind and they will learn at no other.*
> —*Edmund Burke*

I joined a group of kids in cruelly making fun of him, an act which upset me, when I thought about it, for years. I can only explain it in terms of my feeling, as early as the age of eight, that by needing and accepting his help and comfort I had compromised myself, and took it out on him.

The generalization—that men find it difficult to accept help from other men—is then given a lengthy but simple illustration, the story of the author's summer camp experience.

Sometimes the paragraph develops not just one example but several, as in this one written by Arthur Herzog, from *The B.S. Factor:*

> Copy Cant is familiar in advertising (no wonder copywriters are called *copy* writers), but it is more prevalent than is generally realized in fields that take pride in their intellectuality. Consider the title chains of books. Betty Friedan's *The Feminine Mystique* had such a tiny print order and low visibility that *The New York Times Book Review* did not review it. (True, a newspaper strike was in progress, but the *Times* caught up with other books.) "Mystique" became popular and soon mothered a dozen books with "mystique" in their titles: *Jewish, Southern, Masculine,* etc. David Riesman's *The Lonely Crowd* (also neglected by the *Times*) brought out the "crowd" books. Richard Rovere's *The American Establishment* established "establishment" in titles, just as Charles Schulz's *Happiness Is a Warm Puppy* sired a litter of "happiness is" titles.

The writer supports his generalization, that publishers copy successful titles, by offering four examples: titles based on *mystique, crowd, establishment,* and *happiness.*

If we return now to the paragraph on music, we can ask whether there are any examples that would develop the generalization that music is enjoyable because it relaxes and brightens the mood. Here is a possible revision of our paragraph, one that develops it by an example:

> I enjoy listening to music no matter what I am doing. Music always makes me feel relaxed and brightens my mood. For example, when I am driving to school in the morning I switch on the car radio and tune it to WJJD. Listening to C&W music, with its simple ballads of betrayal and lost love, its familiar themes like "goin' back home," its uncomplicated guitar rhythms, helps me fight the tension of the expressways. What I see are menacing semis or crazy Jeeps, what I hear are horns, engines, and screaming brakes, what I smell is diesel exhaust. But my heart and mind are at peace because the music has carried me away from the city, out to some little town in the hills.

The generalization has been fleshed out by one detailed example.

Alternatively, several examples could be used, each in lesser detail, as Arthur Herzog did in his paragraph on "Copy Cant." Our paragraph on music might now look like this:

> I enjoy listening to music no matter what I am doing. Music always makes me feel relaxed and brightens my mood. If I'm studying, some light classical music provides a soothing background and still allows me to concentrate. If I'm working around the house, driving the car, or talking with friends, soft rock is what I choose. For parties, however, I like good hard rock—the harder the better—or else rap music. And sometimes, especially when I am driving to school in the morning, I might tune in a C&W station just to bring a breath of fresh country air into the smog-laden and noisy atmosphere of the expressways.

Do you see how this paragraph and the one preceding it both use the example pattern, in other words *generalization + illustration(s)?* Without the illustrations the original paragraph is empty, almost trivial. Examine your own writing to see whether you can give life to some bare statements by appropriate example. By the way, isn't the word *generalization* another way of saying "topic sentence"? Once again we see how frequent and how useful such sentences can be.

A2. List of Reasons

Could you develop your paragraph by giving a **list of reasons?** This is the second most frequent method of development. Here is an example, by Wendell Berry, from *A Continuous Harmony:*

> Odd as I am sure it will appear to some, I can think of no better form of personal involvement in the cure of the environment than that of gardening. A person who is growing a garden, if he is growing it organically, is improving a piece of the world. He is producing something to eat, which makes him somewhat independent of the grocery business, but he is also enlarging, for himself, the meaning of food and the pleasure of eating. The food he grows will be fresher, more nutritious, less contaminated by poisons and preservatives and dye, than what he can buy at a store. He is reducing the trash problem: A garden is not a disposable container, and it will digest and reuse its own wastes. If he enjoys working in his garden, then he is less dependent on an automobile or a merchant for his pleasure. He is involving himself directly in the work of feeding people.

In the first sentence, Berry states that gardening is an excellent way to help the environment. He then lists, in the six sentences that follow, a total of seven reasons the statement is true (the third sentence contains two separate reasons). Here is another example, this time written by a student:

> The recent decline in the popularity of religion has two principal explanations. The first is that people feel less need for it. Whereas in earlier times people turned to religion for consolation in the midst of calamities such as the Black Death, or for strength as they faced the challenges of colonizing a new world, now modern medicine has practically erased the danger of fatal epidemics and modern technology has made work physically effortless. The second reason is that popular attitudes have changed. People used to call on religion to explain those things they could not otherwise understand. Now they are inclined to look for "scientific" answers and to place their faith not in priests, ministers, or rabbis but rather in "experts" who profess to have a solution for everything.

The paragraph develops through its explanation of two reasons for the decline of religion.

If we were to elaborate on the music enjoyment topic by listing reasons for listening to music, it might look like this:

> I enjoy listening to music no matter what I am doing. One reason is that music entertains me while I'm doing certain routine chores such as straightening my room or washing the dishes. Furthermore, music seems to relax me, to break the tension of a hard day or an anxious moment. The lyrics of certain songs can also have a special meaning; when Jim Croce says he wants to "put time in a bottle," he echoes what I have often felt myself. A final reason for listening to music is its effect on my mood. When I hear a track from a good CD, I am not only entertained, I am actually happier, brighter than I was before.

Four reasons are given for the statement that opens the paragraph.

A3. Classification

Could you develop your paragraph by means of **classification?** Paragraphs that use this pattern develop the topic by breaking it down into its categories or classes. In other words, if you want to say more about Subject X, you might divide Subject X into subtopics; if Subject X is musical instruments, you could discuss wind instruments, stringed instruments, and percussion instruments. Alternatively, using a different principle for the classification, you could divide musical instruments into instruments for orchestra, instruments for popular music, and so on. Either way, you now have more to say about the topic—you can develop it further.

For example, when Mortimer Adler wanted to write about book owners, he was able to divide them into three classes:

> There are three kinds of book owners. The first has all the standard sets and bestsellers—unread, untouched. (This deluded individual owns woodpulp and ink, not books.) The second has a great many books—a few of them read through, most of them dipped into, but all of them as clean and shiny

as the day they were bought. (This person would probably like to make books his own, but is restrained by a false respect for their physical appearance.) The third has a few books or many—every one of them dogeared and dilapidated, shaken and loosened by continual use, marked and scribbled in from front to back. (This man owns books.)

We could also revise our paragraph on enjoying music by using classification, perhaps like this:

> I enjoy listening to music no matter what I am doing. Music usually has two effects on me. The first is relaxation: No matter how trivial or frustrating the day has been, listening to a favorite CD or two eases me out of my irritated mood. As my attention gets absorbed in the music I feel soothed, then calmer and more peaceful. The second effect might seem a paradox, but it is equally true: music gives me energy. Especially on a Friday or Saturday night, when I want to party with friends, nothing can give a better emotional high than some good tracks by Nirvana.

This paragraph develops the effects of music on the writer. We can just as easily imagine paragraphs classifying the kinds of music or the sources of musical harmony.

By the way, you may have noticed a strong similarity between this paragraph and the earlier revised paragraph that gave four examples. There is a difference, however. In the above paragraph, the intent is to categorize the effects of music. This purpose is fulfilled by listing two and only two effects, a list that presumably exhausts the effects of which the author is aware. In the earlier paragraph, the intent was simply to offer some examples. The paragraph listed four; presumably the list could have been shorter or longer, because it did not propose to be a complete classification.

A4. Comparison/Contrast

Can you develop your paragraph by **comparison and contrast**? With this method you explain the topic more fully by showing its similarities to and its differences from another member of the same category. Consider as an example the following paragraph, in which the critic Matthew

Arnold finds both similarities (comparisons) and differences (contrasts) between poets Robert Burns and Geoffrey Chaucer:

> Yet we may say of [Burns] as of Chaucer, that of life and the world, as they come before him, his view is large, free, shrewd, benignant—truly poetic, therefore; and his manner of rendering what he sees is to match. But we must note, at the same time, his great difference from Chaucer. The freedom of Chaucer is heightened, in Burns, by a fiery, reckless energy; the benignity of Chaucer deepens, in Burns, into an overwhelming sense of the pathos of things—of the pathos of human nature, the pathos, also, of non-human nature. Instead of the fluidity of Chaucer's manner, the manner of Burns has spring, bounding swiftness. Burns is by far the greater force, though he has perhaps less charm.

Sometimes writers will restrict themselves to just similarities or just differences. William Murray, for example, having already explained what qualities all surfers share, then devotes a paragraph to showing the differences between one kind of surfer and another:

> Most surfers are just nice kids from white middle-class families. They will graduate from college, take jobs, get married and become fathers, and soon they will be surfing once or twice a month, if at all. They will teach their children how to surf, and they will retire gracefully to the outdoor barbecue, the bar and the television set, captured by white collars and brown shoes. But there is another class of surfer that is becoming more and more evident, a hard-core minority of fanatics who are past their teens and for whom life has become an endless summer in search of the perfect wave. It is this dedicated group for whom surfing is a metaphysics that dominates the competitive scene, establishes the pecking order on the beach, and sets the styles of this American subculture based almost as much on language and looks as on skill in the water, though the latter is still the basic prerequisite for status.

How might this comparison-contrast pattern apply to our music paragraph? Here is another possible version of it:

I enjoy listening to music no matter what I am doing. Music always makes me feel relaxed and brightens my mood. When music is playing it has the same effect on me as talking with friends—my attention is diverted from my problems and I feel calmer, more relaxed. Yet music is different from conversation because it is much more subject to my control. I can hear what I want, when I want. I can change CDs, turn the volume louder or softer, even turn the player off completely. None of this is possible in conversation unless I want to bring a quick end to some friendships.

Both comparison and contrast appear very clearly in this paragraph.

A5. Definition

The last question you might ask is whether you can develop your paragraph by giving a **definition** of its topic. Many terms we use quite commonly have several meanings, and often it is useful to explain precisely which meaning is intended. Definition paragraphs make your meaning clearer. Examine this paragraph by the famous scientist and writer Jacob Bronowski, from *The Reach of Imagination:*

I am using the word *image* in a wide meaning, which does not restrict it to the mind's eye as a visual organ. An image in my usage is what Charles Peirce called a *sign*, without regard for its sensory quality. Peirce distinguished between different forms of signs, but there is no reason to make his distinction here, for the imagination works equally with them all, and that is why I call them all images.

Bronowski cautions us that he will not employ the word *image* in its narrower sense as something we picture in our mind's eye. He uses definition to show that an *image* for him will be a sign, and the meaning of the rest of his essay thus becomes clearer.

Here is another example, this one by C. R. Gallistel:

Behavioral neurobiology tries to establish the manner in which the nervous system mediates behavioral phenomena. It does so by studying the behavioral consequences of one or more of the following procedures: (a) destruction of a

[on being asked to define jazz]
Man, when you got to ask what
it is, you'll never know.
—Louis Armstrong

part of the nervous system, (b) stimulation of a part, and (c) administration of drugs that alter neural functioning. These three techniques are as old as the discipline. A recent addition is (d) the recording of electrical activity. All four procedures cause the animal at least some temporary distress. In the past they have frequently caused intense pain, and they occasionally do so now. Also, they often impair the animal's proper functioning, sometimes transiently, sometimes permanently.

Notice that both Bronowski and Gallistel, in order to clarify their definitions, have to borrow from other patterns or techniques. Bronowski uses comparison and contrast— the similarities and differences between his use of *image* and Charles Peirce's use of *sign*. Gallistel has to explain what behavioral neurobiology *is* by explaining how it is *done*.

We return to the music paragraph one last time. To develop the paragraph by means of a definition pattern it might be rewritten something like this:

I enjoy listening to music no matter what I am doing. Music for me is any sound that has a rhythm to it. That definition includes of course the more conventional kinds of music, such as classical, jazz, rock, or rap. But it also includes the swish of cars on the wet street outside my window, or the repetitious thwack of the Ping-Pong ball coming up from the basement, or even the sound of my own humming. As long as I can feel rhythm, I can hear music, and music relaxes me and brightens my mood.

You might not use the word *music* in the same way as the author of that paragraph, but at least you understand what she means.

There are other patterns besides the five familiar ones just described. And these five patterns themselves do not always occur in a "pure" form. Very often a paragraph will contain parts of more than one pattern. You might remember that Jacob Bronowski's definition of *image* contained a contrast, in this case a contrast between his definition of the word and the definition offered by Charles Peirce. If you are giving reasons or explaining causes, do not hesitate to enrich your paragraph by giving examples or definitions wherever they might be helpful.

Furthermore, developing a paragraph and giving it order are often one and the same process. If you arrange a list in logical order or tell a story chronologically, you are also using a pattern of development. The important point about paragraph development is that it need not be left to chance. There are questions to ask, patterns to use, processes to work out, as this section has shown. What you are looking for are ways to stimulate your imagination so that it can supply the added information that makes the difference between sketchy paragraphs and thoughtful, penetrating paragraphs.

The important point about paragraph development is that it need not be left to chance. There are questions to ask, patterns to use, processes to work out, as this section has shown. What you are looking for are ways to stimulate your imagination so that it can supply the added information that makes the difference between sketchy paragraphs and thoughtful, penetrating paragraphs.

EXERCISES

1. Develop two of the topics in each of the following categories into full paragraphs, using the methods prescribed. Or, you may prefer to choose your own topics.

    A. Develop by example (either one detailed example or several undetailed ones):

    role models
    vacation places
    salesclerks
    cheating
    success
    political changes in Europe

    B. Develop by a list of reasons:

    choice of a major
    voting in national elections

importance of friendship
Israeli-Palestinian conflict

C. Develop by classification:

bosses
friends
rock groups
sports

D. Develop by comparison and contrast:

liking and loving
community colleges and universities
"pure" science and "applied" science
movies in theaters and movies on TV
Romance languages and Germanic languages
pain and gain
evolution and revolution

E. Develop by definition:

failure
representative government
tenderness
social sciences
hero (or heroine)
justice
propaganda

2. Choose one of the topic sentences below. Write a paragraph using any one of the patterns of development listed in Exercise 1. Then write it again, using a different method of development. Finally, write the paragraph a third time, this time mixing two or more methods of development.

A. My neighborhood differs from any other section of the city.
B. Sexually explicit TV programs are a disgrace to the society that supports them.
C. Modern "conveniences" only make life more complicated.
D. When in trouble, punt.
E. You can tell nerds right away.

3. Below you will find four student-written paragraphs that need further development. Rewrite them, choosing any method of development discussed in this chapter.

   A. Life runs in cycles. My first day in college reminded me in several ways of my first day in high school.
   B. Is there an absolute truth? Each person has his or her own belief. Since not everyone has the exact same life, no one's truth will apply to all.
   C. I like the sounds of nature. They keep me alert yet make me feel relaxed and peaceful. I try to hear the sounds of nature whenever I can.
   D. Freedom is a precious commodity, but we could lose it. Everybody says they value freedom. But what are they doing to preserve it? Nothing.

4. What methods of development are used in the following student-written paragraphs? Study them closely.

   What happened to the local beauty shops, the ones named "Marge's" or "The Powder Box"? They were simply decorated: two or three chairs in the waiting room with copies of *True Confessions* on a tray table; four sinks, four setting chairs, four hairdryers. The "beauticians" worked at small counters cluttered with pins, clips, rollers, and hair spray. Pictures of boyfriends or movie stars lined the mirrors, and the mirrors were set against a background of floral wallpaper and a plain white linoleum floor. These shops weren't much to look at, but the service was good, the beauticians amiable, and the cost low.

   Now these same shops have grown into "salons," with Art Deco interiors. Graphic walls, chrome-and-leather chairs, hanging plants, and New Age music provide a much less personal atmosphere. After customizing your hair for two hours, the "hair stylist" (now a *he*) will insist you redo your face to go with the cut. Behind him stands an elongated counter with his own private stock of beauty supplies, and when he presents his bill you realize why he never reveals his last name.

B. PARAGRAPH SEQUENCES

Earlier we compared sentences and paragraphs to show how similar they are. In this section I want to draw out the comparison a little further. What you know about developing sentences can help you in developing paragraphs.

B1. Sequential Structures

Here is a paragraph written by E. M. Forster from his essay, "What I Believe":

> No, I distrust Great Men. They produce a desert of uniformity around them and often a pool of blood too, and I always feel a little man's pleasure when they come a cropper. Every now and then one reads in the newspapers some such statement as: "The coup d'état appears to have failed, and Admiral Toma's whereabouts is at present unknown." Admiral Toma had probably every qualification for being a Great Man—an iron will, personal magnetism, dash, flair, sexlessness—but fate was against him, so he retires to unknown whereabouts instead of parading history with his peers. He fails with a completeness which no artist and no lover can experience, because with them the process of creation is itself an achievement, whereas with him the only possible achievement is success.

Suppose we separate the paragraph into sentences and then arrange it so that each sentence modifies or adds details to some preceding sentence. That way our paragraph would look like a sentence that has been divided into its clauses and phrases. The Forster paragraph would look like this:

No, I distrust Great Men.

> They produce a desert of uniformity around them and often a pool of blood too, and I always feel a little man's pleasure when they come a cropper.

>> Every now and then one reads in the newspapers some such statement as: "The coup d'état appears to have failed, and Admiral Toma's whereabouts is at present unknown."

Admiral Toma had probably every qualification for being a Great Man—an iron will, personal magnetism, dash, flair, sexlessness—but fate was against him, so he retires to unknown whereabouts instead of parading history with his peers.

He fails with a completeness which no artist and no lover can experience, because with them the process of creation is itself an achievement, whereas with him the only possible achievement is success.

The first sentence (*No, I distrust Great Men*) establishes the topic. The second sentence explains or modifies the first. The third offers an example of the second, so we mark it as modifying the second, just as we do again when the fourth turns out to be an explanation of the third. The final sentence compares Admiral Toma's failure with the failure of artists or lovers and therefore operates on still a fifth level, as a comment on the fourth sentence.

The value of rewriting the paragraph this way is that we can now clearly see the pattern this paragraph follows. The paragraph develops in an orderly, logical way, each sentence growing in sequence out of the one preceding it.

Read the last sentence of the paragraph. Is there any way you could guess that this final sentence is a natural subdivision of the "topic" *I distrust Great Men*? I don't think so. On the contrary, the connection between them becomes clear only when you see how this fifth sentence grows out of the fourth, how the fourth in turn grows out of the third, and so on back to the first. Thus we can say that all the other sen-

tences *depend on* the first sentence, but they are not necessarily *subdivisions* of it.

The following paragraph by Robert Coles, from "The Children of Affluence," is another excellent example. It discusses the children of the very rich. Here it is, arranged to show how in this case each sentence is an independent, equal, parallel unit:

> It is a complicated world, a world that others watch with envy and with curiosity, with awe, anger, bitterness, resentment.
>
> It is a world, rather often, of action, of talk believed by the talkers to have meaning and importance, of schedules or timetables.
>
> It is a world in motion—yet, at times, one utterly still: a child in a garden, surrounded by the silence acres of lawn or woods can provide.
>
> It is a world of excitement and achievement.
>
> It is an intensely private world that can suddenly become vulnerable to the notice of others.
>
> It is, obviously, a world of money and power—a twentieth-century American version of both.
>
> It is also a world in which children grow up, come to terms with their ample surroundings, take to them gladly, deal with them anxiously, and show themselves boys and girls who have their own special circumstances to master—a particular way of life to understand and become a part of.

The first sentence limits the paragraph to its subject, the world of the child from a wealthy family. Yet all the other sentences offer separate but equally important details about that world. So all the sentences are parallel to each other—a fact emphasized by their similar opening words—rather than growing one from another, as was the case with the sequence in Forster's paragraph.

But you are probably troubled now by a more practical concern. Granted, most paragraphs can be arranged and analyzed in these ways. How can this knowledge help you to be a better writer?

First, an understanding of these sequences enables you to see the defects of paragraphs that you know are weak but that you don't know

> *Composition is for the most part, an effort of slow diligence and steady perseverance, to which the mind is dragged by necessity or resolution.*
> —*Samuel Johnson*

how to improve. In the following example a student writer describes the problems some drivers encounter:

> No matter how efficient some people think they are when they drive, their habits irritate others. The driver at the head of a single lane of traffic goes ten miles per hour under the posted limit. Cars back up for blocks behind him. Horns are honking, people are shouting and swearing. Now, that person may think he is being properly cautious when in fact he is holding up traffic, which is as annoying as another mistake, never turning down the high beams on the headlights. There are other errors, too, like following too close or failing to use the turn signal.

This paragraph came back to the writer with the notation that it "lacks coherence" and "needs development."

At first the writer did not see what these comments meant. Then he decided to arrange the paragraph sequentially. When he did, the reasons for these faults became clear. His attempt at an arrangement looked like this:

No matter how efficient . . .

> The driver at the head of a single lane . . .

> > Cars back up for blocks . . .

> > Horns are honking . . .

> > Now that person may think . . .

> There are other errors too. . . .

This pattern is unsatisfactory, however. Obviously the second sentence is an example of the bad driving habits the topic sentence describes, so we can be comfortable marking this sentence as dependent on the base sentence. Sentences three and four also offer no problem—they clearly depend on the second. But how about the fifth sentence, the one beginning *Now, that person may think . . .* ? We can make it modify the second sentence, too, because it says still more about the slow driver. But to do so we must ignore the second half of it. The second half of the fifth sentence tells about still another bad habit, using high beams, and therefore it belongs in the same position as the second sentence. Our puzzlement is then increased further when we read the last sentence. This final one contains both the third and fourth examples of bad driving habits, yet its position as only the second "middle-level" sentence shows that the paragraph in its current form allows for only two such habits.

So one way to see how this paragraph "lacks coherence" is to realize that the paragraph lists four examples of bad driving habits but structurally makes room for only two of them. Giving each of these habits a separate-but-equal sentence of its own would go a long way toward restoring coherence.

This attempt to rearrange the paragraph also shows why it is not adequately developed. Notice that the first bad habit, slow driving, is stated in the second sentence and then developed by three succeeding sentences. Yet the second bad habit, using high beams, gets only a dependent clause tacked on to the fifth sentence, and the last two habits, tailgating and improper signaling, must share the final sentence. If all four habits could be developed in about as much detail as the first one, the paragraph would be better proportioned.

Here is how the student writer revised the paragraph to eliminate the weaknesses of the original:

> No matter how efficient some people think they are when they drive, their habits irritate others. For example, a driver at the head of a single lane of traffic goes ten miles per hour under the posted limit. Cars back up for blocks behind. Horns are honking, people are shouting and swearing. Now, that person may think he or she is being properly cautious, but in fact he or she is holding up traffic. A second example, equally annoying, is the driver who never dims headlights.

The painful glare of those high beams, especially if they come at you from around a curve, can be frightening and dangerous. Then of course we can't forget the tailgater. If you cruise an expressway at 65, he hangs off your rear bumper like he was slipstreaming you in the Daytona 500. If you encounter him on city streets, he is sure to give you a sharp jolt at the stop sign, then blame you for stopping too quickly. A close relative of the tailgater is the nonsignaler. This last source of irritation has the habit of drifting into the right lane and then, without the least hint or warning, swerving across in front of you and turning left onto a side street, leaving in her wake a screech of brakes and a chorus of angry horns.

The paragraph now has a coherent structure and a full, pro-portioned development. The revised version is also, you might notice, a good example of the "development by ex-ample" pattern discussed on pages 152–154. These are complementary methods, two ways of getting to the same goal.

So if your instructor makes the general comment that your paragraphs lack coherence or lack development, or if he or she makes such comments about particular para-graphs, one way to learn what needs revising is to examine how the sentences relate to each other in the paragraphs. The patterns that emerge when you try to arrange them this way can help you identify where you went wrong and what you can do to improve.

The second practical advantage is that such knowledge can also help you while you are writing. Suppose, for ex-ample, you are writing a paper about the role of computers in modern universities. Early in the process of writing the paper you find you must say something about the uses to which computers are put. A paragraph on "uses of the com-puter" begins to take shape in your mind.

Before you begin to write, however, think for a moment. Which of the arrangements we discussed seems more ap-plicable here? Quickly you realize that the paragraph will contain a list, with all the items on the list—all the uses of the computer—having equal value. Let's assume you can think of three main uses: faculty and student research, academic record keeping, and administrative services. A rough outline of a paragraph already begins to emerge:

Uses

1. research

2. records

3. services

Such outlines need not be written. Their sole purpose is to remind you of the general form your paragraph will take.

Now you can write the paragraph, fleshing out this initial design. As you take up each of the three uses, more details, explanations, and examples of each occur to you, and you incorporate them into additional sentences beyond your three basic ones. But these additional sentences will always depend on the three sentences that form the original sequence. Here is a paragraph that might result from using such a method:

Despite their cost, computers are essential to a university because, in addition to word processing, they serve three main functions. First, they enable both faculty and students to undertake research that would be impossible otherwise. Students and faculty members from all departments and disciplines now find computers to be necessary research tools, especially as they access the resources of the Internet. Even humanities departments, for example, now use computer-produced word counts to study an author's literary style. The second function of computers is academic record keeping, including such tasks as recording grades, issuing transcripts, and tallying class rolls. This work was formerly done by hand, so computers in this case save money and help pay for themselves. Finally, computers are used to keep track of the myriad items and activities that are part of any large and complex organization. Computers are involved in every kind of administrative service, from printing the payroll checks to taking inventory of the pencils.

B2. Repetition and Parallelism

When we discussed repetition in Chapter 2, we praised artful repetition within sentences. But repetition can also occur from one sentence to another sentence, so that the entire paragraph can be drawn together by the use of **repeated phrases.** Consider again the paragraph by Robert Coles, the one in which he describes the world of rich children:

> It is a complicated world, a world that others watch with envy and with curiosity, with awe, anger, bitterness, resentment. It is a world, rather often, of action, of talk believed by the talkers to have meaning and importance, of schedules or timetables. It is a world in motion—yet, at times, one utterly still: a child in a garden, surrounded by the silence acres of lawn or woods can provide. It is a world of excitement and achievement. It is an intensely private world that can suddenly become vulnerable to the notice of others. It is, obviously, a world of money and power—a twentieth-century American version of both. It is also a world in which children grow up, come to terms with their ample surroundings, take to them gladly, deal with them anxiously, and show themselves boys and girls who have their own special circumstances to master—a particular way of life to understand and become a part of.

Every one of the seven sentences in this paragraph contains the phrase *it is a world.* Yet so artful is Coles in the way he varies this phrase that we are never conscious of boredom or monotony.

Sometimes in going from one sentence to another writers repeat not only phrases but also grammatical structures. Repeating grammatical structures can be called **parallelism.** The excerpt form Robert Coles shows parallelism. Here a student describes the view from her dorm room window late at night:

> Cars going down the street, turning left into the parking lot. Sidewalks a gray streak, followed by a green patch of grass and then a gray streak of road. Room lights in Stebler Hall going on or off in irregular patterns, but mostly off. A

couple passing by on the sidewalk, whispering to each other like people usually do when it's very late. Then all is quiet and I am left alone in the silence and the growing darkness, wondering at the mystery of it.

Each sentence except the last begins with a noun—*cars, sidewalks, room lights, couple*—that will be the focal point of that sentence. The nouns are not repeated, but the form of the sentence is. (You probably noticed, by the way, that these parallel sentences are also sentence fragments. The writer has used them deliberately to give the effect of a catalog, in this case a catalog of the objects that attract her attention as she looks out the window.)

How might this help you develop a paragraph more fully? Suppose you had been writing a brief essay on bilingual education. Suppose further that you had written the following paragraph:

> Whether or not we should preserve cultural diversity through bilingual education is a difficult question to answer. Arguments for these programs assert that society benefits from accepting a wide variety of cultures, while opponents say that such education only divides the country.

If you were asked—perhaps by your instructor through a written comment on a draft, perhaps by a classmate at a small group session—to develop the paragraph further, your knowledge of repetition and parallelism might give you still another way to begin.

Your initial focus might be on the second sentence. It identifies two views about bilingual education (pro and con) and gives the primary justification for each. Clearly here is a place where more can be said. Beginning with the proponents, can you search for repetitions and parallelisms that allow you to say more about their views, develop their views more fully? Certainly the word *cultures*, for example, begs for a fuller definition: Which cultures, how wide the variety in those cultures? Then the word *benefits:* Which benefits, and how extensive are they? Then on to the opponents, where the issues might

Writing isn't hard; it's no harder than harder than ditch-digging.
—Patrick Dennis

center on the word *divides:* Divides why, divides in what ways?

The result of a search for repetitions and parallelisms as applied to these questions might be a revision like this:

> Whether or not we should preserve cultural diversity through bilingual education is a difficult question to answer. Proponents of these programs assert that society thus recognizes and accepts the diversity of the cultures that make it up, cultures ranging from Nigerian to Ukrainian, from Mexican to Korean, from German to Indian. When society accepts a culture, it makes the members of that culture feel more at home, more confident in their values and abilities, and thus more eager to contribute something back to society. Opponents of these programs say that such education only divides the country—divides Asians from Hispanics, Africans from Europeans. Having a single language for education helps emphasize what we have in common rather than what separates us, thus promoting the strength that comes from unity.

Can you see how this paragraph is better because it is more fully developed, and that the development includes—in fact depends on—repetitions and parallelisms? You probably noticed the parallel lists ("from Nigerian to Ukrainian . . ." or "Asians from Hispanics . . .") and the parallel grammatical structures (for example, *more at home, more confident, . . . and thus more eager*). Such development gives the paragraph a new level of detail and a new kind of clarity. In fact, you might even have noticed that my own explanatory words themselves contained repetitions (*Suppose . . . Suppose, perhaps . . . perhaps, divides . . . divides*) and parallelism (*to say more about their views, develop their views more fully* or *which cultures, and how wide the variety*).

A word of caution. We have considered each of these patterns, sequences, and repetitions separately and in their purest forms, so that we could understand them more easily. This better understanding should lead to increased awareness, and increased awareness will lead to increased use. Most writing combines all of these sequences and methods. The following paragraph by Susanne Langer, from "The Prince of Creation," illustrates this mixture:

> The answer is, I think, that man's mind is *not* a direct evolution from the beast's mind, but is a unique variant and therefore has had a meteoric and startling career very different from any other animal history. The trait that sets human mentality apart from every other is its preoccupation with symbols, with images and names that *mean* things, rather than with things themselves. This trait may have been a mere sport of nature once upon a time. Certain creatures do develop tricks and interests that seem biologically unimportant. Pack rats, for instance, and some birds of the crow family take a capricious pleasure in bright objects and carry away such things for which they have, presumably, no earthly use. Perhaps man's tendency to see certain forms as images, to hear certain sounds not only as signals but as expressive tones, and to be excited by sunset colors or starlight, was originally just a peculiar sensitivity in a rather highly developed brain. But whatever its cause, the ultimate destiny of this trait was momentous; for all human activity is based on the appreciation and use of symbols.

Two sentences, the second and the last, depend directly on the topic sentence and therefore give the paragraph structure. At the same time we find the second sentence modified by four sentences that grow out of it. We can also observe several patterns of development at work: explanation (second sentence), cause and effect (third), example (fifth), cause and effect again (sixth). And while there is little parallelism from one sentence to another, we can see a great deal of parallelism *within* sentences.

I should conclude this chapter with a second word of caution. The importance of full paragraph development does not mean all paragraphs must be long ones. Quite the contrary. Sometimes you will find opportunities for the deliberately short paragraph. When you need an attention-getting opening paragraph, when you want your concluding paragraph to offer a "punch line," when you wish to give special emphasis to one or two sentences: on these and other occasions a short paragraph will serve you well. Like the extra-short sentences we discussed in Chapter 2, brief paragraphs are quite acceptable if used deliberately and knowledgeably. But I think you should master the material in this section on paragraph de-

> *If we have a correct theory but merely prate about it, and do not put it into practice, then that theory, however good, is of no significance.*
> —*Chairman Mao*

velopment before you decide whether you are ready to make these exceptions.

Short, underdeveloped paragraphs are a common weakness in student writing. But sometimes I do encounter seemingly endless paragraphs, perhaps even an entire paper that consists of nothing but one interminable paragraph. Almost always, however, this extra length comes not from a fuller development of the topic but rather from a failure to see natural divisions in the subject matter; such papers are really several shorter paragraphs that have been lumped together, like a casserole made of leftovers. If you have written paragraphs of this sort, carefully study the suggestions for paragraph unity offered in Chapter 4.

EXERCISES

1. Find the weaknesses both in coherence and in development in the following student-written paragraph. Suggest how the paragraph could be rewritten to eliminate those weaknesses.

> War is nothing more than a racket. It creates business and profit for the businessman, opens up jobs for the unemployed, and creates a rise in the economic wealth of a nation. War is the ways and means of bringing one country and another country together to fight for what they believe is right. During wartime a country is as closely knit as it will ever be. There is no more discrimination between race, creed, or color, just an inborn need to put all our forces together and head for victory, which is a word with many meanings. Victory possibly is the ending of a war or the proving of a point. All in all "to the victor belongs the spoils" because he receives power, land, wealth, and the loser back-

tracks to find out where he went wrong. So in conclusion war is just a business to bring wealth and power, nothing more and nothing less.

2. In the following selection from President John F. Kennedy's inaugural address, identify the parallelism and repetition, both between paragraph and paragraph and between sentence and sentence.

To those old allies whose cultural and spiritual origins we share, we pledge the loyalty of faithful friends. United, there is little we cannot do in a host of new cooperative ventures. Divided, there is little we can do—for we dare not meet a powerful challenge at odds and split asunder.

To those new states whom we welcome to the ranks of the free, we pledge our word that one form of colonial control shall not have passed away merely to be replaced by a far more iron tyranny. We shall not always expect to find them supporting our view. But we shall always hope to find them strongly supporting their own freedom—and to remember that, in the past, those who foolishly sought power by riding the back of the tiger ended up inside.

To those peoples in the huts and villages of half the globe struggling to break the bonds of mass misery, we pledge our best efforts to help them help themselves, for whatever period is required—not because the Communists may be doing it, not because we seek their votes, but because it is right. If a free society cannot help the many who are poor, it cannot save the few who are rich.

To our sister republics south of our border, we offer a special pledge—to convert our good words into good deeds—in a new alliance for progress—to assist free men and free governments in casting off the chains of poverty. But this peaceful revolution of hope cannot become the prey of hostile powers. Let all our neighbors know that we shall join with them to oppose aggression or subversion anywhere in the Americas. And let every other power know that this hemisphere intends to remain the master of its own house.

To that world assembly of sovereign states, the United Nations, our last best hope in an age where the instruments of war have far outpaced the instruments of peace, we renew our pledge of support—to prevent it from becoming merely a forum for invective—to strengthen its shield of the new and the weak—and to enlarge the area in which its writ may run.

Finally, to those nations who would make themselves our adversary, we offer not a pledge but a request: that both sides begin anew the quest for peace, before the dark powers of destruction unleashed by science engulf all humanity in planned or accidental self-destruction.

3. Examine two of your most recent papers. For each paragraph, determine which pattern of development you used. What do you conclude from this review of how you have tended to develop paragraphs up until now? What do you conclude about how you can improve your paragraphs in the immediate future?

4. Using the same essays as in exercise 3, do you see places where you could have used an unusually short paragraph to give an important idea special emphasis? Do you see paragraphs that could profit from being developed at much greater length?

5. Again using the same essays, underline the transition words, phrases, and sentences you used. What can you conclude about how effective your use of transitions has been?

The English
Language:
Grammar

One of the minor plagues of my life is the ritual question, "What do *you* do?" I have learned over the years that if I say I'm an English professor, I had better wince, because immediately my questioners will step back in mock horror and proclaim, "An English teacher! I'd better watch my grammar!" Yet what they then proceed to "watch" is not grammar at all, but rather the kinds of words they use.

I have a similar experience when I ask freshmen what they expect from a composition course. The usual answer is "Grammar and stuff like that." But if I ask what *grammar* is, I am told it is "rules about what words to use" or that it "tells what words mean." Nope, I reply. *Usage* is the description of standard and nonstandard uses of words. *Semantics* is the study of what words mean. Then what could *grammar* possibly be? Puzzled frowns.

The truth is, most people have only the vaguest idea of the meaning of grammar, and they usually associate it with making mistakes when speaking. Here are some other misconceptions: (1) most errors in writing are grammatical errors; (2) study of grammar is necessary to speak and write well; (3) only a few select people (English teachers?) have ever mastered grammar.

The surprising truth is that (1) most "errors" are in semantics or usage, not in grammar; (2) many people have become excellent writers without ever undertaking any formal study of grammar; and (3) everybody—including you—knows a great deal about English grammar and probably has known it since learning to speak.

You doubt this last truth? Then consider this sentence: *Sam has new five quarters.* Immediately you recognize that this isn't good English, that it should be *Sam has five new quarters.* If asked why the first version was wrong, you might or might not be able to give the technical explanation (i.e., that English word order requires adjectives of number to precede adjectives of quality). But you intuitively know how to fix it, and you've probably known this grammatical truth (because that's what it is) ever since you were a small child. Everybody who speaks English knows English grammar; otherwise what they speak would not be English! The only difference is that some people can be explicit about their grammar and some cannot. Speaking is just like walking: all of us know how to do both, but only a few—grammarians in one case, physiologists in the other—can tell us what we are doing.

Let's examine this idea of grammar more closely. Part A of this chapter will discuss grammatical fact and theory and their respective uses. Then, in Parts B, C, and D, we will see how grammar can be applied to your writing. You may be surprised at how few writing problems turn out to be grammar problems, and you may be equally surprised to see how easily the grammar problems can be remedied. The exercises at the end of each part will help you strengthen your knowledge of the grammar of standard written English (or what some people call "edited American English").

A. What Is Grammar?

Grammar is just another name for an explanation of how a language works—in other words, for the grammatical facts about that language. For example, in the French language a negative is formed by putting *ne* before the verb and *pas* after it: *Je ne parle pas anglais* ("I do not speak English").

> *Grammar, which knows how to control even kings . . .*
> —*Moliére*

This is a grammatical fact about French. Similarly, in English negatives are formed by adding an auxiliary verb plus *not* ("I *do not* speak French"); this is a grammatical fact about the English language.

A1. Facts Versus Theories

Please notice the use of *grammatical fact*, rather than the more common term *grammatical rule*. We often speak of grammar as if it were a set of rules. This is unfortunate, because it suggests that somebody "out there" makes up regulations the rest of us have to follow. *Rule* implies power, authority, control. Those who make rules can also change them. If the state says you cannot exceed 50 miles per hour on a certain highway, it is perfectly free to lower that limit to 45. But languages do not operate like highway rules. What some people call rules are really just statements of fact, explanations of how language works. I cannot change these facts, nor can you or anybody else.

To go back to our recent example, suppose I am convinced that *not speak* ought to be an acceptable present-tense form in English, without an auxiliary: *I not speak English*. The word *not* already conveys negation; the auxiliary verb *do* is unnecessary and should be eliminated. This makes perfect sense, but I can't do it. The reason is that the English language—English grammar—does not work that way. It is a *fact* that to form negatives you must add *not* and use an auxiliary verb like *do*. *I not speak English* is simpler and more sensible, but it's not grammatical.

So grammar on a simple level is a set of facts about a language. These facts of course do not exist in isolation. They are related to each other in various ways, and some people study these relationships in order to form more comprehensive explanations about how the language as a whole works. It is easy enough to say that we form negatives by adding *not* plus an auxiliary, but it is much harder to explain how we form verbs in the English language or how we construct sentences. Those who study these relationships and offer theories about them are called *grammarians*.

While you don't need to know theories, you do need to know basic language facts. As we noted, you probably have known most of them ever since you were a preschooler. If you read and write extensively, maybe you already know intuitively all the facts a good writer must know. But if you are like most students, you may not be sure about a few simple but important facts. This is especially true of facts that are more applicable to written English than to spoken English.

A2. Written English

Why are the facts of written English a special problem? There are two reasons. The first is that writers have to be more precise, because they do not have the same resources available to them when they write as they do when they talk. No gestures, no voice inflections, no chance for answers to ritual feedback questions: "Y'know?" "Okay? " "Get me?" To compensate for this lack of feedback, writers want to be as clear as possible, which means that certain grammatical facts that can be ignored easily in speech cannot be ignored in writing. For example, we will be discussing pronoun reference in the next section. In conversation, pronoun reference causes no difficulty; we can augment our pronouns by pointing or nodding the head, and if the person or thing to which the pronoun refers is still not clear, a listener can stop us and ask who or what we mean. But in writing we have to make sure the pronoun reference is explicit.

The second reason is that written English links all those people who use the language. The dialect of a Scotsman, for example, might be almost unintelligible to you, just as your dialect might puzzle him. But if both of you *write* what you want to express, these barriers disappear and you share common ground. Because written English must cross all boundaries in nationality, region, class, and culture, it has certain requirements that all who write the language have agreed to observe. Therefore the written language is somewhat more formal. When we write we are more conscious, for example, of matters such as verb endings. The care we take in observing these conventions is the small price we pay for the great privilege the written language gives us: the privilege of telling others, some of whom are quite different from us, what we know and what we feel.

Any grammatical problems you have may stem in large part from the fact that you know the spoken language quite well but have less experience with writing. The facts that are essential to both speaking and writing almost everybody knows. The facts that apply more to writing than to speaking are another matter. The purpose of this chapter, therefore, is to acquaint you with those

> *[Writing is] the great bond that holds society together, and common conduit, whereby the improvements of knowledge are conveyed from one man and one generation to another.*
> —*John Locke*

facts most often unfamiliar to student writers. Knowing them and seeing how they apply to your writing is probably all you need to do to eliminate "bad grammar" as a cause of ineffectiveness in your writing.

The lesser-known facts about written English can be drawn from surprisingly few areas, mainly pronouns, modifiers, and verbs. The remaining parts of the chapter take up each of these three in turn. Please recognize that these issues are vital to your success as a writer. If what you write is ungrammatical, I think you can guess what kind of a response you are all too likely to get from many readers. Whether your reader is a teacher or a friend or a supervisor, the best reaction you can expect is puzzlement, and more often than not the reaction will be irritation and perhaps outright rejection ("Why can't this person use good English?").

Now that might seem unfair. You will perhaps wonder why the reader didn't care more about what you were saying than how you were saying it ("It's clear what I *mean*, isn't it?"). Fair or not, however, such criticisms will be made, and your writing won't communicate as well as it should, it won't accomplish what you want it to accomplish. Consequently, if you wish to be an effective writer, there is no alternative but to take command of the material covered in the rest of this chapter.

You can use the chapter in one of two ways. If you prefer, you can go over recent papers you have written to identify the grammatical problems you have encountered. (Remember to note only *grammatical* problems—punctuation errors, for example, are considered in another chapter.) Then locate and carefully study the sections in this chapter that relate to your particular problems. The list of common abbreviations for correction symbols given on the inside back cover of this book may give you some idea of where to find the discussion you are looking for; if that fails, try the index.

The second way to approach the rest of this chapter—and this might be the better method if grammar is a common or severe problem for you—is to proceed directly through the rest of the chapter all the way to the end. That way you have an overview of the principal facts, some of which may seem new and may need to be studied a second time.

Please note that some parts of this chapter, and indeed some other parts of the book, use grammatical terms such as the *parts of speech* (e.g., *noun, verb, adjective, adverb, pronoun, conjunction, preposition*). Other grammatical terms (e.g., *case*) may also make occasional but necessary appearances. Usually their meanings will be clear, but if not you can consult the Glossary of Grammatical Terms (pages 483–497).

EXERCISES

1. The claim has been made in this chapter that you already know a great deal about English grammar, even if you cannot be explicit about grammatical terms. Examine the following three groups of sentences. State in your own words the most important similarities and/or differences among the various sentences that make up each group.

   A. My aunt writes quite often in haste.

   Quite often my aunt writes in haste.

   My aunt writes in haste quite often.

   Quite my aunt in haste writes often.

   B. The police officer begged the demonstrators to remove the sign.

   The police officer ordered the demonstrators to remove the sign.

The police officer promised the demonstrators to remove the sign.

C. The New England Patriots defeated the St. Louis Rams in the Super Bowl.

The St. Louis Rams were defeated by the New England Patriots in the Super Bowl.

The ones that the New England Patriots defeated in the Super Bowl were the St. Louis Rams.

2. What are the differences in meaning of the following terms: *usage, grammar, semantics?*

3. Ask a random sampling of people—including people older and younger than yourself—what they understand by the word *grammar.* Are there any similarities in their responses? Do their replies exhibit any confusion about the meaning of the term?

4. Prepare a short paper describing your own training in grammar. Be sure to include answers to the following questions:

A. In what grades was grammar taught in a formal way?

B. What were you told about what grammar is?

C. What, specifically, were you taught in the way of grammar?

D. What attitude toward grammar did your teachers convey?

E. What attitude toward grammar did you yourself have?

F. What were the reasons for this attitude?

5. Check a recent group of papers you have written. Ignore all the corrections on your papers that have to do with punctuation, word choice, spelling, paragraph structure, and content. Of the remainder, how many are errors in grammar? Of these, how many have to do more with the written than the spoken language (i.e., errors in verbs, pronouns, or modifiers)? Do the results of your investigation bear out the claims made in the fourth paragraph on page 181?

B. FACTS ABOUT PRONOUNS

Words that can be used in place of a noun or noun phrase are called **pronouns.** Like nouns they can change to distinguish between singular and plural (*I* versus *we, mine* versus *ours*). They can also indicate gender (*he, she, it*), person (*you, she*) and case—whether they represent a subject or an object (*who* versus *whom*). In general, pronouns can perform the same functions as nouns.

What makes pronouns different is that they have no meaning of their own. A rose is a rose is a rose, as Gertrude Stein once remarked—but what is a *which?* Pronouns can't make sense until we take into account the persons or objects to which they refer—in other words, until we take into account what are called their **antecedents.** Take this sentence, for example:

> The guard inspected my purse thoroughly, although he seemed embarrassed about the whole matter.

The pronoun *he* in this sentence means little by itself, but in context we know that it quite clearly refers to the antecedent noun *guard.*

This section will discuss the most important facts about pronoun forms and about the relationships between pronouns and their antecedents.

B1. Pronoun Forms

We noted that pronouns can change form when they change in number, gender, person, or case. People make few errors in number, person, or gender (when is the last time you wrote *It are going to bed?*). So our consideration of pronoun forms really gets down to matters of case.

When we discuss the relationship of a noun, pronoun, or adjective to other words in a sentence, we are discussing case. Concretely this means answering such questions as "Is the word a subject? a direct object? an indirect object?" Case is usually determined in English by position in the sentence. In a sentence such as *The train is coming,* for example, we

Who would succeed in the world should be wise in the use of his pronouns.
—*J. M. Hay*

say the noun *train* is the subject because it occupies the subject position. Problems of pronoun case are often abbreviated by *case, ca,* or simply *pron* ("pronoun").

Let's begin with the subjective case—in other words, with **subject pronouns.** Eight pronouns can fill the subject position in a sentence:

Subject Pronouns

Person	Singular	Plural
1	I	we
2	you	you
3	he, she, it	they

She and *I* are going.

We will be back in a half hour.

Who and *whoever* used as subjects are also in the subjective case:

Who is going?

Whoever he is, he must love books.

Goethe was the author *who* most influenced Thomas Mann.

Ordinarily you won't have too much trouble with pronouns in such sentences, as long as the sentences are short or relatively simple. The tricky parts come when sentences get more complex or when common speech patterns differ from those required in formal writing.

The first pitfall to negotiate occurs when two subjects are used with only one verb—the so-called **compound subject.** Do you see any problem in this sentence from a student paper, for example?

The center fielder and her ran for the fly ball at the same time.

In this instance *her* is not the preferred pronoun form. It may have sounded correct to the writer, but the difficulty becomes clearer when the other half of the compound subject, *center fielder,* is left out:

Her ran for the fly ball at the same time.

Clearly undesirable, right? Immediately you know to use the subject form *she* rather than the object form *her*. If you have a compound subject, always apply this same test (leaving out the other half of the compound subject) to determine whether you have used the best pronoun. If the pronoun acts as a subject, it must be in the subject form.

Similarly, people often write *us* in a subject place rather than *we*, when the pronoun is used alongside a subject noun:

Us Tareyton smokers would rather fight than switch.

Smokers, the noun used in conjunction with the pronoun, acts as a subject. Therefore, formal writing would require the subject pronoun *we: We Tareyton smokers* . . . Again, apply the simple test of leaving out the other part of the subject, in this sentence *smokers*. You would not say, *Us would rather fight than switch*. So the test gives you a clear indication of which pronoun form is the necessary one.

Pronouns can also directly follow a form of the verb *to be*. When they do, they must be in the subject form. This sentence from a student paper is therefore correct:

Her friends suspect it is she who sets off the fire alarms.

She is the proper pronoun here because it is in the subject form, as it must be when serving as a *complement* to the linking verb *is*. But you may have been tempted to use *her*. If so, the reason is a natural one: In speech we quite often

use the object form of the pronoun after the verb *to be*, just as we would if the verb were not *to be*. If someone comes home and you call out "Is that you?" the natural response is "It's me." But in writing, at least in formal writing, the subject pronoun forms should be used in cases like these.

Now let's consider the **objective case**, which also has eight forms:

Object Pronouns

Person	Singular	Plural
1	me	us
2	you	you
3	him, her, it	them

Are the children coming with *us* or going with *them?*

The assistant coach gave *it* to *me.*

Whom is also in the objective case (it functions as an object):

With *whom* do you wish to speak?

Whom did they call first?

Pronouns in the objective case can function in three main ways:

1. as direct objects:

   Whom is the clerk helping?

   Did Tom invite *you* to the party yet?

2. as indirect objects:

   Teresa told *us* the secret.

   The boss promised *them* a raise.

3. as objects of prepositions:

   Is the secretary talking to *him* or to *her?*

   With *whom* are the Aquinos staying?

In speaking, many people use *who* as an object instead of *whom,* especially in questions: *Who is the clerk helping? Who are the Aquinos staying with?* The reason is that people are used to having a subject near the beginning of a sentence, so they use the subjective case *who.* (Questions reverse the normal word order, so in these cases the objects begin the sentences, not the subjects.) In formal writing, however, *whom* should be used as an object form.

Note also two facts that correspond to points made earlier. Remember we said that if a pronoun is used immediately before a noun subject, it has to be in the subject form (*We smokers*). By the same token, if a pronoun is used immediately before a noun object, it must be in its object form:

Schools must give us taxpayers our money's worth.

Here, *taxpayers* is an indirect object. Also, when a sentence has compound objects one of which is a pronoun, the pronoun must be in the objective form:

My numerous childhood illnesses brought my mother and me closer together. *Vladimir Nabokov*

Here again you could apply the simple test of removing the other object (*my mother*) and seeing what is left. You would not write, *my illnesses brought I*, so *me* has to be the proper pronoun form.

The third case to be considered is the **possessive.** Let's consider both possessive pronouns and possessive adjectives here:

Possessive Pronouns

Person	*Singular*	*Plural*
1	mine	ours
2	yours	yours
3	his, her, its	theirs

Possessive Adjectives

Person	*Singular*	*Plural*
1	my	our
2	your	your
3	his, her, its	their

Whose is also in the possessive case:

Whose is this?

Pablo Neruda was the poet *whose* work won him a Nobel prize in 1971.

In general, you probably don't have trouble with these possessive forms. In the phrase *my coat*, you know that *my* modifies *coat* and serves as an adjective just like *old* or *big* or *white*. And if someone says, *Whose is this?* referring to your coat, there is no problem choosing the right posses- sive pronoun for the answer. But there is one case in which possessive adjectives are sometimes forgotten, and that is before a subject with an *-ing* ending:

> I was nervous about *his* driving the car.

> We were happy about *their* moving to a new house.

Note that the possessive adjectives *his* and *their* are used, not the object forms *him* and *them*.

I should close this section on pronoun case forms by pointing out three more little grammatical facts. The first is that *them* should not be used instead of the demonstrative adjectives *these* or *those: Please hand me those keys on the table* (not *them* keys). Second, reflexive pronouns (those with the *-self* ending) are not used as objects in writing un- less both the pronoun and the subject of the sentence refer to the same person, as in *Narcissus loved himself.* In speech people often use the reflexive pronoun as an object without such a precondition, as in *André picked up some tuition refund forms for Brenda and myself.* Since the reflexive pronoun *myself* does not refer to the subject of the sentence (*André*), formal writing requires the normal object form:

> André picked up some tuition refund forms for Brenda and *me*.

Finally, when the words *than* and *as* appear in a sentence with a comparative adjective or adverb, some detective work may be required on your part before you know what pro- noun form is needed to go with them. Here are two examples:

> That's the only exam where he did as well as I.

> Coffee affects you more than me.

In the first example, the subject form *I* is used, because *I* is the subject of the clause *I did* (where *did* is understood). In the second example, the object form *me* is used, because *me* is the object of the clause *it affects me* (where *it affects* is understood). These little sticklers don't occur very often, but when they do, you will know which pronoun form to use if you can figure out what understood words have been omitted.

B2. Pronoun Agreement

Pronouns get their name from the fact that in most instances they take the place of nouns. By doing so they perform a useful function. If we did not have them we would have to use the noun itself, again and again. Our prose might look like this:

> Ali grabbed the garbage bag, but Ali saw the garbage bag was leaking, so Ali shoved the garbage bag inside a second bag.

How much better it is to use pronouns:

> Ali grabbed the garbage bag, but he saw it was leaking so he shoved it inside a second bag.

Although pronouns enable us to make a sentence more concise, we cannot lose sight of the fact that each pronoun is replacing a word; this word, the *antecedent*, appears elsewhere, usually in the same sentence. While it usually precedes a pronoun, the antecedent can sometimes follow a pronoun within a sentence:

> Although I don't have *it* now, I can get *the money* to you tomorrow.

And sometimes the antecedent is found in a preceding sentence:

> Natasha handed me *the tickets*. I put *them* on top of the dresser.

A pronoun must agree with its antecedent in number. In other words, the pronoun is singular if the antecedent is singular, plural if the antecedent is plural. (Pronouns also agree in gender and person, but native speakers hardly ever make mistakes in those areas.) Agreement in number is usually a simple matter:

> If *she* treats the body like a pincushion, *[Emily] Dickinson*
> also treats pincushions like bodies. *Camille Paglia*

But in a few instances agreement is not so simple. If in
one of your papers a pronoun or possessive adjective is
circled and the abbreviation *agr* is written next to it, you
have probably encountered one of these problem cases. Take
the situation where the antecedent is *each, either, neither,*
or an indefinite pronoun such as *everyone* or *somebody:*

> Each team member must clean out his locker before May
> 31st.

> Somebody had left her sweater in my room.

Formal writing requires singular possessive adjectives for
these antecedents, as in the sentences above. In everyday
conversation, however, most of us are likely to use the plural possessive adjectives in such cases—*their locker, their
sweater.* Therefore when we write we have to resist a strong
temptation to use those plural forms.

These last two example sentences bring to mind an important issue related to this topic: the use of the generic *he.*
The two preceding example sentences are acceptable as is,
because in the first *his* refers to people who both writer
and reader knew were male, and in the second *her* refers to
a person who both writer and reader knew was female. The
same holds true for sentences in this book where I use *he* or
she to refer to various student writers because I know the
author's gender. But what happens when the person referred
to could be either male or female? This important issue is
discussed in Chapter 8, on pages 287–290.

There are two other circumstances in which agreement
in number is not so easily determined. The first of these
circumstances is when the possessive adjective has two or
more antecedents. Believe it or not, the English language
then allows for four possibilities:

1. If the antecedents are joined by *and*, always use a plural possessive adjective:

> Mr. and Ms. Benitez both needed *their* word processor.

2. If the antecedents are joined by *or* or *nor* and the antecedents are both plural, use a plural possessive adjective:

   Neither planes nor tanks have established *their* value in the Middle East conflict.

3. With *or*, if the antecedents are both singular, use a singular possessive adjective:

   Either Phil or Ted will pick us up in *his* car.

4. Again with *or*, if one antecedent is singular and the other plural, the possessive pronoun or adjective agrees in number with the antecedent closer to it in the sentence:

   Either Karen or her sisters will come to get my cell phone, so please leave it out where *they* can see it. [*they* because the plural *sisters* is closer to the pronoun than singular *Karen*]

The other circumstance that might puzzle you occurs when the antecedent is a **collective noun,** such as *crowd, family, team, group, class,* or even the word *collection* itself. Sometimes collective nouns are used in the singular, sometimes in the plural. To determine whether you should use a singular or plural possessive adjective, decide whether the antecedent will be considered as a single unit acting in unison or as a collection of separately acting individuals. If the former is true, make both the verb and the possessive adjective singular:

   The team is ready for *its* biggest game of the year.

If the individuals that make up the unit act separately, make both the verb and the possessive adjective plural:

   The team opened *their* lockers.

Here the team acts as a collection of individuals; *its locker* would indicate that the team shared one big locker. This matter is subtle, but sometimes your easiest clue is to decide which verb form seems "natural" and then to coordinate the possessive adjective or pronoun with it. Another solution is to insert the word *members* after the collective noun (and you can even leave *members* in the sentence):

> The team members opened their lockers.

B3. Pronoun Reference

Let's assume now that your pronoun has the right case form according to its function and the right number form according to its antecedent. There is another issue to consider: Will your reader have any difficulty in knowing what the antecedent is? Every pronoun needs a clear antecedent, a **pronoun reference.** If it does not have one, the sentence should be revised to eliminate any possible confusion for the reader. (Common abbreviations for problems with pronoun reference include *ref, pro ref,* and *amb ref.*)

The first type of problem is what can be called **ambiguous reference.** *Ambiguous* means capable of being understood in more than one way; ambiguous reference means that the pronoun has more than one possible antecedent. Consider this example:

> Debra agreed with Yolanda that she ought to run for Student Senate.

Does the pronoun *she* refer to Debra or Yolanda? In other words, does Debra agree that she herself ought to run, or does she agree that Yolanda should? Either is possible— it's ambiguous—although only one meaning is intended. Here is another example:

> On Saturday I polished my car and straightened up my room; it still needs a lot more work.

Which needs more work—the car or the room?

To eliminate ambiguous references, the cure is usually simple enough: Cut out the pronoun and repeat the intended antecedent:

> Debra agreed with Yolanda that Yolanda ought to run for Student Senate.

> On Saturday I polished my car and straightened up my room; the room still needs a lot more work.

> *If things were to be done twice, all men be wise.*
> —*proverb*

The cure is certainly easy. The difficult part is knowing when the pronoun is ambiguous. After all, *you* know the intended antecedent, so you have no reason to pause over the sentence as you proofread your paper. Furthermore, there are many cases where the pronoun is technically ambiguous but where no confusion results:

> Nancy stroked the cat's fur. She wished the heat was not quite so oppressive.

In theory *she* could refer to the cat or to Nancy, but the intention is so clearly to refer to Nancy that the sentence needs no revision.

The only helpful procedure is to read your own writing insofar as possible with the eyes of a stranger. Don't ask yourself whether your writing is clear to you; instead ask whether it will be clear to someone else. Look at your use of pronouns in that way and maybe the problem pronouns will be easier to identify. Above all, watch for sentences that mention two items or two people of the same sex and then follow them with a singular pronoun, as in the Debra/Yolanda example. That's the most frequent source of ambiguity.

A second kind of problem occurs when a pronoun by its position seems to refer to one antecedent but actually refers to another. Thus:

> The canoe tipped sideways, throwing Paula and me into the water. She sure was hard to handle, especially in the rapids.

The position of the pronoun *she* would at first lead you to think that it referred to Paula, its nearest possible antecedent. But the remainder of that second sentence makes it obvious that the antecedent is the canoe. This problem is not really the same as ambiguous reference, because readers eventually determine which antecedent is intended. But they do experience a momentary and rather amusing confusion!

Here is another example from student writing:

> Keats was attacked by the reviewers, so much so that Shelley even thought his death might have been caused by those attacks.

At first glance, *his* might seem to point to *Shelley* as the antecedent. But then we realize that *Keats* is necessarily the choice, especially since it would be awfully difficult for Shelley to think about the attacks if he himself were dead. So the sentence needs to be revised:

> Keats was attacked by the reviewers, so much so that Shelley even thought Keats's death might have been caused by those attacks.

Again, if you have this problem, the cure is to read your writing with the eyes of a stranger, insofar as possible.

A third type of problem is a close relative of the second. If the antecedent and its pronoun get separated by too many other words, readers may forget what the antecedent was by the time they get to the pronoun. And if they forget the antecedent they have to stop and go back to determine it, which causes a temporary delay in reading. Here is an example of the problem, called **remote reference:**

> At last I finished stuffing the envelopes. Slowly I cleared off the desk, recapped my pen, and shoved the wastebasket out of sight; then I pulled on my jacket and went to put them in the mail.

Of course *them* must have *envelopes* as its antecedent—there is no other logical possibility. The difficulty is that the antecedent is so remote from the pronoun. It is better in this case to clarify the passage by repeating the antecedent: *went to put the envelopes in the mail.*

The fourth and last type of problem is **vague reference,** which can happen when a writer uses *it, which, this,* or *that* to refer to a whole idea rather than to a single noun. Sometimes using pronouns in this way causes no difficulty; this sentence, for instance, reads clearly:

> We spent the whole week loafing on the beach, which gave us a good tan if nothing else.

We readily understand that *which* refers to the whole activity described in the independent clause. But on other occasions the reference is not quite so clear:

> The governor's budget proposes heavy cuts in welfare and mental health along with a big increase in highway construction. This is folly, unless he wants to commit political suicide.

This might refer to the increase for highways, or perhaps to the proposed cuts, or maybe to the entire budget. The antecedent for *this* is so vague that the pronoun carries no clear meaning of its own. Better to revise it:

> The governor's budget proposes heavy cuts in welfare and mental health along with a big increase in highway construction. This entire proposal is folly, unless he wants to commit political suicide.

See to it that whenever possible the pronouns *it, which, this,* and *that* have concrete, namable antecedents. Make a special effort to avoid the vague, indefinite uses of *it:*

> POOR: It says in the paper that more snow is coming.
> REVISION: The paper says more snow is coming.

(Of course you will not be able to avoid fixed idioms with the pronoun, as in the phrase *It's snowing.*)

EXERCISES

1. Choose the appropriate word to complete each of the following sentences. Explain your choice.

  A. Either the dean or the president will sidetrack the proposal, although each will do it for (their/his) own separate motives.
  B. (Who/Whom) did you give my glasses to? [formal writing]
  C. The American family needs to have (its/their) values examined.
  D. Why do most elementary school systems neglect (us/we) overachievers?
  E. (Who/Whom) is calling, please?

   F. I bought two Dr. Peppers for my sister and (me/myself).

   G. The sheriff and his deputies each had (his/their) own role to play in the archetypal plots of the old Grade B westerns.

   H. Mina and (she/her) think only about grades, never about their social lives.

   I. My roommate thinks she needs twice as much sleep as (I/me).

   J. A crowd will take on a character of (their/its) own, becoming docile or turning mean, perhaps even violent.

2. Some of the following student-written sentences have a problem in pronoun usage; some do not. If the sentence is correct as is, put a checkmark next to it. If the sentence needs to be changed, make the necessary alterations.

   A. Us kids always stuck together whenever the adults pushed us.

   B. The sage realizes the young poet's need for his wisdom.

   C. He may look overweight, but let me assure you he is twice as fast a runner as me.

   D. I put the books on the table, then turned on the CD player, poured myself a Pepsi, adjusted the lamp, changed my shirt, and read the mail; finally I faced the fact that I was going to have to study them.

   E. I bought myself a new pair of jeans, just to make myself feel better.

   F. Every day my mother straightens up the living room and then washes dishes, but it soon needs doing all over again.

   G. Him and the insurance agent went to the garage to check on the damage estimates.

   H. The prosecutor and my lawyer agreed that she should have investigated the case more thoroughly.

   I. It said on this sheet what we were supposed to do.

   J. Probably I would not have gained this knowledge about myself for many more years.

   K. One learns their hidden traits when they enter into close personal relationships.

   L. The teacher accused me of deception, hypocrisy, manipulation—how could I defend myself against it?

M. We contestants grew restless, waiting for the judge to finish his endless list of rules.

> *God does not much mind bad grammar, but He does not take any particular pleasure in it.*
> —*Erasmus*

3. Rewrite the following student paragraph so that each pronoun is the correct one and has a clearly defined antecedent with which it agrees. Also, make sure the paragraph has a consistent point of view—don't let it switch from second person (*you*) to third person (*they*) and then back to second person without good reason.

I looked forward to Mondays and Thursdays. It was at these times that I would work as a page in the House of Representatives. Your expectations about this job are usually shot down the first day you work. The number of representatives there are relatively few—I could usually count them on my fingers. I would sit back and look at the high walls of the House chamber and what a grand sight it was; they were loaded with tradition and beauty. The chamber itself is characteristic of the serious business conducted within its walls. The walnut rostrum is directly in front of an American flag hung vertically and they have wreaths hanging from the rostrum that tell you about union, justice, tolerance, and liberty. Us pages could gaze at this splendor all morning long, because they usually gave us almost nothing to do. Sometimes we would fetch them coffee, or you might have to go out and buy somebody their morning paper if he had forgotten to pick up one earlier. It was never anything important, like take this to the speaker and see how I should vote. It was mostly a matter of us sitting around and them paying us for it.

C. FACTS ABOUT MODIFIERS

Imagine a world of nothing but subject, verb, and complement. Our prose would look like this:

> I took a bus. The bus was late. I arrived late. Class had begun. I was embarrassed.

In short, we would be writing like third graders.

Much of the difference between how a
third grader writes and how you write lies
in your much greater experience at using
modifiers. Given similar data, you might
have written the small paragraph above
somewhat like this:

*Comment is free, but
facts are sacred.*
—Manchester Guardian

> I took a bus, which was my first mistake. As usual the bus
> was late, very late. Consequently I arrived after class had
> begun, and I had to suffer the acute embarrassment of see-
> ing the teacher glare icily at me as I took my seat.

Part of the greater maturity evident in this paragraph
comes from such aspects as increased sentence length and
the use of pronouns. But the most important aspect is the
use of modifiers such as *which was my first mistake* (sentence modifier), *very* and *icily* (adverbs), *after class had
begun* (adverb clause), and *acute* (adjective).

Because modifiers are so important a part of your style,
of anybody's style, you need to make sure you use them as
effectively as possible. To do that, you should first be aware
of the forms modifiers can take.

The most familiar modifier is the **adjective.** Adjectives
usually modify nouns: *green blouse.* Sometimes they follow
linking verbs such as *is: the sky is **dark.*** They have comparative and superlative forms: *little, littler, littlest.* Furthermore a group of words—a phrase, a clause—can act as an
adjective: *the hunter **in the red jacket.*** Other parts of speech
can become adjectivals—in other words, can fill an adjective position: *the **brick** wall* (noun used as adjective).

Adverbs are the second major category of modifiers.
They usually modify verbs (*she smiles **easily***), *adjectives*
(***barely** warm soup*), or other adverbs (***very** quickly*). They
often have the characteristic *-ly* ending. Adverbs are like
adjectives in that they can be compared (*more **easily,** most
easily*). Their position can be occupied by adverbials (*she
goes **today**—noun used as adverb*) or by adverbial phrases
or clauses (*she laughs **when she shouldn't***).

A third important kind of modifier, the **sentence modifier,** is a word, phrase, or clause that modifies not a noun or

a verb but rather the whole sentence to which it is attached. Let's look at the example presented earlier:

I took the bus, which was my first mistake.

The clause *which was my first mistake* modifies neither bus nor took. Instead, it can be understood properly only if it is seen to qualify the entire main clause: *I took the bus.* Therefore, the *which* . . . clause is said to be a sentence modifier. Here are two other examples:

In the cafe, he tells me the story of his life. *Albert Camus*

Miraculously, no one was hurt. *newspaper item*

In these two examples, the prepositional phrase *In the cafe* and the adverb *Miraculously* modify the remainder of the sentences in which they are found.

So modifiers come in three major forms: adjectives (including adjectivals and adjectival phrases and clauses), adverbs (including adverbials and adverbial phrases and clauses), and sentence modifiers. Now what you need to know are the principal pitfalls writers must avoid if they are going to use these modifiers effectively.

C1. Forms of Modifiers

First pitfall: The sentence *seems* to invite an adverb but in fact requires an adjective. Like this one from a student journal:

I felt bad when the exam was over—so much endurance had brought such little joy.

The sentence is correct, but you can hardly be blamed if you thought that the adjective *bad* should have been replaced by the adverb *badly*. After all, we are used to adverbs in that position, immediately following a verb. The reason we use the adjective rather than the adverb is that the verb *feel* is one of a small group of verbs that act like the verb *to be*. These verbs are often called **linking verbs** because they do just that—they link subject and complement. The most frequently used linking verbs are *be, be-*

come, seem, appear, and some verbs associated with the senses—*feel, look, smell, sound, taste.* The complement of a linking verb is an adjective:

The basement smells musty.

The wind became violent.

That reply sounds childish.

Perhaps the simplest way to understand how linking verbs work is to imagine them being replaced by the most common linking verb, *to be.* Immediately you would recognize that an adjectival form has to be used. Replace *The wind became violent* with *The wind was violent.* (You would not write, *The wind was violently.*) In the preceding examples, the adjectives that follow the linking verbs clearly modify the subjects of the sentences (*musty basement, violent wind, childish reply*).

Note that when *feel, look, sound,* and other linking verbs are not used to link subject and complement but rather have or can have an object, they are modified by adverbs, not adjectives:

With Adjective (linking verb)	With Adverb (nonlinking verb)
The music sounded beautiful to me.	He sounded the alarm frantically.
Don't you feel good?	I felt for the door cautiously in the darkness.
She looked happy and relaxed.	She looked skeptically at the salesclerk.

Just as adverbs are sometimes used mistakenly in place of adjectives, adjectives are sometimes used mistakenly in place of adverbs. Do you see any problems in this sentence?

Larry speaks real slow, as if each word required a great effort.

In speech the sentence might be quite acceptable. But in writing two problems arise. The first is that *real* is being used as an intensifying adverb—in other words, as a syn-

> God loveth adverbs.
> —Joseph Hall

onym for *very*. When the word is an adverb, it must have its adverbial form, *really*. The second problem is that *slow* also occupies an adverbial position, because it modifies the verb *speaks*. You might lose sight of that fact because adverbs usually follow immediately after the verbs they qualify. But in this case *slow* has been bumped over one place by the intensifier *really*. As long as the word functions as an adverb, it needs an adverbial form; thus *slowly* is the right word. A rewritten version of the sentence would look like this:

> Larry speaks really slowly, as if each word required a great effort.

(In the rewritten example, *very* would sound better than *really*.)

Remember, too, that adjectives and adverbs have comparative and superlative forms:

Positive	*Comparative*	*Superlative*
hot	hotter	hottest
good (adjective), well (adverb)	better	best
late	later	latest
typical	more typical	most typical
quickly	more quickly	most quickly

In formal writing the comparative forms should be used when two items or qualities are being compared, as in this example from a student paper:

> Of the two older Woody Allen movies I have seen so far, *Bananas* is clearly the better one.

Better should be used rather than the superlative *best*. However, use the superlative forms for three or more items:

> To affect the quality of the day, that is the highest of arts.
> *Henry David Thoreau*

C2. Position of Modifiers

Problems with modifiers can also arise when a modifier is out of position, although it may be in the proper form. A

misplaced modifier—abbreviated *mis mod, m m,* or *mis pt*—results in confusion for the reader.

My favorite example of a misplaced modifier comes from a headline in our student newspaper a while back:

Laura Allende Speaks of Terror and Repression at Loyola

Now, what the author of that headline meant was that Ms. Allende, daughter of the late president of Chile, had spoken about terror and repression in her own country. But the position of the adverbial phrase *at Loyola* makes it seem as if the terror and repression are much closer at hand, and the result is unintended humor. To eliminate this confusion, the phrase should be moved back to its proper adverbial position right after the verb *speaks:*

Laura Allende Speaks at Loyola of Terror and Repression [in Chile]

For another example of a misplaced modifier, consider this sentence from a student's paper:

The computer is also used to recall master lists of all a com-pany might own for inventory purposes.

The position of the phrase *for inventory purposes* confuses the reader. Does the author mean that the computer recalls lists of all that the company owns, or merely lists of all that the company owns for inventory purposes? Obviously she means the former, and our confusion is only temporary. But still, that temporary confusion would not have happened if the phrase had been placed immediately after the word *used:*

The computer is also used for inventory purposes to recall master lists of all a company might own.

Here is one more example of a misplaced modifier, in this case just a simple adverb:

I am more and more convinced that I ought not become a doctor lately.

The placement of *lately* at the end of the sentence confuses us, because we wonder how a future event (becoming a doctor) can be said to have taken place "lately." Of course what has been taking place lately is the self-convincing. So when the adverb is put closer to the verb it modifies, the confusion disappears:

I am more and more convinced lately that I ought not become a doctor.

Sometimes the misplaced modifier cannot be corrected simply by putting it in a different position in the sentence. In these cases the modifier will be found to have no word or group of words that it modifies, and so while it "makes sense," grammatically speaking it is dangling there by itself, with no direct connection to the rest of the sentence. The result is what is called a **dangling modifier** (common abbreviations: *d m, dng, dgl, dangl mod, dangl part*[iciple]; occasionally *coh*[erence]). Here is an example from a student paper:

Lacking enough money, the Florida trip was a disaster.

Lacking enough money seems to modify the subject noun *trip*. But it can't—how would a trip lack money? Instead the phrase modifies the unnamed person who took the Florida trip. To correct the sentence, we could name the person who took the trip and make that person the subject of the sentence:

Lacking enough money, I considered the Florida trip to be a disaster.

There are other ways of adjusting the sentence to eliminate the dangling modifier and still retain the same meaning, such as converting the modifier into a clause:

Because I lacked enough money, my Florida trip was a disaster.

You won't have too much difficulty finding a good solution. The trick is in recognizing danglers in the first place. Your best bet for catching most of them is to doublecheck yourself any time you open a sentence with a phrase, making sure the phrase modifies the subject if it is acting as an adjective. If necessary, change the sentence until it hangs together the way it should.

By the way, dangling modifiers occur most frequently at the beginning of a sentence, but that is not the only place we encounter them. Do you know what is wrong with this example and how to revise it?

> The house lights were turned down, waiting for the actors to appear on the bare stage.

An expectant audience, yes—but expectant *house lights?*

EXERCISES

1. In the following sentences, choose the appropriate adjective or adverb. Assume the writing is formal.

   A. It is (real/really) exciting to get e-mails from friends when you are away at school.
   B. Stand (close/closely) to your partner.
   C. We can (sure/surely) do better than you predict.
   D. The university chorus welcomes anyone who can sing (well/good) enough to pass a simple audition.
   E. The guitarist played as (loud/loudly) as he could, to hide the fact that he was the (weaker/weakest) of the three musicians.
   F. To most drinkers bourbon tastes (smoother/more smoothly) than scotch.
   G. When you look at both the Hancock Building and the Sears Tower from a distance, the latter is clearly the (more/most) impressive.
   H. When she gets those migraines she feels (miserable/miserably).
   I. We would then sneak into our parents' room as (quiet/quietly) as possible.
   J. The doctor felt the wound (careful/carefully), probing for splinters of glass.

2. Write four sentences that show the pattern of subject + linking verb + adjective-as-complement. Use each of the following four adjectives as your complements.

Jaunty   scarlet
heavier   most pungent

3. Revise the faulty modifiers in these student-written sentences. Be sure you know *why* the modifiers need to be revised or repositioned.

   A. Violent shows should be put on TV late at night; this would reduce the chances of children viewing them substantially.

   B. She talked real fast and I had a hard time following her.

   C. Hearing about the detour, the expressway seemed a much better choice.

   D. The back bedroom is the warmest of the two.

   E. There has been an increase in the controversy about the development of nuclear energy over the years.

   F. Being a devoted baseball fan, the designated-hitter rule seems a travesty.

   G. I look back on the day and see it completely different.

   H. The conductor spends a lot of time talking about his grandchildren on our train.

   I. The golfer shouted "Fore!" as loud as he could, and we ducked real quick.

   J. After checking several sources, this paper will conclude that *in vitro* conceptions are not morally wrong.

4. Examine three of your most recent papers. Circle the modifiers you find, whether words, phrases, or clauses. How often do you use modifiers? Are there any grammatical errors apparent in your use of them? How do you think you might improve your use of modifiers?

5. Compose complete sentences using the following openers. Be sure the opening modifiers are directly tied to the subject.

   A. Having explained the reasons for their decision . . .

   B. To avoid failing the course . . .

   C. When feeling boisterous . . .

   D. By determining the wind direction . . .

   E. Grabbing a fresh pencil . . .

D. FACTS ABOUT VERBS

Verbs, like pronouns, cause a disproportion- ately large share of the problems writers can encounter. If verbs are troublesome for you,

> *Form is power.*
> —*Thomas Hobbes*

most likely the difficulty will be either verb form (*v, vb, tense, tnse, t*) or verb agreement (*agr, v, vb*). We should begin with form.

D1. Verb Form

You know that most verbs have three quite regular forms: a present-tense base, a past tense (base + *-ed*), and a past participle (auxiliary verb + base + *-ed*). The past participle form is always used with an auxiliary such as a form of *to have.* Here are some examples:

Base	Past Tense	Past Participle
join	joined	(have) joined
spill	spilled	(have) spilled
slap	slapped	(have) slapped

In the last example, incidentally, the consonant *p* is doubled in the past and past participle to preserve the vowel sound of the base; what would *slaped* sound like? The verb endings themselves are unchanged. So, to use our first ex-

ample, in the present you *join,* in the past you *joined,* and in the so-called perfect or compound tenses you *have joined, had joined,* or perhaps *will have joined.*

While regular verbs predominate in our language, there are also hundreds of irregular verbs, including some of the most important ones. "Irregular" means just that—irregular and therefore unpredictable. Some of them are irregular in both the past tense and past participle although those two forms are still identical: *cling, clung, (have) clung; grind, ground, (have) ground.* Others are different in all three parts: *be, was, (have) been; know, knew, (have) known; write, wrote, (have) written.* Just to be contrary, there are still others that are *alike* in all three forms: *bet, bet, (have) bet; hurt, hurt, (have) hurt.* Trickiest of all are those with alternate forms: *leap, leaped* or *leapt, (have) leaped* or *(have) leapt; stink, stank* or *stunk, (have) stunk.*

Nevertheless you know from experience how to use most irregular verbs. Perhaps the easiest way to resolve doubts you might have is to consult this list of the most "mischievous" ones:

Base	Past Tense	Past Participle
am, are, is	was, were	been
arise	arose	arisen
bear	bore	borne (*or* born)
beat	beat	beaten
bid (*ask, entreat*)	bade	bidden
bind	bound	bound
blow	blew	blown
break	broke	broken
burst	burst	burst
choose	chose	chosen
creep	crept	crept
deal	dealt	dealt
dive	dived, dove	dived
eat	ate	eaten
flee	fled	fled
forbid	forbade	forbidden
freeze	froze	frozen
hang (*suspend*)	hung	hung
hang (*execute by hanging*)	hanged	hanged
lay (*place, set down*)	laid	laid
lead	led	led
lend	lent	lent

lie (*recline*)	lay	lain
mean	meant	meant
prove	proved	proved or proven
ride	rode	ridden
ring	rang	rung
rise	rose	risen
see	saw	seen
seek	sought	sought
send	sent	sent
set	set	set
shake	shook	shaken
shine	shone *or* shined	shone *or* shined
shrink	shrank *or* shrunk	shrunk
sing	sang *or* sung	sung
sink	sank *or* sunk	sunk
sit	sat	sat
sleep	slept	slept
spin	spun	spun
spit	spat	spat
spring	sprang	sprung
steal	stole	stolen
swear	swore	sworn
swing	swung	swung
tear	tore	torn
thrive	thrived *or* throve	thrived *or* thriven
wear	wore	worn
weave	wove	woven
weep	wept	wept
wring	wrung	wrung

Many mistakes that people make with irregular verbs come from trying to make them regular. This may take the form of assuming the past and past participle forms are alike when they aren't: *We begun studying last night* (instead of *We began studying last night*). Or it may take the form of assuming the verb isn't irregular and therefore adding the regular -*ed* ending to the base: *The old man spitted into the gutter* (instead of *The old man spat into the gutter*).

Another set of difficulties occurs when writers use forms that are familiar in spoken English but not in standard written English. The solution, of course, is not necessarily to change the way you speak but rather to learn the forms you will need to use when you write.

Sometimes people write what they *think* they hear; familiar examples are *could of* instead of *could have* or *would of* instead of *would have*. In student papers I often encounter sentences like this one:

> There was no way I could of satisfied my father's demands.

The writer has heard a contraction of *could* and *have*, *could've;* when pronounced, it sounds just like *could of*, and so the latter is substituted. A similar example is *could care less:*

> He could care less what anyone else thinks of his funny clothes.

The phrase is really *couldn't care less*, as becomes clear when you think about its meaning. But in speech the *couldn't* is often slurred over so quickly that the *-n't* ending gets lost, and then it ends up getting lost on paper, too.

Other problems of this sort arise when a student's spoken dialect has verb forms that are not found in standard written English. In writing it is better to use the forms of standard written English. Briefly, here are some facts about standard written English that every writer should know.

1. A form of the verb *to be* must be used in each of the following situations:

   a. when it is the only verb in the sentence:

   > She is a smart girl. [Not *She a smart girl.*]

   > They are noisy. [Not *They noisy.*]

   b. When it is used with a verb with an *-ing* ending, either past or present:

   > He is working. [Not *He working.*]

   Note that *be* plus a present participle, e.g., *he be working*, is a form that is not used in standard written English.

2. When *been* is used with a present participle, it is preceded by a form of the verb *to have:*

> She has been sleeping. [Not *She been sleeping* or *She done been sleeping.*]

3. If the past-tense or past-participle ending is *-ed*, it is always added to the written form of the verb, whether or not it is pronounced:

> We defeated their debate team yesterday. [Not *We defeat their debate team yesterday.*]

> He had shined his shoes before he left for ROTC drill. [Not *He had shine his shoes before he left for ROTC drill.*]

So far the verbs we have been discussing have been in the indicative mood, but there is another mood called the **subjunctive.** One main use of the subjunctive is to express something hypothetical or contrary to fact; for instance, the subjunctive is used after *as if:*

> He spends money as if he *were* Bill Gates.

> She talks as if she *were* a real expert.

The meaning of these sentences is quite different from present-tense factual statements in the indicative mood: *He is Donald Trump. She is a real expert.*

Here are some other examples in which the subjunctive is used to express a hypothetical idea:

> If I *were* stranded on a desert island, I'd like to be with you.

> Imagine that Shakespeare *were* alive today—how would he write?

The subjunctive is also used to express a wish, in which case the plural past tense is used even if the subject is singular:

> I wish we *were coming* with you.

> I wish I *were* thin.

Finally, the subjunctive mood is used to express something necessary or mandatory:

It is essential that he *be* there by noon.

I insist that they *be given* fair treatment.

The teacher asked that she *pay* attention and *do* her homework.

Notice that the difference between the subjunctive and indicative forms is that in the third-person singular present tense the form is like the *I* form (*that she pay, that he study, that she do*), except the verb *to be*, where *be* is used for all persons (*that I/you/he be*). In the past tense, *were* is used for all persons of the verb *to be* in the subjunctive (*if I/you/ he were*).

D2. Subject-Verb Agreement

To discuss subject-verb agreement, there is really only one fact to announce: Verbs must agree with their subjects in number—singular verb for a singular subject, plural verb for a plural subject. Sounds simple, but it's not—otherwise this chapter would not have a section devoted to the topic! You know that singular subjects take singular verb forms: *The lectern needs a microphone.* And plural subjects take plural verb forms: *The tables need candles.* The difficulties occur in situations where it is not immediately apparent whether the subject should be considered singular or plural.

We can begin with subjects that are usually considered singular and therefore take a singular verb:

1. Collective nouns such as *staff, team, family, group,* and *collection,* even though they comprise more than one member, are considered a single entity:

   The graduate faculty *is* so designated because its members are capable of directing research projects and dissertations.

   Recall, however, that there are occasional exceptions to this rule—see pages 196–197.

For there be women, fair as she, Whose verbs and nouns do more agree.
—Bret Harte

2. Nouns of time, money, weight, and measurement may sometimes be plural in form but always take singular verbs:

Ten ounces *is* all I can spare you.

Eighty cents *is* now a cheap price for a cup of coffee.

3. Indefinite pronouns such as *anybody, everybody, anyone, everyone, one, each, either,* and *neither* all take singular verbs:

Each of us *hopes* to win.

Neither *deserves* to be fired.

But *any* and *none* can be used with either a singular or a plural verb, depending on the context:

Several suitors ask for the princess's hand but *none have* a chance.

For question 5 *none* of the above *is* the correct answer.

A second category of subjects includes those that can take either singular or plural verbs, depending on the circumstances:

1. Compound subjects joined by *or, nor, but also,* and *but not* have a verb form that depends on whether the part of the compound subject closest to the verb is itself singular or plural. If the part of the subject closest to the verb is singular, use a singular verb:

Not only the referees but also the timekeeper *was* confused.

Here the singular noun *timekeeper* is closer to the verb than the plural *referees,* so the verb is singular.

If the part of the subject closest to the verb is plural, use a plural verb:

Either Ray or his parents *own* the car.

Here the plural *parents* is closer than the singular *Ray,* so the verb is plural.

2. When relative pronouns are used as subjects, the verb form depends on the antecedent. If the antecedent of the relative pronoun is singular, the verb is singular:

He is the only rock star who *turns* me off.

The antecedent of *who* is the singular *star*, so the verb is singular, *turns*.

If the antecedent is plural, the verb is plural:

She is one of those people who *are* always complaining.

The antecedent of *who* is the plural *people* (not *one*), so the verb is plural, *are*.

Finally we can note some special situations in which it is easy to make mistakes:

1. When a subject is separated from its verb by a clause, and when the last word of the clause is a noun different in number from the subject, confusion can result. Here is an example from a student exam:

The current system of elections have other flaws besides voter apathy.

The mistake was in seeing *elections* as the subject and then using the plural verb *have*. But if you disregard the phrase *of elections* and harken back to the real subject, *system*, the necessity of using the form *has* becomes clear:

The current system of elections *has* other flaws besides voter apathy.

2. Not all subject nouns ending in *-s* are plural:

Statistics *is* my favorite subject.

(But *statistics* could be plural if not referring to the subject of study, as in "These statistics do not lie.")

3. Compound subjects joined by *and* must always have plural verb forms:

The blue jay and the starling *drive* away other birds.

You might be tempted to look only at the part of the subject closest to the verb—that is, the singular *starling*—and make the verb singular. But the complete subject is the compound subject *blue jay* + *starling*—therefore requiring a plural verb.

4. When the word order is inverted, and a complement different in number from the subject comes before the verb, it is easy to make the mistake of having the verb agree with its preceding complement rather than with the subject that follows:

Awaiting the victor *are* two small trophies.

The example is correct because *trophies*, not *victor*, is the subject—the usual word order has simply been reversed. A similar case arises when a sentence begins with *there:*

There are no longer any silent men in the world today. *Max Picard*

There is a space filler; *men* is the real subject and must have a plural verb. *There is* would be acceptable only if the subject were singular.

Of course, the facts just discussed—facts about pronouns, modifiers, and verbs—are not all the facts about English grammar. You already know most of the other facts; otherwise you wouldn't be able to communicate in English at all. This chapter includes only those facts that apprentice writers often do not know, especially the facts that apply to writing but not always to speech.

Remember also that this chapter has focused only on grammar. In the case of verbs, for example, this has meant talking about potential mistakes in such areas as case, mood, and agreement. But several other important matters about verbs do not appear in this chapter because they do not involve grammatical mistakes. To cite one instance, learning the strengths and weaknesses of using the passive voice (discussed in Chapter 3, page 106) is just as or perhaps more important for your increased mastery of English prose.

Please be aware, too, that it is not always possible to make clear distinctions between problems of grammar and other types of writing problems. For example, our discussion of verb forms in conversation versus verb forms in writing might be considered usage rather than grammar. By the same token, the section on "shifts" in Chapter 2 might well be included as part of grammar. Just remember that labels are not nearly as important as facts. This book is trying to give you the facts you need to be a more informed writer.

EXERCISES

1. Choose the correct verb form in the following sentences:

   A. Three wrecked cars and a dilapidated van (crowds/crowd) their driveway.
   B. The reward for our labors (were/was) strawberries and ice cream.
   C. Arrowheads (lay/laid) buried in the soil for those adventurous enough to dig for them.
   D. My new T-shirt has (shrunk/shrunken) since it was washed.
   E. Thirty pounds of lime (was/were) never enough to cover the lawn.
   F. He (dealed/dealt) the cards quickly, almost impatiently.
   G. The coaching staff (hope/hopes) to recruit at least two high-scoring guards to replace this year's graduating seniors.
   H. Everybody in the back rows (hears/hear) only an occasional sentence or two of the lecture.
   I. The frozen water had (burst/bursted) the pipes.
   J. Either two hours of painting or one hour of chorus (satisfy/satisfies) the fine arts requirement.

2. Revise any of the following student-written sentences that are incorrect:

   A. Three hours are all the time I need to study Spanish.
   B. She lended me her comb in the restroom.
   C. Most puzzling to Inspector Clouseau is three small clues that he stumbles on during his investigation.
   D. The baby be sleeping now and I can write this paper.
   E. A widespread incidence of rashes were reported to the health department.
   F. The bull sprung from behind the tree and charged us.
   G. The most unfair of all these regulations are the one dealing with child-support payments.

H. When he let out our secret I could of killed him, because we might be suspended or even expelled.

I. Logistics are the biggest problem when you plan a graduation party.

J. I had always shrank from such a responsibility, but now I had no choice.

K. There was speculation that the government might try to clamp down on campaign activities by special interest groups.

L. Acknowledging that the lot of today's women are different, we still find many cases of discrimination in employment.

M. The economy should rebound sharply during the next six months.

N. She staying after class today to talk with the instructor.

O. The complications that result here is that the same bullet could not have hit Kennedy and Governor Connally, too.

P. Last night I was once again lead into temptation and bought a six-pack.

Q. I replied very firmly that I could care less.

3. Locate a fairly long passage from a magazine or a book. Study the verbs. Note especially the following:

A. verbs in the passive voice (if any)

B. shifts in voice, tense, mood (if any)—see Chapter 2.

C. frequency of forms of verbs *to have* and *to be*

Then study the verbs in three pages of your own writing according to the same three criteria. Do you see any differences in your use of verbs?

4. Write two or three paragraphs describing your movement from one place to another, such as from one part of the campus to another, from home to school or work, or from city to country. Put all the verbs in the present tense.

Now rewrite the same description, changing all the verbs to the past tense. Do you see any differences in *effect* resulting from this change? What would happen if you rewrote many of the sentences in the passive voice?

5. Study the use of verbs in the following passage by Annie Dillard. What do you observe?

A weasel is wild. Who knows what he thinks? He sleeps in his underground den, his tail draped over his nose. Sometimes he lives in his den for two days without leaving. Outside, he stalks rabbits, mice, muskrats, and birds, killing more bodies than he can eat warm, and often dragging the carcasses home. Obedient to instinct, he bites his prey at the neck, either splitting the jugular vein at the throat or crunching the brain at the base of the skull, and he does not let go. One naturalist refused to kill a weasel who was socketed into his hand deeply as a rattlesnake. The man could in no way pry the tiny weasel off, and he had to walk half a mile to water, the weasel dangling from his palm, and soak him off like a stubborn label.

6. The example paragraph by Annie Dillard presented in question 5 embodies a writing style rich in vigorous, action-oriented verbs. But sometimes the nature of the subject calls for a style richer in nouns and stingier in its use of verbs. Consider the following:

The problem of why the theory of knowledge is not taught in the schools is relatively easy to see. Epistemology is, after all, a dangerous subject. If we start to question the validity of statements, then the teachers themselves come under question. All assertions about education, established forms of religion, government, and social mores will also be subject to justification on the grounds of how they are known to be true. For parents and teachers who have not been through the experience of exploring how we determine facts, it would be unnerving to have their children continuously questioning the roots of knowledge. Inquiry is indeed a challenge to the acceptance of things as they are. *Harold J. Marowitz*

Write a short paragraph on the use of verbs and nouns in this passage. Do you see how, compared to the Dillard excerpt, the different nature of the subject here requires a greater use of nouns and much less emphasis on vivid, exciting verb choices?

Conventions: Punctuation

Conventions are quite simply customs. In other words, they are agreed-upon ways of doing things, and they succeed precisely because everybody agrees they mean one certain thing and not another. For example, in the United States the custom is to greet a friend with a handshake. But in Eastern Europe you must greet a friend with nothing less than the traditional hug that the Russians call the *obyátiye*. Neither the handshake nor the *obyátiye* is "better"; each is simply the custom for its own part of the world.

In language the conventions are just as arbitrary—and just as necessary. For example, there is no special reason why sentences have to end with a dot we call a period. Instead we could use an *x* or maybe a slash or any one of a hundred other marks. All of these other marks are just as logical or illogical as the dot. But the English language among others has the custom or the convention of the period dot, and we must accept this custom if we wish to be understood when we write.

This chapter takes up those conventions that consist of marks within or near words that help us organize those words and see their relationship to other words. In short, it discusses punctuation. In the next chapter we will turn to other kinds of conventions, such as abbreviations and capitalization.

A note on how to use the chapter. Part A focuses on those conventions that often allow a writer some freedom and flexibility. Unlike question marks, for example, which are always used in certain prescribed ways, these devices— commas, semicolons, dashes—can sometimes be an opportunity for choice and therefore a part of your style. Even if your writing is generally free of punctuation errors, you should find this material helpful in making you a more sophisticated and versatile writer.

The conventions that do not allow so much flexibility are treated in Part B. You will probably want to use them when you are in doubt about how to punctuate a particular passage or when an instructor calls your attention to a particular error in one of your papers.

A. PUNCTUATION CHOICE

Punctuation is perhaps the most common category of errors in student writing. Usually such errors are signaled by red circles and by such symbols as *punc*, *pn*, or *p*, or perhaps by silent correction of the offending mark. Often these corrections are met with a helpless shrug—after all, what is a comma here or there anyway? Such a reaction is natural, although shortsighted. Proper punctuation is sometimes vital to the clarity of a sentence, because without it writers risk being misunderstood. They also court the irritation of their readers, because many people equate correctness in punctuation with maturity in writing style.

Nevertheless, in many situations the presence or absence of a certain punctuation mark *is* a matter of free choice. In these cases (and these cases only), if you shrug your shoulders when someone recommends a change, your reaction might be a proper one. This section tries to show you the difference; in other words, it explains which punctuation customs are never broken, which ones are sometimes broken, and which ones are simply matters of taste. Learning to punctuate effectively is not difficult—it just requires a little patience and attention to detail.

Furthermore, if you can understand *why* these conventions exist in the form they do, you will find it much easier to observe them. Most punctuation is based on common sense, not mystery. This section stresses the common-sense basis for punctuation customs, and it combines this emphasis with discussions of how and why writers

The difficulty in life is the choice.
—*George Moore*

are sometimes led astray. With this information, punctuation ought not be a mystery to you.

Al. Commas

When we talk, we often use short pauses accompanied by a slight change in inflection. These pauses enable us to catch our breath, but more important they tell listeners how to group the words they are hearing so they can understand us better. In writing, commas represent those pauses. Sometimes, as in a long sentence, they just let us catch our breath:

> It should be noted here that the poet laureate's office isn't quite as vulnerable to grandstanding as the NEA, since it is operated with the library's cache of private trust funds.
> *Daniel T. Max*

Sometimes they group words in ways that are vital to the meaning of the sentence:

> If you don't know how to cook, all the food in the refrigerator is of no use at all.

Examine that last sentence, from a student paper, more closely. Picture it without the comma, in fact the way it was originally written by its author:

> If you don't know how to cook all the food in the refrigerator is of no use at all.

Do you see how the sentence is confusing without the comma? You would read it as telling about cooking "all the food in the refrigerator," and only a puzzled rereading enables you to sort out the true meaning. This example should eliminate once and for all the idea that commas and other forms of punctuation are not important. However unintentional his mistake may

have been, the writer of that sentence misled his readers by
omitting the comma.

So **commas** are used for clarity and for reflecting natural speech rhythm. Both of these reasons are important.
Sometimes the presence of a comma is justified by one,
sometimes by the other, sometimes by both.

Neither reason alone is sufficient to explain all commas.
In the following sentence, for example, the natural pace of
speech would not allow for much of a pause, yet the commas are necessary:

> December 7, 1941, is the date of the attack on Pearl Harbor.

The commas allow the reader to see the relationships within
the series of numbers. In other sentences commas are not
needed for clarity, but they do give the reader a helpful pause:

> We allow time for talking about general writing problems or
> about selections from a reader, but the focus is always on
> the student's evolving essay.

In this case, the comma not only gives pause but serves a
grammatical function: it separates two independent clauses
joined by a coordinating conjunction.

Perhaps the most familiar use of the comma is to *separate items in a series*, if the series consists of three or more
things:

> Joyce comes closest, but the strongest influences are out of
> the past—the Bible, Marlowe, Blake, Shakespeare. *Will-
> iam Styron*

> Symbols, myths, and legends are just as important to us as
> they are to primitive peoples.

> Such an ill-considered, hasty, and dispiriting view of life must
> cause her immense misery.

> He talks quickly, confidently, eagerly.

The items in the series need not be single words. We punctuate phrases and clauses the same way as long as they form
a series:

> The alley was littered with boxes of garbage, plastic bags of leaves, and a scattering of abandoned toys.

> He was entirely rid of his nervous misgivings, of his forced aggressiveness, of the imperative desire to show himself different from his surroundings. *Willa Cather*

The only exception occurs when the items themselves have much internal punctuation and semicolons are therefore required (see page 242).

One caution: The most common mistake students make when they punctuate items in a series is to put an extra comma after the last item in the series:

> Groucho, Chico, Harpo, and Zeppo, were the four Marx Brothers.

This writer was accustomed to following each item in a series with a comma, so he extended the principle to the last item, too, and put a comma after "Zeppo." Such a mistake is understandable because it is based on a valuable principle. But the last item should always run directly into a verb that follows, and therefore the comma after "Zeppo" must be eliminated.

A second required use of the comma is to *mark off free modifiers*. An example of a free modifier (also called a *non-restrictive* modifier) is the short clause *who owned a harness repair shop* in the following sentence:

> When she was twenty-two years old her father, who owned a harness repair shop, died suddenly. *Sherwood Anderson*

Such modifiers can be cut from the sentence without affecting the meaning of the words they modify. In this case, the meaning of *father* would not change even if the modifying clause were left out. Bound (or restrictive) modifiers, on the other hand, directly affect the meaning of the words they modify and should not be set off by commas:

> The people who had been waiting stood up with their mouths open. *Frank O'Connor*

The clause *who had been waiting* explains which people; in other words, it is tied, or "bound," to *people*. If the clause were to be marked off by commas, In other words if it were to be set aside as just an optional expression, the meaning of the sentence would be markedly different:

> The people, who had been waiting, stood up with their mouths open.

The principle here is simple: Free modifiers are separated from the rest of the sentence by commas; bound modifiers are not. Free modifiers can include words, phrases, and clauses:

> My father, angry, shouted into the phone. [words]

> Here and there a piece of timber, stuck upright, resembled a post. *Joseph Conrad* [phrase]

> What if his search, which had been so thorough and so painstaking, was now about to pay off? [clause]

Free modifiers are set apart by commas preceding and following them, unless of course the modifier comes at the end of the sentence:

> The man gave a kind of twisted grin, showing where the teeth had been knocked out above the new scar. *Robert Penn Warren*

Bound modifiers, on the other hand, are not marked off by commas:

> The waves that come at high tide are even more formidable.

> The saddest of all is the tarnish that has appeared on the American sense of history. *Jan Morris*

The two clauses *that come at high tide* and *that has appeared on the American sense of history* both modify nouns. Because they are bound to *waves* and *tarnish*, because they explain *which* waves and *which* tarnish are meant, no commas are possible.

The reason for making a distinction between free and bound modifiers becomes clear if you compare the following two versions of the same sentence:

> The newspaper, which came late Friday afternoon, had a small death notice on the obituary page.

> The newspaper which came late Friday afternoon had a small death notice on the obituary page.

The first sentence marks off the clause by commas and therefore makes it a free modifier. The second sentence, however, uses the clause to specify *which* newspaper—the one that came late Friday afternoon, not some other one. The clause is now bound—bound, in this case, to *newspaper.* Do you see the difference in meaning between the two sentences? Do you also see that this difference is conveyed by the presence or absence of the commas? And if you read the two sentences aloud, can you "hear" the commas in the version with the free modifier?

This distinction is not an easy one. Student writers sometimes err by putting in commas where they should not:

> Two police officers came to our school and the one, who did most of the talking, asked for permission to interview me.

The writer clearly wanted the clause *who did most of the talking* to distinguish one police officer from the other—the one who talked more rather than the one who talked less. But the commas set off the clause as a free modifier, so the police officer remains unspecified.

Similarly, commas are often left out at times when their presence is essential, as in this example:

> We sent a petition to the provost who could not ignore it.

Of course this student writer was thinking of only one provost—*the* provost—when she phrased the sentence. But the absence of a comma after provost makes the clause that follows a bound clause, as if it were singling out this provost from all other provosts (the one *who could not ignore it* versus the ones, presumably, who could). That is not what the author meant. So the comma is necessary to make the final clause a free modifier and eliminate the misreading.

Another convention about the comma is that it can *set off direct quotations.* If a quotation opens a sentence, put a comma at the end of it, just before the quotation marks:

"I want to write a letter to Mom," Sandy said.

But the comma is omitted if the quotation ends with a question mark or exclamation mark:

"Can you imagine anything more absurd?" she cried to a friend. *E. M. Forster*

If the quotation ends the sentence, put a comma after the word that precedes it:

Susan added, "Oh yes, you know all the authors faithfully research their periods." *Janice Radway*

Again there is one exception. When the quotation and the words ahead of it must go together to make a complete sentence, the comma is left out:

Culler tells with an abundance of fresh documentation the story "of Newman's education, of his work as the educator of others, and of his educational thinking as expressed in *The Idea of a University.*" *Martin Svaglic*

Here no comma precedes the quotation, because it is not an independent statement. Instead, the quotation completes the sentence begun with the words before it.

Finally, if the quotation is interrupted by other words, two commas are needed. One follows the first part of the quotation, just before the quotation marks; the other follows the inserted words:

"Well, bright boy," Max said, looking into the mirror, "why don't you say something?" *Ernest Hemingway*

Note that *why* is not capitalized in this example. The reason is that the second part of the quotation simply continues the sentence begun in the first part.

Another required use of the comma is *to organize dates, addresses, and numbers*. These customs are probably quite familiar to you. Earlier we saw how a comma helps the reader distinguish the year from the date of the month: "December 7, 1941, is the date . . . " In addresses, commas usually separate the street from the city, the city from the state, and the state (plus any zip code) from the remainder of the sentence:

Mail your order to 330 South Palm Drive, Miami, FL 06415, and allow four weeks for delivery.

We group numbers into convenient three-digit units by commas:

The population of Chattanooga is 179,082.

An operating budget of $58,786,225 is projected for fiscal 2003.

Commas are also used to *set off informal letter salutations*, as to friends and relatives:

Dear Ned,   Dear Grandma,

And, finally, commas can *separate abbreviations following a proper noun from the noun itself:*

Xerox, Inc., recently announced the acquisition of a new subsidiary.

Rita Bilodeau, Ph.D., has resigned from her post as director of student services.

We have been discussing standard uses of the comma, cases in which everyone would agree that commas are necessary for clarity. It should be pointed out here that a comma must be used in any case where a sentence might not be clear without it; look, for example, at this defense of conservatism by the poet Alexander Pope:

Whatever is, is right.

Without the comma, the sentence might be puzzling. Here are other examples:

CONFUSING: Then I was really worried for Stephanie rarely stayed at the library beyond 10:30.
REVISION: Then I was really worried, for Stephanie rarely stayed at the library beyond 10:30.
CONFUSING: If I am allowed to predict the future of commodity brokering looks bright.
REVISION: if I am allowed to predict, the future of commodity brokering looks bright.

The reader is tempted to understand the original sentences as saying the writer was *worried for Stephanie* or was going to *predict the future.* In both examples a comma prevents such a misreading.

In some cases, though, commas are not obligatory—they are a matter of choice. Let's move on to these other cases.

Commas can *mark off an introductory word, phrase, or clause.* Here are several examples from professional writing:

> Nevertheless, it's delightful to be back. *Anthony Burgess*

> Of earthly possessions, Isadora had little enough to leave. *Janet Flanner*

> As I look back upon my own conception of Esau, he is not nearly as clear and definite a personality as Jacob. *W. E. B. DuBois*

If introductory words or word groups are short enough, some writers prefer not to separate them from the rest of the sentence by a comma. These examples are also drawn from professional writing:

> Happily we discover that sermons which seriously try to interpret that supreme event possess a moving power out of proportion to the wisdom of their content. *William Sloane Coffin*

> A few days later a hunting party of Cheyennes sighted a column of bluecoats camped for the night in the valley of the Rosebud. *Dee Brown*

> If this punishment is right the criminals must have a lot of property. *Clarence Darrow*

Note how commas are not used after the opening words, phrases, and clauses; there is no comma after *Happily, A few days later,* or *If this punishment is right.*

When you are in doubt about whether to use a comma with introductory words, your best bet is to let your ear be the guide. Read the sentence in question aloud. Do you "hear" a comma—in other words, do you hear a slight pause between the introductory words and the remainder of the sentence? If so, insert the comma; if not, leave it out. Before leaving the comma out, however, make sure the sentence will not be confusing without it.

Another use of the comma is to *separate parenthetical expressions*. Normally, if a group of related words has been taken from its customary position in the word order of a sentence and put into another position, that new position is signaled by commas before and after:

> The nineteenth century was, for the intellectuals of Western Europe, a comfortable period exuding confidence and optimism. *E. H. Carr*

The phrase *for the intellectuals of Western Europe* appears between the verb *was* and its complement *a comfortable period*—hardly the usual place. Ordinarily the phrase would appear at the beginning, as an introductory phrase, and the verb and complement would be joined (*was a comfortable period*). Because of this displacement, the phrase is set off by commas. Similarly, the phrase *like you* in the following sentence would normally come at the end, after *spirit*:

> Remember, he is not, like you, a pure spirit. *C. S. Lewis*

The earlier position of the phrase requires a pair of commas. Parenthetical expressions are those that do not have a necessary part in the structure of the sentence—they could be put within parentheses and the sentence would still be complete and understandable. They resemble free modifiers, except unlike modifiers they are not tied to specific words in the sentence. Such parenthetical expressions are also set off by commas before and after:

> Many laughed then, as we may be tempted to do, at all those absolute physicians of the soul. *George Santayana*

> That method, I think, is a recipe for disaster on a scale unimaginable only a decade ago. *political pamphlet*

The clauses *as we may be tempted to do* and *I think* are parenthetical, hence the commas.

Sometimes, however, parenthetical expressions are short enough to allow the author to omit the commas:

Quite often when I was on one of my food-collecting expeditions I came across chimpanzees unexpectedly. *Jane Goodall*

The clause *when I was on one of my food-collecting expeditions* is not isolated by commas, most probably because the author realized that commas would slow down the reader too much.

How do you know when parenthetical expressions are short enough so the commas can be eliminated? Again the answer is "by ear." If you sense a pause when you read a sentence aloud, put in a comma; if not, leave it out. (Once again you should make sure that leaving out the commas will not make the sentence confusing.)

Whatever your choice, however, be consistent. Parenthetical expressions within a sentence are set off either by two commas or by none. The author of the following sentence felt the tension between two or none, but she resolved it in the wrong way by using only one:

Society for Blake, has stifled man's spirit and actions.

The writer needs to add a comma before *for* or remove the one after *Blake*.

Another important but variable use of the comma is to *separate the independent clauses of a compound sentence*. Remember that compound sentences have two main clauses, each of which could stand by itself as a sentence. When two main clauses are joined into one sentence by a conjunction such as *and*, *but*, or *yet*, a comma before the conjunction helps the reader keep the clauses distinct:

My class was wearing butter-yellow piqué dresses, and Momma launched out on mine. *Maya Angelou*

Half a man's lifetime is devoted to what he calls improvements, yet the original had some quality which is lost in the process. *E. B. White*

Simple enough so far. The variation in punctuation again comes with variation in length. If the independent clauses are reasonably short, the comma can be left out:

> Seventh graders were not tested but the sixth and eighth graders were.

At the other extreme, two unusually long independent clauses are often separated by a semicolon rather than a comma, simply because the reader welcomes the "heavier" pause that the semicolon provides:

> Form for the poet is the bit and the bridle without which (unless you are an acrobat) you cannot ride your horse; but for the writer of prose it is the chassis without which your car does not exist. *W. Somerset Maugham*

This recommendation of the semicolon becomes almost a requirement if the independent clauses are themselves punctuated by several other commas:

> After all, we are only bound to play our own parts and do our own share of the lifting; and as in no case that share can be great, so in all cases it is called for, it is necessary. *William Morris*

The semicolon after *lifting* allows the reader to separate the two parts of the compound sentence, because it contrasts with the comma that precedes it and the two that follow.

Please note that the comma appears when the independent clauses are joined by a conjunction. If there is no conjunction, a semicolon must be used instead:

> Bull in pure form is rare; there is usually some contamination by data. *William G. Perry*

Alternatively, of course, the two clauses could be converted into separate sentences:

> Bull in pure form is rare. There is usually some contamination by data.

Often student writers are unaware of this important difference, and the result is a **comma splice**—in other words, two independent clauses "spliced" together by a comma even though no conjunction introduces the second clause. These are examples from student papers:

> Beyond the forests are steep cliffs, at the bottom of the cliffs are huge, moss-covered boulders.

> The key to understanding this concept lies in the word "myth," it carries an elusive meaning.

> The street was typical of the neighborhood, it was deserted by day but vibrant and pulsing at night, especially Saturday night.

> The EPA tests revealed the presence of benzene, this is a highly toxic chemical.

In each case the first independent clause is not followed by a conjunction (i.e., no conjunction after *cliffs, myth, neighborhood,* and *benzene,* respectively). Therefore, the comma is not the best form of punctuation. Such comma splices, also called run-on sentences, can be eliminated in a number of ways:

1. Add a conjunction:

   > Beyond the forests are steep cliffs, *and* at the bottom of the cliffs are huge, moss-covered boulders.

2. Use a semicolon:

   > The key to understanding this concept lies in the word "myth"; it carries an elusive meaning.

3. Divide the material into separate sentences:

   > The street was typical of the neighborhood. It was deserted by day but vibrant and pulsing at night, especially Saturday night.

4. Make one clause dependent on the other:

   > The EPA tests revealed the presence of benzene, which is a highly toxic chemical.

Once more, however, I should note an exception. The tendency in modern prose is to let short independent clauses

be joined by a comma even
if no conjunction is present:

She wants to be a part of all
this, she wants to do this
thing. *Tom Wolfe*

Probably by now you are
accustomed to my saying
there are "variations" and

I had a delightful day. In the morning I worked on my latest play, and I ended up putting in a comma. Then I had lunch, and in the afternoon I thought about that line some more. I finished by taking the comma out.
—attributed to Oscar Wilde

"exceptions." You realize that some conventions for the comma are inviolable rules, some depend on circumstances, and some depend on taste. Let's study a sentence that shows examples of each:

Of course, it doesn't, and nobody really expects it to, but even so I hardly supposed that Hitting Away would gallop off with the Withers Stakes, as he did at Aqueduct last Saturday. *New Yorker*

The sentence as punctuated by its author contains four commas. One comma, the last one, is required by the *rule* that all free modifiers must be marked off this way. Another comma, the third one, is required by *circumstance:* it precedes a conjunction (*but*) that joins two independent clauses that are long enough to make the comma indispensable. The two earlier commas, however, are present because of the author's *taste.* The first of them marks off an introductory phrase (*Of course*), but the phrase is short enough so that the comma could be left out. The second comma is like the third in the way it precedes a conjunction (*and*) joining two independent clauses, but the two clauses are so brief that punctuation might not be necessary. Note also that the author chose *not* to insert commas around the phrase *even so*, although technically he or she could have.

In short, there are no less than *eight* ways to punctuate this sentence, each of them equally "correct"! Besides the original, here are the seven legitimate alternatives:

1. Of course, it doesn't, and nobody really expects it to, but, even so, I hardly supposed that Hitting Away would gal-

lop off with the Withers Stakes, as he did at Aqueduct last Saturday.

2. Of course it doesn't, and nobody really expects it to, but even so I hardly supposed that Hitting Away would gallop off with the Withers Stakes, as he did at Aqueduct last Saturday.

3. Of course, it doesn't and nobody really expects it to, but even so I hardly supposed that Hitting Away would gallop off with the Withers Stakes, as he did at Aqueduct last Saturday.

4. Of course it doesn't and nobody really expects it to, but even so I hardly supposed that Hitting Away would gallop off with the Withers Stakes, as he did at Aqueduct last Saturday.

5. Of course it doesn't, and nobody really expects it to, but, even so, I hardly supposed that Hitting Away would gallop off with the Withers Stakes, as he did at Aqueduct last Saturday.

6. Of course, it doesn't and nobody really expects it to, but, even so, I hardly supposed that Hitting Away would gallop off with the Withers Stakes, as he did at Aqueduct last Saturday.

7. Of course it doesn't and nobody really expects it to, but, even so, I hardly supposed that Hitting Away would gallop off with the Withers Stakes, as he did at Aqueduct last Saturday.

Which one do I prefer? Possibly the second or the fourth. Your taste, however, might differ from mine, just as the author's did.

Right now you might be tempted to shrug your shoulders and wonder how you could ever understand the use of commas. Furthermore, you may be wondering whether the comma errors marked on your papers by your instructor are really errors at all. Because the use of commas is often a matter of taste, why should his or her taste supplant yours?

Let's address the second issue first. True, some occasions for using the comma are matters of taste. But most are not. The majority of commas are determined by rules or by circumstances rather than by taste, as a careful reading of almost any prose passage will show. So the chances are good that the problem noted by your instructor is a situation in which the presence or absence of a comma is not a matter of free choice at all. And even if your problem *is* one of those cases in which taste comes into play, remember that taste is partly a product of experience. Since your instructor's experience is greater than yours, weigh his or her suggestion carefully, although the final decision rests with you.

As to the first issue, whether or not the proper use of commas can ever be learned, don't be discouraged. It's all much simpler than it seems. In fact the material here probably can be summed up in two suggestions that cover almost every circumstance:

1. Make sure you know the situations where commas are always required (items in a series, free modifiers, direct quotations, dates, addresses, numbers, abbreviations following names).
2. For cases where circumstance or taste governs the comma, your ear can be your guide. Even in those circumstances where a comma is absolutely necessary, such as with long introductory phrases, long parenthetical expressions, or long independent clauses joined by a conjunction, you will almost invariably hear a slight pause when you read the sentence aloud. That pause is your clue to put in the comma, just as it is a clue in matters of taste as well.

A2. Semicolons and Colons

Although semicolons and colons are similar in name and appearance, they serve quite different purposes, as this section will show.

We have already anticipated most of the uses of the **semicolon** in our discussion of commas. Recall that a semicolon can *separate two independent clauses when they are not joined by a conjunction:*

> [A] semicolon in its right place is a thing of beauty.
> —C. Colwell and J. Knox

She stood in a frozen attitude; her breath was released in a sigh. *Tennessee Williams*

Even if a conjunction is present, however, you might still want to use a semicolon to join especially long independent clauses. For example:

What might have been, I don't know; but I applied for, and was given, eight months' writing time. *Tillie Olsen*

Despite the fact that the second independent clause begins with the conjunction *but,* Olsen used a semicolon because both clauses are fairly long. Note that this was a matter of choice—Olsen would not have been "wrong" had she decided to use a comma, although the semicolon is perhaps a wiser choice because it creates a more definite separation of the clauses.

Also, semicolons are necessary to *mark off long items in a series,* especially when those items have internal punctuation. The reasoning is simple. The length of the items makes it desirable to give readers a greater "catch-your-breath" pause between each item. Furthermore, if the items in the series have commas within them, these commas will not be distinguished easily from the commas that separate the items themselves. Semicolons can solve both problems:

It was supposed and taught that there had been, quite concretely, a creation of the world in seven days by a god known only to the Jews; that somewhere on this broad new earth there had been a Garden of Eden containing a serpent that could talk; that the first woman, Eve, was formed from the first man's rib, and that the wicked serpent told her of the marvelous properties of the fruits of a certain tree of which God had forbidden the couple to eat; and that, as a consequence of their having eaten of that fruit, there followed a "Fall" of all mankind, death came into the world, and the couple was driven forth from the garden. *Joseph Campbell*

The most common misuse of the semicolon is putting it between clauses when one of the two clauses is not fully independent. *When a semicolon joins two clauses, both clauses should be capable of being complete sentences.* If a fragment appears in either position, some other kind of punctuation is needed. Here are two examples from student papers, both of which are incorrect:

> Since the sterno cans seemed to be unobtainable; the gang set out to find another method of keeping warm.

> After that, I understood better why Chris was my parents' favorite; his vulnerability.

In the first example, the words to the left of the semicolon form a dependent clause (note how they begin with the subordinating conjunction *since*). They do not form a complete sentence. A comma must replace the semicolon, allowing the dependent clause to link up with the independent clause (*the gang* . . .). In the second example, the writer probably mistook a semicolon for a colon. *His vulnerability* is not a sentence; it acts as an *appositive* and should therefore be set off by a colon, as we'll see shortly in the discussion of the colon.

Some modern writers are abandoning the insistence on no fragments on either side of the semicolon, especially when the fragment contains an understood subject and verb. Hunter S. Thompson, for example:

> Worse, I needed two sets; one for myself and another for Ralph Steadman, the English illustrator who was coming from London to do some Derby drawings.

Although the words to the right of the semicolon do not form a complete sentence, Thompson trusts us to understand *I needed* as the implied subject and verb: *[I needed] one for myself and one for Ralph Steadman.* However, since many readers do not approve of using semicolons this way, I'd advise you to avoid this use of them.

As for **colons,** we just noted their principal use: to *mark off appositive explanations and constructions.* (The preceding sentence is our first example!) An **appositive** adds to or explains a word or word group that precedes it. You can understand this easier by looking at another example:

The ego develops canny mechanisms for dealing with the threat of id impulses: denial, projection, and the rest. *Jerome Bruner*

Here *denial, projection, and the rest* is an appositive construction that explains the noun *impulses*. The student sentence from the previous page would, if punctuated correctly, offer another example of an appositive:

After that, I understood better why Chris was my parents' favorite: his vulnerability.

(When an appositive appears earlier in a sentence, it is usually marked off by commas as a free modifier: *The reason Chris was my parents' favorite, his vulnerability, suddenly dawned on me.*)

Colons can *precede any explanation or elaboration of what was said in the first part of a sentence:*

Now, it is clear that the decline of a language must ultimately have political and economic causes: it is not due simply to the bad influences of this or that individual writer. *George Orwell*

Often the explanation takes the form of a list or a series:

In the manifest story the events happen in space and time: first, going into the ship's belly; then, falling asleep; then, being thrown into the ocean; then, being swallowed by the fish. *Erich Fromm*

Notice, by the way, that because his list of events is a long one and because each item has a comma within it, Fromm separates the items with semicolons rather than commas.

Keep in mind that colons do *not* follow forms of the verb *to be* or verbs such as *include*. Thus, the colons should be deleted from the following examples:

The social sciences include: anthropology, sociology, political science, and psychology.

The dangers to avoid are: overexertion, dehydration, and sun poisoning.

The other important use of the colon is to *precede a formal quotation:*

The host announced: "Dinner is served."

In such sentences the colon is an alternative to a comma. The colon makes for a "heavier" break between the speaker and the quotation itself.

Colons also help to *organize numbers, Bible citations, book titles,* and *formal letter salutations:*

9:35 p.m.

Deuteronomy 2:14-15

Paul Ricoeur's *Interpretation Theory: Discourse and the Surplus of Meaning*

Dear Ms. Connell:

A3. Dashes

Like colons and semicolons, the hyphen (-) and dash (—) are similar in appearance. But the functions of the two are quite different. In this section we discuss dashes; hyphens are covered in the next chapter.

Dashes are often used as an alternative to some other form of punctuation. In fact, no less than five other punctuation marks can be replaced by a dash:

Hands shaking, dying for a cigarette, he found the pants— a size small but still a fit. *Richard Goldstein* [alternative to comma]

A third of all Americans—more than 70 million people—are optionaires, a higher percentage of affluent citizens than any other large nation has produced. *Celeste MacLeod* [alternative to parentheses]

It had been a long few days and I had scrutinized too many
details of four vicious killings and something in my mind
flailed out now—Jesus Simpson, murderer, cold-blooded
killer, compassionate, sensitive, sentimental. *Joe Eszterhas*
[alternative to colon]

There were five of us at DePauw who were religious re-
jects—myself, one Roman Catholic, one Greek Orthodox,
one Lutheran, and one Jew. *Margaret Mead* [alternative to
semicolon]

His name was Mayhew, it was written out in enormous red
letters across the front of his helmet: MAYHEW—You'd better believe it! *Michael Herr* [alternative to period]

When do you use a dash instead of one of these other
punctuation marks? There are no set rules. Sometimes you
will want to use a dash for the sake of variety. Sometimes a
dash helps because you have already used its alternative
(for example, parentheses) earlier in the sentence and can't
use it again—like in *this* sentence! And sometimes a writer
relies on dashes just because he or she likes them. Norman
Mailer, for example, can't get through a paragraph without
several dashes, often as many as ten or twelve.

One suggestion I would make is to avoid an excessive
number of dashes, because they might give a breathless sort
of tone to your writing. This suggestion applies with special
force to more formal writing situations, such as research
papers, business letters, speeches, and résumés.

EXERCISES

1. The following sentences illustrate a variety of examples
   of punctuation. Some of the sentences are punctuated
   correctly and ought not to be punctuated any other way.
   Mark these sentences with the letter *C* (correct as is).
   Some are punctuated in an acceptable way, but other
   punctuation would also be acceptable. Mark these sentences with the letter *V* (variable), and be prepared to
   explain the acceptable alternative(s) and your preference. Some are punctuated incorrectly. Mark these with

an *I* (incorrect), making sure you know why the sentence needs revision and what the correct punctuation would be. All of the sentences are from student papers.

To err is human, but when the eraser wears out the pencil, you're overdoing it.
— *J. Jenkins*

A. There are three types of students in colleges today; the nerd, the party animal, and the jock.

B. He feels he is losing power in the world, the power to succeed and to prove to himself that he still has this power, he beats his wife.

C. Is it true that you come into this world alone and that you die alone?

D. I should mention one more anxiety that all college students male or female experience during their college years.

E. To change a tire you need; a spare tire, a jack and a lug wrench.

F. Finally I want to talk about whether capital punishment reduces crime.

G. Who could convict 2 Live Crew of obscenity when they restricted admission to adults; and offer a satirical view of society at that?

H. Amateurs who have never played the game suddenly become experts.

I. Then it happens the first fight, the undying love these two people vowed for one another changes.

J. Open marriage is a flexible concept allowing each partner to draw on his or her own special qualities.

K. She has some special interests like making clothes which are very plain and simple looking but neat; cooking for she loves to eat, and just having a good time.

L. A team of misfits challenging the softball champions of Park Ridge should not expect to win, but we did.

M. Would you please be seated.

N. The lotus-shaped stage opened and Mick Jagger came strutting up to the microphone.

O. A topic sentence is often quite terse because it will be amplified by the paragraph that follows.

P. An upset win over the Packers gives them a good chance for the division championship.

Q. The world has waited eighteen years to hear of me: I'm afraid it will have to wait eighteen more.

R. After Mr. James was finished with my hair I was taken to the henna department and introduced to Mr. Phillip.

2. In the following sentences: (1) delete any commas or semicolons that should not be present, (2) circle any commas or semicolons that could be left out at the writer's discretion, (3) change commas to semicolons or vice versa whenever such a change is required, and (4) insert any needed punctuation.

A. Underneath the windows were bushes, most of the bushes were gardenias with large white flowers.

B. It is a stately clock ticking away the time hour after hour.

C. All of a sudden, the organ began "Pomp and Circumstance" and I was on my way marching with the music through a large crowded auditorium.

D. The morning was gray and chilling cold, everyone seemed warm though, because almost everyone on the bus was asleep.

E. I got out of bed and headed for the kitchen; but after looking at the clock I decided I ought to start for the university right away.

F. The sound that occurs when the firecracker goes off, depends on where you are standing; how far from the explosion.

G. My brother is taller, skinnier, and darker skinned, than I am.

H. The streets are no longer lined with trees but, the neighborhood still has a homey feel to it.

I. When I looked up, I saw several members of the other team watching our warm-up, an audience like that only made us feel more pressure.

J. Little did I know, that within a period of three months I would change my mind.

K. Some of Browning's best-known poems include "The Bishop Orders His Tomb," which describes the reflections of a corrupt Renaissance prelate, "Fra Lippo Lippi," which tells about an earthy monk, a man given more to sensuality than to sacrifice, despite his religious vocation, and "Love Among the Ruins," a love poem set in modern times.

L. Everyone, who thought Bush was wrong about his policy toward Pakistan, should have written his or her senator immediately.

M. His loud, abrasive, voice rang in my ears.

N. Now, as adults, they demand behavior of their children, that often exceeds both the child's mental and physical capabilities.

3. The dash is much undervalued as a punctuation mark in most student writing. Find two or three articles or stories in a popular magazine. How often do you encounter dashes? What other punctuation marks could be used instead? Does the frequency of dashes vary from one writer to another?

B. PUNCTUATION REQUIREMENTS

Some conventions have flexibility, but others are more rigid. We turn now to the punctuation marks that don't usually offer options.

B1. Periods and Other End Punctuation

A **period** is the written representation of the falling inflection we hear at the end of every declarative sentence. Ordinarily you are never puzzled about using periods to end sentences or legitimate sentence fragments:

I'd like to learn more about Tibetan Buddhism.

Me, too.

However, you should note one unusual case. Sometimes a writer wishes to make a request, but for the sake of politeness he or she poses the request as a question. In such cases the word order is the same as the word order for a question, but no "answer" is expected. Here is an example:

Would you please send me a copy of your recent article on nutrition.

A period is the best end punctuation for this polite request, despite the questionlike word order.

The period, by the way, has other uses besides ending sentences. It can separate numbers written as decimals:

7.286	$4.59	9.6%	12.36 oz

It can end abbreviations:

Mr.	Ms.	Mrs.	Ph.D.
N.Y.	ibid.	A.M.	A.D.

A series of three spaced periods form what is called an **ellipsis,** which has a number of uses. One is to show that words have been deleted from a quotation:

> Starting as an apprentice, Leyland . . . was able to take over the company by the age of thirty.

Also, the ellipsis can show that a thought has been interrupted or broken off:

> Maybe I should . . . and yet, the more I think of it, I'm convinced I shouldn't.

Usually an ellipsis appears within a quoted sentence, as in the examples above. Sometimes, however, the words to be left out occur at the end of the quoted sentence. Then the ellipsis follows the period that signals the end of the sentence, so the result is *four* spaced dots, three for the ellipsis and one for the period:

> Special procedures govern registration for these classes. . . . These procedures are outlined below.

Two other marks besides periods can punctuate the end of a sentence. The first is the **exclamation point,** which gives special emphasis to a sentence. Here is a brief passage by the writer Thomas Merton:

> Sermon to the birds: "Esteemed friends, birds of noble lineage, I have no message to you except this: be what you are: be *birds*. Thus you will be your own sermon to yourselves!"
>
> Reply: "Even this is one sermon too many!"

Merton's passage illustrates another fact about exclamation points—they are more common in dialogue than in other forms of writing.

Modern prose style is sparing in its use of exclamatory sentences. If a writer uses such sentences too often, the reader may become annoyed because he or she thinks the writer is relying too much on an artificial way of getting attention. This is the kind of writing I mean:

> The old drunk was just one of my experiences! Since I travel on the bus quite frequently, I get to see some pretty weird people sometimes! I am just grateful there are plenty of sane people left!

The student who wrote this paragraph wanted these concluding sentences of her paper to be lively and dramatic. Unfortunately, she did not choose the most effective means. Exclamation marks galvanize the reader like a mild electric shock. If you administer these shocks too often, the reader gets accustomed to them and finally sees them only as an annoyance.

Too many exclamation marks might even make your writing read like Queen Victoria's letters, such as this one to her daughter:

> My poor, dear darling child!
>
> How dreadfully vexed, worried, and fidgety I am at this untoward sprain I can't tell you! How could you do it? I am sure you had too high-heeled boots! I am haunted with your lying in a stuffy room in that dreadful old Schloss—without fresh air and alas! naturally without exercise and am beside myself. Only do take care and let some fresh air into your room and do get yourself carried out at least to get air!

That kind of fervor overstays its welcome.

The other alternative end punctuation is the **question mark.** Its most common use, of course, is for the direct question:

> Yet what do we live for, except to live? *D. H. Lawrence*

> How are we to bring order into this multitudinous chaos
> and so get the deepest and widest pleasure from what we
> read? *Virginia Woolf*

Questions are known by their inverted word order. In other words, a direct question like *Will you go tonight?* has a word order different from the normal declarative sentence, *You will go tonight.* (Indirect questions are treated differently—for example, *He asked if you are going tonight.*)

Sometimes a question is included as part of a regular declarative sentence, as in these examples from student papers:

> And then—are you following me?—the two long pieces
> should be cut at least one inch shorter.

> "Should I water the geraniums?" she asked.

Note that no comma follows the question mark in this example. Less frequently the question mark is used in a series:

> How much of them do you want to sell? And for how much?

Sometimes it may appear within parentheses, expressing the writer's doubt about a preceding fact:

> Wordsworth was about thirty years old (?) when he and
> Coleridge published *Lyrical Ballads.*

B2. Quotation Marks

Quotation marks have a number of uses; one is to set off a short direct quotation. (Longer quotations, usually of three or more sentences, should appear in indented block form). Nearly everyone is aware of this use of double quotation marks:

> As John Anderson says, "The psychic income of the job is
> far less than it once was." *Sanford Ungar*

Student writers are more often confused by other issues, such as: Where do quotation marks go in relation to other punctuation marks? Which quoted passages begin with capital letters and which do not?

The most commonly asked question is whether quotation marks come before or after a comma or period. The rule is very simple: Periods and commas *always* go inside quotation marks:

> "If he gets his way," Spence declared, "we will have a new supernational community dominated by the multinational corporation." *Jeremiah Novak*

The closing quotation marks follow both the comma after *way* and the period after *corporation*. (Putting commas and periods outside of quotation marks is actually British style.)

Colons and semicolons are different—the quotation marks come *before* them:

> Indeed, I am a compulsive reader, a "print nut"; if there is nothing around to read, I will study the labels on ketchup bottles. *S. M. Miller*

Exclamation and question marks depend on circumstance. If the quoted passage itself is a question or exclamation, the quotation marks come *after:*

> "There is a young man waiting for me?" he asked at the reception desk. *Mary Manning*

Suppose, however, the quoted passage is not itself an exclamation or question, but the entire sentence, which includes a quotation, does offer an exclamation or question. Then the quotation marks will appear *before* the end punctuation:

> How stupid I was to keep on insisting on "my rights"!

> Do you know the words to "My Way"?

As for capital letters, the custom is simple. Begin all quotations that are complete sentences with a capital, just as you would any other sentence:

> "My boy," I say, "you and your friends are very shrewd." *Page Stegner*

The complete quoted sentence begins with *My boy*, so *My* is capitalized. *You* is not capitalized, even though it is the first woɪd of the second part of the quotation, because it is not the first word of the full quoted sentence.

Quoted phrases or clauses do not begin with capitals and are worked in as part of the sentence in which they appear:

> He spoke with gusto of a "strong, independent, aggressive" presidency—but for what? *Christopher Lydon*

If a quotation contains still another quotation, this second quotation is defined by single quotation marks:

> "I told [my mother] that I wrote *Monkey Business* and she ignored me. 'Marvelous remarks,' she said. 'How does [Groucho] think them up?'" *S. J. Perelman*

The single quotation marks are always inside the double ones.

All quotation marks, whether single or double, come in pairs. Occasionally a writer forgets to put in the concluding set, thereby puzzling his or her reader, as in this example from a student paper:

> My father always says, "Get a good education. He never went beyond the seventh grade, so he has a great reverence for schooling.

Because the writer neglected the closing quotation marks after *education*, we at first think the second sentence is part of what the father "always says." Then, partway through, we realize this sentence is *about* the father and could not be spoken by him, so we backtrack and start the sentence again. This inconvenience would have been avoided had the writer checked her use of quotation marks during proofreading.

The only time quotation marks are not used in pairs is when a quoted passage is more than one paragraph long. In these cases each new paragraph opens with quotation marks, to show that the quotation continues, but no closing quotation marks appear until the very end, lest it seem as if the quotation were ending sooner than it really does:

> ". . . We went back to the hulk and reshipped our cargo.
> "Then, on a fine moonlight night, all the rats left the ship.
> "We had been infested with them. . . ." *Joseph Conrad*

There are no closing quotation marks after *cargo* or *ship* because the quotation continues in the next paragraph.

Quotation marks can also designate certain titles. Titles of short stories, magazine articles, songs, poems, essays, and shows are among those eligible:

D. H. Lawrence's story "Market Day"

Joan Didion's article "Why I Write"

the hymn "Rock of Ages"

T. S. Eliot's poem "The Journey of the Magi"

the TV show "Friends"

A writer can use quotation marks to show that a word is being used in a special way. In the following sentence, for example, the author intends the word *wonders* to be taken ironically rather than literally:

Now people go there for the "wonders" and the wild mountain scenery. *Anthony Brandt*

Slang words, especially, are often treated this way. But with slang, student writers are more likely to use quotation marks too often rather than too seldom. If you have good reason to use slang, don't apologize for it by adding unnecessary quotation marks. Apologize in this way only when you want to express disapproval of the words themselves. Compare these two student-written sentences:

WEAK: We had just started to put up the tent when the most "godawful" storm arose.
GOOD: I was amused by his complaint about how "heavy" the information was I had given him.

In the first, the author obviously intends *godawful* as the adjective that best describes the power of the storm. Consequently he would have been better off if he had either left out the apologetic quotation marks or chosen a different adjective. In the second sentence, by contrast, the author apparently does not approve of the word *heavy* as a synonym for important, and by the quotation marks she disassociates herself from what she considers weak slang.

B3. Apostrophes

Apostrophes are examples of punctuation within a word. Probably no single mark is omitted more often than the poor apostrophe, especially when it is used with nouns to show possession. Possession is indicated by an apostrophe followed by an *s:*

the tenant's lease	the children's clothes
somebody's book	Roberto's pen
Denver's bus station	Delores's watch

If the noun is plural and ends in *s*, the apostrophe follows the *s:*

old wives' tales	plumbers' rates
the Nguyens' dinner party	the girls' playthings

The purpose of the apostrophe in these cases is simple: to help the reader distinguish between regular plurals (e.g., *two cars*), singular possessives (*the car's muffler*), and plural possessives (*the cars' mufflers*). Granted, we cannot "hear" the difference in these sentences if they are read aloud. But a simple apostrophe offers the reader a very real convenience.

Apostrophes are also familiar in contractions and other places where they help show that a letter or letters have been omitted. For example, take this sentence spoken by Huck Finn:

> Jim said the moon could 'a' *laid* them; well, that looked kind of reasonable, so I didn't say nothing against it. *Mark Twain*

The apostrophe in "didn't" shows where the *o* has been left out of *did not.* We use many contractions like this in writing, such as *I'll, I'm, can't, shouldn't, we'd, don't,* and *it's.* The apostrophes in Huck's *could 'a' laid them* are different. This is not a standard contraction. Rather, it shows that certain letters are not heard in speech. The full phrase would read *could have laid them,* but Twain uses one apostrophe to replace the *h* and another to replace the *ve* to show us that in Huck's dialect these letters would not be pronounced.

Be careful to distinguish between pronoun usages that are possessive (and *don't* take an apostrophe) and those that are contractions:

> The governor of Colorado has signed a bill renaming his state's El Paso Community College "Pikes Peak Community College." At least one Colorado legislator, Rep. Joel Hefley, had argued hard for an apostrophe in the new name—"Pike's Peak," he thought it should be—but he lost.
> —newspaper item

Possessive	Contraction
its	it's
your	you're
whose	who's

The apostrophe is also used to form the plurals of certain letters, abbreviations, and words, especially abbreviations with periods and italicized words or letters:

two *not*'s   Ph.D.'s   *x*'s and *y*'s

But otherwise

the three Rs   ABCs   GIs

B4. Parentheses, Brackets, and the Slash

Parentheses are used to enclose explanations or other incidental material. The important criterion for deciding whether a group of words can be put within parentheses is this: Can you leave the group of words out of the sentence and still have a complete sentence? If you can, parentheses might be appropriate, because the words are incidental—or "parenthetical"—to the sentence. If you cannot leave them out, avoid the parentheses. Here are some examples:

> For it was not the British (whoever they were!) who "made" the poem's vision of golden daffodils compelling, but the poem itself. *Shirley Lim*

> The trouble with *mother* and *father* of course is that they suggest authority (as well as love), and thus strike an undemocratic note in the family. *Morton J. Cronin*

> Every living thing (and perhaps many a dead one as well) pays heed to that call. *Aldo Leopold*

> The three main hypotheses regarding the first question are that the mark stands for (1) Advertising, (2) Advantage, and (3) Adventitious. *Jacques Barzun*

Everything within the parentheses in these examples could be left out and the sentence would still be complete structurally. Note, by the way, that no other punctuation ever precedes an opening parenthesis and that punctuation following a closing parenthesis (like the comma in the second example) goes outside the parenthesis. Of course the words within the parentheses can have their own internal punctuation, which can even include a period if the parenthetical remark is a full sentence:

> I can only assume that where R. S.V. differs in meaning from K.J.V., the translation has improved. (Considering the immense advances in archeology, philology, and other sciences since 1611, this is a reasonable assumption.) I am also willing . . . *Dwight Macdonald*

Parentheses do offer some choice. The example sentence by Aldo Leopold, for instance, could also have been written with the parentheses left out or with the parentheses replaced by commas or dashes:

> Every living thing and perhaps many a dead one as well pays heed to that call.

> Every living thing, and perhaps many a dead one as well, pays heed to that call.

> Every living thing—and perhaps many a dead one as well—pays heed to that call.

If you read the four alternatives carefully, you will see that the difference is in the stress given to the phrase *and perhaps many a dead one as well*. No punctuation gives the phrase least stress—the phrase becomes fully subordinated to the rest of the sentence. Parentheses give slightly greater stress but still subordinate it. Commas provide still more emphasis, and dashes the most. The ability to choose well among these alternative forms of punctuation is a valuable skill that enables a writer to fine-tune the reader's image of what is being said.

Because their shapes and functions are similar, parentheses are sometimes confused with **brackets**. Just remember that brackets are squared rather than curved and that brackets are used to set off comments or explanations by the author within passages he or she is quoting. These explanations include filling in words that were absent or represented by pronouns in the original but that the reader now needs in order to understand the passage out of context:

> "[Darwin] laughed much at this, and came back to it over and over again." *Theodore Baird, quoting Carlyle*

> "With few exceptions, this [i.e., ne'er-do-wells becoming pioneers] seems to be the case in the settlement of all new countries." *student paper quoting Eric Hoffer*

Both the name *Darwin* and the phrase *i.e., ne'er-do-wells becoming pioneers* were not written by the authors of the quoted passages, Carlyle and Hoffer. Instead they were inserted by the writers quoting the passages, to help us understand them. Because neither was written by the original author they must be put within the brackets.

Brackets are also used for parenthetical material that falls within existing parentheses:

> The Book of Leviticus (which gives the rules and regulations by which they [the Israelites] lived) follows Exodus.

The **slash** is found in short poetry quotations, to show the division between the lines of a poem. Here is part of a poem by Christina Rossetti, "Memory"; the slashes show where each new line begins: "I watch there with clear eyes, / And think how it will be in Paradise / When we're together."

Occasionally a slash will join alternative words and indicate that they are options:

> We are pulled out of the space/time continuum.

> The traditional he/she/it singular pronouns are no longer sufficient for our language.

In the first example, and perhaps the second, hyphens would have been acceptable.

Needless to say, we are familiar also with the slash (and other punctuation) as part of Internet addresses:

http://www.salonmagazine.com/feb98

Punctuation marks make up the largest category of conventions in the English language. But there are other conventions, too, as we shall see in the next chapter.

EXERCISES

1. The following passages have no punctuation whatsoever. Punctuate them as well as you can. In situations where you have a choice, be ready to explain the decisions you make.

    A. I noticed the other salespeople staring and grinning at us and then I felt the color rising to my cheeks

    B. That year 1910 was an important one in Mexico the Mexican Revolution began

    C. The worlds highest capital La Paz Bolivia is at an altitude of 11900 feet

    D. Depressants have unusual effects on the body a lack of interest in ones surroundings an inability to move or talk slowing of the pulse and a deepening depression sometimes accompanied by a deadening of all sensations

    E. The doctor i e the one in the green coat entered my room and looked gravely at the information on my chart why was he frowning so much

    F. In many underdeveloped countries a strong system of kinship or friendship such as compadrazgo in Spanish America serves as insurance does in richer nations the system provides for help in times of trouble

    G. What will tuition be next year he asked

    H. Mt Washington 6288 feet tall is the highest peak in New Hampshire

    I. What an exciting finish

    J. Anyone and I mean anyone who criticizes Steve criticizes me

K. One Renaissance bishop claimed that the world was created at 900 am on the morning of October 23 4004 BC

L. During Easter vacation I spent endless hours applying for any type of job clerk typist waitress secretary you name it

M. Did you know that Tarot cards precursors of modern cards have four suits swords cups coins and clubs These four suits of the Tarot deck represented the four social classes of medieval society swords for nobility cups for the clergy coins for the tradespeople and clubs for the peasants

N. In some islands of Micronesia huge stone coins as big as twelve feet in diameter are used as currency theres not much problem with theft even though the money lies around in the streets

O. I don't believe we will run out of petroleum in thirty years as some scientists have predicted how about you

P. The Tsar Czar spelling confusion still puzzles me

2. Punctuate the following passages by adding quotation marks:

A. Don't you dare go was exactly what he said to me, observed Philip.

B. Probably everybody is familiar with the poem Stopping by Woods on a Snowy Evening.

C. Aren't you afraid your parakeet will fly away? I asked. I don't care, Helen said. I wish he would. He really is a pain. The parakeet came up close to her ear and gave her a loud kiss. Get away from me, you stupid bird!

   Face it, I said. He loves you. You'll just have to bear it. Secretly I was laughing to myself

   Did Janice tell you what Sammy did the other day? I said no. Well, she licked her lips, Janice was sitting at the kitchen table . . .

D. If I hear I Believe I Can Fly one more time I think I'll destroy his stereo piece by piece.

E. Have you read Borges's story The Yellow Rose? he asked me.

3. Write sentences that would be examples of the following:

   A. a polite request
   B. a direct quotation containing within it another direct quotation
   C. an indirect question
   D. items in a series, the items being long and having internal punctuation
   E. a quoted sentence with words omitted at the end
   F. a sentence with a parenthetical expression
   G. a question that interrupts a regular sentence
   H. a quotation introduced by a colon
   I. a quotation with a pronoun that must be explained by words in brackets
   J. an exclamation
   K. a sentence with a parenthetical expression set off by dashes
   L. a quotation with words omitted partway through
   M. a direct question

4. Insert apostrophes in the following words or phrases wherever they are needed.

   everyones favorite
   its [contraction of it is]
   its [possessive pronoun]
   two Hs
   couldnt
   theres
   five M.A.s
   Philips house
   for old times sake

5. Examine the ways—both conventional and unconventional—that Tom Wolfe uses punctuation in the following passage from *The New Journalism*. What punctuation marks does he use? In which places do you find him exercising a *choice*, i.e., where could a different kind of punctuation be used? What reasons do you think Wolfe had for making the choices he in fact made?

The Novel seemed like one of the last of those super-strokes, like finding gold or striking oil, through which an American could, overnight, in a flash, utterly transform his destiny. There were plenty of examples to feed the fantasy. In the 1930s all the novelists had seemed to be people who came blazing up into stardom from out of total obscurity. That seemed to be the nature of the beast. The biographical notes on the dust jackets of the novels were terrific. The author, you would be assured, was previously employed as a hod carrier (Steinbeck), a truck dispatcher (Cain), a bellboy (Wright), a Western Union boy (Saroyan), a dishwasher in a Greek restaurant in New York (Faulkner), a truck driver, logger, berry picker, spindle cleaner, crop duster pilot . . . There was no end to it . . . Some novelists had whole strings of these credentials . . . That way you knew you were getting the real goods . . .

By the 1950s The Novel had become a nationwide tournament. There was a magical assumption that the end of World War II in 1945 was the dawn of a new golden age of the American Novel, like the Hemingway–Dos Passos–Fitzgerald era after World War I. There was even a kind of Olympian club where the new golden boys met face-to-face every Sunday afternoon in New York, namely, the White Horse Tavern on Hudson Street . . . Ah! There's Jones! There's Mailer! There's Styron! There's Baldwin! There's Willingham! In the flesh—right here in this room! The scene was strictly for novelists, people who were writing novels, and people who were paying court to The Novel. There was no room for a journalist unless he was there in the role of would-be novelist or simple courtier of the great. There was no such thing as a *literary* journalist working for popular magazines or newspapers. If a journalist aspired to literary status—then he had better have the sense and the courage to quit the popular press and try to get into the big league.

8

Other Conventions

I spoke at the beginning of the last chapter about conventions, such as the handshake versus the *obyátiye*. Punctuation is not the only kind of custom or convention that applies to written language. In this chapter we will discuss two other kinds of conventions—in other words, two other kinds of agreed-on arrangements. The first has to do with how words can be represented on the page—specifically, how we italicize, boldface, capitalize, hyphenate, abbreviate, and numerate. The second has to with the agreed-on preferences for one kind of word choice over another.

A. REPRESENTING WORDS

Let's take a nice simple word: "second." Besides the way we just represented it between the quotation marks, we could also—depending on our needs at the time—italicize it, boldface it, capitalize it, hyphenate it, and abbreviate and numerate it, thusly: *second,* **second,** Second, sec-ond, 2nd. For each of these possibilities this section of the chapter explains both the customs and the needs governing the customs.

A1. Italics

On the classic television show *The Honeymooners*, Jackie Gleason played quick-tempered bus driver Ralph Kramden. At least once in each episode Ralph would glare at his wife and then snarl, "You're a real sweetheart, Alice." She would growl back and the fight would be on.

That sentence became a trademark for the show: "You're a real sweetheart, Alice." But suppose we encountered the sentence all by itself, in written form. Read out of context, the sentence could be the tenderest, most loving sentiment. No written version would convey Ralph's exasperated, sarcastic tone of voice. To convey tone we must rely on additional words as I have done with *snarl*, *exasperated*, and *sarcastic*.

So the written language can never fully represent the spoken language. Even when the words are the same, many important aspects of speech such as pitch, tone, and accent must be sacrificed. This is the price we pay for that great advantage of writing, the ability to address others without limitations of space or time.

Although writing can never duplicate speech, writers are not by any means helpless. Many devices narrow the separation. For example, the use of italics allows a writer to emphasize one word at the expense of another. Contrast these two sentences:

Who *do* you think I am?
Who do you think I *am*?

The first suggests surprise—"Apparently you have mistaken me for someone else; who am I really?" The second suggests outrage—"How dare you address me this way, don't you realize how important I am?" Italics let the writer distinguish these tones by showing which words to stress.

In print we recognize italics by their slanted type: *like this*. Handwritten or typewritten manuscripts represent them by underlining, <u>like this</u>.

Most of the time italics appear because custom requires them. For example, they help to *designate titles of books, plays, long poems, movies, paintings,* and *magazines* and are used for *names of ships* or *planes:*

Rolling Stone (magazine)	*Paradise Lost* (long poem)
Othello (play)	*A Beautiful Mind* (movie)
Angela's Ashes (book)	*Constitution* (ship)
Mona Lisa (painting)	*Los Angeles Times* (newspaper)

In the following sentence observe how the two magazine titles and the book title are italicized, but the title of the essay, which was not published as a separate book, remains in quotation marks:

> He combined the gist of the *Nation* piece with his earlier *Partisan Review* attack on V L. Parrington, and he used the new version, called "Reality in America," as the lead essay in his influential book *The Liberal Imagination*. *Leo Marx*

Italics also identify *words from foreign languages*. These include phrases or single words used as part of a sentence:

esprit de corps (French)	*ruah* (Hebrew)
Weltanschauung (German)	*arrivederci* (Italian)
de jure (Latin)	*shinyo* (Japanese)

> With him it was the *offensive à outrance*—the headlong attack. *John Fowles*

Longer, self-sufficient passages from another language can be treated the same way:

> *Philosophieren*, says Novalis, *ist dephlegmatisieren, vivificieren*. *Walter Pater*

Words or phrases that originated in another language but that have been fully adopted in English—words such as *fiancé* (from French), *prima donna* (from Italian), and *status quo* (from Latin)—are not put in italics. Your dictionary can help in doubtful cases. (Then why, you might ask, were those words italicized in this paragraph? Read on.)

Italics can set off *words used as examples:*

> If in addition to the analysis of metaphor a glossary is compiled of key words, such as *law, facts, nature, species, variety, variation* . . . it will appear that Darwin's verbal universe is expressed and his language system complete. *Theodore Baird*

The most frequent use of italics is one that is a matter of choice. Writers can use italics to give *special emphasis*. Sometimes the emphasis falls on a single word:

> At least the *idea* of education which Adams, solitary and recusant, imposed upon himself was an exemplary idea. *Louis Kronenberger*

Sometimes it falls on a group of words:

> They smiled sympathetically to let him know that *they knew,*
> *they understood, they were very sympathetic. Joyce Carol*
> *Oates*

And sometimes it falls on a key sentence. Italics therefore
single out that sentence from the surrounding ones, perhaps
because it offers a summary or a conclusion:

> Few of us take the pains to study the origin of our cher-
> ished convictions; indeed, we have a natural repugnance to
> so doing. We like to continue to believe what we have been
> accustomed to accept as true, and the resentment aroused
> when doubt is cast upon any of our assumptions leads us to
> seek every manner of excuse for clinging to them. *The re-*
> *sult is that most of our so-called reasoning consists in find-*
> *ing arguments for going on believing as we already do.*
> *James H. Robinson*

By all means use italics for emphasis—otherwise you
deprive yourself of a valuable way to direct your reader's
attention. Student writers too often neglect the opportunities that italics, like dashes, can provide. My only caution is
the same caution that applies to other means of emphasis,
such as exclamation marks and one-sentence paragraphs:
Be sparing, don't overuse. If italics appear too frequently,
their effect is lessened, in the same way that good food is
enhanced by the delicate use of seasoning but destroyed by
recklessness. Again be warned by an example from Queen
Victoria:

> My dearest Uncle, . . . The *peace negotiations* occupy ev-
> ery one; *if* Russia is *sincere,* they will end most probably in
> peace; but *if* she is *not,* the war will be *carried* on with *re-*
> *newed vigour.* The recollection of last year makes one *very*
> *distrustful.*
> England's policy throughout has been the *same, singu-*
> *larly unselfish,* and *solely* actuated by the *desire* of *seeing*
> *Europe saved* from the *arrogant* and *dangerous pretensions*
> of that *barbarous power* Russia—and of having *such safe-*

guards established for the *future*, which may ensure us against a *repetition* of similar *untoward events.*

I repeat now, what we have said from the beginning, and what I have *repeated* a *hundred times*, if *Prussia* and *Austria* had held *strong* and *decided* language to *Russia in '53*, we should *never* have had *this war!*

I dare say the poor uncle must have been thoroughly exhausted by the time he finished that letter. So much excitement could kill a man.

A2. Boldface

We just saw how one use of italics is to give special emphasis. With the advent of the personal computer, writers have still another way of providing emphasis: putting a word in boldface, like **this.** Boldfacing has always been used in books, but previously it required the efforts of a typesetter. Now it is available to the rest of us at the touch of a command key. Whereas italics means putting a word into a wholly different type font ("slanty writing," someone has called it), a boldfaced word is in the same type font but the lines are simply thicker, more noticeable and therefore "bolder."

Italics and boldface are sometimes used interchangeably, but there are differences in the customs about them that writers should respect. Generally, boldfacing is restricted to two situations: *marking off subsections of a text*, and *giving special emphasis.*

The first of these can be illustrated by a segment from an article by Caroline Bird:

> . . . According to estimates made by the economist Fritz Machlup, if we had been educating every young person until age 22 in that year of 1970, the bill for higher education would have reached $47.5 billion, $12.5 billion more than the total corporate profits for the year
>
> **The Baby Boom Is Over**
> Figures such as these have begun to make higher education for all look financially prohibitive . . .

Here the boldface subtitle marks off, and shows the focus of, the next part of her article on college costs. By a similar principle, boldface can sometimes be used to designate the speakers in a dialogue, as in this example:

Student: I like the paragraph. It flows well.
Instructor: What do you mean by the word "flows"?

Occasionally, too, writers find the need to use boldface to set off, for example, the names of authors from the lists of book titles following their names.

In using boldface to provide special emphasis, writers do tread on the territory normally reserved for italics. Use boldface only rarely, perhaps to call attention to a key term during the discussion of a complicated subject, as in this example:

A third corporate strategy, **restructuring,** involves reforming the habits of both management and employees.

You may have noticed how this book uses boldfacing in a similar way.

Continue to use italics for all those special needs mentioned a page or so ago, such as titles, foreign words, and examples.

A3. Capitalization

The history of capitalization in the English language is a story of steady decline. There was a time when writers capitalized almost every noun, as well as many other words that they thought deserved special emphasis:

I HAVE only one thing more to say on the Occasion of the Union Act; which is, that the Author of the Crisis may be fairly proved from his own Citations to be guilty of High Treason. *Jonathan Swift*

But the trend toward diminishing the use of capitals has been a consistent one. It reaches its extreme nowadays in certain greeting cards:

happy birthday! i finally figured out a way to cure my inferiority complex! i'm going to stop comparing myself to you!

Of course the cus-
toms most of us follow
are neither as insistent
about preserving capi-
tals as Jonathan Swift
nor as liberal about dis-
pensing with them as cer-
tain greeting card com-
panies. You probably
know the obvious places
where we all capitalize:
*the first person singu-
lar pronoun (I), people's
names, and the first
word of a sentence or
legitimate fragment.*
These usually offer no
difficulty. Moreover, we saw how to capitalize direct quota-
tions in the last chapter.

Instead, most problems with capitalization occur in one
specific area: *names other than people's names.* Which names
are capitalized and which are not? It depends on how specific the name is. In general, the more specific the name (in
other words the closer it comes to identifying one particular
person, place, or thing), the more likely it is to be capitalized.

Here are some concrete situations where writers are often in doubt about whether to capitalize. If the word names
a specific day, month, event, or period, do capitalize it:

Tuesday   the Battle of Gettysburg
the Protestant Reformation August

If it names a less clearly defined time, such as a season, do
not:

summer   the old days
the medieval period   autumn

If the word names a specific institution, do capitalize it:

U.S. Department of Labor   Archmere Academy
University of Oregon   Newberry Library

If it names a general category of institutions, do not:

libraries	graduate schools
recreation departments	city hospitals

If the word names a specific college course, do capitalize it:

Sociology 101	Advanced Organic Chemistry
French 2	Studies in Victorian Literature

If the word names a general subject area, do not:

chemistry	a psychology course
the mathematics exam	composition

If the word refers to a specific geographical place, do capitalize it:

Fifth Avenue	the West
North Dakota	Southern hospitality

If it just refers to a general direction, do not:

eastern journey	travel west
go north on a certain road	take the third street

If the word names a specific group or party, do capitalize it:

the Democratic candidate	the Romantic poets
the Orthodox Church	the Socialist Party

If it names a general concept, do not:

all democratic governments
orthodox (i.e., conventional) ideas
a romantic mood
socialist goals

If the word names a title that refers to a specific person or is part of a person's name, do capitalize it:

President Lincoln	Queen Juliana
Grandma	Professor Somerville

If the word names a category of people, do not:

several presidents
kings and queens
my grandmothers
a professor's obligations

*If you would not be forgotten,
as soon as you are dead and rotten,
either write things worth reading,
or do things worth writing.
—Ben Franklin*

One temptation to which some writers fall victim is the urge to give words special emphasis through capitalization. Consider this sentence, for example:

> How dare these hypocrites violate the Supreme Law of the Land?

The author of that sentence was quite indignant and wanted to show how presumptuous her opponents were. Therefore she tried to give a Supreme Court decision a certain extra dignity by calling it the "Supreme Law of the Land," all in capitals. But no specific law, institution, or concept bears that title, and so she needs to find a different way of giving voice to her wrath. (*Supreme Court*, of course, would have capitals because it is an institution.)

We use capitals in two other places that sometimes cause difficulty. One is the matter of *sacred names*. Most such names, whether they refer to persons or to texts, are capitalized:

the Holy Spirit   the Torah
the Koran   the Buddah
the Bible   the New Testament

Note that the sacred books are not italicized. A word like *Bible*, for example, is not treated as if it were simply a book title.

The other place we should think about capitals is in *titles of works*, where every word is capitalized except conjunctions, articles, and short prepositions. Capitalize even these words if they are the first or last word in either a title or subtitle:

"If This Goes On . . ." (short story)
Gosford Park (movie)
The Autobiography of Malcolm X (book)

Aristotle Contemplating the Bust of Homer (painting)
"The Loneliness of Being Black" (essay)

Here you'll notice that conjunctions (*and*), articles (*the*), and short prepositions (*of*) remain uncapitalized except when in the first (*The*) or last position (*On*). But just because a word is short doesn't mean it should be lowercase: Always capitalize nouns, pronouns, verbs, adjectives, and adverbs whatever their length.

A4. Hyphens

Remember that although the hyphen and dash are similar in appearance, they are quite different in function.

Hyphens can be seen as a form of internal punctuation; in other words, they occur within a word, like apostrophes do and therefore might even be considered an aspect of spelling.

A hyphen is used to *join the separate parts of several types of compound words.* These compound words include:

1. compound nouns, where two or more words are linked to form one noun:

   mop-up   get-together
   city-state   weigh-in
   self-interest   by-product

2. compound adjectives, where two or more words join to work as an adjective preceding a noun:

   a top-to-bottom appraisal   cradle-to-grave security
   death-dealing blow   multiple-choice question
   problem-solving techniques   up-to-date technology

3. compound numbers:

   forty-eight   seventy-seventh
   nine-tenths   one-third

The difficult question for most writers is whether to hyphenate certain word groups. Compound numbers offer no problem—they are always hyphenated. Compound nouns are a little harder. Sometimes they have hyphens (for example, *mop-up* or *city-state*); sometimes they don't (for example, *card catalog*). What principle can explain why *crossbeam* is one word, *cross-examination* is a hyphenated compound, and *cross section* is two separate words? Your dictionary is the best help: Look up the word in question and hyphenate or not as the dictionary shows. If the compound does not appear in the dictionary, keep the two words separate (i.e., don't use the hyphen to make a compound).

> The hyphen is being done away with—indefensibly, ruthlessly ... [and] if the hyphen goes, so does the very conception of the structure of English.
> —Charlton Ogburn

Compound adjectives are the most troublesome of all. Sometimes your dictionary can help. If the word isn't listed there and if it precedes the noun it modifies, your safest bet is to hyphenate the compound. In such circumstances writing the unified word is probably wrong, because all single words should appear in the dictionary and this one doesn't. More generally, hyphens are usually necessary for clarifying compound modifiers preceding a noun, unless part of the compound is an adverb ending in *-ly* (such as *badly needed vacation*). In many cases words that are hyphenated as compound adjectives are not hyphenated when used as nouns. Compare:

a cause-and-effect relationship
the cause and effect of rising prices
hand-to-mouth existence
living from hand to mouth
a problem-solving task
engaged in problem solving

Another use of hyphens is to *mark off prefixes in certain words*. Some prefixes are always separated from the base word by a hyphen:

ex-president   self-determination
quasi-religious

Most, however, are separated only under special circumstances:

1. when the base word is capitalized:

   pro-Bush   non-Asian
   ultra-Marxist   anti-Semitism

2. when the hyphen distinguishes between two words that are written alike but mean quite different things:

   to re-cover (furniture) vs. to recover (from an illness)
   a co-op (store) vs. a coop (for chickens)

3. in some cases when the last letter of the prefix and the first letter of the base word are the same:

   anti-intellectual   semi-independent

For the most part, however, common prefixes (*pre-*, *post-*, *re-*, *inter-*, *un-*) are not separated from the rest of the word. When in doubt, check your dictionary.

Hyphens are also used to *divide a word into syllables.* Sometimes you must hyphenate a word because only part of it can appear at the end of one typed line and the remainder of the word must appear at the start of the next line. (Nowadays with computers writers normally do not have to make this adjustment, but with longhand or typewriters it can still happen). In such cases the word should be divided wherever the syllables divide. For example, the word *indulgent* can be hyphenated two ways: *in-dulgent* or *indul-gent.* I should offer two cautions, however. Don't hyphenate words consisting of a single syllable, such as *through,* or words of fewer than six letters. And don't separate compound words anywhere but at the hyphens they already have (i.e., *mother- /in-law* or *mother-in-/law* but not *mo-/ther-in-law*).

A5. Abbreviations

An abbreviation is just a different way of writing a word. *Dr.* is shorter than *Doctor,* but a reader will "say" them both the same way. Theoretically we could abbreviate almost every longer word in the language. Having two systems for representing words would be too confusing, however, so we abbreviate only in a few common, agreed-upon places.

The most familiar abbreviations are *courtesy titles and degrees:*

Dr. Catherine Sikorski	Ms. Carole Holmberg
Sen. James Winston, Jr.	Michael Cipolla, Ph.D.

Courtesy titles are not abbreviated, however, when they do not precede a person's name:

The senator is seriously mistaken.
Have you called a doctor?

A few *expressions that derive from foreign languages* are always abbreviated; most are pronounced as abbreviations:

A.M.	etc.	P.S.
P.M.	B.C.	e.g.
i.e.	A.D.	Ibid.

Sometimes a set of initials is so familiar that the organization or object it represents is known more by the initials than by the full name. These well-known initials become the common abbreviation, usually written without the period punctuation:

CBS	NATO
URL	FM
FBI	DNA

The most common mistake student writers make in their compositions or papers is to abbreviate place names, days of the week, or units of measurement, which should not be abbreviated:

Fifth Avenue	minute
Great Britain	ounces
Mount Everest	megabytes
Saturday, December 2	inches

Of course abbreviations for such things might be quite proper in letters, newspaper articles, or recipe books, where space is at a premium. But in most college writing the custom is to spell them out.

A6. Numbers

Numbers can of course be expressed in figures (7/8, 14, 987) or written out as words (seven-eighths, fourteen, nine hundred eighty-seven). Are there customs about when to use the former and when to use the latter?

One general principle you can use is this: Spell out the number in words if it is one or two digits or if it starts a sentence. Otherwise use the numeral.

Thus, if the number is between one and nine (single digit) or ten and ninety-nine (double digit), write it out:

three	twenty-two
eight	seventy-one

But when you get to three digits or more, use the numerals:

167	418,689
2,614	61,772,327

So a person might have thirty-two dollars and enjoy a temperature of sixty-seven degrees, while someone else may have $216 and be sweltering in 105-degree heat.

No matter how many digits it has, a number beginning a sentence is always spelled out:

> Two hundred fourteen dollars short: She was going to be stranded in Cleveland. (Not "214 dollars . . ." or "$214 . . .")

There are certain other conventions worth noting. First, while the numbers preceding *o'clock*, *noon*, and *midnight* or expressing approximate time are always spelled out (*four o' clock, twelve noon, half past six*), expressions of exact time use numbers: 3:06 P.M. Also, figures are always needed for addresses (67 Hazelcrest Lane), ratios (5 to 2), percentages (21 percent), sports scores (Bulls win 90–88), dates (May 12), routine identifications (Interstate 10, Channel 22, 98.6 FM), and pages and other divisions (page 5, Chapter 15, line 42, scene 4).

Most fields have style guides that outline preferred uses of spelled-out numbers versus figures; be sure to consult these style guides when you write for specific courses or disciplines.

EXERCISES

1. Practice the use of italics to give emphasis by writing a half-dozen sentences in which you stress certain key words or phrases by means of italics. Then go back through two of your recent papers and see whether there are places where you could have used italics to your advantage. Compare these papers with some articles from a popular magazine; does the magazine use italics more often, and if so, how and where?

> *Whatever you would make habitual, practice it, and if you would not make a thing habitual, do not practice it.*
> —*Epictetus*

2. In the following passages, capitalize and italicize according to the principles explained in this section:

   A. virginia woolf's father was the philosopher and critic sir leslie stephen, the editor of cornhill magazine. in 1904 she and her brothers and sisters moved from hyde park gate to 46 gordon square in bloomsbury. by 1912 virginia had married one of her brother thoby's friends, leonard woolf, and she soon published her first novel, the voyage out.

   B. some of the material developed by the nebraska curriculum development center is available under the title the rhetoric of short units of composition.

   C. when he returned to the united states from europe, baldwin lived in greenwich village in new york city. his first book after his return was the collection of essays titled nobody knows my name, which was quickly followed by the novel another country. two plays also appeared: blues for mister charlie, produced by the actor's studio, and the amen corner, which played on broadway. his early essay "notes of a native son" continues to be widely anthologized because of what it says about black-white relationships, although baldwin insisted that he did not want to be known "merely as a negro writer."

3. Comment on the use of italics and capitalization in the following passage:

   For on the one hand, I think it is possible to hold that ideologies *have a history of their own* (although it is determined in the last instance by the class struggle); and on the other, I think it is possible to hold that ideology *in general has no history*, not in a negative sense (its history is external to it), but in an absolutely positive sense.

This sense is a positive one if it is true that the peculiarity of ideology is that it is endowed with a structure and a functioning such as to make it a nonhistorical reality, i.e. an *omni-historical* reality, in the sense in which that structure and functioning are immutable, present in the same form throughout what we can call history, in the sense in which the *Communist Manifesto* defines history as the history of class struggles, i.e. the history of class societies.

To give a theoretical reference-point here, I might say that, to return to our example of the dream, in its Freudian conception this time, our proposition: ideology has no history, can and must (and in a way which has absolutely nothing arbitrary about it, but, quite the reverse, is theoretically necessary, for there is an organic link between the two propositions) be related directly to Freud's proposition that the *unconscious is eternal*, i.e., that it has no history. *Louis Althusser*

How would you describe the *readability* of this passage (for most readers, anyway)? We grant the difficulty of the subject matter: do you think the passage would have been even *more* difficult if the author had not made extensive use of italics?

4. Insert hyphens in the following words or phrases wherever they are needed. Unite parts of words that are separated unnecessarily. If you are in doubt, let your dictionary help.

child rearing	three quarters
re enforce	up to date plan
semi autonomous	far reaching effects
post doctoral	anti intellectual
great great grand mother	anti American
follow up	six tenths
quarter back	self esteem

5. In a popular news magazine such as *Time* or *Newsweek*, read through a few of the articles, circling every abbreviation you can find. What seems to be the policy of this magazine regarding abbreviations? Then take a somewhat different kind of magazine—say *The Atlantic*, *Harper's*, or the *New Yorker*. Does the policy here seem to be different? If so, can you guess at a reason that might account for the difference?

B. WORD CUSTOMS

Just as there are alternative ways of representing words (italics versus boldface, for example), so, too, there are choices to be made among words themselves. In other words, two choices may be equally "correct" grammatically, but convention or custom will award strong preference to one choice over the other. In this section of the chapter we will examine some of the most noteworthy of these customs.

Note that many of these issues could have been considered in other parts of the book—slang in Chapter 1, for example, or sexist pronouns in Chapter 6. But the fact that all of them are governed by current convention makes this an appropriate place to discuss them.

B1. Language Level

Let's begin with the spoken word rather than the written word. Suppose you have a test scheduled for a Tuesday morning, but on the same day at the same hour you have a court date to answer a summons for a speeding ticket. To your roommate you might say, "I've gotta be in court at nine on Tuesday morning. For sure I won't be back in time for Walker's bio test. Hope the old guy lets me take a makeup." But when you approach the venerable Dr. Walker himself, you unconsciously adjust your language: "Excuse me, sir, I have to be in court next Tuesday and so I must be absent from the midterm. Would it be possible for me to take the examination at some later time?"

Your adjustment is a recognition of the fact that each situation has a level of language appropriate to it. In conversation with a friend, you use the language conventional for that situation: contractions ("bio"), informal terms ("old guy"), and idioms ("for sure"). But when the situation calls for more formal language, you use that instead. Otherwise you would run the risk of not persuading your listener. Dr. Walker probably would not be surprised to hear that he has been called an "old guy" or worse. But he might not respond well if you called him that directly.

Writing is like speaking. Each writing situation has a language convention for and appropriate to it, depending in large part on the writer's expectations about what the reader wants to hear. Two key terms often used to describe these levels of language are *formal* and *informal*.

Formal language is the language of the public situation, when the writer's intended audience is not someone he or she knows personally. In such circumstances writers tend to be more careful, choosing words and arranging sentences to show an acknowledged lack of intimacy between themselves and their readers. They would probably also use fewer contractions and avoid certain words or phrases that might seem inappropriate (or would put the words in quotation marks to show an awareness that they have a nonliteral value or slang tone). For an example of formal writing, you need go no further than your nearest textbook. Business, government, and academic writing all use formal language.

Informal language, on the other hand, presupposes an

intimacy between author and reader, as in letters or e-mails exchanged by old friends; it makes use of more contractions, more of the unbuttoned language usually found in everyday conversation. This is a good example:

> I got so depressed and fed up with the Rev and his Holy Bobble that I swung with the collection one night (a cool 83 cents) and went out looking for trouble.

I figured I'd given the Rev more than 83 cents worth of happiness. Twofold happiness, in fact. When he first saw me, he thought he'd found the 13th Disciple. Later, when the true nature of the beast became apparent, he was able to say he had personally encountered the Anti-Christ. So it was kicks coming and going.

Contractions (*I'd, the Rev*), slang (*swung, cool*), and plays on words (*Holy Bobble*) characterize this writing as very informal.

Formal and informal writing should not be thought of as two distinct categories, all writing being clearly one or the other. Instead you can visualize them as overlapping:

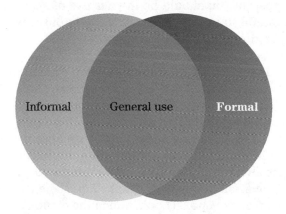

In the shaded area, where the overlap occurs, are the great majority of words and phrases. These words are for general use in both formal and informal writing.

The darker area represents those words usually found only in formal writing. These are often words with specialized meanings, such as *dichotomous* or *serotinal*, that are not normally part of our conversation or writing but that in certain circumstances have a legitimate purpose. Formal language can also include more complicated sentence structures, and it will always respect standard usages (see the Glossary of Usage).

The lighter area represents those words that ordinarily do not find their way into our prose except in our most informal moments. They include slang and other nonstandard usages:

1. *Slang.* Slang is a way of speaking or writing that often involves the use of exaggeration to produce a special effect. Old words can be given new meanings—*freak* to describe reacting with unnecessary excitement, for example, or *high* to describe being intoxicated by drugs or alcohol. New extensions of old meanings can also be created—*Dude!*, for example, to address a friend with affection. Everybody uses slang. It gives language much of its verve and humor. But slang is much more common in speaking than in writing, and much more common in informal writing than in formal. So the more formal your writing situation, the more sparing you should be in your use of slang and the more careful you should be in following the old adage "When in doubt, don't."

Slang, of course, is quick changing, ephemeral. Just a few years ago it was "hip" to call someone a "square," but now only "squares" would use either word. Slang can become more formal with time (dignity comes with age for words, too) and therefore ceases to be slang. Some people have the erroneous idea that slang is bad. Because it is sometimes ephemeral and inappropriate, they mistakenly believe that it is always harmful. "A pox on them," as Shakespeare would have said in his best Elizabethan slang, and he did not mean chicken pox. (Look it up in the dictionary.)

2. *Informal, colloquial.* The line that separates words in this category from slang is hazy at best. "Informal" words (the term *colloquial* is fast disappearing because it was found to be misleading) are just what you might expect: words that are found much more often in speech and informal writing than in more formal contexts. They differ from slang insofar as they lack some of the exaggeration usually characteristic of good slang. Take the word *wiseacre*, meaning an annoying know-it-all. It lacks the dramatic extension of meaning found in a word like *freak*, but at the same time it is perhaps out of place in very formal situations.

The same cautions that were mentioned about slang words can also be applied to informal words. These words are acceptable in themselves. But the more formal the writing situation, and the more removed you are from intimate conversation, the less likely it is that such words will be effective. It's like a man arriving for dinner at an expensive restaurant without a coat and tie; there's nothing morally superior about a coat and tie instead of jeans and a T-shirt—it's just a matter of appropriateness.

3. *Obsolete, archaic.* These terms describe different degrees of being outdated. An *obsolete* word (or one meaning of that word) is one that was once used in a certain way but is no longer. *Archaic* applies to a word that is fast becoming obsolete—it is rarely used with a certain meaning, and then only in unusual contexts. An example of an obsolete word is the verb *cope* used to mean "meet (someone) in combat." *Cope* does not have that meaning anymore (it has others, of course). Compare it with a word like *withal*, which is still in use but is swiftly becoming archaic, or at least some of its meanings are. You are not likely to use obsolete words, but you might occasionally stray into an archaicism, especially when you are trying too hard to sound impressive in highly formal writing.

4. *Vulgar.* I don't suppose I need to do much explaining here. A *vulgar* word is one that is taboo, at least in polite circles, whether in speech or in writing. I assume it is clear that you would not use vulgarity in any situation except a highly informal one—perhaps when you are using dialogue in a personal-experience paper.

5. *Nonstandard, substandard.* Both of these terms imply the existence of standard English, the language of educated speakers when they are being conscious of what and how they speak. *Nonstandard* is a deliberately bloodless term used to describe what some people would call "bad English." It includes words almost everybody uses—a familiar example is *ain't*—and words that are used by some people and not others, such as *learn* meaning "teach": "I'll learn him not to contradict me." Some people make the distinction between words disapproved of by many but occasionally acceptable (*nonstandard*) and words that are always thought to lack prestige (*substandard*).

Most of us make frequent use of nonstandard words and forms. But in writing we recognize that such words offend many readers and therefore hinder communication with them. Because other alternatives are available, it is best to avoid nonstandard usages whenever possible. Again, dialogue may be a necessary exception.

If you have inadvertently used a nonstandard word or phrase, an excellent first resource is a glossary of usage such as the one in this handbook. But if a glossary is not handy, the dictionary will give a helpful albeit briefer explanation. It just ain't true that *ain't* ain't in the dictionary.

B2. The Pronoun "I"

One convention that students often bring to college is expressed something like this: "You shouldn't ever use the pronoun *I* in formal writing." In this matter custom is changing. If you have been told never to write in the first person (to never use *I* or *we*), you may wish to modify your practice.

The older custom was not without its reasons. It held that avoiding the first-person pronouns forced writers to think more impersonally, more broadly, and more analytically. The more carefully and analytically writers thought, the more persuasively they wrote, and persuasive writing is after all the goal. (In such writing the use of the third-person pronoun *one* often creeps in to replace the first-person pronoun. Do you see how, for example, *One observes* sounds more impersonal, more analytical, than *I observe?*)

But the power of this convention has waned. Part of the reason may be the seeming hypocrisy of the older custom: Why say *One observes* when what you really mean is *I observe?* Another part might be the increasing tendency toward informality in our society, as evidenced in everything from "casual dress Fridays" in business offices to the current state of student attire. (Your grandparents' generation would have worn dresses and suitcoats to class; your parents' generation would have worn neatly pressed but casual clothes; as for your generation . . .)

Whatever the reason, it is now acceptable to use *I* or *we* in many formal writing situations. If you mean yourself personally, use *I;* if you mean both you and all your readers, maybe *we* would be appropriate. This textbook, to cite but one example, does sometimes use *I* and *we* in these ways—the very first paragraph of this chapter serves as an example.

But still a caution is advisable. In formal writing you do intend, after all, to be persuasive, and often most persuasive writing does take a broader, more analytical, more impersonal stance. Do not use the first-person pronouns unless the person or persons to whom they refer are clear and their "presence" in the writing is both timely and appropriate. When in doubt, take the broader view.

B3. Pronouns and Sexist Language
What pronoun should be used in this sentence?

> Each laboratory worker must show _____ security pass before entering.

Their would be inappropriate because the antecedent is clearly singular. If we assume that the workers are both male and female and if the only third-person singular possessives are *his, her,* and *its,* which do we choose?

The original solution was the so-called generic *he,* where *he* and its derivatives (*his, him, himself*) could refer to any group made up of both males and females. In other words, the pronoun *he* served two functions: In some circumstances it referred to one or more antecedents who were clearly male, and in other circumstances it referred to human beings in general, male or female. A few of the example sentences in this book, because they were taken from works written many years ago, show this pronoun use. In our example, the traditional solution would have been to use the possessive adjective *his:*

> Each laboratory worker must show his security pass before entering.

Those who used it would have said that the context tells the reader that *his* must be taken generically to refer to all laboratory workers, male or female. Some writers today, especially if their writing habits were formed decades ago, still use the generic *he*.

But customs—conventions—can change over time. Many people in recent years have objected to the use of *he* to refer to all human beings. They believe the pronoun is so firmly linked in our minds with the male sex that it can never be free of sexual bias. We may *say* that the pronoun refers to both males and females, but subconsciously—or even consciously—we *think* male. Such mental habits can bias readers and reinforce stereotypes of male dominance. Consequently, most writers and editors today, following current practice, would write our example sentence in one of three ways:

> Each laboratory worker must show *his or her* security pass before entering. [adds feminine possessive adjective]

> Each laboratory worker must show a security pass before entering. [cuts possessive adjective entirely]

> Laboratory *workers* must show *their* security passes before entering. [converts subject to plural]

In all three versions, the use of *his* to refer to what could be a woman has been eliminated.

You can usually avoid offense by cutting pronouns or possessive adjectives or by casting sentences into the plural, as in the second and third of the preceding revisions. When these solutions prove impossible and you must use the singular, use *his or her* or some other device for acknowledging both sexes, if both are intended. A few thorny sentences may still remain, sentences where no alternative to a singular pronoun is really satisfactory and where the reference occurs several times over a long passage. In these cases, the generic *he* may be unavoidable, but otherwise I would advise staying clear of it.

This issue of pronoun reference relates to some larger issues regarding sexist language. You know of course that language can hurt, and you would never offend by using racial or ethnic slurs in your writing. You also know that you cannot expect a fair hearing from your readers if you use insulting language related to someone's age, national origin, sexual orientation, or disability. But some writers do not so easily recognize how language can sometimes belittle women and they therefore quite unintentionally use sexist language.

For example, some occupations have changed dramatically in recent years. Where it used to be possible to write *policeman* or *mailman* with full confidence that the job holder was male and *stewardess* with full confidence the job holder was female, there are now plenty of women in the first two professions and plenty of males in the third. Writers must respect these changes by using *police officer*, *mail carrier*, and *flight attendant*, respectively.

Some professions or roles offer a choice of terms. If department *chairman* can be ruled out because not all who fulfill that office are male, some prefer *chairperson* while others choose *chair* or *head*. Defenders of *chairperson* think the other two conjure up ludicrous images of talking chairs or acting heads, while proponents of *chair* or *head* think *chairperson* is too cumbersome. Another example is the passé term *Congressman;* should it be *Congressperson* or *Representative?*

Only in the few cases where there are balanced pairs of words, such as *actor/actress,* can writers use terms for professionals that distinguish men from women, and even here some prefer *actor* for both sexes. In no case would you want to use condescending terms such as *lady lawyer* that imply something odd about women having such a position. The simple principle here is that people should be treated equally, and nothing in a writer's language should imply otherwise. (See Exercise 3 at the end of this chapter for other examples.)

Just as you would not use fireman (since *firefighter* implies that women can also have that job), so, too, should you treat men and women equally when it comes to providing information about them. If *Mr.* allows for the male in question to be married or unmarried, use *Ms.* (rather than *Miss* or *Mrs.*) to allow the woman in question to keep her marital status a private matter. If you refer to men by their last names only in certain contexts (e.g., *Shakespeare*, *Hemingway*), give women the same consideration: *Austen*, *Woolf* (not *Jane Austen* and *Virginia Woolf* unless you would also be using *William Shakespeare* and *Ernest Hemingway*).

You should be aware, too, that language customs are evolving on these issues. For example, most writers now agree to not use the terms *mankind* or *man* as if they referred to all people, especially since good alternatives such as *humankind* are usually close to hand. But at the same time many people think the city of Portland, Oregon went a wee bit too far when it ordered that *manhole covers* be renamed *personhole covers*. Try to be both sensitive and sensible.

B4. Avoiding the Verb "To Be"

You might remember the suggestion back in Chapter 3 about not using the passive voice. Some people take this suggestion to heart with another bit of conventional wisdom: "Avoid the passive voice." We have seen that avoiding passives may not be possible, or if possible, may be undesirable. But the conventional wisdom turns out to have its value after all, because it focuses attention on verbs, and especially on all verbs that use some forms of the verb *to be* (passive voice requires one of these forms). Adopting the convention in its broadest sense—i.e., focusing on your uses of *to be*—can be of singular value in helping you write better.

Remember that *to be* is a linking verb (page 202) and that it comes in several forms (*am, are, is, be, been, was, were, being*), either by itself (*I am, they were*) or tied to others (*are speaking, is being sought, have been informed*). The problem with *to be* in any of its forms is that it is so, well, *inactive*, so *passive*. It sets up a kind of equation, so that when you write, for example, *the glass is empty* you establish an equation between the glass and emptiness (*glass = empty*). Thus the verb, one of the two absolute essentials in an English sentence, contributes less than perhaps it could to the "what's happenin'" of that sentence. Wherever you can do it gracefully, change the verb to eliminate any ver-

sions of *to be*. See if that doesn't make your writing more
vivid, more active, more vital.

Let's illustrate with an example. Circle all the forms of *to
be* in the following paragraph:

> The question of preserving cultural diversity with or with-
> out bilingual education is difficult to answer. Arguments for
> these programs assert that society is only benefited from
> the acceptance of a wide variety of cultures while opponents
> are suggesting that bilingual education is a costly way to
> divide America. Clearly bilingual education is having a dis-
> ruptive potential when it is used to segregate different
> ethnicities. However, it is clearer still that America has been
> thriving on cultural integration for two centuries and that
> bilingual programs might be the deciding factor in the pres-
> ervation of this ideal.

I assume you circled *is* in the first sentence; *is . . . benefited, are suggesting,* and *is* in the second sentence; *is
having* and *is used* in the third sentence; *is clearer still,
has been thriving,* and *might be* in the fourth.

Now suppose you revised the paragraph by finding better alternatives for the *to be* verbs:

> How should America answer the difficult question of
> whether bilingual education preserves or destroys cultural
> diversity? Arguments for these programs assert that society
> only benefits from the acceptance of a wide variety of cul-
> tures, while opponents suggest that bilingual education di-
> vides us in a costly way. Clearly bilingual education has a
> disruptive potential when used to segregate different
> ethnicities. However, it is clearer still that America has
> thrived on cultural integration for two centuries and that
> bilingual programs might constitute the deciding factor in
> the preservation of this ideal.

Granted, problems remain. But do you see how this second version is crisper, more mature than the first? And do
you see how this improvement came about simply through
changing the *to be* verbs into a paragraph that now contains
ten active verbs and only two instances of *to be*?

EXERCISES

1. What words in the following student-written passage allow us to describe the passage as *informal* writing? Why?

   I knew the minute he walked in the door that we had a live one on our hands. He tried to look around the lobby casually, but he caught me watching him, so he made a bee line right for my counter. Obviously he was checking us out for an alarm system.

   He came slowly toward me with a half-smile on his face. Trying to cover up his nervousness, I thought. Well at least he isn't a pro. That's all we needed. Our Holiday Inn had been operating for only six months, but already five color TV sets had been ripped off. So I was determined to get this guy.

2. The controversy about whether *he* can refer to all people or just males has been widely debated. Write a short summary of the controversy. In preparing the summary, include some or all of the following activities:

   A. Determine the policy in effect for your local newspaper.
   B. Check the section on pronouns in a composition handbook published at least thirty-five years ago (your library will probably have some older editions) and see what advice it gives.
   C. Jot down what you can remember about what you were taught in grade school and high school on this issue.
   D. Determine what seems to be the policy in use for this textbook; do the same for Allan Bloom's bestseller, *The Closing of the American Mind*.
   E. Decide whether you will follow the policy recommended on page 290 and why you will or will not follow it. Whatever the choice may be, what reactions can you expect from readers?

3. What nonsexist word or term could you use to replace the following?

   A. weatherman
   B. forefathers

C. saleswoman

D. spokesman

E. foremen

F. anchorwoman

G. aviatrix

H. businessmen

4. The following passage by William Faulkner was written in 1932. Rewrite the passage using nonsexist language. Keep the vigor and pungency of Faulkner's original.

> Poor man. Poor mankind. . . . Man performs, engenders, so much more than he could or should have to bear. That's how he finds he can bear anything.

5. Improve the following paragraph by changing as many of the *to be* verbs as possible:

> The interest of critics today is often with the interpretive and relational aspects of reading. On the interpretive level, depending on their training and affiliations, they might be engaging in a New Critical close reading, or pursuing etymologies, or asking about the hermeneutical strategies of individual readers. On the relational level, the interest of critics was at one time biographical—how is the novel a reflection of the person who wrote it? Now critics are more likely to situate the work in a cultural context or show how it is complicit in some ideology.

The Writing Process: Prewriting

When you learn to drive a car, you study dozens of separate skills, from turning the ignition key to applying the brakes. Yet driving a car is not merely the sum of those skills, like adding up shifting + steering + acceleration + braking. Although you learn all of these skills independently, you still must be able to combine them into one overriding skill: the ability to pilot a 3,000-pound machine safely even when it is hurtling down an expressway at 55 miles per hour. Furthermore, when you are on that expressway and some idiot cuts right in front of you, there is no time to say to yourself, "Now I must push hard on my brake and then I must check the mirror to see if I can change lanes and then I must steer to the left." People become accident statistics that way. Instead, you must be able to use your skills *instinctively* and *simultaneously*.

So too with the complex skill of writing. We have talked about many separate skills in this book. But good writing is not just the sum of those skills, it's not a matter of good words + good sentences + good paragraphs + good punctuation. Instead you need to combine, to integrate those skills. This means learning to use them instinctively and simultaneously, as you confront the challenges every writer must meet in college work.

In short, this is the chapter where we put it all together. Just as there is a time for putting aside the driver training manual and getting behind the wheel, so, too, there is a time for shifting the focus away from separate writing skills and toward the successful combination of those skills in a good college paper.

Most papers you will write in college are going to be short ones—let's say five pages or fewer. That is where we should begin. This chapter considers that part of the process of writing short papers that some call **prewriting:** the activities of finding a topic and thinking it through. The next chapter discusses those parts of the process in which you plan and write a first draft, while Chapter 11 takes up the final part of the process, *re*writing, otherwise known as revision. Bear in mind, too, that we could just as logically have begun the whole handbook here, with prewriting, and then moved on to consider words, sentences, and paragraphs later, as part of rewriting. In fact, your instructor may have chosen just such an arrangement.

You should not think of this division of the writing process into stages as you would a recipe. Good writers do not say, "I just finished stage two, now it's on to stage three." Writing, I said a moment ago, is a *process*. We study the composing process just as we do any other process: as a series of continuous actions that bring about a certain result. Many of these actions go on simultaneously. Often a writer is planning and writing and revising all at the same time.

Nevertheless, we can look at that writing process unfolding through time, as these chapters try to do. Separating the continuous action into stages allows us to analyze it clearly and conveniently.

Moreover, these chapters can be valuable if you are using this text as a resource book for particular writing errors and your instructor's comments always seem to be variations on certain familiar themes: "paper needs better organization"; "topic insufficiently developed"; "provide more examples." The comments might not bother you so much except for the fact that they are often accompanied by a grade that shows that the instructor means something important by them. What you need is a more successful strategy for developing the papers you write. These chapters can offer special help here.

Or suppose your problem is agony of the spirit: A certain stage in the writing process causes you almost unbearable pain. Perhaps it's the stage of deciding what you will write about. Or maybe you have little trouble deciding what to write about but can never figure out how to get started. What you need is a different way of approaching the task, plus some tips on how others—including professional writers—have met it successfully. Any one of Chapters 9 through 11 might help, depending on which one seems most directly related to your needs.

A. EXPLORING TOPICS

Quite often there's no mystery about the topic for your paper because your instructor will have decided for you. Sometimes he or she will name a single topic; at other times he or she will provide a list and allow you to choose; at still other times he or she will prescribe a specific topic area and ask you to adapt it to your own interests or circumstances. Instructors provide topics for any number of good reasons. Most often their intent is not to restrict your freedom but rather to give order to your experiences in ways that enhance your intellectual growth.

If your instructor has named a topic or provided a list, you should not conclude that the prewriting activities have already been done for you. Quite the contrary: You still need to narrow your subject, assess your information, think critically about your topic, and adapt your topic to the needs of your presumed audience. The later parts of this chapter will address these needs.

But in the meantime we will examine those situations where the instructor has left the determination of a topic strictly up to you.

A1. Finding a Topic

This situation may be familiar:

Scene: a student's room, late at night. *Cast:* only one—the student writer (you?). *Plot:* student is in conflict partly with himself or herself ("Why didn't I start this stupid thing sooner?"), mostly

> *I am still of the opinion that only two topics can be of the least interest to a serious and studious mood—sex and the dead.*
> W. B. Yeats

with a seemingly intractable paper due the next morning. As the curtain rises on this tearful melodrama, our hero or heroine is heard to mutter, "What can I write about? What can I *possibly* write about?"

First principle: You can write well only about what you know. I learned that principle the hard way when I was a freshman in college. One week the instructor asked us to write a short story. I wrote what I thought was an exciting little story. It was all about a circus performer (a knife-thrower, as I recall); it had a spine-tingling climax and it was written in my very best style. But the story came back to me accompanied by one short sentence of dismissal: "You don't know anything about circuses."

The instructor was right. I didn't know anything about circuses and therefore could not write familiarly about them. Writers must stick to what they know. You can supplement what you know by reading more and learning more, of course. But that's not going to help much at midnight on the night before the paper is due. So the wisest step is to take a short inventory of what you know, thus giving yourself a chance to see what material you could use for the paper.

What *do* you know? First of all, you know yourself—your life history, your fears, your dreams, your successes and failures. If the paper can be autobiographical or descriptive, perhaps you need go no further. Let your mind play freely over your past and your present. Every memory or idea that occurs to you occurs to you for a reason. After all, hundreds of things happen to people every day that they promptly forget and never remember again. Try to unravel the thread and find out *why* some particular memory or idea lingers, because in that reason may lie the secret of how you can make the story appeal to someone else. For example, almost everybody can remember his or her first day of school, not because each person's first day is so different from anyone else's but rather because that day is an important rite of passage for everyone.

You also know lots of information about a wide variety of subjects. Jobs, hobbies, friends, interests, books you've read, TV programs you've seen, subjects you've studied in or out of school—you know something about all of these and more. If your paper will explain or describe something, these are the places to search.

And you have opinions, too. When you talk to friends, what excites you? What makes you enthusiastic, or irritates you, or arouses your indignation? If your opinions interest a friend during a conversation, they could be made to interest a reader, too.

So far we have been talking about ways you can use your own experiences as material for your essays. What other kinds of strategies can you use for finding a good topic?

One possibility is **brainstorming.** Sometimes this activity forms part of the classroom experience, and your instructor may encourage brainstorming sessions either for the class as a whole or within small groups. Sometimes, too, you will be encouraged to brainstorm as a group outside of a class. And you always have the option of undertaking this exercise on your own whenever you think it might prove useful.

Brainstorming simply means jotting down, often as quickly as you can, *all* of the ideas, associations, objects, events, and comments that come to mind. Free associate, the way you would if you were playing charades. If a thought flits into your consciousness, put it down, even if it seems ridiculous or you have no idea how you could ever use it. Don't censor yourself. Let one idea or image suggest another, and be as specific and as concrete as possible. Keep on going. Don't worry

yet about finding any patterns or formulating any thesis statements.

Then, when you or your group feels as though the images and ideas are slowing down, you can let the brainstorming come to a natural stop. Now is the time to start looking for patterns. Do you see in all these heterogeneous notes a few common threads—perhaps some questions to be asked and answered, some problems to be solved, some comparisons to be made, some objections to be raised? Perhaps an explanation to be given, a process to be described, a case to be argued, an experience to be conveyed? Out of the brainstorming notes you will find one or more clusters of ideas and images that you can use, which in turn will stimulate new ideas and images as you begin to write. Meanwhile, the remaining notes—probably the large majority of them—can be consigned to temporary and then perhaps permanent oblivion.

You can also try a variant of brainstorming called **free writing,** in which you write as fast as you can, again in a kind of free-associating way, for a planned period of time (say ten minutes). Because you don't begin with an agenda, the effect is to liberate you from writer's block. In the end you have some sentences down on paper, out of which can emerge some ideas for a more focused piece of writing.

Some writers, while they may find brainstorming helpful, prefer to have a more planned, more systematic resource to which they can turn for ideas. They like to keep and draw on a **writer's journal.** In fact, your instructor may have required or encouraged you to begin such a journal. A writer's journal differs from a diary. In a diary the writer enters all of those events that make up daily life: classes attended or not attended, e-mails written and received, conversations held, phone calls made, TV shows watched, meetings or social events planned or undertaken. A writer's journal, on the other hand, is both less and more than a diary. It is less insofar as it leaves out most of what falls under the category of "what I did today." But it is more than a diary because it includes everything that the writer thinks might sometime prove useful. Newspaper articles and selected quotations from books and interesting facts would all be included. So would things you heard or overheard people say, theories a professor advanced in a class, events you participated in or heard about or saw on the

> *If a man cares enough about tiddledy winks, his book about tiddledy winks will be a great book.*
> —*Matthew Bruccoli*

TV news. A good journal will include your feelings and some memories and whatever insights or ideas the day seems to have afforded. If good paper topics or interesting ideas or even just good sentences, phrases, or words occur to you, you should jot them all down, perhaps by carrying the journal around with you. Then, when the time comes for finding and focusing on a topic, the material will already be there, ready to handle, and the planning and writing can begin.

So, the important issue really is not "What am I going to write about?" Almost anything can make a good topic. During one week, for example, the nationally syndicated columnist Bob Greene wrote about the following five topics: (1) a sixty-year-old thief dying of emphysema, (2) advice to the lovelorn from a mailroom employee, (3) a man whose only profession is getting his name in the paper—149 times so far, (4) a dancer who strips for Jesus, and (5) a botched kidnapping attempt in a small town. In themselves these certainly are not subjects of world-shattering importance. Yet Greene manages to make readers care about them and share his fascination.

The secret is not what you write about—it's saying something interesting about the topic no matter what it is. Consequently, you must be excited about the subject yourself before you can make it interesting to others. Good writers have something they are burning to say. Once you have settled on a subject that is important to you, you are ready to communicate that fascination to others.

So just for the moment take *any* area of interest to you. Your task is to find a good paper topic within that area of interest. Alternatively, if your instructor has given you a topic or list of topics, you want to figure out how to develop it. In either case, the key to whether a paper will be successful lies in your answers to three important questions:

- Can I narrow this subject area to a manageable size?
- Do I have sufficient information on the subject?
- Can I adapt the subject to my reader?

If the answer to each of these three questions is yes, the prospect of a successful paper lies before you.

Let's explore how to answer the first of these three questions.

A2. Narrowing the Subject

First you need to know whether you can narrow the potential subject. Here is how that process works if the assigned topic is broad or if you select your own topic.

Suppose one area of interest that occurs to you is the job you had last summer. Suppose further that the job was at a fast-food franchise, say a Burger King. At first blush that job may not seem like fertile territory for a paper topic. But don't dismiss it too quickly. Give some thought to whether your job experiences can provide a focused topic after all.

For many people the most natural way to look at a subject is the chronological way. In other words, they see an experience just as they would a story, proceeding from beginning to end. Look at your time on the job in this chronological way. If you examine it closely, many small topics might emerge: (1) "how and why I was hired," (2) "my first day on the job," (3) "the up times and down times during the summer," or (4) "when and how I left the job." Doubtless the list could be longer.

But the chronological approach is far from the only way to look at an experience. Instead of considering the job according to a time frame, first day to last day, you could analyze a slice of it. For example you could ask yourself some questions about what you saw and did on any *typical* day. Then you might get several quite different topics: (1) "my duties on the job," (2) "rush periods versus slack periods," (3) "best and worst parts of the job," (4) "the amount of money a franchise makes each day," (5) "people I worked with," (6) "my pay and how I spent it."

If you think about the job still further, you will probably find that you also had opinions about it. Sometimes these opinions were about personal issues, but sometimes they

> *Some of my best [ideas] have come to me at the kitchen sink.*
> —*Agatha Christie*

were about larger public ones: (1) "the food we eat at such places is good (bad) and inexpensive (overpriced)"; (2) "Americans spend too much money on convenience foods" (or "convenience foods make possible an easier, better life for all of us").

Please notice two things about this analysis of topics derived from a job experience. First, these topics lend themselves to a wide variety of types of papers. If your instructor requires a personal experience paper, for example, you could use "how I was hired," "my first day on the job," or "the rush period." If an expository paper is needed—that is, one that explains something—then "my duties" or "the money a franchise makes" or "types of customers" would be eligible. If the paper should be argumentative, either "the food is good (bad)" or "the value of convenience foods" would do quite well; both could be framed as statements about which people can legitimately differ.

These last topics are also a reminder that a paper topic need not show its origin in personal experiences. You could write about Americans spending too much on convenience foods without ever once mentioning that you had worked at Burger King. Similarly, you could write an expository paper on "how people get jobs" without discussing the particular job-hunting experiences that led you to your conclusions.

The second thing to notice about this analysis is that so far we have moved down only one level of generalization, from your job in general to particular aspects of that job. Sometimes, however, you will have to move down more than one level. Suppose what had first occurred to you was not "my job at Burger King" but rather "the crazy jobs I've had."

Then you would have had to restrict the subject from jobs in general to the Burger King job in particular, then maybe to "the good things about my job," and perhaps finally to a still more specific topic, such as "the best thing about my job." We might diagram your thinking like this:

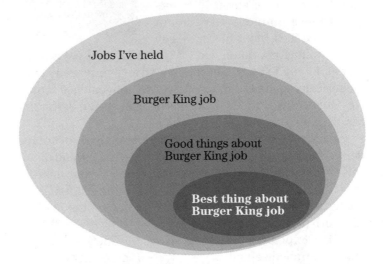

Jobs I've held

Burger King job

Good things about Burger King job

Best thing about Burger King job

Thus you would have moved from the general to the more specific. Please note, however, that before you begin writing you will still need to connect this specific topic *area* into a thesis *statement* (see page 365).

The clue to choosing a good topic therefore lies in a simple bit of advice: You should say a lot about a small subject area rather than a little about a large subject area. For nine papers out of ten, this advice is applicable and extremely important. In fact, the principle behind the advice is so important that it could almost be elevated to the status of a rule worth memorizing: *A lot about a little is better than a little about a lot.*

Why is this so? The reason is the same one that governs the writing of paragraphs: the need for sharp focus. You might recall the analogy of the binoculars in Chapter 4, how we have to adjust the focus knob precisely before we can get a clear view. We said that a paragraph must also have a sharp, precise focus before it can be clear to a reader. The same thing holds true for papers and essays.

Let's change the analogy somewhat. Have you ever had the experience of comparing a beautiful scene and a photograph of that same scene? The photograph will show all the familiar details, but there is much the camera has not captured. Important qualities, like breadth and depth and the sheer splendor of it all, are somehow diminished or lost. The picture is *of* the scene but is *less* than the scene. Conversely, you can look at a close-up picture of a person or an object and see things that you never observed in "real life." The camera holds up for your attention details you could have seen but didn't. In these cases the picture is *of* the scene and *greater* than the scene.

Writers are like cameras. When they try to offer a huge, panoramic view of a subject, they often fail. The subject is so much more than the few details that can be offered about it that the subject dwarfs the treatment. But when a writer examines a small part of the subject closely, in great detail, the close-up reveals what we readers might have thought or seen but did not, and we react with both surprise and gratitude.

EXERCISES

1. The list that follows contains experiences almost everybody has had or situations most people have encountered. Choose five of them; then, for each one, arrive at four separate topics: one narrative topic (telling a story), one descriptive topic (describing a person, a place, or an object), one expository topic (explaining something), and one argumentative topic (defending a position on an issue about which people can differ).

   A. First day in secondary school
   B. A job
   C. A crowd of which you were a part
   D. Travel—short or long trip
   E. Separation from a friend
   F. Love—familial or otherwise
   G. Choosing a college
   H. A conflict with authority

2. Narrow each of these topics to a scope suitable for a three-page paper:

A. Recent political scandals
B. The advantages of family life
C. U.S. policy toward Iraq
D. Portrayal of children on TV programs
E. Dating patterns in high school

3. Either in a group or by yourself, brainstorm the following topic areas. When you have finished, determine what kind of paper topic might emerge.

A. divorce
B. *Nightline*
C. cocaine addiction
D. Hawaii
E. hip-hop music
F. physical fitness

G. basketball
H. Alzheimer's disease
I. democracy
J. surrogate mothers
K. new SATs
L. AIDS research

4. Keep a writer's journal for three weeks. Faithfully record every idea, every experience, that seems remotely relevant. Fill at least a couple of pages every day. How can you use the journal for paper topics?

B. CRITICAL THINKING

Suppose now that you have found or been given a topic and that you have been able to answer yes to the question of whether the subject area can be narrowed to a manageable size. A second question asks you to find out how you can have something worthwhile to say about the topic.

The way to explore, to think through, your topic is to engage in the kinds of mental activities that go under the general term of **critical thinking.**

Critical thinking is a very broad term that includes all the mental processes aimed at solving problems. So it includes the systematic questioning and the problem-solving techniques discussed in the next section, but it can also include, for example, the daydreams, musings, and stream-of-consciousness free writings discussed in the previous section

There are two ways to slide easily through life: to believe everything or to doubt everything; both ways save us from thinking.
—*Alfred Korzybski*

when they are purposeful activities. Critical thinking also includes the evaluative and analytic thinking that characterize the argumentative writing we will discuss in the next chapter. In fact, I think you can see that the ability to think critically on a wide variety of topics might be said to define what a college education is all about!

For our purposes, critical thinking will mean to assess the amount of information about the topic you have or must acquire, analyze the nature of that information, ask questions about the topic in ways that yield the kind of material you will need for writing your paper, and think carefully about the needs of your potential readers.

B1. Assessing Your Information

The very process of narrowing a topic also makes you aware of what you know and don't know about it. When you examine a subject chronologically, analyze its constituent parts, or sort out your opinions about the public policy issues it raises, you are thinking critically about the topic and simultaneously reminding yourself of what you might know (e.g., a typical work day at Burger King) and what you might not know (e.g., how much money Americans spend on fast food).

Most of the time the answer is going to be yes, you do have enough information to enable you to say something interesting about a topic. The fact that you have chosen a topic means that it interests you; interest in turn stems from experience and therefore knowledge. This is especially true if the topic is a narrative or descriptive one. Your own life history affords all the "data" you need for writing the paper. When you have decided on topics such as "my first day on the job" or "those frantic rush hours," you know already that your own experiences can give you all the information you need.

Sometimes, however, you will decide you don't really have enough information on a particular topic. For example, suppose the topic that oc-

> *Nothing will sustain you more potently than the power to recognize in your humdrum routine, as perhaps it may be thought, the true poetry of life.*
> *—Sir William Osler*

curs to you is "the profits of a Burger King franchise." If you never saw daily tallies of receipts or annual financial statements, you probably do not have enough data to write about this topic. If you saw the receipts for only a few days, those data won't help much unless you know whether the days were good, bad, or average. Furthermore, before you start writing, you probably ought to know something about operating costs and about the relative size of this franchise compared to others. If there is no way to get the needed information, you should drop the subject and work on something else.

However, if the information can be found, you needn't abandon the topic. After all, writing about a subject offers an excellent chance to learn something new. Maybe you can get the information easily, perhaps by checking some books or notes that are nearby, perhaps by conducting interviews or by making a phone call or two; then the topic might still be a good one. Notice the word *easily*. For a short paper you are not usually expected to go beyond the resources readily available to you.

Another possibility: You know the information exists, but getting it will require extensive work in the library or at the computer searching the Internet. Such a topic might be perfect for a longer library/research paper. Chapter 12 will discuss this kind of paper in detail.

Perhaps you are not sure at first just how much information about a subject you really do possess, or perhaps you need to think through a subject more carefully before you begin to write. Then you may find it valuable to engage in **systematic questioning.** Questions can be useful ways of finding out about a subject.

For instance, if the possible topic is "a typical Burger King franchise" (using our earlier example), here are some questions you might ask:

- What does a Burger King franchise look like from the outside?
- How is the interior arranged, and why is this arrangement used?

- How many employees does a typical franchise have, and how much are they paid?
- What types of jobs do these employees perform? What kinds of foods are served, at what prices?
- What is the quality of the food, and how does it vary?
- What kinds of customers does a typical franchise attract?

By asking questions such as these, you avoid the time-wasting habit of thinking aimlessly about a subject. Instead you have set up a systematic method of inquiry. As a result of applying that method, you will know whether or not you have sufficient information for a paper, and—presuming the information is enough—you will have pinned down the material that can go into the paper when you write it.

Sometimes you can use questions that help you view a potential subject as a problem. Looking at the subject as a problem enables you to think about it in a systematic way, just as you would any other problem, whether it be fixing your car or mending a broken friendship. When you think about any problem, you go through at least the following four questions:

- Why is this problem really a problem?
- What are the possible solutions to the problem?
- What goals must be met by any possible solution to the problem?
- Given the goals, what is the best solution?

Suppose your Burger King experience suggests a topic such as "Americans spend too much money on convenience foods." If you view this proposed topic as a problem, your thinking might go like this:

- Why is spending money on convenience foods a problem? (Immediately you would think of several reasons: the large amount of money spent each year, the poor nutritional value of many fast foods, the waste of resources that could be devoted to other purposes, the assault on America's taste buds, the decline of cooking skills . . .)
- What possible solutions are there? (These would range from such severe measures as outlawing convenience

foods to milder steps such as educating the public, perhaps through the schools.)
- What goals must be met by any possible solution? (Clearly,
any solution must be simple, practical, respectful of liberty, and—above all—effective.)
- What is the best solution? (Perhaps you will call for an
advertising campaign designed to acquaint the buying
public with the nutritional risks they incur and with the
enormous amount of money they waste.)

Once more, by using a set of questions, you will have gathered the available material and learned whether or not it is
enough to support a paper.

B2. Evaluating Your Information and Ideas

One of the hardest things for most people to do is think critically about their own thinking. But that's what a writer must
do if she or he is going to write persuasively on any topic.

If you reflect for a moment on the kinds of things you are
willing to say to others, I think you will agree that your
thoughts can be described several different ways, depending on the degree of certainty you have or wish to express.

For example, you can have a thought that might be called
a **feeling,** a **hunch,** or a **guess.** Thus, you might have a feeling ahead of time that you are going to do well on a certain
exam, even though the subject has always been difficult for
you. Or you might have a hunch that the underdog will pull
off a major upset in a sports event. Or you might guess that
it will rain soon, because the weather forecaster has said
there's a chance of showers and you can hear a rumble of
thunder in the distance.

Now suppose you are compelled to put some money behind your feeling, hunch, or guess. Most people will start
to feel anxious, because they know perfectly well that they
might do poorly on the exam, or that the favorite may indeed win, or that the distant rumble might pass and the
skies remain clear. In other words, the degree of certainty
for a feeling, hunch, or guess is low. (That does not, of
course, mean that people will not act—or bet money—on

their hunches, as racetrack and casino owners will happily attest.)

At the other extreme from the hunch is what we call a **fact.** Facts are statements that we all agree are true because we can test them. Thus, if I say that water boils at 100 degrees Celsius, or that the World Cup was held in Korea and Japan in 2002, or that the largest city in Great Britain is London, people will accept these as factual statements, either because they "know" them on their own or because they can easily verify them. Facts usually have empirical evidence to back them up. Scientific experiments support the claim about boiling water, for example. Media accounts and testimonies from firsthand experience confirm the timing and venues of the World Cup, while atlases and almanacs provide comparative population data for cities in Great Britain. I'm sure that somewhere out there you might find a person who would deny one or more of these facts, but all reasonable people would accept these as true statements, at least for the time they are made. (London, after all, was not always the biggest city in England.)

Facts have special value for a writer. Because they are agreed-upon or verifiable truths, they offer powerful support for the validity of a writer's opinions. If a fact is well known, you can be assured your reader will accept it. If the fact is well established but not well known, you need to point your readers toward the sources that will allow them to verify it. (But the trick, of course, is to make sure that a fact really is a fact. Read on . . .)

Between hunches and facts comes a wide area of thinking that we describe with words like *theory, opinion,* and *belief.* Each implies differences in the degree and kind of certainty.

Theories, for example, combine a number of facts and findings into an overall explanation of how these facts fit together, how the patterns observable in them can be accounted for. We are most familiar with this process in scientific reasoning, for example the way a higher lung cancer rate among smokers (fact) led researchers to the theory that smoking causes lung cancer. But we construct theories in every aspect of our daily life, even though we may not be conscious of it. Based on your observations of other students, you may have developed a theory, for instance, that instructors give better grades to students who smile a lot and who contribute in class. As a result, you may strive to smile and speak up more in class to see if you can get a better grade (testing your theory).

Opinions are statements about what seems to be true, what you judge is probably true. Thus, you can have opinions about politics ("Governor Smith is the best governor this state has ever had"), about areas of study ("history is a fascinating subject"), about sports figures ("Shaquille O'Neill is the best center playing the game today"), indeed just about every aspect of what it means to be human. You think that Smith is a great governor, but you know perfectly well that not everybody shares your opinion—that in the last election, for example, 45 percent of your fellow citizens did not share it. We are all quite free in expressing our opinions. Without them conversation would wither, not to mention talk shows on radio and television. But while we express these opinions freely, and while we may hold them fervently, we know that they are not agreed-upon statements in the same sense as statements about the boiling temperature of water.

Beliefs are statements that you are convinced are true, statements you feel you should act on. Beliefs are more general and more purposeful than opinions. Thus, you may have political beliefs, religious beliefs, or philosophical beliefs. You might even be prepared to lay down your life for a belief—as many people have done. Of course, people do not always act on their beliefs, even if they know they should. An example of the way an opinion and a belief can meet would be for someone to have a strong belief in the principles of the particular political party Smith belongs to and therefore to state an opinion about what a great governor Smith is. Acting upon that belief might include not only voting for Smith but volunteering to work in his reelection campaign.

How does an awareness of these differences help you think through your topic and then write a good paper?

First, you can come to understand what your reader will accept without needing any proof, what your reader will accept but only with adequate proof, and what your reader will quite possibly not accept at all unless your writing is unusually persuasive. Ask yourself, with regard to each idea you propose to offer in a paper, the following questions:

- Is this idea an agreed-upon and widely known fact? (If so, your reader will probably accept it easily.)
- Is this idea an agreed-upon fact but one known only to specialists? (If so, you can use it, but your reader will be persuaded only if you cite a reputable source for your information.)
- Is the idea one of your firmly held beliefs, something that motivates your actions? (No idea may be more important to write about, but recognize that not everybody shares your beliefs, and write accordingly.)
- Is the idea one of your opinions? (Again, you must recognize that others may not agree—which does not, of course, mean that you should avoid such ideas, only that you should let your reader know that you recognize the difference between an opinion and a fact.)
- Is the idea a hunch, a guess? (If so, label it that way.)

Thinking through the development of your topic in this way helps you become aware of where you will have to concentrate your persuasive energies. Also, nothing turns readers off more than a writer who seems not to be recognizing that his or her opinions are just that, not universally accepted truths.

Second, you can apply the same set of questions to material you read, even (especially?) material you read to give you ideas for your paper. Is this author giving sufficient and verifiable proof for the idea he or she is advancing? Is the author offering what is really an opinion but treating it as if it were a fact? How much of what the author says here is governed by the author's beliefs? What *are* those beliefs, as far as you can determine? How widely shared are the beliefs? How well does the author distinguish (perhaps implicitly) among beliefs, opinions, and facts? How well does the author defend his or her beliefs, opinions, and theories? You therefore become a more critical—that is to say, a more thoughtful and reflective—reader. The last thing you'd want to do is not notice that a writer has been treating as a fact what is really his or her opinion and then replicating that problem by importing the idea into your writing and treating the source as "proof" of your own opinion.

B3. Adapting to the Reader

And so we come to the last question: Can you adapt your subject so that it suits your reader? The ability to take into account your audience is an important writing skill.

Before you know whether the subject can be adapted, you must answer a more fundamental question: Who is your reader? Sometimes an instructor will provide this information when assigning the paper. "Address this paper to a classmate," or "Write the paper as if your reader is someone who knows nothing about your subject." In these cases you know who your reader is supposed to be. But if you have not been given such instructions, try to visualize a possible reader. Will it be a classmate? your instructor? a friend? When I say "visualize the reader," I mean just that. Picture him or her in your mind's eye. If your reader is a

category of people, such as "classmates" or "college instructors," take one particular person and let that person stand for all the other members of the category.

Then ask some questions about this reader. First, can you assume an interest in the topic, or must you *make* the reader interested?

Going back for a moment to the job at Burger King, some topics derived from that experience are easily adapted to any audience. Whether your reader will be a classmate or the instructor or a friend, you can assume first of all that the reader knows only a few surface details about your job.

(Some classmates may have had jobs similar to yours, but the majority have not.) As for the reader's interest, some topics have a ready appeal. Most people have eaten enough hamburgers at fast-food franchises to be interested in some "inside information" on how the food is prepared or on how an employee can ever manage to survive the pressures of rush hour.

But other topics have more limited appeal. The economics of a franchise might be an interesting subject for a business course, but it might not do as well in a freshman English course if it will require highly technical explanations. So you might have to rule that topic out, simply because, although it interests you, it cannot be adapted for your intended audience. (If you *can* adapt it, of course, so much the better.)

Still other topics will interest readers only if developed in certain ways. A paper on "my first day at the job" is not inherently exciting. To succeed, you must *make* it interesting. Perhaps you can do so by showing the funny things that happened, in which case the humor of your paper justifies its claim on your reader's time. Perhaps you will stress the terrors of that first day, and you can involve your reader in your plight by making him or her share your feelings—after all, you can count on your reader having gone through similar days at one time or another.

Then, too, it's not just a matter of what interests your reader: You also have to take into account what you think your reader probably *knows* and probably *believes*.

Now that you have defined and even pictured your potential reader, how much does this reader already know about the proposed topic? The differences here can be enormous. Think about these intended readers—about the possible range in their ages, about their educational level, about any specialized kinds of knowledge they may have, about any shared experiences. In other words, what knowledge can you presume and what must you be sure to explain? What will your reader have to have in order to make sense of what you are about to say? You want to give whatever information is necessary without insulting your reader's intelligence by presuming ignorance where none exists.

Also, what opinions and beliefs might your readers have that will color their response to your topic? Identify the potential range of political and religious beliefs, of ethical principles, of shared assumptions about personal and social life. Think, too, about the commonly held opinions in the group that you will be addressing. How likely are they to agree with you? What ideas will most likely be convincing to them, and how can those ideas be supported? What kind of change in your reader's opinions do you hope for, and how might you best achieve that goal? Reflect just as carefully on the beliefs and opinions you hold in common with your reader, so that in your paper you can capitalize on these shared convictions.

Just remember the one important question every reader asks: "Why should I read this?" First get an answer. Then keep both the reader and the answer in mind as you write the paper. That's part of the secret of powerful writing.

EXERCISES

1. How much information would you need before you could proceed on the following topics? How readily do you think that information can be obtained?

   A. The characteristics of a typical premed student
   B. Advertising revenue for college newspapers
   C. Grade inflation
   D. Discrimination against women in the restaurant industry
   E. The rise in single-parent families

2. Assume your reader is a classmate. What assumptions would you make about your reader's reaction to the following topics? How much interest is he or she likely to have? How much prior knowledge?

   A. Air pollution in your town or city
   B. The 1952 presidential election
   C. Factors influencing success in college courses
   D. The coal strike of 1978

E. Professors' salaries

F. Computer malfunctions as a cause of automobile engine stalling

G. Campus food services

H. The events of September 11, 2002

3. Now assume that your reader is the instructor of your course. Using the same topics as in the previous question, what changes in your assumptions are necessary? Are there any topics for which you would not have to change your assumptions?

4. Find a back issue of one or more of the following magazines: *Cosmopolitan, Reader's Digest, Field & Stream, Jet,* and *The American Scholar.* What assumptions about its readers does each magazine make? How do the advertisements bear out these assumptions?

5. Choose one of the following possible topics:

right-to-die legislation
Human Genome Project
2002 World Series
Ming dynasty

What facts do you know about this topic? What beliefs or opinions do you have? Any theories or hunches? Then how about potential readers—what might be *their* theories or *their* opinions; what facts might *they* possess?

10

The Writing Process: Planning the Paper

People have been thinking and talking about how to write for thousands of years. Back in the fourth century B.C. the philosopher Aristotle said that as far as he could tell, writing consisted of invention (deciding what to say), arrangement (deciding how to organize it), and style (deciding what words would best express it). Observe that of those three segments, two of them take place before the writer ever puts down a single word!

Your success as a writer therefore depends in no small measure on the ability to think through a topic before starting to write. Notice I didn't say think *about* the subject. Anyone can spin wheels for an hour: "Well what should I say ... nah, that's dumb ... but maybe I could ... still and all ... that's no good either." Such thinking gets you exactly nowhere. What I am talking about is the ability to think *productively*, so you know where to start. This chapter offers suggestions on how to make your "thinking time" bear fruit. Therefore, you could call it another aspect of prewriting.

Of course, writers use a variety of planning methods. Some writers like to plan everything in great detail ahead of time, then write quickly. Others like to have just a kernel idea to begin with; they do the rest of their thinking as they go along. Some writers use written outlines; others do not. This chapter will respect such differences in method. But no matter what method you use, *some* foresight, *some* planning is necessary.

In the previous chapter we discussed how you can find something to write about. Quite often, however, you will not have that problem, because your instructor will tell you what to write about. Some college writing assignments are very specific, such as this one from a political science course:

Write a paper of 2,500 words on the topic of why the term *interest group liberalism* is a better term for the phenomenon we used to call *pluralism*.

Others will simply describe in a more general way the kind of paper you are to write, like this one from an ROTC course:

Write on any aspect of national security that interests you.

And even if the subject has been left completely up to you and you have found a topic, you still need to know how to proceed with that topic.

In this chapter we will divide writing assignments into six major categories, requiring different approaches, or strategies. Five of these six categories, divisions of Part A, are each headed by a question about a specific writing assignment; for instance, "Does the assignment ask you to tell about something that happened?" Once you have answered yes to one of the five questions, you will know which category of writing assignment you are dealing with and you can proceed to the description of that specific category. For each type of assignment I have provided examples of topics taken from a variety of courses within the past several years; you can compare your own assignment to these to make sure you have the right category. Whether your instructor has given you a topic or you have chosen one yourself, you can use these five questions to formulate an approach to your assignment.

The sixth type of writing assignment, creating an effective and persuasive argument, has its own special requirements. Argumentative writing is the focus of Part B.

A. DEVELOPING YOUR TOPIC

Now that you have your topic, gathered the necessary information about it, thought it through critically, and assessed the audience for your paper, you can plan what you are about to write. Begin by asking yourself the following five questions about the topic. Whenever the answer to a question is "yes," consider the planning advice that follows.

A1. Does the Assignment Ask You to Tell About Something That Happened?

"Something that happened"—this phrase covers several possibilities. It can mean something that happened to you:

> Write a brief autobiography recounting the major steps in your mathematical education. [from a mathematics course]

> Tell about an experience that made a deep impression on you. [from a composition course]

> Describe a personal experience in which you encountered what you interpreted as prejudice. [from a psychology course]

It can also mean something that happened to people you know and even people you don't know. Most often this last group is made up of people who have participated in important events about which you have learned:

> Describe the sequence of actions taken by President John F. Kennedy during the Cuban Missile Crisis of 1962. [from a history course]

These topics require you to tell a story. For this reason, they are often called assignments in **narrative writing.** Please note that here narrative writing does not mean fiction, such as novels or short stories. Rather, the stories you are asked to tell are true stories, and you draw them from either your own experience or your knowledge of somebody else's experience. Your task is to convey the *significance* of the experience to your reader.

You know how some people tell a joke well? And how other people always blow the punchline or ruin the joke some other way? Think of someone you know who tells stories very well, and then think of the qualities that make for good storytelling. The good joketeller or storyteller has at least two important gifts: (1) a good memory, especially for significant details, and (2) a sense of timing, building the

> *Life is painting a picture,*
> *not doing a sum.*
> *—Oliver Wendell Holmes*

story up to its dramatic conclusion ("So then the cowboy goes up to his horse the third time and he says . . ."). These same two gifts, the use of detail and the timing that gives a story its "punch" or its "point," characterize the well-written narrative paper.

First you need **details.** If you are writing about yourself, a big hurdle is recognizing the fact that your experiences *can* be interesting to others, that people do want to hear about what has happened to you. But you will hold their attention only if you can re-create your experience for them. You must make them see, feel, and hear what you saw, felt, and heard. It is natural to fear that a detailed account of your experiences will be boring. Conquer that fear. Make your story come alive with sharp, vivid, familiar details.

We worry that a detailed story will tire readers. But in fact the easiest way to bore them is to give a very general story covering a lot of territory. That's why those "my summer vacation" papers in high school were so deadly. Instead you need to take a very few incidents in your life and develop them with significant details. Moreover you must weave the details into a story that will have meaning for your reader, so that he or she will know why that story should be told.

Here, for example, is the first paragraph of a narrative paper in which the writer tries to cover too much:

> It can be quite difficult to pinpoint one event in my life that could honestly be considered an insight. Since there are many events that determine one's moral values, a great many factors must be considered. Growing into an adult is one event. There are many changes you go through in order to reach maturity. Also friends help you develop into a social being and I have been very fortunate in this respect. Another element I can think of is job responsibility. Owning a car, as I have for the last three years, is another event in my life that has been quite important.

The paragraph is deadly dull. It attempts too much, it offers no concrete details, and it needs to be trimmed (notice the excess words and the cumbersome passive voice).

Here is the opening of that same narrative paper after the author limited it to a single experience that she wanted to create in detail:

> "Miss Tychanski, come up here!" The summons roused me from the fitful doze that usually overcame me during English class. Suddenly I felt the adrenaline flowing, and my face must have turned scarlet. Ms. Roberts was clearly angry, and as I approached her desk I could see her nostrils flaring, as if she was restraining herself only with great difficulty. I was about to undergo an experience that would drastically change my concept of what it means to be just or fair in this world.

Do you see how the second version absorbs our attention much more readily? It's the details that do it, along with the implied promise that the story will carry an important message.

Even when the story you are telling is about someone else, perhaps an important historical figure and his or her role in a major historical event (for example, President Kennedy and the Cuban Missile Crisis), details still play an important role. First, list all the details and incidents you can think of that apply to the story. Then consider the length of the assignment and choose the most significant details and incidents, leaving aside lesser ones you simply can't squeeze in. When you write the story, be as specific as you possibly can.

The ordering of events for a narrative paper is almost always very simple. The order is by *time*—this happened and then this and then this—chronological order. Good transitions between sentences and paragraphs (discussed in Chapter 4) make clear the cause-and-effect relationship between the events in the story. The reader sees not just how Event B happens *after* Event A, but how Event B happens *because of* Event A.

Even though the order of the paper is determined by the sequence of events you are describing, you still need to plan how to tell the story. Planning in this case means keeping in mind the second quality of a good storyteller: **timing.** Remember that a writer must build a story—give it punch even if it lacks a punchline.

To make sure that your story has good timing and builds to a conclusion, ask yourself, "What is the point of this story? Why am I telling it?"

Sometimes the reason will be obvious. If you tell about an incident that was especially funny, exciting, or dangerous, your reader will know why the story is important. In such cases you simply build the story so that the funniest or most exciting or most dangerous part occurs near the end, at a moment toward which the whole story has progressed.

Many other stories are not inherently funny or dramatic. Instead they are valuable because of what they can teach us about human life. As long as the story has a point—in other words, as long as it can have meaning for the reader as well as for you—it is worth telling. In writing such narratives you need to keep in mind the point—the meaning—of the story. The incidents and details should be selected and described in such a way as to lead the reader toward this central meaning. Yet a caution is necessary: let the events *suggest* the meaning. Don't bludgeon the reader with your "message." If the details of the story can't suggest the meaning by themselves, maybe you need a different story.

In summary, if you tell a story, here are some steps you can follow:

1. List as many details as possible, especially sensory details, the ones that can make the reader relive the experience with you.
2. Tell the story in chronological order, using as many of the details as possible.
3. Arrange the story so that it leads up to a natural conclusion or "point."
4. Let the story suggest its own meaning.

A2. Does the Assignment Ask You to Describe Something?

Many paper topics require you to describe something or someone, as in these two topics from composition courses:

Describe the ugliest or the most beautiful place you have ever seen.

Describe in detail someone you knew at your high school, whether classmate or teacher.

Assignments that require **descriptive writing,** as it is often called, can be found in other types of courses, too:

Describe seven pieces of art based on Greek and Roman mythology that can be found in the Art Institute of Chicago. After naming the title and the artist, tell in detail what the piece looks like and what mythological story it represents. [from a mythology course]

Observe a group of people waiting in line; write a two-page summary of what you see. [from a sociology course]

Select a communication event, such as a hospital emergency room or a courtroom trial. Observe the event for a minimum of one hour, and then give a detailed account of what you saw. [from a communication course]

The mere presence of such words as *describe* or *description* does not guarantee that the topic calls for descriptive writing. Sometimes these words are used together with other words to mean something else. For example:

Describe an ethnic community's linguistic, cultural, and social contributions to Buffalo, New York. [from a linguistics course]

Here the word *describe* is used as a synonym for *summarize.* If the assignment does not require you to go beyond what you receive from your five senses, if you are free simply to describe what your senses tell you, then the assignment is for descriptive writing. On the other hand, if you must rely on other data, or if you must analyze or interpret, then the assignment may include descriptive writing but belongs also to some other category (most probably extended definition or elaboration on a topic, discussed in Section A5 of this chapter).

The first need for a descriptive paper is a **plan.** When you describe something, you will provide lots of details about it, and those details must be organized in a sensible way.

Many kinds of plans are possible: You can describe an object, for example, by starting at the left side of it and working toward the right, by working from its top to its bottom, or by starting with its most important feature and then moving to features of lesser importance. The kind of plan is often not as important as the existence of a plan, because without one, your details will seem haphazard and confusing.

Plans for descriptive papers are really the same as plans for descriptive paragraphs. Do you remember the Joan Didion paragraph in Chapter 4 (page 141), where she drew our attention from the mountains to the seacoast town of Guaymas and then out into the bay, following the route of a traveler along Highway 15? Here is a longer description, also by Joan Didion. Observe how this time the author first views the subject from "higher up," from a greater distance, then comes in close to show us features typical of the landscape and the towns. The passage is taken from *Slouching Towards Bethlehem.*

Let us try out a few irrefutable statements, on subjects not open to interpretation. Although Sacramento is in many ways the least typical of the Valley towns, it is a Valley town, and must be viewed in that context. When you say "the Valley" in Los Angeles, most people assume that you mean the San Fernando Valley (some people in fact

By the work one knows the workman.
—La Fontaine

assume that you mean Warner Brothers), but make no mistake: we are talking not about the valley of the sound stages and the ranchettes but about the real Valley, the Central Valley, the fifty thousand square miles drained by the Sacramento and the San Joaquin Rivers and further irrigated by a complex network of sloughs, cutoffs, ditches, and the Delta-Mendota and Friant-Kern Canals. . . . The Valley road, U.S. 99, three hundred miles from Bakersfield to Sacramento, is a highway so straight that when one flies on the most direct pattern from Los Angeles to Sacramento one never loses sight of U.S. 99. The landscape it runs through never, to the untrained eye, varies. The Valley eye can discern the point where miles of cotton seedlings fade into miles of tomato seedlings, or where the great corporation ranches—Kern County Land, what is left of DiGiorgio—give way to private operations (somewhere on the horizon, if the place is private, one sees a house and a stand of scrub oaks), but such distinctions are in the long view irrelevant. All day long, all that moves is the sun, and the big Rainbird sprinklers.

Every so often along 99 between Bakersfield and Sacramento there is a town: Delano, Tulare, Fresno, Madera, Merced, Modesto, Stockton. Some of these towns are pretty big now, but they are all the same at heart, one- and two- and three-story buildings artlessly arranged, so that what appears to be the good dress shop stands beside a W. T. Grant store, so that the big Bank of America faces a Mexican movie house. *Dos Peliculas, Bingo Bingo Bingo.* Beyond the downtown (pronounced *down*town, with the Okie accent that now pervades Valley speech patterns) lie blocks of old frame houses—paint peeling, sidewalks cracking, their occasional leaded amber windows overlooking a Foster's Freeze or a five-minute car wash or a State Farm Insurance office; beyond those spread the shopping centers and the miles of tract houses, pastel with redwood siding, the unmistakable signs of cheap building already blossoming on those houses which have survived the first rain. To a stranger driving 99 in an air-conditioned car (he would be on business, I suppose, any stranger driving 99, for 99 would never get a tourist to Big Sur or San Simeon, never get him to the California

he came to see), these towns must seem so flat, so impoverished, as to drain the imagination. They hint at evenings
spent hanging around gas stations, and suicide pacts sealed
in drive-ins.

The second key item in a good description is the use of
abundant details. In the preceding selection, notice how
many details are worked into the description. Ms. Didion
did not simply tell us there were occasional towns, she
named them. She did not simply tell us the Sacramento Valley was flat. Instead she tried to make us *feel* how flat it
was: We see the arrow-straight highway, the unvarying landscape, the peeling paint in the impoverished towns.

The Didion passage gives us many carefully chosen details, included because the writer wants to give us a specific impression. Good writers never include details just for
their own sake. Often they select ones that will help them
create a **dominant impression.** A landscape, a building, a
room, even a person, will have one characteristic that is more
striking than the others. A writer will fasten on this characteristic as a focusing point for his or her description. Ms.
Didion chooses words that give the impression of monotony,
both in the landscape and in the lives of the people who
inhabit it. This same principle applies to descriptive assignments such as the ones given earlier for courses in mythology, sociology, and communication. For the works in the
art museum, the people waiting in line, or the courtroom
trial, what dominant impression could a writer choose as
the focus for his or her description?

By the way, as writers we tend to think first of visual details, or what we have seen. Yet we have five senses, not
just one. Are there ways to include in your description what
you have *touched, smelled, heard, tasted?* The following
sentence by Norman Mailer, about the city of Chicago, includes all five senses:

> A great city, a strong city *with faces tough as leather hide
> and pavement* [touch], it was also a city with faces where
> the faces took on the broad beastiness of *ears which were
> dull enough to ignore the bleatings* [sound] of the doomed,

noses battered enough to smell no more the stench [smell]
of every unhappy end, *mouths*—fat mouths or slit mouths—
ready to taste the gravies [taste] which were the reward of
every massacre, and eyes, simple pig eyes, *which could look
the pig truth in the face* [sight]. [italics added]

Admittedly that sentence is unusual, but it points up the kind
of sensory awareness that makes for good description.

The last important item in a good description is a **fresh
choice of words.** Think about these words from the Didion
passage: *ranchettes, sloughs, seedlings, scrub oaks, leaded,
amber, tract, blossoming, drain.* Or these from the Mailer
sentence: *beastiness, bleatings, stench, slit, gravies, massacre.* Do you know the meaning of most of these words?
Would you have thought of using them in an essay? Most
people would answer yes to the first question, but no to the
second. In other words, good description requires not so
much that you learn new words—although new words can
help—as that you use more of the words you already know.
(Chapter 1 can offer guidance here.)

A3. Does the Assignment Ask You to Explain the Cause of Something?

Research is usually just another name for exploring *how*
and *why* questions. How does monetary policy influence
the business cycle? Why do these chemicals react this way?
Why does this poem affect us the way it does? Whether carried on in the academic world or in some other community,
research is basically an attempt to find out the cause of
things. Therefore it should come as no surprise that many
college writing assignments are directed toward finding
causes. Some examples:

Write a paper of five to ten pages explaining the reasons for
the recent population explosion in nonindustrial nations.
[from an anthropology course]

Write an original paper of approximately five pages double-
spaced in which you explain the cause of a chemical phenomenon not discussed in class. [from a chemistry class]

Sinclair Lewis says that Babbitt leads a life of "barren hearti-
ness"; write a short (two- to three-page) paper explaining
how Lewis could arrive at that judgment of Babbitt. [from a
literature course]

Cause-and-effect relationships can be very simple: You
flip the switch, a light fails to turn on, and you find that the
cause of this failure is a burned-out bulb. These relationships can also be very complex. What caused the Persian
Gulf War? Dozens of possibilities come to mind, such as
American need for oil, Iraqi aggression toward Kuwait, Arab-
Israeli tensions, George Bush's pride, Saddam Hussein's
pride—the list could go on and on, and all the entries on the
list could be plausible.

If your assignment is to write a paper involving **cause and
effect,** three steps should be part of your planning. First,
determine the **emphasis** of the paper, especially whether
the emphasis is on causes or on effects. The above three
topics for college papers all emphasize finding causes: the
cause of the population explosion, of a chemical phenomenon, or of a judgment. But some topics, particularly in the
natural sciences and the social sciences, emphasize effects:

Trace culture's effect on maturation. [from a psychology
course]

Lab report: three to five pages, reporting the effects observed
from performing the experiment on p. 171. [from a physics
course]

The point is that in most cases you will be given causes
and asked to find effects, or else you will be given effects
and asked to find causes. Be sure to know in which direction you are supposed to move.

Then it's time to do some **listing**—listing the causes or
listing the effects, as the case may be. Put down as many as
you can think of—prune them later if you must. If you are
listing the results from lab or field experiments, be sure you
include all the results, not just some of them.

The last step before you write is **evaluation.** If you are
writing about causes, examine each possible cause care-

fully—in other words, subject it to still more critical thinking. Ask some questions. Is the cause very close in time to its effect? If so, is there another cause, still fur-

> *Find out the cause of this effect,*
> *Or rather say, the cause of this defect,*
> *For this effect defective comes by cause.*
> —*William Shakespeare*

ther back in time, that is equally responsible? *More* responsible? (That burned-out bulb is the immediate cause of the light failing to go on. But the causal relationship may not be as simple as it first appears: After all, the bulb burns out after 750 hours of use because the manufacturer built it that way, and the manufacturer in turn built it that way because the American economy depends on planned deterioration.) Just because one event occurs before another, is the first necessarily the cause of the second? (Israel and certain Arab countries experienced tensions for a long time before 1991, but does that mean the Gulf War broke out *because* of their tensions?)

More questions. Is a cause sufficient by itself to explain the effect or is it only one among several others? (Saddam Hussein's pride might have contributed to the war in the Gulf, but it was certainly not the only factor.) Must this cause be present before the effect can take place, or could other causes produce the same result? ("American need for oil" gives a partial explanation for our interest in the Gulf region, but the Japanese also had that interest and did not involve themselves so directly.)

Answering these questions forces you to be careful and precise in writing about the causes you have listed. And by reversing the direction of the questions, you can learn to be just as precise when your task is to write about effects.

Consider the following passage from Alvin Toffler's *Future Shock:*

> The culture shock phenomenon accounts for much of the bewilderment, frustration, and disorientation that plagues Americans in their dealings with other societies. It causes a breakdown in communication, a misreading of reality, an inability to cope. Yet culture shock is relatively mild in comparison with the much more serious malady, future shock.

Future shock is the dizzying disorientation brought on by the premature arrival of the future. It may well be the most important disease of tomorrow.

Future shock will not be found in *Index Medicus* or in any listing of psychological abnormalities. Yet, unless intelligent steps are taken to combat it, millions of human beings will find themselves increasingly disoriented, progressively incompetent to deal rationally with their environments. The malaise, mass neurosis, irrationality, and free-floating violence already apparent in contemporary life are merely a foretaste of what may lie ahead unless we come to understand and treat this disease.

Future shock is a time phenomenon, a product of the greatly accelerated rate of change in society. It arises from the superimposition of a new culture on an old one. It is culture shock in one's own society. But its impact is far worse. . . . Most travelers have the comforting knowledge that the culture they left behind will be there to return to. The victim of future shock does not.

Take an individual out of his own culture and set him down suddenly in an environment sharply different from his own, with a different set of cues to react to—different conceptions of time, space, work, love, religion, sex, and everything else—then cut him off from any hope of retreat to a more familiar social landscape, and the dislocation he suffers is doubly severe. Moreover, if this new culture is itself in constant turmoil, and if—worse yet—its values are incessantly changing, the sense of disorientation will be still further intensified. Given few clues as to what kind of behavior is rational under the radically new circumstances, the victim may well become a hazard to himself and others.

Now imagine not merely an individual but an entire society, an entire generation—including its weakest, least intelligent, and most irrational members—suddenly transported into this new world. The result is mass disorientation, future shock on a grand scale.

This is the prospect that man now faces. Change is avalanching upon our heads and most people are grotesquely unprepared to cope with it.

Do you see how Toffler's emphasis is on the *effects* of the two causes he has named (culture shock and future shock)? Do you see the implicit list of these effects? (The list starts with "bewilderment, frustration, and disorientation"; you should have no trouble continuing it from there.) And do you see the careful weighing of relationships in sentences like the third one, which says that future shock is a "much more serious malady" than culture shock?

A4. Does the Assignment Ask You to Compare or Contrast?

"Comparisons are odious," goes the old saying. But without them we would be handicapped in making our ideas clear to others. In fact, the ability to see resemblances and differences is so important a sign of intellectual maturity that many college writing assignments require you to make use of it. Here are some examples:

> Compare the political process of Great Britain with the political process of France. [from a political science course]

> Give your intelligent reaction to one of the books on the following list by comparing it to the book you reported on earlier in the semester. [from a sociology course]

> Compare the Lamarckian and Darwinian theories of evolution. [from a natural science course]

> Compare the concepts of justice in Scott's *Heart of Midlothian* and Dickens's *Bleak House*. [from a literature course]

Technically, to **compare and contrast** means to *find similarities and differences*. But in practice, as the four preceding examples show, the word *compare* by itself has come to mean finding both; the word *contrast* by itself means to find differences only.

So what makes for a successful comparison? The first step is again a simple **listing.** Put down all the similarities you can detect, then all the

No comparison, no judgment.
—Edmund Burke

differences. (Only the second kind of list is necessary if your task is to contrast.) Be thorough; make the list as complete as possible.

Your next step is to establish a **ranking.** Granted that Item A and Item B can be compared in fifteen ways, but which ways are more important and which less? You will fare better if you take the most important points of comparison and describe them in detail. Irrelevant or trivial points only distract the reader and waste the space you could be devoting to more productive discussion. For example, if you are contrasting two-year and four-year colleges, you may want to stress the fact that technical courses such as auto mechanics are often taught at the former but seldom at the latter. On the other hand, the fact that your cousin Alfred liked his two-year college but did not like his four-year college most probably does not merit your reader's attention.

The final step is determining a **pattern.** Suppose your contrast of community colleges and four-year colleges results in a list of four important differences—size, cost, curriculum, and faculty—so you will contrast them using these four criteria. One pattern would involve proceeding first through the two-year colleges and then through the four-year colleges, like this:

    I. Two-year colleges
      A. size
      B. cost
      C. curriculum
      D. faculty
    II. Four-year colleges
      A. size
      B. cost
      C. curriculum
      D. faculty

Alternatively, you could go through each basis of contrast, item by item, looking first at the two-year college and then immediately contrasting it with the four-year college. Your pattern would look like this:

I. Size
  A. two-year colleges
  B. four-year colleges
II. Cost
  A. two-year colleges
  B. four-year colleges
III. Curriculum
  A. two-year colleges
  B. four-year colleges
IV. Faculty
  A. two-year colleges
  B. four-year colleges

Item-by-item patterns like this one usually allow for more specific, more detailed comparisons. Simpler subjects might suit the first pattern more easily, especially since that pattern enables you to avoid the danger of the "ping-pong" effect, one of the risks of an item by item pattern. The important point is that you must have a pattern, because it organizes your comparison or contrast and makes it easier for your reader to follow your thinking. Remember that your reader will want to know the significance you are giving to the similarities and differences you describe.

Consider the following paragraphs by Bruce Catton from "Grant and Lee: A Study in Contrasts" as an example of good comparison-contrast writing:

> Back of Robert E. Lee was the notion that the old aristocratic concept might somehow survive and be dominant in American life.
>
> Lee was tidewater Virginia, and in his background were family, culture, and tradition . . . the age of chivalry transplanted to a New World which was making its own legends and its own myths. He embodied a way of life that had come down through the age of knighthood and the English country squire. America was a land that was beginning all over again, dedicated to nothing much more complicated than the rather hazy belief that all men had equal rights and should have an equal chance in the world. In such a land Lee stood for the feeling that it was somehow of advantage to human

society to have a pronounced inequality in the social structure. There should be a leisure class, backed by ownership of land; in turn, society itself should be keyed to the land as the chief source of wealth and influence. It would bring forth (according to this ideal) a class of men with a strong sense of obligation to the community; men who lived not to gain advantage for themselves, but to meet the solemn obligations which had been laid on them by the very fact that they were privileged. From them the country would get its leadership; to them it could look for the higher values—of thought, of conduct, of personal deportment—to give it strength and virtue.

Lee embodied the noblest elements of this aristocratic ideal. Through him, the landed nobility justified itself. For four years, the Southern states had fought a desperate war to uphold the ideals for which Lee stood. In the end, it almost seemed as if the Confederacy fought for Lee; as if he himself was the Confederacy . . . the best thing that the way of life for which the Confederacy stood could ever have to offer. He had passed into legend before Appomattox. Thousands of tired, underfed, poorly clothed Confederate soldiers, long since past the simple enthusiasm of the early days of the struggle, somehow considered Lee the symbol of everything for which they had been willing to die. But they could not quite put this feeling into words. If the Lost Cause, sanctified by so much heroism and so many deaths, had a living justification, its justification was General Lee.

Grant, the son of a tanner on the Western frontier, was everything Lee was not. He had come up the hard way and embodied nothing in particular except the eternal toughness and sinewy fiber of the men who grew up beyond the mountains. He was one of a body of men who owed reverence and obeisance to no one, who were self-reliant to a fault, who cared hardly anything for the past but who had a sharp eye for the future.

These frontier men were the precise opposites of the tidewater aristocrats. Back of them, in the great surge that had taken people over the Alleghenies and into the opening Western country, there was a deep, implicit dissatisfaction with a past that had settled into grooves. They stood for democracy, not from any reasoned conclusion about the proper ordering of human society, but simply because they had grown up in the middle of democracy and knew how it worked. Their society might have privileges, but they would be privileges each man had won for himself. Forms and patterns meant nothing. No man was born to anything, except perhaps to a chance to show how far he could rise. Life was competition. . . .

So Grant and Lee were in complete contrast, representing two diametrically opposed elements in American life. Grant was the modern man emerging; beyond him, ready to come on the stage, was the great age of steel and machinery, of crowded cities and a restless, burgeoning vitality. Lee might have ridden down from the old age of chivalry, lance in hand, silken banner fluttering over his head. Each man was the perfect champion of his cause, drawing both his strengths and his weaknesses from the people he led.

Yet it was not all contrast, after all. Different as they were—in background, in personality, in underlying aspiration—these two great soldiers had much in common. Under everything else, they were marvelous fighters. Furthermore, their fighting qualities were really very much alike.

Each man had, to begin with, the great virtue of utter tenacity and fidelity. Grant fought his way down the Mississippi Valley in spite of acute personal discouragement and profound military handicaps. Lee hung on in the trenches at Petersburg after hope itself had died. In each man there was an indomitable quality . . . the born fighter's refusal to give up as long as he can still remain on his feet and lift his two fists.

Daring and resourcefulness they had, too; the ability to think faster and move faster than the enemy. These were the qualities which gave Lee the dazzling campaigns of Second Manassas and Chancellorsville and won Vicksburg for Grant.

Do you see the pattern behind this comparison and contrast? Chart it on a piece of paper. If you can see how Catton arranged his discussion, you have before you a good model for writing this kind of essay.

A5. Does the Assignment Require an Extended Definition or Elaboration on a Particular Topic?

The four types of papers explained so far all have certain words or phrases that help you recognize them, such as *tell the story, describe, explain the causes, compare.* But quite often you are not asked to analyze the topic in so specific a way. Instead the topic is simply named, and you are expected to **elaborate** on it: i.e., to say more about it, to explain it, to analyze it, to develop it. This type of writing assignment is more common than any other.

Some assignments require you to elaborate on the meaning of a particular term. This is called an **extended definition.** Here are some examples:

Define justice. [from a philosophy course]

Write an extended definition of one of the following: ripoff, X-rated, funky. [from a composition course]

Explain Augustine's concept of God. [from a religion course]

Other assignments ask you to explain the most important ideas in a particular book (the familiar **book report**). Some books on which students have been asked to report recently include the following:

Allan Bloom's *The Closing of the American Mind* [from an education course]

Viktor Frankl's *Man's Search for Meaning* [from an anthropology course]

Suzanne Langer's *Philosophy in a New Key* [from a philosophy course]

C. Wright Mills's *The Power Elite* [from a political science course]

Michael Arbib's *Computers and the Cybernetic Society* [from a mathematics course]

Fritjof Capra's *The Tao of Physics* [from a physics course]

Vine Deloria Jr.'s *Custer Died for Your Sins* [from a history course]

Paula Giddings's *When and Where I Enter* [from an Afro-American studies course]

Most commonly, the topic for the paper is simply stated by itself:

Courtly love in medieval Spanish literature [from a Spanish course]

Policing and personal liberty after September 11 [from a criminal justice course]

Zen and the art of math learning [from a mathematics course]

The Enron accounting scandal [from a business course]

Principal aims and characteristics of *The Acts of the Apostles* [from a religion course]

Campaign finance reform [from a government course]

Concepts of honor in Renaissance drama [from a literature course]

Brief history of ichthyology [from a biology course]

These last topics, depending on the length required and on their relative difficulty, might also be appropriate for the library research paper (see Chapter 11). For the time being, as long as we assume that any research needed for them is easily accomplished, we can treat them as short papers.

To write papers on these topics, first be sure you can **define terms.** You cannot write about courtly love in medieval Spanish literature until you are fully certain what *courtly love* means. If you are discoursing on policing and personal liberty, what do you mean by *policing?* (For example, if the National Guard stands guard at an airport, is such activity an example of policing or not?) An assignment that asks you to relate Zen and math learning obviously means more by Zen than simply the doctrines of a particular Eastern religion; instead Zen should be taken in a wider sense, one that includes a whole complex set of attitudes toward who we are and how we live and think.

> *If you're not able to
> communicate successfully
> between yourself and
> yourself, how are you
> supposed to make it with
> strangers outside?*
> —*Jules Feiffer*

Not every paper will require a defini-tion of terms. An essay on the Enron ac-counting scandal, for example, might not need such an exercise. (Then again it might—what exactly is the "scandal" anyway?) And even if you do have to clarify some terms for yourself, you might not have to repeat those defini-tions explicitly in the paper, especially if you can be confi-dent your reader knows them. But the value of defining terms lies in the added understanding of the subject this process gives to you, the writer. Furthermore, you will be clued in to those situations where you must give an explicit defini-tion in the paper itself.

Next comes the stage in which you **gather information.** Most probably, as I said before, this process will not be very lengthy for a short paper. (Book reports are the obvious exception.) While you are brainstorming the topic or look-ing up information on it, be sure to take notes on what you discover. Jot down or record any relevant fact, no matter how trivial, because it is much easier to discard material than it is to remember what you have forgotten. If the infor-mation gathering gets too lengthy, or if you must use the library or the Internet or type the paper in a special form, turn to Chapter 11 for further guidance.

Then **select.** Not everything can be dumped into the pa-per just because you happen to know it. Consider the pre-scribed size of the paper and adjust your expectations to it. Remember that each page will contain only one or two fully developed paragraphs, on the average, and that no signifi-cant point should get anything less than one paragraph. So if you are writing a four-page paper on the Enron account-ing scandal and you expect to make eleven important points, you had better think again. Our rule, you will recall, is that a lot about a little is better than a little about a lot.

Respect for that same rule suggests the fourth step: **am-plify.** Now is the time to put to use those paragraph devel-opment skills we discussed in Chapter 5. Classify, compare, contrast, define. Above all, illustrate by examples. Never assume that just because your discussion is clear to you, it must therefore be clear to someone else. Be patient, cover the ground thoroughly, in detail, so that your understanding of the topic is conveyed as clearly and directly as possible to your reader. If you cannot make your point clearly, perhaps you do not understand the subject as well as you think you do!

The following very short essay by Bertrand Russell called "What Good Is Philosophy?" shows the virtues we have been discussing:

> If you wish to become a philosopher, you must try, as far as you can, to get rid of beliefs which depend solely upon the place and time of your education, and upon what your parents and schoolmasters told you. No one can do this completely, and no one can be a perfect philosopher, but up to a point we can all achieve it if we wish to.
>
> "But why should we wish to?" you may ask. There are several reasons. One of them is that irrational opinions have a great deal to do with war and other forms of violent strife. The only way in which a society can live for any length of time without violent strife is by establishing social justice, and social justice appears to each man to be injustice if he is persuaded that he is superior to his neighbors. Justice between classes is difficult where there is a class that believes itself to have a right to more than a proportionate share of power or wealth. Justice between nations is only possible through the power of neutrals, because each nation believes in its own superior excellence. Justice between creeds is even more difficult, since each creed is convinced that it has a monopoly of the truth of the most important of all subjects. It would be increasingly easier than it is to arrange disputes amicably and justly if the philosophic outlook were more widespread.
>
> A second reason for wishing to be philosophic is that mistaken beliefs do not, as a rule, enable you to realize good purposes. In the Middle Ages, when there was an epidemic of plague, people crowded into the churches to pray, thinking that their piety would move God to take pity on them; in

fact, the crowds in ill-ventilated buildings provided ideal conditions for the spread of the infection. If your means are to be adequate to your ends, you must have knowledge, not merely superstition or prejudice.

A third reason is that truth is better than falsehood. There is something ignominious in going about sustained by comfortable lies. The deceived husband is traditionally ludicrous, and there is something of the same laughable or pitiable quality about all happiness that depends upon being deceived or deluded.

You can see how Russell has defined a term (*social justice*), gathered his reasons and selected three of them (one to each paragraph), and then provided examples of each reason (e.g., sectarian strife, the medieval plagues, and deceived husbands).

EXERCISES

1. The following are topics that illustrate each of the five planning methods described in Part A. Use them as starting points for papers:

   A. narration:

      Write about an experience that revealed something heretofore unknown about a friend or a member of your family.

      Tell about an event whose significance became clear to you only after the event was over.

      Write a short essay describing a recent political event. Make sure the essay has a point.

      Give a brief history of your mathematical education to date.

   B. description:

      Describe your room in a way that enables us to learn something about who you are.

      Write a character sketch of someone you remember from your childhood.

      Describe the building that most typifies for you the college you attend.

Describe a statue, painting, or other art work you have encountered locally or while traveling.

C. cause and effect:

Why did you decide to attend college?

Why is violence so prevalent in the movies and on TV?

How do you account for the fact that almost half of the American people do not vote in national elections?

Describe the effects that have followed from the end of Soviet control over Eastern Europe.

D. comparison and contrast:

Compare two sports with which you are familiar.

Compare and contrast two of your college teachers in terms of their teaching styles.

Compare commuter students to resident students.

Contrast two political candidates who have stood for office in your area or in the country as a whole.

E. elaboration:

What does "equality of opportunity" mean?

Explain the biological process called cloning.

Summarize a book you have read recently in your major field and explain its significance for someone who wants to understand that field better.

Explain what calculus is to someone who has never had a course in it.

2. Examine the last few papers you have written. To which of the five categories does each belong? Or are any of them papers that defend an opinion or make an argument (see Part B)? Can you see any ways in which you could have improved those papers by following the planning methods described in this section?

3. Below you will find a variety of types of topics. Decide which of the five methods is best for each. How would

you go about planning papers on these topics? (Don't
be concerned if you don't have enough information to
actually write the paper.)

A. Describe an occasion when you made a deep personal com-
mitment to some future goal.
B. The Scopes "monkey" trial.
C. What similarities and differences do you see between the
Stalinist purge trials of the 1930s and the American "red
scare" of the late 1940s and early 1950s?
D. Define *cyberpunk*.
E. Summarize your moral philosophy. What do you think are
the causes for your holding that philosophy?
F. England and the rise of industrialism.

B. DEFENDING OPINIONS AND ARGUING ISSUES

You might be surprised to know that on the average almost
one-fifth of all your writing assignments in college will require you to defend a belief or conviction. This type of paper is most frequent in upper-division (junior and senior)
courses. Sometimes the issue will be defined for you; your
task is to choose one side of the issue and defend it:

Are humans aggressive due to nature or nurture? [from an
anthropology course]

Can prisons rehabilitate offenders? [from a criminal justice
course]

Select an environmental consequence of nuclear generating plants; make a value judgment about this consequence,
using any ethical framework you wish, so long as you *defend* your reasons for or against. [from an ecology course]

Should an antiabortion amendment be approved? [from a
political science course]

Other assignments will offer more latitude for you as a
writer, such as these two topics from philosophy courses:

Write an essay stating and defending your position on the
topic "what it is to be a human being."

Develop and defend your *own* position on any issue you choose (e.g., freedom) by considering reasonable objections to it of the type the authors of this course would make.

Some people make a distinction between **opinion papers,** in which you simply state what you think about a particular issue, and **argumentative papers,** in which you present both sides of an issue and then urge your reader to believe something or do something. In both cases, however, you are called upon to explain yourself and therefore you must be clear, logical, and persuasive. The factor that unites all the topics of this category is the freedom given to you to stake out your own position. Presumably the instructors who framed the topics listed previously did not care whether you chose nature or nurture, did not care whether you thought prisons could rehabilitate or not, did not care whether you thought human beings are apes or angels. They would grade you, not on whether you chose the "right" side, but rather on *how well you defended the side you chose.*

B1. Developing Your Defense

So the first thing you must do in writing this kind of paper is to decide what your opinion on the topic is and then **summarize your opinion,** if possible in a single sentence. (In most cases, you will already have an opinion based on your reading for the course or on class discussions; if not, you may need to read more, ask some questions.) In writing opinion papers, it is absolutely essential to clearly express your opinion in a sentence, called a *thesis sentence* (to be discussed further in the next chapter). After all, you cannot defend your thesis until you have stated it clearly and concisely.

Once you have written a possible thesis sentence—in other words, a one-sentence summary of your opinions—apply two tests to find out whether it is usable. First: Is the thesis sentence a question? If so, rule it out. No question can be a thesis sentence for an argumentative paper, because a question does not tell us your conclusion. Don't write: "Are humans aggressive by nature or nurture?" Instead write, "Humans are aggressive by nature, not nurture" (or vice versa). Second: Does the thesis sentence offer an opinion that everybody would agree with? If so, again rule it out. Opinion papers thrive on controversy. If no reasonable person could disagree with what you say, then no controversy exists and your paper is an example of one of the five earlier categories. For example, this thesis sentence is unacceptable: "The aggression in human nature is a troubling problem." Who could quarrel with that statement? But start naming causes, or start naming solutions, and you will have no difficulty finding a genuine controversy. Just ask yourself if the statement you have chosen to defend is one about which people of sound mind can differ.

Then you need to **define terms.** If you claim that people are aggressive by nature, what do you mean by *nature?* Do you mean just biological heredity—i.e., the genes received from one's parents? In that case I might be born aggressive and you might be born peaceable, simply because our parents have given us "bad" genes or "good" genes. Or do you take *nature* in a wider sense to include the biological inheritance everyone receives as a human being? In that case you might find some propensity for aggression in all of us, perhaps because we are descended from certain aggressive species of primates. The meaning you assign to the term *nature* will clearly affect the conclusions you reach. Furthermore you owe your reader the chance to decide whether he or she agrees with you without any confusion over what a word means.

Next you should decide whether to support your opinion by *inductive reasoning, deductive reasoning,* or *practical reasoning.* Each of these types of reasoning deserves more detailed discussion, so we consider them in the next section.

Now you are ready to **marshal the reasons for your opinion.** Put them down in order: 1-2-3-4. You may not want to itemize them quite so directly in the essay itself, but at the planning stage you will find it useful

> *Thinking is the activity I love best, and writing is simply thinking through my fingers.*
> —*Isaac Asimov*

to have such a list. The list will help you outline your paper, and it can also show weaknesses in your argument. (If you have only one reason for your opinion, and that reason is itself not very strong or convincing, maybe you had better give the matter more thought!)

Finally, take pains to **refute objections to your opinion.** I said earlier that you should be defending an opinion with which people of right mind can differ. Picture those reasonable opponents—in fact, make them your intended readers. Show them, patiently and respectfully, why you believe your opinion is more valid, or tenable, than theirs. Think of their most likely objections and respond as intelligently as you can to those objections.

This short essay by the conservative economist Milton Friedman, "Prohibition and Drugs," can serve as an example of these five steps:

> "The reign of tears is over. The slums will soon be only a memory. We will turn our prisons into factories and our jails into storehouses and corncribs. Men will walk upright now, women will smile, and the children will laugh. Hell will be forever for rent."
>
> This is how Billy Sunday, the noted evangelist and leading crusader against Demon Rum, greeted the onset of Prohibition in early 1920. We know now how tragically his hopes were doomed. New prisons and jails had to be built to house the criminals spawned by converting the drinking of spirits into a crime against the state. Prohibition undermined respect for the law, corrupted the minions of the law, created a decadent moral climate—but did not stop the consumption of alcohol.
>
> Despite this tragic object lesson, we seem bent on repeating precisely the same mistake in the handling of drugs.

On ethical grounds, do we have the right to use the machinery of government to prevent an individual from becoming an alcoholic or a drug addict? For children, almost everyone would answer at least a qualified yes. But for responsible adults, I, for one, would answer no. Reason with the potential addict, yes. Tell him the consequences, yes. Pray for and with him, yes. But I believe that we have no right to use force, directly or indirectly, to prevent a fellow man from committing suicide, let alone from drinking alcohol or taking drugs.

I readily grant that the ethical issue is difficult and that men of goodwill may well disagree. Fortunately, we need not resolve the ethical issue to agree on policy. *Prohibition is an attempted cure that makes matters worse—for both the addict and the rest of us.* Hence, even if you regard present policy toward drugs as ethically justified, considerations of expediency make that policy most unwise.

Consider first the addict. Legalizing drugs might increase the number of addicts, but it is not clear that it would. Forbidden fruit is attractive, particularly to the young. More important, many drug addicts are deliberately made by pushers, who give likely prospects their first few doses free. It pays the pusher to do so because, once hooked, the addict is a captive customer. If drugs were legally available, any possible profit from such inhumane activity would disappear, since the addict could buy from the cheapest source.

Whatever happens to the number of addicts, the individual addict would clearly be far better off if drugs were legal. Today, drugs are both incredibly expensive and highly uncertain in quality. Addicts are driven to associate with criminals to get the drugs, become criminals themselves to finance the habit, and risk constant danger of death and disease.

Consider next the rest of us. Here the situation is crystal clear. The harm to us from the addiction of others arises almost wholly from the fact that drugs are illegal. A recent committee of the American Bar Association estimated that addicts commit one-third to one-half of all street crime in the U.S. Legalize drugs, and street crime would drop automatically.

Moreover, addicts and pushers are not the only ones cor-
rupted. Immense sums are at stake. It is inevitable that some
relatively low-paid police and other government officials—
and some high-paid ones as well—will succumb to the temptation to pick up easy money.

Legalizing drugs would simultaneously reduce the amount
of crime and raise the quality of law enforcement. Can you
conceive of any other measure that would accomplish so
much to promote law and order?

But, you may say, must we accept defeat? Why not simply
end the drug traffic? That is where experience under Prohibition is most relevant. We cannot end the drug traffic. We
may be able to cut off opium from Turkey—but there are
innumerable other places where the opium poppy grows.
With French cooperation, we may be able to make Marseilles
an unhealthy place to manufacture heroin—but there are
innumerable other places where the simple manufacturing
operations involved can be carried out. So long as large sums
of money are involved—and they are bound to be if drugs
are illegal—it is literally hopeless to expect to end the traffic or even reduce seriously its scope.

In drugs, as in other areas, persuasion and examples are
likely to be far more effective than the use of force to shape
others in our image.

Notice how Friedman has taken sides on a controversial
issue (the prohibition of drugs), clarified the grounds upon
which he will argue (expediency, not ethics), itemized his
reasons (effect on us, effect on addict), and refuted his opponents (drug traffic cannot be ended). You may not agree
with his conclusion, but you cannot help but admire the
persuasiveness of his argument. Similarly, your instructors
may not agree with the conclusions you reach, but they will
reward papers in which you defend your opinions clearly
and intelligently.

B2. Using Inductive, Deductive, and Practical Reasoning

Part of the critical thinking necessary for defending an opinion or creating an argument involves deciding on the most

appropriate kind of reasoning process to use. In some ways the distinctions we are about to make are somewhat artificial: In the real world people defend their opinions as best they can with a mixture of all three kinds, and doubtless you will often find yourself doing so, too. But you can clarify your thinking and write more persuasively if you are aware of the options available to you and the special needs of each.

Inductive reasoning is the accumulation of examples that, taken together, suggest a conclusion. When you count automobiles on the highway and then conclude that 40 percent of them are of foreign manufacture, you are reasoning inductively—thousands of cars are the examples that allow you to state your conclusion. Inductive reasoning depends heavily on data, statistics, and observation of experiments, and as such it is often the preferred method for constructing scientific arguments.

If you are going to argue inductively, make sure you have gathered as many facts as you can to support your conclusion. The success of your paper will depend on how persuasive your evidence is. Ask yourself whether there are counterexamples that could weaken your argument. Make sure, too, that you don't exceed what the evidence will allow. If 51 percent of the people responding to a questionnaire answer a certain question one way, you might safely conclude that a majority of those responding hold a certain opinion. That does not mean that everybody holds it, or even that a "great" majority holds it. It does not even mean that a majority of all people agree with the 51 percent of those polled, unless you can show that the population answering the questionnaire is a representative sample of the population at large. Going back to the example of the cars of foreign manufacture, the percentage of such cars is higher on the east and west coasts of the United States and also higher in urban rather than rural areas; how representative of the country as a whole was the place where you gathered your data? Then, too, there's a definitional question again—is a Mitsubishi assembled in Illinois more "foreign" than a Ford assembled in Mexico?

Deductive reasoning, by contrast, begins with a principle and then shows conclusions that follow from that principle. When you begin with the principle that frustration leads to aggression, when you further observe that Nation A has been very frustrated recently, and when you then conclude that Nation A is likely to become aggressive, you are reasoning deductively.

If you are going to argue deductively, make sure that the general principles from which you reason are unassailable. There is little profit in claiming that Nation A is aggressive because "everybody is aggressive." Who says your general principle is correct? Instead you must begin with a principle everybody accepts. If your principle is open to question, concentrate first on making the principle itself clear and persuasive, perhaps through inductive reasoning. Then you can proceed to deductive reasoning—to drawing conclusions from the principle—with greater safety and confidence. Even so, you must be careful to follow the formal rules of logic. What's wrong with this little bit of reasoning?

All collies have long hair.

My friend Juan has long hair.

Therefore, Juan is a collie.

As we've seen, inductive and deductive reasoning often work together: Gathering data, for example, may allow a writer to arrive at a general principle for which he or she can then deduce several consequences. The philosopher Stephen Toulmin, observing these connections and the fact that we rarely find writers using inductive or deductive reasoning in their "pure" state, has proposed that we consider a third kind of reasoning as a model for constructing arguments. Few writers can gather *all* the evidence that inductive reasoning might require before being able to reach a definitive conclusion. Fewer still wish to put together the formal proofs, with their unassailable logic, that the rules of deductive reasoning require. Instead, writers will satisfy and persuade readers if they make statements that are "reasonable"—that everybody will accept either because they are already predisposed to do so or because the writer offers enough support to make the statements acceptable.

Practical reasoning, as this kind of thinking is called, consists of making or arriving at summary statements or conclusions called *claims*. Claims function like thesis statements; in other words, they are statements that writers "claim" are true and that they believe "have a claim" on the reader's attention and assent. To accept a claim, readers expect both *data*—evidence of some kind—and a *warrant*—some explanation that links the data to the claim. Thus, you might wish to claim that the United States needs to reform the way it finances congressional campaigns; support for such a claim would come from data (such as statistics on how much a typical campaign costs these days) and from warrants (such as stating that too much time spent raising money means too little time listening to constituents' needs).

No matter what kind of reasoning you use, be careful not to fall victim to those weaknesses in reasoning we call **fallacies.** While rhetoricians have identified many types of fallacies and have given them some complicated Latin names, we can restrict ourselves to the few that occur most frequently.

The major cause of fallacies is presuming too much on the basis of the evidence available. So if the initial question is whether or not Mike Tyson should be banned from boxing for biting off Evander Holyfield's ear and other offenses, and if in your essay you make a claim about the value to boxing that will follow once Tyson has been banned, you have presumed an answer to the first question rather than having proved it (a fallacy called *begging the question*). Similarly, if you observe that a particular political party took power two years ago and claim that the state's economy is better off now because of that election, you are assuming a cause and effect based simply on the timing of the two events; in fact, the improved economy might have many other possible causes. Notice that identifying this fallacy (called *false cause* or, in Latin, *post hoc propter hoc*) does not mean you are "wrong" in your thinking; it simply means that you must prove, and not merely assume, that what happened earlier caused what happened later.

Another presumption occurs when a writer takes one or two examples and then makes the *hasty generalization* that these examples typify the whole. Thus, if you watch one episode of a TV show and conclude that this will be a great series, you have moved to a conclusion too quickly, without sufficient data. In other cases, a writer will offer readers a *false dilemma*. If you claim that for a country to progress economically it must choose between totalitarianism and democracy, you presume there are no other alternatives; the examples of several countries in Asia and Latin America would trouble your argument.

Still another kind of presumption occurs when a writer, to back up a claim, *appeals to some outside authority*. If that authority is an expert, the appeal may help. But, as a counterexample, does it really matter, in deciding which long-distance carrier to use, that basketball player Michael Jordan endorses the beleaguered Worldcom? If the outside authority is "what everybody believes"—the consensus belief of most people today—and your argument is that your reader should jump on this bandwagon, too—well, how persuasive was the argument 600 years ago that "everyone knows" the sun revolves around the earth? And if the appeal is to the reader's knowledge of someone's character, as in those cases where the writer attempts to discredit an argument by disparaging the character of the person who makes the argument, how persuasive was the claim, made by an opponent, that a congressman's views about a pending bill had to be wrong because the congressman was known to be a homosexual? In short, appeals to authority may be quite proper, but don't misuse them, and don't ask them to do your work for you.

One last word about planning your paper. Sometimes an assignment will require more than one approach. For instance, this assignment from a history course combines the opinion paper and elaboration on a topic:

This essay of three typed pages should show an understanding of the main idea in Segundo's book and should also include your own opinion of this main idea.

This assignment, from a philosophy course, combines the opinion paper, elaboration on a topic (extended definition), and comparison and contrast:

For the major project you will be required to summarize the theories about free will offered by any two authors we have read; after summarizing them, show the contrast between them and (if you wish) express a judgment about which theory you accept.

Obviously you will need to combine the suggestions made under each relevant heading before you are ready to start the paper. As an example of writing that combines two or more types of approaches, read again the short selection from Alvin Toffler's *Future Shock* (pages 337–338). The passage is primarily cause-and-effect analysis, but it also includes definition and elaboration.

EXERCISES

1. The following are topics for opinion papers or argumentative papers. Plan a paper on one or more of these topics. Would you use inductive, deductive, or practical reasoning, or a mixture of reasoning methods?

   Is the use of "mercy killing" legitimate?

   Should the government exercise stricter control over prime-time television programs?

   Is the adulation of sports heroes harmful to children?

   Should teenagers who seek an abortion have to consult with or have the permission of their parents?

2. In the absence of any other proof, what is wrong—fallacious—about the following claims?

   Reelect Governor Smith, or else the state economy will collapse.

I've met two fashion models, and believe me they're all neurotics.

When Prestige University raised its tuition dramatically two years ago, the number of students applying to the university soon also rose, which shows that raising tuition encourages rather than discourages applicants.

If Shaquille O'Neal drinks Pepsi, I should too.

Don't pay to see that movie—everyone knows it's a bad one.

3. Find a topic about which there will be a wide divergence of opinion. Form a group with other members of your class and brainstorm about the topic. What issues does it raise? What opinions do people commonly hold, and on what bases do they hold them? What additional information should a person seek before forming his or her own opinion? Then weigh the opinions, seek out the information, and write a paper developing your own response.

11

The Writing Process: Drafting and Revising

You may have observed that we have been analyzing
the writing process for two full chapters and have
not gotten to the opening sentence of a paper yet.
That's exactly as it should be. Remember, Aristotle said that
two-thirds of the writing process goes on in the head before
ink touches paper. If you have planned well, the actual writing and revising of the paper will proceed more quickly.

This chapter discusses that part of the writing process in
which ink meets paper, no matter whether the ink comes
from a pen, a typewriter, or an electronic printer, and no
matter whether a given sentence is being written for the
first time or rewritten for the seventh. The first version or
draft of a paper is the subject of Part A. Equally if not more
important is the effort a writer puts into revising the paper,
which is the focus of Part B. The special requirements of
writing essay exams form the agenda of Part C.

A. DRAFTING

You have brainstormed, you have explored, you have assessed, you have planned. Now comes Aristotle's final step,
putting your carefully planned thoughts into words, the very
best words for the expression of those thoughts.

A1. Two Preliminaries: Thesis Sentence and Outline

Before you try to write the first sentence of a paper, take a
moment to write a more important sentence: your **thesis.**
What is a thesis sentence? It's simply a statement of what
the paper is about. In order to tell "what the paper is about,"

a good thesis sentence does more than just name a topic, it goes on to summarize briefly what you will say about the topic. For example, the first of the two sentences below simply names a topic, while the second offers a real thesis sentence:

This paper is about cybernetics.

This paper contends that cybernetics, because of the opportunity it offers to free us from mindless routine, is the single most promising development in contemporary American life.

A good thesis sentence is direct, straightforward. It does not ask questions. Instead, it answers questions, provides solutions, and tells us the writer's purpose.

I recommend that you write a good thesis sentence, perhaps on a separate index card, before you start any paper that is not narrative or descriptive. The reasons are two very practical ones. First, the thesis sentence reminds you of the task you have undertaken. It stands as a kind of summary statement for all that mental activity described in Chapters 9 and 10. Second, the thesis sentence can be kept next to you as you write the paper. As you finish each paragraph you can ask yourself, "Does this paragraph contribute in some way to the task described in the thesis sentence?" If the answer is no, you have an immediate warning that you are straying from your topic.

Most textbooks about writing tell you that you should always draw up an **outline** before you start to write. The problem with such advice is that many excellent writers have never used an outline in their lives. Alberto Moravia, for example, claimed that his novels were "not prepared beforehand in any way." Furthermore, those writers who do use outlines rely on them in quite varying degrees. Some create very detailed outlines and adhere to them slavishly. Norman Mailer wrote *The Naked and the Dead* only after compiling a whole file drawer full of notes and a complete "life history" for each projected character. Others jot down just a few key words and don't worry if they change their minds later on.

All of these writers order their thoughts clearly. The difference is that for some the process is internal and for others it must be to one degree or another external—in other words, written down, outlined.

Too many writers are premature; they should organize their ideas before writing a piece. I do tremendous organizational layouts on any pieces before I actually write them. I take notes on matchbook covers, napkins, anything.
—Woody Allen

So what can I tell you about outlines that would be both true and useful? Just this: If no instructor has ever criticized the order of your paper, if instead your papers are complimented for their coherence and their clear structure, then don't concern yourself with outlines. Apparently your internal processes for creating order are sufficient for your purposes. All your reader cares about is the result, not the means for attaining those results. But if you are like most of us, you need all the help you can get. Here is where an outline can help. It offers a chance to summarize those plans we discussed in Chapter 10. Once you have defined your tasks, use the outline as a way to list the strategies you will use. Also, the outline can remind you of the main divisions of your topic and can help you distinguish between larger and smaller categories. Of course, you should not be a slave to your outline—after all it's *yours*, and you can always change it later if necessary.

In general, the shorter and simpler the paper, the shorter and simpler the outline. For a three-page paper on cybernetics for example, this might be a sufficient outline:

Thesis: Cybernetics affects every aspect of our lives positively.
  I. Definition of cybernetics
 II. Applications
    A. At home (examples)
    B. At school (examples)
    C. At work (examples)

But a larger, more complicated paper, especially the kind of paper we will discuss in Chapter 12, needs a different outline. For example, following is the outline I used in writing this chapter. If you look carefully at both the outline and the chapter, you will see that the final product *resembles* the outline but is not identical with it. Outlines are slaves, not masters.

Chapter 11: Drafting and Rewriting
Intro
   I. Drafting (illustrated by examples drawn from professional writing)
      A. Opening—stories, surprises, metaphors, quotations, questions, emotions, etc..
      B. Thesis sentences
      C. Outlines
      D. Writing the paper
      E. Endings—avoid repetition
   II. Proofing and Revising
      A. Rewriting—"speeders" and "bleeders"
      B. Word processing
      C. Format—type, ms., margin, title, following instructions
      D. Proofreading—symbols, etc.
   III. Writing Essay Exams
      A. Sample questions
      B. Preparing for the test
      C. Writing the exam: 4 steps

A2. Getting Started

Do you sometimes find it almost unbearably painful to write the first few words of your paper? Are there times when the blank sheet just stares back at you, defying you to think up a good opening sentence?

If so, you have a case of writer's block. Some cases are severe, some mild, but all are painful and frustrating. One comforting thought is that you share this malady with almost everyone who has ever tried to write. The novelist William Styron, for example, bemoans "the pain of getting started each day," and concludes: "Let's face it, writing is hell." Other writers report the same frustration. Irwin Shaw revealed that "each morning I wake up with fear and trembling, knowing the typewriter is waiting for me." James Jones, the author of *From Here to Eternity*, took a half hour each day just to convince himself he was ready to write. Then, once he was "convinced," he smoked ten more cigarettes, drank a half dozen cups of coffee, and reread yesterday's mail—all this before he put down a single word!

I can't offer you some magic elixir that will make the problem go away—if I could do that, I'd have bottled it and sold it to Styron, Shaw, and Jones. What I can do is suggest remedies that others have tried and found helpful. Experiment with them. If an idea works for you, use it. If it doesn't, discard the idea and try another.

Here, in no particular order, are some possible remedies for "writer's block."

1. *Use a cassette recorder.* Many people can say what they want to put down even though they can't write it. If you can compose orally, by all means do so, even if it's just the opening paragraph. Perhaps a simple listing of your ideas will be helpful. Then replay the tape and write down what you hear. This transcript will often give you at least a start, a rough draft from which you can begin the actual writing.

2. *Skip the opening paragraph.* Go directly to the second or some later paragraph, one you can write quickly. Then later on you can return to the opening, and by that time the block will be gone.

3. *Exercise vigorously for a short period of time.* This suggestion may seem frivolous, but it is based on a sound physiological principle: An increase in the oxygen supply to the brain often results in increased efficiency. Anything to break the deadly cycle of "How shall I start? How shall I start?" is bound to be helpful.

4. *Try rituals.* In other words, use rituals that free your memory and allow ideas

> *The last thing one settles in a book is what one should put first.*
> —*Blaise Pascal*

to come forward. No rules govern what makes a good ritual—each writer's rules are individual, usually based on something that happened on a day when he or she was particularly creative. Ernest Hemingway used to sharpen twenty pencils before he began to write (and then composed standing up at a typewriter!). Willa Cather read a passage from her Bible. Thornton Wilder took a brisk walk. It's not *what* you do that is important. The value is in the ritual itself, because it liberates your imagination, it makes you say, "Now I am ready to write."

5. *Practice free writing.* In Chapter 9 we saw how free writing (making your fingers "fly" as quickly as possible for a specified period of time) could provide ideas for a focused essay. This technique can also break up writer's block. Getting *anything* down on paper can free up the mind and hand to get *something*—some focused, specific something—down as the first draft begins.

Now also is the time to think about those suggestions for good opening paragraphs made back in Chapter 4 (pages 127–130). Would it help to open with an anecdote? A quotation? A question? An expression of strong emotion? Some figurative language? A surprise statement? A brief and lively introduction?

A3. The Complete Draft

I cannot tell you "how to write," a magic formula that will make all the right words tumble out onto paper. No one can. Writing is still in many ways a mystery, as with all the really important things in life.

But I can give you a few recommendations you should keep in mind as you write. These suggestions do not remove the mystery, but they help confine it:

1. *Follow your outline.* No outline can be of any service unless it is used. Once you have written a successful outline, which in turn is based on the strategy you have chosen, the direction of your paper should be clear. If the paper will compare and contrast, for example, you will already have

decided what similarities and differences to discuss and what emphasis you will give to each point. The paper can now almost write itself.

If you have one strong idea, you can't help . . . repeating it and embroidering it. Sometimes I think that authors should write one novel and then be put in a gas chamber.
—J. P. Marquand

2. *Develop each issue fully.* We saw earlier in the book that the secret of a good sentence is development of its core idea and the secret of a good paragraph is development of its topic. This is also true on the level of the complete essay. Your paper will be clear and convincing in proportion to the amount of detail you provide. Only by amplifying each point you make with stories, examples, or explanations can you help your reader come close to your view of the subject. Of course, good development doesn't mean being repetitious or wasting words. Instead, it means realizing how clear and how detailed you have to be to bridge that gap between your understanding of the subject and your reader's. The paragraph development skills of Chapter 5 will help you achieve these goals.

Here is where it may become necessary to change your outline. Sometimes as you begin developing a particular part of the paper, you may discover that a full treatment of this section will carry you much further than you had thought. You realize you have started on a topic worthy of a paper in its own right. Conversely, there are times when you begin an issue and then realize you have nothing much to say about it—you can't treat it in detail because you don't *know* any details. In both cases you may have to go back to the outline and do some crossing out or rearranging. It is better to eliminate a subtopic than to leave it undeveloped or allow it disproportionate space.

Similarly, you might find new ideas occurring to you as you write, ideas that had escaped your attention when the outline was drawn up. Jot down those ideas when they come (it's surprisingly easy to forget them). Then see how they can be worked into the outline in a sensible way, so that they will find a place in the completed paper.

3. *Assess your tone.* While you are writing, pause to think about the reader you have envisioned for your paper (Chap-

ter 9). Have you been keeping that reader's interests and need in mind? In particular, thinking about the kinds of words you have been using, what kind of tone (Chapter 8) has been established: a formal tone, an informal tone, or a humorous one? Does it seem to be the right tone for persuading your readers?

4. *Use effective transitions.* You have both an outline and a thesis statement next to you as you work. But remember that your reader must rely on you for guidance. Transitions between paragraphs make clear your intentions. You and the reader are like two bicyclists, one following the other; transitions are the hand signals by which the leader tells the follower which way he or she proposes to go.

In Chapter 4 we discussed the various kinds of transitions: contrast words, comparison words, time or place words, consequence words, example words, summation words (see pages 123–126). These same transitions can be used as the mortar that binds together the building blocks of your paragraphs. Here, for example, are the opening words of eight paragraphs that make up one section of Alvin Toffler's book *Future Shock:*

For most people, the first such juncture . . .

In the past . . .

A second critical life juncture . . .

A third significant turning point . . .

Among the more conventional couples of tomorrow . . .

This third marriage . . .

Not all of these marriages will survive until death, however, for the family will still face a fourth crisis point . . .

Of course . . .

Observe how Toffler keeps the reader right on track with these transitions—we can almost tell how the essay develops just by reading the transitions.

I suggested earlier that you keep the thesis sentence by you as you write. When you begin a new paragraph, ask yourself whether you have created a good transition between the previous paragraph and this new one. Then check the transition against the thesis sentence: Does the transition suggest how this new paragraph furthers the development of the topic defined by your thesis sentence? If it doesn't, should it?

5. *End the paper effectively.* Here is your chance to use those good ending paragraphs we discussed in Chapter 4. Can you conclude by picking up on a story, a quotation, or a theme used at the beginning? Can you stimulate your reader's interest by speculating about the future or proposing a question for further thought? Do you have a concluding anecdote or quotation? How about a surprising twist? Remember not to stray onto the dull ground of the "in this paper I have said" kind of ending.

EXERCISES

1. Go over some recent papers you have written. Did you use an outline? If not, try to outline the papers now, after they are completed. Can you come up with clear, simple outlines? If you cannot, perhaps your papers would have been more coherent had you used outlines.

2. Again looking at those papers—did you have a thesis sentence for each? If so, write them out. If not, see what difference clear thesis sentences might have made.

3. Choose *one* of those recent papers, the one that seems to you most deficient. Revise it, making sure you: (1) develop an outline, (2) write a thesis sentence, (3) offer an effective opening paragraph, (4) develop each subtopic fully, and (5) finish with a lively concluding paragraph. How much of an improvement did these five steps make?

4. Locate two or three magazines aimed at the general public. Which techniques discussed in this chapter were used in the articles? How do they engage the reader's attention and make him or her want to read further?

B. REVISING THE PAPER

Finally the words are down on paper. However, the difference between unsuccessful writers and successful writers

> *The main rule of a writer is never to pity your manuscript . . . . I say that the wastebasket is a writer's best friend.*
> —Isaac Bashevis Singer

is often this: Unsuccessful writers think they are now done, while successful writers know they are not. These successful writers know that they must revise—that is, they must engage in "re-vision," seeing it all again, seeing it another time, but differently. And they know that this rethinking of a paper is not the same as proofreading it.

B1. Rewriting the Paper

Somewhere along the way you were probably advised always to write a first draft and then to rewrite completely. If you are like most people, you agree with this advice in theory, but you hardly ever follow it.

Most people don't rewrite, because they don't take the time. Like the character in the scenario I described in Chapter 9, they finish a paper on the night before it is due. The most they have time for is reading through the paper quickly, trying to spot grammar or spelling errors. This last activity is an important one, but it is not rewriting. The proper name for it is proofreading (see B4, later in this chapter).

You may expect me to exhort you to give up your sinful ways and promise to rewrite every paper from now on. Perhaps I will, perhaps I won't. Whether you should always write a second draft depends on the circumstances. It depends in particular on how you write the first draft, on whether you are what I call a "speeder" or a "bleeder."

A speeder is someone who races through the first draft of a paper quickly and easily. He or she doesn't worry about each word, each sentence—the important thing is to get *something* written. This kind of writer works like a sculptor in clay: First one gets a large amount of material, shapeless but pliable; then one forms it, going over it carefully and slowly, working and reworking the original lump until it resembles what one first imagined. Speeders know that much of their creative energy will go into the rewriting process, and so they use the quick first draft much as sculptors use that first lump of clay.

Many professional writers work this way. Georges Simenon, the great master of detective novels, finishes his first draft of a book in only a little over a week. Anthony Trollope used to work even faster: 5,000 words a day, week after week, pen dashing across paper. If your habits of composition indicate that you are a speeder, you must then allot a significant amount of time for rewriting. Second and maybe third drafts are essential parts of how you write, and if you do not include them your writing will suffer. Anita Loos, for example, claims she rewrites every piece about twenty times.

What does it mean to write a second draft? Usually it means *writing the paper again*, from first screen to last. You change, add, subtract, and reorder at every step of the way. If you simply go back over a first draft, deleting a few words here and inserting a few there, the improvement will be very slight. Instead, you need to invest just as much energy in the second draft as you did in the quickly written first draft. Simenon, for example, sets aside one day of rewriting for every two days spent in the first writing.

Then come the bleeders. These are writers who sweat blood as they compose, writers for whom every word is an agony, "every sentence a victory." William Styron, who you may recall said that "writing is hell," finishes only two or three handwritten sheets each day.

If you are a bleeder, you rewrite, too, but you do it in your head rather than on the screen or on paper. Consequently, your first draft may be much closer to the final product than it is for a speeder, because like Styron you have a "need to perfect each paragraph—each sentence even—" as you go along. You still need to revise, to check language and organization. But you can probably work directly with the first draft rather than completely rewriting the paper.

No special advantages go with being either a speeder or a bleeder. Both have to rewrite, both have to invest time in thinking about alternative ways of communicating with their readers, both have to proofread their final copy. Poor writers are the ones who speed but don't rewrite, or who speed when they should bleed.

> *Ther nys no werkman,*
> *whatsoevere he be,*
> *That may bothe werke*
> *wel and hastily.*
> *—Geoffrey Chaucer*

Revising is not something you do once, after everything else is complete. Instead it is a constant, ongoing process. Even if you are a speeder, the very act of rejecting one word and choosing another means that you are revising while you write. Every writer revises at every stage. The only difference is whether his or her composition habits require a second full draft before going on to the finished paper.

If revision is a constant process, of what does that process consist? Clearly, revising means engaging in at least the following five activities: (1) deleting words, (2) adding words, (3) substituting one word or group of words for another word or group of words, (4) changing the order of words, and (5) combining groups of words. These activities can be performed on a handwritten text, a typed text, or a word processor screen (see B2). And when we say add, delete, or change the order of words, we could be talking about adding, deleting, or reordering *many* words, indeed whole sections of a paper, as we shall see later on.

Perhaps you can see the revision process most clearly through an example. Here are two paragraphs that appeared earlier in this book (page 181):

> The truth is, most people have only the vaguest idea of the meaning of grammar, and they usually associate it with making mistakes when speaking. Here are some other misconceptions: (1) most errors in writing are grammatical errors; (2) study of grammar is necessary to speak and write well; (3) only a few select people (English teachers?) have ever mastered grammar.
>
> The surprising truth is that (1) most "errors" are in semantics or usage, not in grammar; (2) many people have become excellent writers without ever undertaking any formal study of grammar; and (3) everybody—including you—knows a great deal about English grammar and has known it since learning to speak.

Now here is the original draft of those paragraphs (which was originally one paragraph), plus handwritten revisions:

The truth is, most people have only the vaguest idea of ~~what grammar is,~~ the meaning of grammar, and they usually associate it with making mistakes when speaking. Here are some other misconceptions ~~about grammar:~~ (1) study of grammar is necessary to speak well and write well; (2) most errors in writing are grammatical errors; and (3) only a few select people (English teachers?) have ever mastered grammar. The surprising truth is that (1) many people have ~~written quite well~~ become excellent writers without ever ~~undertaking~~ undertaking any formal study of grammar; (2) most "errors" are in semantics or usage, not in grammar; and (3) everybody— including you—knows a great deal about English grammar and ~~you have been aware of this~~ has known it since learning to speak.

If you examine the changes between the first draft and the final version of the paragraph, you will find examples of each of the five kinds of revisions mentioned above. In particular you can note: (1) words crossed out (*what grammar is* in the first sentence, *about grammar* in the second sentence); (2) words added (*study of* in the third sentence, *surprising* and *ever* in the first sentence of the second paragraph); (3) words substituted for others (*become excellent writers* replaces *written quite well*); (4) changes in word order (points 1 and 2 are switched in both paragraphs); (5) groups of words combined (*knows a great deal about English grammar* and the separate clause *you have been aware of this since learning to speak* are now combined into *knows a great deal about English grammar and has known it since learning to speak*). My purpose in making

Editing is the most companionable form of education.
—Edward Weeks

these changes was to give the passage a clearer order and a better wording. In *none* of these changes was I "correcting an error." Instead I was simply trying to improve my writing by making it clearer to you, the reader. This improving process is what we mean when we talk about revision.

So far we have been talking about revisions that are largely stylistic, changes that some people call **editing.** In fact, everything we have discussed in the first eight chapters of this book, from words to sentences to paragraphs to conventions, all could be said to belong to this process of editing what you have written.

But remember that re-vision means reseeing, which means that you have to resee *what* you have written (content) just as much as *how* you have written it (style). To resee also means that you will have to rethink, replan, reorder, and perhaps delete or add, not just words or sentences but paragraphs or whole sections of the paper. This is your chance to think about the paper as a whole, in light of the entire writing process as described in Chapters 9 and 10, and then to undertake some major changes to make the paper better. While many students find it easy to edit and proofread, fewer have the courage to genuinely rethink their entire effort. If you have this courage, you will improve your writing immensely.

Here are some questions to ask yourself as you rethink the paper:

- Going back to the notes I took when doing the preparatory critical thinking—in other words, when I was assessing my information, conceptualizing the reader, and planning the essay—have I followed the plan I set for myself, or has my intention somehow evolved into something different? What *is* my real intention, my purpose, as I would express it now? Is my tone appropriate for that purpose?
- Do I find that valuable ideas that came up then, when I was planning, have somehow been left out as I wrote this first draft? If so, how can I incorporate them now?

- Going back to my thesis sentence and/or outline, have I fulfilled the promise implicit in them?
- What information or details have I left out that I must add if I am going to be persuasive on this topic?
- Are there additional examples I can use to strengthen my points?
- Have I used material that, truth be told, I really don't need? If I am adding material elsewhere, is there some material that now, by comparison, seems less important and therefore worthy of deleting?
- Do I need to change the order of my paragraphs in order to make the paper proceed more logically or smoothly? What else can I do to clarify my organization and meaning?
- Is my treatment of the topic balanced—that is, is each part given an appropriate treatment, or is one part developed too much and another too little?
- If I have defended my opinion or developed an argument, what might a reasonable opponent say by way of objection to the claims I am making? How can I strengthen my argument against those objections?

So far we have assumed that you are revising this paper on your own. But your instructor may also wish you to engage in **peer revision.** This activity, modeled on what professional writers do, means that one or more of your peers—usually fellow students—will help you by making suggestions, providing reactions, finding strengths and weaknesses, observing connections between paper and assignment, commenting on organization or style, and noting errors that need correction. Sometimes these recommendations may come from an e-mail partner or partners. Profit by these suggestions, of course bearing in mind the fact that you carry the ultimate responsibility for your own work. In turn, always be as helpful to your peers in their writing as you hope they will be to you.

Your instructor will also be concerned with the way you revise, and he or she may ask you to hand in a draft that can be returned with advice on how to revise more effectively. Alternatively, these drafts are sometimes "handed in" by e-mail, with the instructor then interacting with students about the paper by exchange of e-mail messages. Naturally you will want to give the **instructor's suggestions** the most careful attention, no matter how they are received. No one likes to be told that his or her writing is less than perfect, but the suggestions are for your benefit. Ask questions when you don't understand a symbol or a comment. If your instructor says something like "This paragraph isn't clear," don't just add a word or two; instead, think carefully about *why* it might not be clear, and rethink it entirely before you revise. Similarly, if your instructor asks whether you can "offer further examples," don't settle for a quick one off the top of your head; find several and talk about them in some detail. Nor should you limit yourself to making just the changes the instructor recommends. Those suggestions are for starters, and your instructor will appreciate—and reward—the valuable revisions you make that go beyond what he or she saw as problematic in the draft.

B2. Using the Computer

Most students are now learning to write with word-processing software on the computer, and their ways of revising a paper may be somewhat different. This section will offer some suggestions for making the most effective use of word-processing features.

I am assuming that you have acquainted yourself with the proper ways to operate your software. Be sure you know how to add material, delete material, and move words, sentences, and paragraphs from one place to another. Be sure also that you know how to reformat and how to use the distinctive features of your particular program. This may seem obvious, but I cannot tell you how many times as a teacher I have had a student turn in work with skipped half pages or unusually wide margins or some other disfiguring characteristic, with the explanation of "I didn't know how to make my computer correct this." Whatever else you do, make sure the computer has a good digestion, because instructors no longer accept "the computer ate my paper" as a valid excuse.

For most people, the principal difference between writing the old way and writing on a computer is that the latter permits the writer to revise more easily and extensively as he or she goes along. Instead of writing out a first draft and then typing a second one and then typing a "good" final copy, for example, the writer can undertake multiple drafts, experiment with several possible versions, and then, at the end, generate a final "good" copy with the simple press of a key. Those who write on computers usually report that they revise more because revision is so easy, and therefore they believe their writing has improved. Few who have made the change to word processing ever want to go back to the old methods.

Much of what was said in Section B1 applies here. The five kinds of changes described on page 376—additions, deletions, substitutions, combinations, and changes in word order—can all be made on the computer. It is advisable that you develop ways of reminding yourself of doubtful words, phrases, or sentences—that is, ones that you think are not yet "right" and that you want to revise later. Some people put brackets around the doubtful parts, others use question marks (???) in the text, and still others put a little X in the margin. Whatever the device, the advantage is that you know where to focus your revision efforts; then, when the words or sentences satisfy you, the device can simply be deleted. Another tip is to open a second file where you can store ideas for possible revisions, alternative versions of sentences, and other miscellaneous information that you cannot use right away because you are busy writing but that you do not want to forget when the time comes for revision.

Even though you may do most of your revising as you go along, much like the "bleeders" described in Section B1, you will still profit from generating one "hard copy" draft of your paper before printing out the final copy. A hard copy gives you two advantages. The first is that you can put it away, in a drawer or wherever, so that you can come back to it later and read it with "fresh" eyes. Suddenly you will become aware of weaknesses you had not seen before, because you were too close to your subject, too much in-

volved in writing it. The second advantage is that certain
structural problems are harder to detect on a screen than
on a handwritten or typed draft. These problems include
inadequate or excessive treatment of certain parts of the
topic and disproportionately long or short paragraphs.
These difficulties are less apparent with a computer because the portion of the paper that you see at any one time
on your monitor is smaller than would be true of a typed
draft, so it is harder to keep yourself mindful of the relationships of the parts to the whole. Seeing a hard copy enables you to observe the overall structure and to make any
necessary changes.

If you have access to them, a variety of computer programs have been developed that can help you with your revisions, especially your stylistic revisions. The most familiar are spellcheckers, which are most appropriately used
for proofreading (see Section B4). (Note that spellcheckers
do not find misspellings that are correct in another context—
e.g., here/hear or hint as a typo for lint.) Other programs,
however, help you pinpoint word choice problems, provide
information on sentence length, give you a word count, detect repetitive words and constructions, locate passive-voice
sentences, or identify jargon or sexist language. Of course,
locating such material in no way obligates you to change
something. A passive-voice construction, for example, may
be exactly what you want in a given sentence. But the computer can help by showing you patterns. If passive voice
appears in 40 percent of your sentences, for example, or if
your average sentence length is 11.6 words, or if "There is
. . ." or "There are . . ." begins a third of your sentences, you
know that you have identified a feature of your prose that
bears closer examination.

Discover the joys of experimenting with your word processor. Learn how you can play with verb tense, for example,
or with replacing nouns with pronouns. Freed from the tyranny of black print on white paper, you may find yourself
exercising more creativity in your revising than you did in
your original writing. And the results of such experimentation can be impressive.

B3. Preparing the Final Manuscript

When you put your paper in its final form, you need to observe certain conventions about how it should appear.

First, if you possibly can, **type or print the paper,** preferably using a computer. I can think of at least four reasons for this recommendation. The first two benefit you directly; the second two benefit your reader:

1. Typing or printing eliminates any negative reaction a reader might have to your handwriting.
2. Mechanical errors (such as spelling and punctuation) are easier to spot in cold, impersonal type.
3. Typed or printed papers can be read more easily, thus allowing the instructor to concentrate more on your message than on your medium (i.e., script).
4. Typing or printing eliminates confusion (is that squiggle an *o* or an *a?*)

And, of course, all four reasons ultimately work to your advantage, because the gratitude of an instructor cannot do you any harm. Statistical studies have shown that a typed or printed paper has a better chance of getting a high grade than the same paper untyped. Most instructors—including yours, I am sure—take great precautions to avoid misjudging a paper because of poor handwriting. But why take a chance?

When you type or print out your paper, use unlined, white, $8^{1}/_{2}$-by-11-inch sheets. For typewriters, use a ribbon that is reasonably fresh and make corrections properly, whether through correction fluid or correction strips. If you use a computer, make sure that the printer will give you good, legible, dark copy and that its cartridge is not failing.

Type on one side of the paper only, and leave a one-inch margin on all four sides. To number each page, use the computer's numbering system, or type your name a half inch from the top between

> It was very pleasant for me to get a letter from you the other day. Perhaps I should have found it pleasanter if I had been able to decipher it. I don't think that I mastered anything beyond the date (which I knew) and the signature (which I guessed at) . . . Other letters are read and thrown away and forgotten, but yours are kept forever—unread.
> —T. B. Aldrich to E. S. Morse

the top and right margin, followed by two spaces (no punctuation mark), and the page number (see the sample paper beginning on page 467). On page 1, include the number only.

In the absence of other instructions, on the first page you should type, an inch from the top flush with the left margin, your full name, the instructor's name, the course number and title, and the date, all on separate double-spaced lines.

Next, **give your paper a title.** Center it, in caps and lowercase (not all caps, not underlined, no quotation marks). The title should be a double space below the date. Insert a quadruple space between the title and the first line of the paper. (The rest of the paper, including extracted quotations and any "Works Cited," should be double spaced. The exception is footnotes, if any, which should be single spaced—see Chapter 13).

What kind of a title? It's best if you can find one that is short, informative, and humorous or provocative. Some examples are:

"Brave Words for a Startling Occasion" (Ralph Ellison)

"Howtoism" (Dwight Macdonald)

"Why Stop?" (Mary Hood)

"On the Importance of Being Free" (Walter Lippmann)

"First Aid for a Bus Rat" (student)

"My Emancipation Proclamation" (student)

Notice that a good title is one of the *last*—not first—tasks you complete.

Finally, **respect your instructor's requirements.** He or she may specify certain ways for your paper to be written. You might be asked to include certain information along with the title, such as the course and section number or the date or the instructor's name. You might be asked to staple or not to staple, to fold or not to fold, to have a title page or not to have a title page. Usually there are reasons for these requirements. Simple prudence would suggest that you respect your instructor's wishes in these matters.

B4. Proofreading the Paper

Now you are ready to give the paper a last proofreading before you turn it in. This is not the time for major changes—they will have been made at the rewriting stage. If a major change suddenly becomes necessary, you ought to retype or reprint that section of the paper. Instead, this is the time for catching such things as spelling, punctuation, or typographical errors. Any handwritten corrections should of course be done neatly.

Use standard correction devices. For example, to correct a misspelled word, draw a line through the word and write in the correct word above:

   . . . noting this example and ~~takeing~~ ^{Taking} care not to . . .

To add a missing word, insert a caret (⌃) at the proper place and write the word directly above it:

   This plan, while ⌃not typical, is nevertheless

The same holds true for a missing letter within a word:

   like this.

Two transposed letters can be reversed and thus put right by a curved line (⌒⌄):

   Without knowing the name it is impossible to . . .

And letters accidentally separated can be joined by two arcs:

   no one doubts their sincerity . . .

To show that a new paragraph should begin even though you failed to indent, put the symbol ¶ immediately before the first word of the sentence that should begin the paragraph:

   . . . large and sprawling. ¶ Give your paper . . .

Conversely, the symbol *no* ¶ tells the reader to ignore a paragraph indention you have made and to read the passage as a single paragraph:

ൌ ¶ Use standard correction devices.⌐ For example, to correct a misspelled word, draw . . .

Many writers find it difficult to proofread their own work. A student when shown a paper containing several obvious mistakes will often say, quite sincerely, "But I *did* proofread that paper." When we know what we intended to write, it is often difficult to look objectively at what we did in fact write. A hint: try proofreading your papers backward, last word to first. That method won't turn up missing words or mistakes in sentence or paragraph structure. But it will help you find misspellings and typographical errors, because it divorces your words from their meaning and lets you see them in perfect isolation.

Some instructors encourage **peer editing** as a natural follow-up to peer revision. That's good experience, as long as you remember that the final responsibility rests with the writer and that writers need to internalize editing skills rather than rely on someone else to "save" them. Remember, too, that proofreading is necessary even if you use a computer with a spellchecker; no program can catch errors where the spelling would be correct in another context.

One final caution: Be sure you have saved a copy of the paper before handing it in, either by photocopying it or by saving it to disk on your computer. It's better to be safe than sorry.

EXERCISES

1. Here is a short list of successful essay titles. Why do you think they appeal to readers?

"Stripping Down to Bare Happiness" (Linda Weltner)
"Through the Dark, Glassily" (Richard Gambino)
"The Perils of Obedience" (Stanley Milgram)
"Springtime Reality: Exams 5, Me 0" (student)
"A Few Words About Breasts" (Nora Ephron)
"What You See Is the Real You" (Willard Gaylin)
"Bamboozle Me Not at Wounded Knee" (Terri Schultz)

2. The following passage from a student paper is in severe need of proofreading. Mark it as necessary.

> When I was little I used to wait everyday at the front window with my nose pressed up agianst the glass. My grandma told me thats' why I have a pug nose now, but you know how Gradmas are. You're probably wondering the reason for my stunting the growth of my nose by keeping a virgil at the window. Actually it was a man; at age five the only other man in my life besides my father. My Gradma called him Paddy. my mother called Dad, and to me he was Grandda. Every evening when I heard Grandma setting the table I would be at me station, waiti ng for a figure far in the distance to come limping towards home. He would come belowing in the door just as I hit the peak of my excit-ment and gather me into his arms like a sheperd would gather the smallest of his sheep. Inevita-bly a voice arose from the kitchen: "Paddy, if you get that child all exdited she wont be able to eat her dinner. Then Grandda would straigten up and we both would go overto the piano bench for our evening ritual.

3. If you use a computer, write one paragraph on a specific topic perhaps connected with a paper you are working on. As you write, you will also be revising. Improve the paragraph as much as you can. Keep a log of *each* change you make as you go along, no matter how small.

   Now examine the log. How many changes did you make? How many of them were related to content? How many to improving the style? How many to correcting errors, from typos to sentence fragments? What does the log permit you to conclude about revising using a word processor?

4. If your instructor concurs, try peer revision on your next paper. After this process, answer this question: What did

your peers help you see that you probably would never have discovered on your own?

5. Write a few paragraphs on how over the years you have used machines and technology as part of your writing. Include any home experiences, any grade school or high school or work experiences, and also your current experience in college. Remember that machines can include manual typewriters, typewriters with memories, personal computers, and computer terminals. In what ways have machines helped your writing, as compared with writing in longhand? Where appropriate, comment also on what you have gained as you moved from one kind of technology to another—as you moved, for example, from simpler to more complex kinds of software.

6. Examine your three most recent papers (not necessarily for English class) and note the mistakes that could have been "caught" by more diligent proofreading. What can you conclude about how efficient your methods of proofreading are?

C. WRITING ESSAY EXAM ANSWERS

In one particular college writing situation, the processes of planning, drafting, and revising are especially compressed.

I'm referring to the oft-dreaded essay exam.

Recent research shows that essay questions are included in over half of the examinations given in a typical college or university. Even in business courses or in natural science courses such as biology or chemistry, about one-fourth of all exams include essay questions. For the social sciences and humanities the percentages, as you might expect, are much higher. Perhaps so far your courses have not relied heavily on such questions, but keep in mind that the frequency of essay questions is at its *lowest* in the freshman year and increases steadily as a student progresses to higher-level courses.

Knowing how to write a good response to an essay question will be vital to your academic success. Fortunately, the ways to write good essays can be demonstrated. This section describes a proven method for writing successful essay answers.

C1. A Sample Question

Despite what some students believe, there are measurable differences between good essay answers and poor ones. Instructors do not just grade whimsically, awarding an *A* here and a *D* there as their fancy dictates. The differences between a good essay and a poor essay will be clear to anyone who compares them.

To discover how true this is, read the following two essays, printed here exactly as they were written. Both students had studied for the exam, but one had a successful strategy and the other did not. Observe the differences:

The Question

Summarize the qualities of the Byronic hero. Show how they are manifested in three of Byron's poems: "Lara," "Childe Harold's Pilgrimage," and "Manfred." [30 minutes—from a literature course]

Response 1

The Byronic hero is an archetypal hero of Byron himself. He has more emotions, more capabilities, can suffer better. Basically, his philosophy is "Anything you can do I can do better." In "Lara" Byron mentions that he does in his life, what others fail or don't want to do. (I had a quote memorized from this poem, but I'll be damned I forget it!) In "Childe Harold's Pilgrimage" Byron's hero shows his egocentricism. (There's probably no word like this, but I'll make it up; just like Poe and tintinnabulation.) Byron compares himself with Hamlet, Napoleon, and finally the ultimate Christ. In this poem he says that everyone and their deeds are done in vain. But not Byron. "But I live, and live not in vain." "Manfred" denys everything. He believes we make our own heaven and hell. Manfred tells the abbot, "'Tis not so difficult to die" and he will "die, as I lived, alone." Byron considers himself the perfect hero because man, in general, is corrupting the earth and himself. "I love not Man the less, but Nature more."

Response 2

The Byronic hero is often noble in birth, sensual, intense, strong, alienated from the everyday world, seemingly cool (but actually tender of heart), reflective, restless, idealized, physically handsome, and often cynical or melancholy. "Lara" offers an excellent portrait of all these qualities, for as Count Lara is described we can visual the smile on his lip that is nevertheless cold and removed, and we are told in great detail about his alienation. Looking down from a mountain-top, figuratively, he senses the envy and imperception of those below him. Though he must walk among the "common" people, he will never feel a part of them. Also, poor Count Lara is doomed to a life of difficult love affairs because he has been born so physically attractive. Finally, despite his somewhat concealed contempt (combined with, paradoxically, a true love of humanity) he charismatically draws the attention of all those who meet him.

The restless image of the Byronic hero is what is first illustrated in "Childe Harold's Pilgrimage." Byron describes his self-imposed exile from England to Italy. He has cynically cast England and its current ethical system from his mind and heart. In Italy he seeks a more enlightened people—although, typical of the Byronic hero, he has a cynical attitude toward people in general. Byron does not spare himself any criticism of wasted passions or misdirected energy, however. He equates himself with Napoleon, for both burned their energy (fire) too quickly for their own good. Byron admits to many sensual experiences, and though he speaks negatively of them, he still cannot ignore the attraction of love—even though true love is extremely hard to find. In this poem Byron again refers to the doom he was slated

for because of his physical attractiveness. He certainly expressed great moodiness in the poem, also, and a great deal
of reflection on everything from his own personal failures
to the tragic defeat of Napoleon at Waterloo.

   In "Manfred," Byron portrays a sensitive, reflective man
who is prepared to accept all the consequences of his life.
He has lived the life of the Byronic hero and through to his
end he is skeptical (cynical) of the worth of a religious man
such as the abbot. Manfred believes he is his own salvation
or damnation. He feels alienated from the world and desires
only extinction. Because he has had a tragic love affair, we
can also assume he was physically beautiful and sensual.

   Now ignore for a moment the fact that you did not take
the course on which this question was based. I wager that
the clear superiority of the second response compared to
the first is still quite apparent to you. Without knowing a
thing about English Romantic poetry, you could tell that the
second essay deserves a better grade. Why is this so?

   Let's begin with what the two responses have in common. Both take into account the task the question imposes.
Both refer, quite properly, to all three poems, and both give
considerable evidence of careful reading and diligent study.
Furthermore both observe similar traits in the Byronic
hero—for example, his cynicism and his large capabilities,
especially for suffering. Both even mention similar details:
Childe Harold's comparison of himself with Napoleon,
Manfred's acceptance of the fate he has brought upon
himself.

   In these respects the first essay is successful. This answer has its virtues and we should not neglect them. (Note,
for example, that the first response mentions some details
that the second does not.) But our recognition of the virtues makes us doubly aware of the severe faults that weaken
the answer.

   The very first sentence gets the author off on the wrong
track. The Byronic hero is said to be an archetype of Byron
himself. But where does the question ask the author to talk
about the relationship of the poet to his creations? Granted,

In literature quotation is good only when the writer whom I follow goes my way, and, being better mounted than I, gives me a [ride].
—*Ralph Waldo Emerson*

much can be said about the relationship between Byron and the heroes he describes in his poetry—but say it somewhere else, not here. The author, once in pursuit on this false scent, follows it relentlessly throughout the rest of the essay. Thus fully half of the response is given over to a discussion that is not false, just irrelevant.

This irrelevance is certainly not intended by the writer. But quite soon we encounter other irrelevancies the author ought to have controlled: his quotations. Evidently the writer had taken the trouble to memorize these lines, and by God they were going to fit in somehow—otherwise how would the instructor be impressed? Yet these quotations, while accurate, have in most cases nothing to do with the traits of the Byronic hero. So again considerable space (and time) is wasted.

Then, too, we notice how the essay lacks a coherent structure. It consists of one paragraph only, a shapeless blob sorely in need of discipline. We feel that the author quickly started his pen on that first sentence and never looked back. This lack of both foresight and hindsight is reflected, too, in the errors that disfigure the essay: "egocentricism" for *egocentrism*, "denys" for *denies*, the missing punctuation before "Christ."

The second essay, by contrast, has a very clear structure. Thirty minutes results in three well-developed paragraphs, one on each poem. The greater length of the essay comes from its greater use of detail in each sentence. (It might surprise you to know, for example, that the second essay has only four more sentences than the first, i.e., twenty vs. sixteen.) This greater amount of detail allows the author to say more: to list a dozen qualities rather than a half-dozen, to offer more precise statements about the poems themselves.

Moreover the writer of the second essay sticks more firmly to the task. From the very first sentence, which gets right down to the business of listing qualities, we know that the author has the job in hand and intends to get on with it. Every sentence after the first relates directly to the topic. Yet the paragraphs each have their own point, their own contribution to make: The Childe Harold paragraph, for example, discusses the restlessness of the Byronic hero, a quality that does not apply so strongly to Count Lara.

The second response has its faults: it is occasionally repetitious, it has a weak ending, the word *visual* should be *visualize.* But even more clear is its merit, its evident superiority, over the first response,

I am convinced that many (most?) students who fare badly on essay examinations have studied just as much as the students who do well. Their problem is not a lack of preparation; rather, they are victims of two weaknesses: the wrong *kind* of preparation and no workable strategy for writing the answers. These weaknesses can be cured, as the next sections will show.

C2. Before the Test

As you prepare for a test that will include essay questions, keep in mind the *goals* of such tests. Remember, instructors can grade a multiple-choice test easily: All they need do is see which box has been checked, and often a machine will even do the scoring for them. So if an instructor has chosen to read the answers to essay questions, most probably the reason is that he or she can accomplish certain important learning goals much better with such questions. These goals might include testing the following:

1. The student's ability to distinguish between what is important and what is not so important and to detect general trends.
2. The student's ability to relate, to make comparisons (for instance, of one historical period to another or of one literary work to another).
3. The student's ability to apply the material learned in one course to other fields, to solve other kinds of problems in a fresh, original way.

4. The student's ability to grasp methodology, to understand how a particular discipline works.

As you can see, most instructors use essay questions because they want to know more than whether you have read the textbook and attended the lectures, important as those two activities are. They want to know whether you *understood* what you have read and heard and whether you can *use* it.

Now keep your instructor's goals in mind as you prepare for the exam, because they affect how you prepare. Specifically, they suggest that it will not be enough to simply reread the text and the lecture notes. Good preparation will also require the following steps.

1. *Be sure you see the larger patterns in the material you study.* Memorize facts, yes. But also know which facts are the most important ones and which facts can be related to which other facts—in short, be able to distinguish and relate. Then think of these facts as part of the subject you are studying. For example, if your assignment was to read William Styron's *The Confessions of Nat Turner,* how you review the novel for a test depends on the course for which it was assigned. If the course is U.S. history, you might concentrate on what the novel reveals about a crucial period in the American South before the Civil War. If the course is sociology, you might take special note of what the novel says about slavery as a social institution. If the course is literature, you might study the development of the plot or of the character Nat Turner.

2. *Pose sample questions to yourself.* Because this advice is not uncommon, you may be tempted to dismiss it ("I've tried that and I've never yet guessed correctly which questions will be on the test"). Such a reaction, while quite understandable, misses the point of the exercise. Of course it is unlikely you will guess what questions will be asked. The value of posing questions is that it accustoms you to "handling" your material. The more you work with it, the more confident you become of your ability to respond to questions about it. This reduces the danger of panic, and

your chances of success increase proportionately. The purpose is similar to the one that motivates lifeboat drills on a cruise ship: while in theory everybody might know what to do in an emergency, in times of danger it's better to have had a rehearsal.

3. *Review the verbs commonly used in essay tests.* An essay question imposes some task on you. The nature of the task will usually be defined most clearly by the verbs your instructor chooses. Different verbs mean different tasks. No matter how much you have studied, failure to keep to the required task will cost you heavily. Yet failures of this sort are very common. They account for a high percentage of those cases where a student prepares diligently, only to be frustrated and bewildered by a low grade. Those are the moments when life seems terribly unfair.

Here are the verbs most commonly used in essay questions, together with a description of the tasks they imply. For each I have included an example or two, drawn from actual essay tests given within the last few years in a variety of courses and departments.

a. **To analyze** is to examine something closely and critically; it also might mean to break something down into its parts. Example:

Characters in plays usually face moral and emotional crises; analyze these "crisis points" in two characters from two plays we have discussed. [30 minutes—from a German literature course]

b. **To compare** is to find similarities (and sometimes to find differences, too); **to contrast** is to find differences only. Examples:

Compare and contrast the religion of the Vedas with the religious development of the Upanishads. [20 minutes—from a comparative religion course]

Contrast the basic assumptions, general methodology, and technique of descriptive linguistics with those of anthropological linguistics. [30 minutes—from a linguistics course]

> *"Where I use a word," Humpty Dumpty said, in rather a scornful tone, "it means just what I choose it to mean—neither more nor less."*
> *"The question is," said Alice, "whether you can make words mean so many different things."*
> —*Lewis Carroll*

c. **To define** is to state precisely the meaning of a word or a concept. Examples:

Define what Webster means by *authority*. [20 minutes—from a sociology course]

Define photosynthesis. [10 minutes—from a biology course]

d. **To describe** is to summarize, outline, or in some other way give a brief "picture" of the subject. Examples:

Describe George Kerman's interpretation of America's role in international history. [25 minutes—from a political science course]

Describe the chemical interactions between light and dark reactions of photosynthesis. [20 minutes—from biology course]

e. **To discuss** can mean to describe or identify. Example:

Discuss three types of American diversity. [30 minutes—from an communication course]

It can also mean to react in some way, for example to a quotation:

Discuss this statement: "Renaissance writers made distinctive contributions to a modern understanding of history and the writing of history." [45 minutes—from a history course]

f. **To enumerate** is to list, in 1-2-3 fashion, providing a brief description of each item on the list. Example:

Enumerate the major postwar American strategic doctrines. [30 minutes—from an ROTC course]

g. **To evaluate** is to find both the good and bad points of a particular subject. Examples:

Choose one of the many theories about the origin of agriculture and then evaluate it. [20 minutes—from a botany course]

Evaluate the theories of the neoclassical sociologists (Simon et al.) about formal organizations. [35 minutes—from a sociology course]

h. **To explain** is to make something plain and understandable, usually by giving details about it. Examples:

Explain the motivation theory that helps us understand the behavior of Mr. B. in *Wheels*. [15 minutes—from a business course]

What place did the Enlightenment give to religion? Explain your answer fully. [30 minutes—from a history course]

i. **To identify** is to name and usually to describe briefly. Example:

Identify the two sets of leaders in each House of Congress. [20 minutes—from a political science course]

j. **To outline or summarize** is to condense a large body of material, selecting only the most important parts. Example:

Summarize the contributions of John Dewey to American primary education. [18 minutes—from an education course]

k. **To relate** is to show the connection(s) between one thing and another. Example:

Relate Keats's theory of negative capability to his own poetry. [50 minutes—from a literature course]

l. **To trace** is to show the progress of a subject through time. Example:

Trace the influence of Sir Joshua Reynolds on early nineteenth-century British painting. [25 minutes—from a fine arts course]

Other verbs can appear, too, such as *assess, defend, develop, expand, show.*

The important thing is to learn to recognize all the verbs and to know what they ask you to do. Remember, too, that unless you do this ahead of time, the knowledge will be of little use.

C3. Writing the Examination

Let's assume now that you have undertaken the three-step preparation described in the previous section. Good preparation is very helpful, but it will bear fruit only if you combine it with an effective strategy for answering the question you are asked. This strategy consists of four steps:

1. Categorize the question.
2. Develop an appropriate method of answering the question.
3. Write out the answer clearly, sticking to the topic.
4. Reread the essay.

Step 1. Categorize the Question

With a little experience you will find that you can quickly assign a question to one of the following three categories. (Again, examples are included from real courses.)

1. *Long identifications.* Basically, these questions are just longer versions of the short-answer identifications you have known since grade school. They do not call for any creativity. The instructor is simply testing your knowledge; there is clearly a "right" answer, and if you have studied you are probably home free. Such questions are often introduced by *who, what, where,* or *when. Define, identify,* or *summarize* can also fit into this category. Examples:

   What is a denomination? [5 minutes—from a comparative religion course]

   Define the term *segmentation.* [10 minutes—from a biology course]

2. *Specified relationships.* Here, too, the instructor has in mind what will constitute a good or "right" answer. But in addition to asking you to reproduce certain facts, he or she also expects you to relate these facts to other facts in specific ways. In short, you have to be able to *assimilate* and *distinguish* information.

   Questions that ask you to *compare* or *contrast* often belong in this category. So do questions requiring you to *evaluate, assess, relate, explain, defend,* or *trace*—or questions that begin with *why* or *how.* Examples:

Why would semantics be considered central to any theory of linguistics? [20 minutes—from an anthropology course]

Contrast the post–World War II military alliances with the prewar variety. [25 minutes—from a history course]

3. *Open-ended questions.* Only in this last category do we find questions for which the instructor has no preconceived ideas about what makes a good answer. Instead he or she gives you considerable freedom. The intent is not to invite you to shovel a certain objectionable material. Nor are you required to echo the instructor's own opinions. Rather he or she will be concentrating on *how* you answer. A good essay will reveal knowledge of the subject, but more important it will show that it was written by an intelligent and thoughtful person.

Questions in this third category can also be identified by key words: *discuss, suppose, argue for or against.* Here is an example, taken from an astronomy course:

Imagine that you are a taxpayer in Florence during the year after Galileo published the *Starry Messenger.* Galileo has applied to the government for financial support to further his investigations. Would you urge the government to give him a grant? Why or why not? [30 minutes]

Clearly the instructor will allow you to choose either alternative. The success of your answer will depend partly on your knowledge of Galileo and his times. But it will also depend on your ability to "think out loud" about Galileo's relationship to the political, religious, and economic currents of his day. Here is another example, this time from a literature course:

Devise an alternative ending for two plays we have read. What would be the consequences of your ending for the theme, character development, and structure of the play? Would your ending succeed? Why or why not? [45 minutes]

Again the quality of the answer will depend as much on its *how* as on its *what*.

The importance of categorizing a question should be coming into focus. Immediately you know how much freedom you have in shaping your answer: for the first category, none; for the second, no freedom either, but the answer requires a more complicated mental process; for the third, true freedom, but still more emphasis on your creative powers. Furthermore, since these categories are arranged here in order of increasing difficulty, you can usually expect the time to be allotted proportionately—less time for questions in the first category, more time for the second, still more for the third.

With practice you can categorize essay questions in a matter of seconds. By so doing, you guarantee a safe start.

Step 2. Develop an Appropriate Method of Answering the Question

This means knowing the key verbs defined in Part C2 of this chapter and being able to recognize what task each implies. Once you know the tasks, you can quickly calculate a rough mental outline of your answer. Recall, for example, the question from an anthropology course: "Contrast the basic assumptions, general methodology, and technique of descriptive linguistics with those of anthropological linguistics." Immediately you know to stress only the differences and to divide the answer into three parts. So the answer can be sketched like this:

Assumptions, descriptive vs. anthropological

Methodology, descriptive vs. anthropological

Technique, descriptive vs. anthropological

That outline for answering the question will most likely bring success.

Sometimes more than one task is involved. A political science instructor asked this question: "Define *federalism*, distinguish it from *unitary government*, and give an example of each system within the United States." A good answer

must combine three skills; it might
look like this in outline:

> *All excellent things are difficult.*
> *—Spinoza*

    A. Definition of federalism
    B. Differences from unitary
       government
       1.
       2.
       3.
    C. Example of federalism
    D. Example of unitary government

While you develop an appropriate method, keep in mind also the amount of time you can devote to a question. Your answer should always be as detailed as possible given the time available. Don't overestimate what you can accomplish. On the average, a student can expect to write only about one well-developed paragraph (five or six sentences) for every eight to ten minutes of work. So for a half-hour question expect to complete only three full paragraphs, four at the most.

Step 3. Write Out the Answer, Clearly and Concisely

This stage occupies the most time—perhaps four-fifths of the total. But if you have given sufficient attention to the first two stages (and if you have studied!), the response should come quickly and easily.

Some tips may be helpful. Don't waste valuable time in your opening paragraph on a restatement of the question. Your instructor knows what he or she asked. Instead get directly into the topic. If you have the leisure to develop an opening paragraph, use it to summarize the approach you will take to the question.

Try to make your answer simple and clear. If you are going to enumerate four reasons and you have thirty minutes, give one paragraph to each reason. Be as direct as you can, especially through the use of transitions: "The second reason is . . . ," "The third reason is . . ."

Remember to stick to the topic. Essay questions are not opportunities for you to spill out everything you know about

> *It takes a little talent to see clearly what lies under one's nose, and a good deal of it to know in which direction to point that organ.*
> —*W. H. Auden*

the subject. Limit yourself to what is called for; otherwise you waste time. Suppose, for example, you are taking a literature course and the exam question asks you to analyze the attitude of a certain character toward her daughter. Your first reaction is joyous—you have read the novel, you know the character. But remember, you must *analyze*, that is, break into parts, examine, explain; and you must analyze only the *attitude* toward the *daughter.* Don't tell everything you know about the mother and everything you know about the daughter, just to prove to your instructor that you have read the book. Most assuredly don't get off into issues like plot, setting, interpretation, the author's life, and whether you liked the novel. If you do, your answer can contain many good facts and still be unsuccessful.

Step 4. Reread the Essay

Save a couple of minutes at the end for going back over what you have written, asking yourself questions like these:

- Did I answer all parts of the question?
- Are the facts I used *relevant* ones?
- Did I develop each subtopic sufficiently?
- Did I use enough transitions so my reader can find his or her way through the essay?
- Are there any glaring mechanical errors?

Some deficiencies can be repaired rather quickly at real benefit to you. Others, such as a neglected subtopics, might not be fully repairable in two minutes, but at least you have time for one or two hurried sentences that might limit the damage.

You have probably never seen the essay question analyzed in such detail before. But think of its importance. Psychologists know that students' test-taking skills have an important bearing on whether or not they succeed on tests, regardless of how much they have studied. Despite this fact, most students have spent very little time practicing for essay tests. Since these tests will form a large part both of your writing activity and of your final grades, you would do well to study Part C carefully.

In summary, this chapter has tried to offer you a plan for writing a good short paper. Short papers represent perhaps 60 percent of your written work in college. But the other 40 percent is important, too, and is the subject of the next chapter.

EXERCISES

1. Here are a few essay questions given in recent exams. Of course you are not expected to know the material that would permit you to answer them. But assign them to a *category* and determine which *strategy* would be the most appropriate for someone who has to answer them.

   A. In the years after the Civil War the Great Plains underwent vast and rapid change. How do you explain what happened? [30 minutes—from a history course]

   B. What are the major strengths and weaknesses in Lavoisier and LaPlace's argument that respiration and combustion are perfectly similar? [15 minutes—from a natural science course]

   C. "... but what a man is worth is never known until the hour of danger." Comment on this statement in light of the literature we have read this quarter. [50 minutes—from a literature course]

   D. Compare and contrast the cultural climate of the Eastern and Western states. [30 minutes—from an anthropology course]

   E. Should nine old people decide what law is in the United States? [20 minutes—from a government course]

   F. According to Robert Browning, what qualities must a poet have if he or she is to be successful? Use Browning's own poems as the basis for your answer. [20 minutes—from a literature course]

2. Review three or four recent examinations you have taken that involved essay questions. To which category did

each question belong? What was the appropriate strategy? Did you use it? Outline a good answer for those questions that you did not answer as well as you would have liked.

3. Explain in a few words what these terms require you to do.

A. enumerate   E. evaluate
B. summarize   F. define
C. analyze   G. relate
D. trace

4. Evaluate the strengths and weaknesses of the following essay exam answer to a 20-minute question about how the authors T. G. Boyle and Alice Munro portray the process of growing up in their short stories "Greasy Lake" and "White Swans," respectively. Don't worry that you probably have not read the stories.

Munro's "Wild Swans" takes a very different look at growing up. This young girl who had never been away from home, is going up to Canada (I think). This is a big step in growing up. All the warnings and information given to her really mean nothing until she learns for herself. Therefore the occurrence on the train happens because she didn't know how to stop it—the pervert. But know because she has experienced it all the warning given to her make sense and she is all the wiser.

5. Think ahead about exams coming up in courses you are taking now. For each course, ask the following questions: What seem to be the main *goals* of the course? The major *trends?* What category of questions am I likely to get on the exam? What sample questions can I think of, and how should they be answered? What kind of reading must I do to be prepared?

6. From a recent exam that involved essay questions, choose one question that did not go as well as you would have liked. Impose upon yourself the same conditions as existed at the time of the exam in terms of open or

closed book and the amount of time allotted. Then in some quiet place write the essay again, finishing exactly on time. Compare the two versions. Are you now able to produce a better response to the question? If so, in what ways is it better? If not, are the deficiencies the same or different? How would you relate what you have observed to the discussion of essay exams earlier in this chapter?

The Research Paper: Researching

Perhaps half of your college paper assignments remain to be discussed in this text. This other half, longer research papers, cause a disproportionate share of student illness. Sometimes the illness is real; sometimes it is what we can charitably call psychosomatic. ("Well, see, I couldn't get this paper in on time because I've been real sick, see, and could I have an extension until Monday?") In either case the ailment is usually curable. This chapter and the next try to offer some effective home remedies.

When you think of the research paper, you might also think of footnotes, bibliographies, and other requirements you have heard about. But these other matters, while they are customarily taught in connection with longer papers, can be used on short papers, too. Length itself, however, deters many students. "How can I ever fill up ten pages? I have a hard enough time writing two." This is a natural anxiety, but one that can be reduced.

A. THE SEARCH

Our initial focus will be on the -*search* part of *research*—in other words, how you find and evaluate the material you will use for your paper. You could also call these activities part of the prewriting phase for the longer paper.

A1. Before You Start

You begin just where you might expect—with the fact that you must **choose a topic.** Your first step ought to be to ask a question of your instructor (unless his or her assignment sheet answers the question for you). The question is simple but crucial: Should the paper be an argumentative research paper or not?

Argumentative and nonargumentative research papers are similar in many ways. Both are long, both involve footnotes and a bibliography, both require extensive use of the library and other sources of information, and both follow the same format for the final manuscript. The only difference is that an argumentative research paper must either report something new or stake out a new or controversial position on familiar material. The other kind of paper has no such restriction.

To make this difference clearer, think for a moment about the kinds of work people do that we label *research*. Sometimes they come up with new findings, new physical or chemical laws, new explanations. The biochemist who explains the properties of a new organic compound, the political scientist who collects and analyzes data on a local election, and the literary scholar who publishes a hitherto unknown manuscript are all engaged in the kind of research that reports something new, and they must convince others that their discoveries are indeed new and important. Sometimes, on the other hand, researchers cover well-trodden ground but do so in a fresh, original way. They believe they can offer a new interpretation of an old subject, or they believe that the commonly held opinion on a certain subject is wrong. The biochemist who suggests a new hypothesis about the origin of life, the political scientist who claims we have misjudged the appeal of a certain candidate, and the literary scholar who contends that we have misinterpreted *Hamlet* are all engaged in research, too, the kind that takes a new or controversial position on familiar material.

Many long papers written by students, however, do not contain either of these types of research. Instead they summarize a body of material. Their purpose is to draw a large amount of information from a wide variety of sources, then to condense it into a clear, coherent account. Such papers do not intend to offer discoveries or to argue cases. Because they require extensive work in the library and perhaps on the Internet, they are still research papers, but nonargumentative ones.

The majority of longer college writing assignments are for nonargumentative research papers. Here, for example, is a list of suggested term-paper topics from a European history course:

The Social Protest of Honoré Daumier
The Opium War of 1841
The Assassination of Archduke Franz Ferdinand
The "War Guilt" Clause of the Versailles Treaty
Mussolini's March on Rome
Auschwitz
The Berlin Blockade
The Marshall Plan

None of these (and the original list was much longer) calls for the student to unearth new information or to argue a new interpretation. Rather, he or she is expected to offer a summary of what is already known.

Nevertheless, a considerable number of college instructors do insist on argumentative research papers. A nursing student was asked by her instructor to write a ten-page paper developing either side of the question "Food Additives—Helpful or Harmful?" A student in a political science course was required to analyze a book in the light of these two questions:

Do you find this critique of America persuasive?

What do you think will happen in the next twenty years or so that is related to this criticism?

A history professor prefaces his list of topics with these words:

Remember that you are writing an argument. History is the discipline that develops and revises explanations for groups of events in the past. Take a clearcut position on an issue and sustain it throughout your essay, although you should make the other positions clear as well. Never lose track of the position you are defending.

All of these are examples of argumentative research papers, sometimes referred to collectively as "critical" papers.

Find out right away whether your paper should be argumentative. The answer will have a significant effect on both the topic you choose and the treatment you give to the topic.

If your assignment is to write a *nonargumentative research paper*, you simply need a body of material you can summarize. Sometimes a list of possible topics will be given in class. If not, you can arrive at a satisfactory topic by the same process I described in Chapter 9: surveying what you know and what interests you within the general topic of the course, narrowing the subject area, weighing your information, and adapting the subject to the reader. Answering a series of questions about a possible topic or approaching the possible topic as if it were problematic and in need of solution might also help (see Chapter 10).

In a long paper you need not restrict the topic quite as much as for a shorter paper. Now you have room to give a larger topic the detail it requires. Whereas "The Versailles Treaty" is too general for a three-page paper, you might be able to give it adequate treatment in eleven pages. (But "World War I" is still out.) Nor do you have to be content with a topic for which you already have all the information you need. The instructor who assigns this kind of paper gives you the opportunity—in fact *wants* you—to expand the range of what you know.

If your assignment is to write an *argumentative research paper*, the process works a little differently. First ask yourself whether there is something new on which you can report. Don't automatically assume the answer is no. Many valuable topics lie waiting to be explored, topics that can be researched easily and that will be interesting to others. An example might be student attitudes toward a particular problem: Think what you can accomplish with a tape recorder or a notepad and a few hours of conversation with your friends. Or consider topics about which you happen to have special expertise. One business student worked in the office of a car dealer. With proper permission she used the records at her disposal as the basis for a very good paper on the profit margins and pricing policies of a typical suburban dealership. Researching a new subject might not be as difficult as you think, provided, of course, that the structure of your course allows for such experimentation.

Nevertheless your argumentative research paper will probably exemplify the other type, the kind that argues a position on familiar material. You can follow the same methods for selecting a topic as you would for a nonargumentative paper—that is, the methods described in Chapter 9. But you must take the additional precaution of making sure you have an arguable thesis. An arguable thesis, remember, is one that offers a position on which reasonable people can differ. Often you will not be able to write a thesis statement until after you have researched the issues for a while. The student who wrote a paper on food additives, for example, did not know whether she thought they were harmful or not until after she had evaluated the conflicting testimony. But at the very least you should choose a topic that lends itself to opposing views, and you should realize that at some point you will have to stake out your territory and defend it.

Once you have found your topic (or your instructor has "found" it for you), the next step is to **plan the paper.** Again the composing process is similar to the one described in Chapter 10. Ask the questions to determine whether the paper will be a narrative, a descriptive, a cause-and-effect, a comparison and contrast, an extended definition, or an opinion paper. Then develop a strategy based on the kind of paper you are writing.

Because the material for a longer paper can be unwieldy, outlines are often useful. Naturally the outline for a longer paper will be more complicated than for a shorter one. Start with a **preliminary outline,** because you don't yet know much about your subject. Later you will revise and add to it as your reading and research progresses; soon you will be filling in details and rearranging the order of your subtopics. For now you can be satisfied with a rough idea of where you are going and approximately how you might get there. A preliminary outline on food additives, for example, might look like this:

I. The question (thesis made clear)
II. Definitions (of additives, for instance)
III. Size of the problem
IV. Benefits of additives (list)
V. Risks (list)
VI. Solution?

That outline does not tell you much, but it points the paper in the right direction. After your research is complete you can then draw up the final outline (see page 434). The final outline is your plan for organizing the complete paper. But before we talk about the complete manuscript, we should look at those research activities you need to have finished.

One added note: Argumentative and nonargumentative research papers differ in both topic and approach, but they do not differ in their procedures for gathering and then presenting information. From now on, what I say applies equally to both kinds of papers, although for illustrative purposes I shall use an argumentative research topic.

A2. Finding Printed Sources

The easiest way to show how a long paper gets written is to follow a typical paper from its beginning to its completion.

Suppose you have been narrowing your topic by using the suggestions offered in the previous section. One of your interests, let us further suppose, is capital punishment. The publicity given to this issue in recent years has made you conscious of the moral implications of the death penalty, and you want to weigh those issues carefully and arrive at a logical and defensible judgment about them. You have been told to write an argumentative research paper, so you know that eventually your paper ought to take a firm position on the issue of whether the death penalty is justifiable. You may be inclined toward one position or the other, but you also know that you should explore both sides of the question before you commit yourself.

Just to remind yourself of what comes next, you might draw up a sketchy outline of the topic as you first see it. Like this:

    I. Statement of thesis (for or against)
    II. Brief history of capital punishment in U.S.
    III. Present relevance—Supreme Court decisions, recent cases, etc.
    IV. Reasons to support thesis
    V. Answers to opponents' objections

That is about all you can say right now. This simple outline merely reminds you of what you must do. In fact, it does not even say which side of the case you plan to take—the outline will serve equally well for a defense of capital punishment or an attack on it. Before you can be more specific, however, you will have to learn more about the issue. And that means drawing up a list of sources.

Your first stop is the computer information system at your college library. You know that books can be found under subject headings as well as under author or title, so you look up the *D*'s to check on "Death penalty." You figure the computer screen will show you all the books on that topic your library holds.

Nothing. A big zero.

Next step is the reference section, where you find or ask for one of the most valuable but least-known works: *The Library of Congress Subject Headings*. These two volumes list every imaginable subject heading and then show under what other subject the entry might be classified.

> *Libraries have been very deeply established in the ethic of America. They go right along with the flag.*
> —*Clara Stanton Jones*

In other words, you look up "Death penalty" and it says "See Capital punishment." Therefore, libraries using the Library of Congress cataloging system will list all of their holdings on this topic under the subject heading "Capital punishment." (Some libraries use the older Dewey decimal system, which arranges the call numbers differently—see your librarian for details if you have to make the adjustment.)

Back you go to the computer terminal, this time to check the *C*'s. Success! You find several headings under "Capital punishment—United States." (The computer screen at my library offered over 200 headings, with entries including such relevant ones as "history [of]," "moral and ethical aspects," and "statistics.") Each heading in turn lists one or more books, with some titles appearing under more than one heading. Here is the screen for one of them, reproduced exactly as I found it:

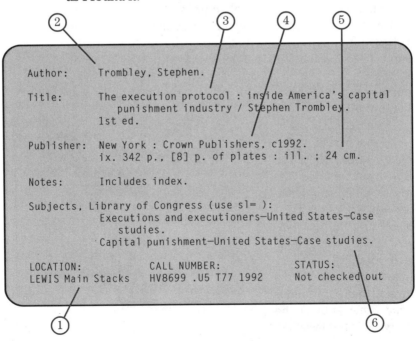

```
②                              ③    ④    ⑤

Author:     Trombley, Stephen.

Title:      The execution protocol : inside America's capital
            punishment industry / Stephen Trombley.
            1st ed.

Publisher:  New York : Crown Publishers, c1992.
            ix. 342 p., [8] p. of plates : ill. ; 24 cm.

Notes:      Includes index.

Subjects, Library of Congress (use sl= ):
            Executions and executioners—United States—Case
                studies.
            Capital punishment—United States—Case studies.

LOCATION:               CALL NUMBER:              STATUS:
LEWIS Main Stacks       HV8699 .U5 T77 1992       Not checked out

①                                                          ⑥
```

The numbers surrounding this sample card point to the places on the card where you will find, in order:

1. *Location, call number,* and *status.* This information tells you where to find the book in your library. The number here is from the Library of Congress classification system; if your library uses the Dewey decimal system, the number will be somewhat different. The "status" section gives you the welcome information that the book should be on the shelves when you get there.

2. *Author.* Stephen Trombley is the author. If he were an editor or translator, his name would be preceded or followed by *ed.* or *trans.*

3. *Title.* The full title is *The Execution Protocol: Inside America's Capital Punishment Industry,* although the last five words could be called the subtitle.

4. *Publication facts.* In this case, you learn that the book was published in New York City by Crown Publishers in the year 1992. Subsequent editions of this book, if any, would have a separate entry.

5. *Book size.* The Trombley book has nine (ix) pages of prefatory material, 342 pages of text, eight pages of plates, and other illustrative material. The size (24 centimeters) tells you the book is not just a small pamphlet. Moreover, you discover that the book contains an index; this index might prove useful for cross-references to other sources.

6. *Subject headings.* This section tells you that this same book is listed under both the subject "Capital punishment—United States—Case Studies" and the subject "Executions and Executioners—United States—Case Studies." Entries will also be found under both title and author.

Now you can begin a list of books on the topic of capital punishment. The Trombley book goes on it, let us assume, and any other books found under this subject heading. Your list might resemble this one:

Bedau, H. A., Death Is Different (HV 8699 US) 1987

Black, Charles, Capital Punishment (HV 8698 B47) 1981 (checked out)

Cabana, Donald, Death at Midnight (HV 8694 C225) 1996

Draper, T., ed., Capital Punishment (HV 299 US C29) 1985 (on reserve)

Meltsner, Michael, Cruel and Unusual (KF 9227 C2 M4) 1973

Szumski, B., et al., eds., Death Penalty: Opposing Viewpoints (HV 8699 US D4) 1986

Wawrose, Susan, The Death Penalty, 1997 (no call # yet—on order)

Instead of a handwritten list you might prefer to enter the books into a laptop computer system or simply to have the library's computer print the full information on every book you select.

Some books you have ruled out, perhaps because they are printed in a language you don't read (such as Karl von Amira's *Die germanischen Todesstrafen*), perhaps because they seem out of date (such as L. T. Beman's *Selected Articles on Capital Punishment*, published in 1925). So far you are content with just the author, a short version of the title, the call number, the publication year, and any information the computer screen might offer about the book's whereabouts. If you have more books than you can possibly read, lean toward the more recent ones or the ones readily available. Later on, if you decide to actually use a book, you will need more information. Be sure to note whether there are any bibliographies listed, because such a book would aid your research immensely. Wouldn't Michael Radelet and Margaret Vandiver's 1988 bibliography on *Capital Punishment in America* be a good source to check?

Now you have the beginnings of a source list for your topic. Books are not the only possibilities, however. Articles in magazines and journals and Internet sources may also be important.

> *Knowledge is of two kinds. We know a subject ourselves, or we know where we can find information on it.*
> —Samuel Johnson

If your library works through an information system, it may be possible to find articles right on the library computer screen or the Internet. Typing in "Capital punishment" produced 427 articles under that heading—far too many to read. So I search the subheadings and come to "Ethical Aspects." This sounds promising for an argumentative paper, so I bring it up:

```
CAPITAL PUNISHMENT—ETHICAL ASPECTS
125    Casting the First Stone <1990>
126    Death Penalty Civilization and Inhumaneness <1990>
127    Death Penalty Debates US USSR <1990>
128    Does It Matter if the Death Penalty Is Arbit <1985>
129    Hard Evidence <1996>
130    Is Capital Punishment Ever Ethical <1995>
131    Justice Civilization and the Death Penalty A <1985>
132    Locke on Punishment and the Death Penalty <1993>
133    Locke on the Death Penalty <1994>
134    Medical Ethics and the Death Penalty <1990>
135    Moral Appropriateness Capital Punishment and <1991>
136    Murder Is Different Review Essay <1989>
137    Night of the Living Dead David Von Drehles A <1996>
138    Not in My Name <1993>
```

--CONTINUED on next page--

Here's a treasure: lots of relevant-sounding titles, listed in alphabetical order. Only a brief version of each title and its date are given, and because of space limitations the screen shows only fourteen articles, although I am also told there are more. I find number 135 intriguing, and when I summon it up, it looks like this:

```
Search Request: S=CAPITAL PUNISHMENT    4 General Indexes (INDY)
WILSON Record -- 135 of 427 Entries Found           Long View
------------------------------------------------------------
TITLE:         Moral appropriateness, capital punishment, and
               the Lockett doctrine.
AUTHORS:       Bilionis, Louis D.
JOURNAL:       The Journal of Criminal Law & Criminology;
               82:283-333 Summer '91
WILSON SUBJECT HEADINGS:
               United States/Supreme Court--Decisions.
               Capital punishment--Ethical aspects.
               Sentences (Criminal procedure).
INDEXED IN:    Social Sciences Index.
ENTRY MONTH:   9112.
```

Now I've got the full title of the article, its author, the journal title, and the number, date, and pages of the issue of the journal in which it appeared. I can go on in the same way, compiling a list of articles that seem likely to be helpful. Again a short form will do:

> Bilionis, "Moral Appropriateness," *J. of Crim.*
> *Law & Criminology* 82 (Summer 1991) 283f

Alternatively, you might be able to push or click on "print" and have the computer issue you a copy of the entry for your file.

If your library's computer system encourages it, you may also wish to begin a **keyword search** among all relevant journals, perhaps using Boolean logic (see page 428). Now you'll be ranging beyond your library's perhaps more limited journal holdings to get a more complete idea (using Web-based reference guides) of what is available in many journals. Offprints can often be purchased or otherwise obtained by your library. Good sources to access articles for a topic like "capital punishment," modified for "United States" only, would be these three:

- PAIS (Public Affairs Information Service). I counted 415 articles accessible by this means alone.
- Wilson Select, Social Sciences Abstract. As the title implies, there is a principle of selection at work here, and within the social sciences you will be provided with abstracts of articles—very handy for deciding whether you really need to see any article in its entirety.
- Academic Search Elite. The articles listed here are from academic journals only, and initially for "capital punishment" you will come up with over 2,000 entries! But further specification—for example, to peer-reviewed articles (in other words, articles in journals where decisions about publication are made by a panel of experts)—results in a much more manageable list of just (!) 153 entries.

Most probably for a topic like this you will concentrate on the last ten or twenty years. But suppose you need earlier material (most computerized information systems only go back a few years), or suppose your library is not yet fully automated. What then?

For popular magazines, use the *Reader's Guide to Periodical Literature*. Of course, this guide cannot include every magazine, but it does offer a generous sampling of articles from popular magazines such as *Psychology Today, Harper's, Newsweek, Time*, and others. Consulting the volume covering the year 1995 and looking under "Capital punishment," you find no less than fifty-one entries. Here is one of them:

Anger and Ambivalence. D. A. Kaplan. <u>Newsweek</u> 126:24-26. Ag 7 '95.

Translated, that entry means that an article with the title "Anger and Ambivalence" by D. A. Kaplan appeared in *Newsweek* magazine. It was published in the August 7, 1995 issue. That issue in turn was part of volume 126, and the article in question began on page 24. A list of abbreviations at the beginning of the *Reader's Guide* can help you do this translating.

The *Reader's Guide* covers the popular press. But you want to know what other experts think, too. What about the scholarly journals not included in the guide?

Your first resource is the *Social Sciences Index*. This series does for scholarly articles what the *Reader's Guide* does for more general articles. The original title for the bibliography was the *International Index;* in 1965 it was renamed the *Social Sciences and Humanities Index*, and then in 1974 it was split into a separate *Social Sciences Index* and a companion *Humanities Index*. Since capital punishment is more closely allied to the social sciences than to the humanities, you would begin with the *Social Sciences Index* for the more recent years.

Again you check under the heading "Capital punishment," and again you are rewarded with several entries. For example, if you are researching earlier years, the volume covering the year from April 1986 to March 1987 lists eleven articles: three from the *Journal of Criminal Law and Criminology*, two from the *Far East Economic Review*, and one each from *Law and Society Review, Journal of Applied Social Psychology, Developmental Psychology, The*

Economist, Journal of Applied Psychology, and *Congressional Digest.* You add the ones that sound most promising to your source list.

Now go back to the computer screen, this time to check your list of articles against the journal holdings of your library. If your library does receive the magazine or journal, note the location of the journal or ask where it is kept. If your library does not receive a particular scholarly journal, cross that article off your list. (For example, of the eight journals listed in the previous paragraph, my university library subscribes to only six.)

If your library does not receive a certain popular magazine, however, don't be hasty in crossing off the article. Many college or university libraries will not purchase a magazine such as *Psychology Today,* but your local city or county library may very well have it, since their clientele is different. Check the local library, perhaps by phone, and find out what they hold. While you are at it, especially if you make a personal visit, don't forget to see what *books* the local library might have that your college library does not.

Two other short steps will complete your search. The reference departments of libraries contain a vast assortment of more specialized bibliographies and reference works. These books might contain valuable leads, so ask your librarian which ones might be the most helpful. Then check on newspapers. Most college libraries carry *The New York Times,* and perhaps other papers as well, on microfilm. Use *The New York Times Index* to locate entries. That way you would not miss the article about the increasing pace of executions that appeared in the *Times* on April 23, 1992.

Now that your initial list is complete, it is time to invade the stacks in search of the books and journals. Don't worry if your list seems long. You won't find everything—books can be misplaced, lost, stolen, at the bindery, or in the hands of another borrower. Furthermore some of the books and articles that you do find will seem, on closer inspection, peripheral to your interests. Use a book's table of contents or the abstract of an article as a way of helping you decide how useful it will be.

Check also to see whether your college library will find the full texts of articles on computer and print them for you. But you might want to ask about cost first!

Remember, too, that this is only a starting list. As you read further you will probably encounter several references to still other books and articles on your topic, and you will find yourself making one or more trips back to the library to supplement your initial collection.

A3. Finding Internet Sources

The Internet is a new and powerful research resource. It has the potential for taking you far beyond your local or university library into a global "library of libraries" where you can access the latest research, discuss developments in virtually any field of human interest (often with leading experts in that field), and find a wealth of up-to-date information.

But doing research on the Internet can also be difficult. Depending on the source, the information can be overwhelming, misleading, unreliable, or just plain wrong. And when you find something worth investigating or using, access to it may be limited or, in some cases, such as military records, restricted. Thus, you will need to use a good research strategy and to exercise sound critical judgment and patience as you work.

To get you started, we'll first take a look at the Internet, then we'll examine some strategies for using it. Finally, we'll explore information systems and research tools available for your research.

The **Internet** can be seen as a vast collection of interconnecting computer *servers* and personal computers located throughout the world. Think of this worldwide network of computers as having several interacting functions: (1) an *exploratory* function that includes search engines and tools; (2) a *collecting*

function, such as information databases and systems; and (3) a *communicating* function, including electronic mail, mailing lists, newsgroups, and chat groups.

Many students new to online searches assume that the Internet and the **World Wide Web** are one and the same. This is not quite accurate. The Internet, as mentioned earlier, is a global network of interconnected computers. The Web, however, is an approach to the Internet. Through the presentation of information in *hypertext*, a linking language that allows you to move among "pages" of the Web, the Web lets you click on highlighted terms—called *hypertext markup language* (html)—to search for text- and image-based information related to your topic of research. Thus, you can progress through Web pages with increasing focus.

You can navigate the World Wide Web conveniently by using a **browser**—a multimedia software program such as Microsoft Explorer, Netscape Communicator, or any of the other Windows- and Macintosh-based programs available on the commercial market. Once on the Web, type the **URL** (*uniform resource locator*) in the Search Box. The URL is an address that lets you access a file or *directory*. It typically looks like this one:

<http://www.webcrawler.com/select/refer.03.html/>

In this case *http:* stands for *hypertext transfer protocol* (the steps necessary to access a file). Then *www.webcrawler.com* indicates the *domain name* (the file location) and */select/ refer.03.html/* provides the *directory path* to the site. The *angle brackets* (< and >) tell you that everything between them makes up the URL address.

Internet **search tools** (or search engines) are divided into two categories: subject directories and text indexes.

Subject directories allow you to search by topic. They include such tools as:

Yahoo! <http://www.yahoo.com>
Library of Congress World Wide Web Home Page
<http://www.lcweb.loc.gov>
Internet Public Library <http://www.ipl.org>

Proceeding from general to specific, you search for information in a subject directory by topic, clicking on the highlighted terms at each site until you hit on the desired information. Be sure to record the URL that appears in the search box—save it as a *bookmark* or print it. This allows you to call up the web site without retracing the hypertext *links* you initially explored.

Search tools for exploring *text indexes* are some of the most powerful engines for researching information. However, they are best used once you've decided on a topic. The reason is simple: Tools for searching text indexes look for *keywords* in an entire article, book, or other text-based document. With millions of such documents on the Web, you are undoubtedly going to turn up an enormous number of entries or *hits* (in the tens or even hundreds of thousands). Therefore, you must refine your search by first selecting a topic.

Like subject directory search tools, search tools for text indexes are too numerous to list in their entirety. But here are a few to get you started:

WebCrawler <http://www.webcrawler.com>
Alta Vista <http://www.altavista.digital.com>
Excite <http://www.excite.com>
Lycos <http://www.lycos.com>
Open Text <http://www.opentext.com>
Infoseek <http://www.infoseek.com>

Let's take a look at Alta Vista, one of the largest and most popular indexes.

Alta Vista is a database of nearly 40 million Web pages. By typing in an URL, you can use Alta Vista to search the Web and *Usenet* (newsgroups) with "simple query" (single keywords) and "advance query" (Boolean connectors, see p. 428) techniques. Alta Vista directs you with on-screen prompts as you focus your research. Searching for key dates, words, and phrases helps you limit the sheer volume of hits possible.

The communicating function of the Internet should not be overlooked in your research. **Discussion groups** are actually open forums on just about every topic imaginable. While not always reliable, the information found in them can help you get on track during the initial stages of your research. Your subscription to a discussion group allows you to interact with others one-on-one; you send, receive, and reply to *postings*, usually with an expert or a fellow enthusiast in your area of interest.

Listserv and *Usenet* are two kinds of discussion groups. They can be entered via the World Wide Web or *Gopher* (the protocol is *gopher://*). Gopher, a text-based program developed at the University of Minnesota, displays information in menus that help you decide what information to "go for."

Internet relay chat (IRC) allows for "real-time" communication. Such tools as *Chat* and *Talk* let you discuss topics one-on-one or in a group as the conversation actually occurs. Unlike e-mail, mailing lists, or discussion groups, IRC is *live* talk; there is no time delay when talking to others. Since IRC is accessible by the general public and is not often used by reliable experts, you should exercise caution when considering opinions expressed by its users.

Electronic mail (**e-mail**) allows you to connect with experts in the field, many of whom are quite willing to assist students with research projects. E-mail addresses are made up of a *user name* (or number) followed by the @ (at) sign, plus the *domain name*—the commercial provider whose computer houses the e-mail box. Here is a bracketed sample of an e-mail address: <jsample@compuserve.com>. Perhaps your college has provided you with your own e-mail address, or perhaps you have subscribed to a commercial service. *Mailing lists*, a subcategory of e-mail, conduct e-mail messages to and from people interested in your particular topic.

Just as you would not take a long automobile trip without some discussion, planning, and a reliable road map, so too you should not begin your Internet search without a plan— a **research strategy** for navigating cyberspace. It's a good idea to work from general to specific. This deductive approach prevents you from getting too specific too soon, thus causing you to overlook areas where your subject is discussed from unsuspected angles or is covered by different disciplines. Although every search strategy has a distinctive approach, yours may benefit from these suggestions:

1. *Brainstorm* a list of what you know about your topic so far: names, dates, places, key words and phrases, ideas, reflections. Jot down everything that comes to mind, but leave space beside each item to add ideas as they surface. The subject headings from your library research may help here.

2. Next, ask yourself what *subject category* of information you need. For example, is it business, literary, artistic, scientific, medical, legal, governmental, educational, sociological, zoological, botanical? Capital punishment, for example, involves law, government, sociology, and ethics, among others.

3. Try to determine the *form of the information* as it might appear on the Internet. Is it likely to be a book? An article? A software program? A computer file? An image, graphic, or table? An e-mail message? A discussion forum?

4. Work with the *correct information system* for your subject, be it a subject directory or a text index. Some information systems include the World Wide Web, Gopher, Yahoo!, Webcrawler, Archie, FTP, Telnet—even Listserv and Usenet newsgroups.

5. Once inside a system—a Web site, for example—follow the *highlighted html*. These hyperlinks let you progress through related topics and information, exploring angles perhaps not previously conceived.

6. *Keep track* of where you go. By printing selected web pages or articles, recording URL numbers, and making bookmarks, you begin building a database for electronic documentation (see Chapter 13, page 454). This process is analogous to noting the call numbers and other identifying information of library books. Bookmarking URLs allows you to home in on key documents without retracing your original search trail.

7. *Strike a balance* between discipline and flexibility. The sweeping and ever-expanding webscape of the Internet

can easily undermine your search strategy. If you don't stay focused on your topic, you can wander into a bewildering universe of varied and divergent topics. However, you should be open to the discovery of a Web site, text index or subject directory that categorizes information under related, but not readily discernible, topics.

8. *Evaluate* your sources. The Internet is packed with unjuried and unedited information. Look for material supported by authoritative documentation, expert names, professional affiliations, and organized presentation. Read section B2 of this chapter very carefully. And, if in doubt about quality, consult your instructor.

English mathematician George Boole developed a three-term system of logic that, when used in combination with keywords in a computer search, renders focused results from a large pool of unorganized information, such as that found on the Internet. Working with terms or "operators"—OR, AND, and NOT—you can narrow your search to bring about an all-inclusive, limited, or one-sided list of titles.

For example, suppose you want Internet information on capital punishment. Your specific interests are capital punishment in the United States and the Eighth Amendment guarantee of protection against "cruel and unusual punishment." Log onto the Internet, and let's suppose you call up Yahoo! at <http://www.yahoo.com>. Locate the subject category of capital punishment by typing the key terms "capital punishment" in the search box. Using *Boolean logic*, you can further refine (or focus) your search by typing a combination of terms in the search box to find desired titles on capital punishment in the United States, more specifically as they pertain to the Eighth Amendment:

1. United States AND Eighth Amendment
2. United States OR Eighth Amendment
3. United States NOT Eighth Amendment
4. Eighth Amendment NOT United States

In the first case, you would raise the fewest number of hits because you are telling Yahoo! to seek articles that contain both "United States" AND "Eighth Amendment" in the titles. In the second, you would hit upon an all-inclusive list because *any* article with either "United States" OR "Eighth Amendment" in its title will surface. In the third and fourth instances, you would use NOT in the search-term string to draw up titles for "United States" only or for "Eighth Amendment" only.

You can extend the logic of Boolean operators by adding related terms and combining the AND-OR sequence with parentheses. The parentheses indicate which combination of terms is explored first. For example, suppose you wanted to include "Fourteenth Amendment" (guarantee of due process of law) to your string of search terms. You would then type the following sequences in the search box, depending on which articles you want to review:

5. (capital punishment in the United States AND Eighth Amendment) OR Fourteenth Amendment

or

6. United States AND (Eighth Amendment OR Fourteenth Amendment).

The result would be a highly focused list of resources.

Now that you have located more material than you could ever use, it's time to begin sorting, evaluating, winnowing.

A4. Taking Notes

Putting together your preliminary list of sources should take you only a few hours. The next step, taking notes on or making other productive use of the material, requires much more time—anywhere from one to four weeks if it is done properly. So begin your project early enough to allow enough time for all the stages. Anything less than a month for a paper of ten pages or more is probably too little time, unless the course you are taking is a highly condensed one. Starting early also gives you the added advantage of being able to ask the library to recall potentially useful books that have been borrowed by someone else.

If you do not already do so, consider doing your note taking on the computer. The capabilities of your software program will determine to a large extent how you take notes. Despite the features of your software, however, you should first develop a system for creating files and organizing your notes based on the outline of your paper. Each note should open with source documentation, including author name, article title, and identifying information such as the URL address—all the better if each note is linked to the outline by a keyword. After you've double-checked the accuracy of your citation, especially the URL (where every letter and every symbol is vital), paraphrase or quote the material appropriate to the major heading or subheading of the file. A simple system of creating a file for every major heading on your outline, with subheadings within each file, may suffice. You can then create separate files to correspond with your paper's overall outline.

If you have a software program with cut, paste, copy, and clipboard features, your task of retyping notes into the rough draft file is greatly reduced. Such features allow you to open more than one file at once, to block sections of text, and then to cut and paste them to another file. Similarly, the clipboard feature of a software program allows you to create notes in a separate—or reserve—file, then to copy them to a major heading file or to the rough draft file of your paper.

One of the more powerful features on the Internet is the ability to download files from another computer to your personal computer. While exploring the Internet, you may find a file on a university or government *server* that supports your research topic. Working with **FTP** (*file transfer protocol*)—steps for transferring files between computers— you can move information from the server to your computer's note-taking file or to the clipboard. Then, it's just a matter of cutting and pasting it to an appropriate subheading within a major heading file. Selected quotations from the newly downloaded file can be electronically transferred from the note-taking file to your rough draft file.

While the procedures for downloading, cutting, copying, and pasting will vary with software programs and your expertise with FTP, what remains constant is the importance of devising a system for setting up files and documenting citations before going online and transferring information.

Plan ahead: it wasn't raining when Noah built the ark.
—poster

If you do not have ready access to a personal computer, you may still prefer to take notes on **note cards.** You will need to keep two types of cards: regular notes and bibliography items.

Make a separate bibliography note card for each book, article, or Internet source you read. Include the author(s) and a full description. For a book the description includes title, publisher, place and date of publication, and (where it applies) the edition and the number of volumes. Also record the call number, or, in the case of the Internet, the URL (uniform resource locator). The value of including the call number or URL is that it enables you to find the source again quickly should you have a sudden need for it after you have returned the book or turned the computer off.

For an article, the description includes the article's title, the name of the journal or magazine, the volume number, the date, and the inclusive pages on which the article can be found. If you put the author's last name in the upper left-hand corner, it will be easy to alphabetize the cards for typing up the final bibliography.

Draw up only one bibliography card for each book or article you use. No matter how few or how many notes you collect from that source, there is still only one bibliography card or entry.

Then set up a file of note cards. Here is where you jot down everything that might prove useful when you write the paper. You can include in your notes several kinds of information:

1. Statements of fact
2. Summaries of important statements by the author whose work you are reading
3. Direct quotations of statements that seem especially important

4. Ideas of your own that occur to you as you read and that you will promptly forget (believe me!) if you don't write them down

Whenever possible these cards or entries should have a subtopic heading in the upper right-hand corner (e.g., *history—20th century; S. Court decisions; arguments against*). This heading is keyed to the preliminary outline and makes it easier to group the notes later, when it is time to write. If you have done a more extensive outline, you can simply key the cards to the outline numbers and letters (II.A.3, for example). Make sure that direct quotations are plainly marked, so you will experience no confusion later on between what was quoted and what was only summarized.

When you encounter long quotations or material such as graphs and tables, consider using a photocopier. Most libraries have one, and for a nickel or a dime you can save several minutes. Be sure to write down the original source on the back of your photocopy.

Knowing what kinds of things go onto note cards or into the computer does not solve the dozens of little practical questions that come up as you read—questions like "Will I ever have any use for this fact or this statement?" Only more experience can give you real help. In the meantime the safest practice is to preserve anything that *might* help. Nothing gives you more confidence in the quality of your final paper than the opportunity to pick only the best out of too much material, and nothing is more frustrating than needing some information you know you encountered but did not record.

EXERCISES

1. If you can, study a long paper you turned in recently. What type of paper was it supposed to be—argumentative or nonargumentative? Did you have a complete file of both bibliographic and note entries? Did you use the resources of the Internet? If yes, was it helpful? If the answer to any of these questions is no, check the rel-

evant sections of this
chapter for guidance on
how you might have im-
proved it.

> *That's the name of the [writing] game—
> words, patience, and revision.*
> —*Irving Wallace*

2. Choose a subject at ran-
dom—like capital punishment—and use the Internet to
research it. Remember to narrow your subject. For example, selecting the topic of capital punishment in the
United States would significantly reduce the number of
hits you would find under the topic of capital punishment alone (as that would include all hits worldwide).
Then consider limiting or defining "capital punishment
in the United States": Should it be limited to U.S. laws,
to discrimination among minorities or the poor, to deterrence?

Do you think Yahoo! or Webcrawler might be the right
search engines to start your search? Why? Are there
other search engines designed for browsing subjects?
What are some search engines used for searching indexes?

3. Explain, in a sentence or two, the meaning of the following terms:

URL	World Wide Web
Boolean operators	Listserv
the Internet	http

B. WRITING THE PAPER

When you have checked all the books and articles and
Internet sources you feel you should read—in other words,
the ones that sounded (from the title or other description)
like they dealt with your topic directly—and when you have
compiled what seems to you like more than enough notes,
you can begin to write.

B1. Outlining and Drafting

First, convert your rough outline into a *final outline.* Now
that you know much more about the subject, you can com-

mit yourself to a thesis and give a detailed and explicit summary of the paper's structure. Here is an example:

Outline
Thesis: Capital punishment should be abolished
  I. History
    A. England
    B. United States
      1. Colonial times and nineteenth century
      2. Twentieth century and today
  II. Reasons for abolition
    A. Directed against a class (i.e., poor, minorities, etc.)
    B. Results from hysteria
      1. Salem witch trials
      2. Sacco-Vanzetti case
      3. Rosenbergs
    C. Mistakes
      1. Lindbergh case
      2. Timothy Evans case
      3. Randall Dale Adams case
      4. Illinois moratorium
    D. Murderers insane
    E. Unconstitutional
      1. Eighth Amendment
      2. 1972 decision
      3. 1976 decision and after—Conservative courts
  III. Refutation
    A. Death penalty deters (but no—see statistics)
    B. Death penalty removes offenders permanently—
      Barzun (but *does* it?)
    C. Revenge (but should we?)
  IV. Conclusion (plea for action)

Such an outline, whether written or put into the computer,
helps give order to what otherwise might be a large, unman-
ageable subject. Notice that the outline presumes you've
made your final decision on the argumentative issue the
paper raises.

    If you have handwritten notes, now you can arrange them
in the approximate order in which you will use them—in

other words, in the order suggested by your outline. The subtopic headings should help. For example, put all the notes on "History—U.S." together and all the notes on "Reasons for abolition—mistakes" together, and so on. You will have a few notes that fit into more than one subtopic and a few that fit into none. Don't worry—just keep them where you can consult them quickly when the opportunity arises.

You are now ready to start the first draft. The composing process here is no different from the one described in Chapter 11: Find a good opening, state a clear thesis, develop each part fully, make careful transitions, and frame a pointed conclusion. Just be sure to note which sentence or which paragraph will need documentation (more on this later).

The only additional suggestion I would make is to be sure that your writing style is relatively formal. That does not mean to use flat committee prose—good writing is lively writing. It simply means you make only a limited use of contractions, colloquialisms, the pronoun *I*, and other signs of informality.

Try to write as clearly and forcefully as possible. Show that you care, that you have something you really want to say.

B2. Evaluating Sources

As you write, you may find yourself using a source that seems untrustworthy or that contains statements that conflict with statements from other sources. Whom should you believe? Which statements will you adopt and which will you reject? You need to be able to *evaluate your sources*, especially those taken from the Internet.

Sometimes you can evaluate sources on the basis of external evidence. If the conflict is over certain facts, and if one source is more recent than the others and reports on studies that make earlier studies outdated, you will prefer the most recent source. If the conflict is over facts and one source is more complete and authoritative than another (e.g., *Webster's Third International Dictionary* versus a cheap paperback dictionary), choose the more reputable source. If the conflict is over opinions and one opinion comes from the *National Enquirer* and the other comes from *The Washington Post*, you might be inclined to give the latter at least the initial preference. If the conflict is over opinions and one writer is an expert in the subject and the other clearly is not, you might want to give more weight to the expert's testimony. (Notice I say *might*—experts can be wrong.)

External evidence is not always enough, however. A book or article may offer an opinion, and you simply are not sure whether you can rely on it. Suppose, for example, that in your investigation of capital punishment you came across the book *Capital Punishment: The Inevitability of Caprice and Mistake*, 2nd ed. (1981) by someone named Charles L. Black, Jr. The very title makes clear Black's position on the death penalty. Furthermore, he seems to make some potent arguments against it. But you want to know whether you can trust Black and his conclusions. Since you are not an expert yourself (although you are fast becoming one), you would like to know what the experts said about Black's argument.

Your first resource is the *Book Review Digest* in the reference department of your library. Since the first edition of Black's book appeared in 1974, you try the 1975 volume and you are rewarded by a list of no less than six reviews, in *America, Choice, Library Journal, National Review, New York Times Book Review,* and *The New Yorker.* Four of these reviews are summarized and excerpted for you. The summaries tell you that Charles L. Black, Jr., was Sterling Professor of Law at Yale University and the nation's foremost authority on constitutional law. In addition, the excerpts are without exception highly complimentary to his book, calling it "persuasive" and a "most concise, complete, and satisfying treatment." Evidently this is a book to be reckoned with, at least insofar as it discusses constitutional law.

These capsule reviews may satisfy you. If not, you can always read the complete reviews in the original journals. Furthermore, you have the opportunity of going on to a second resource, the reviews from scholarly journals indexed in the *Social Sciences Index.*

As for evaluating articles, your chief reliance must be on the source—that is, the journal or magazine itself. Does it have a known bias? If so, does that bias seem to affect the statements you are considering? If your subject is the death penalty, for example, you might not be surprised to find that the conservative *National Review* is for capital punishment and the liberal *Nation* is against it.

Perhaps the greatest advantage to doing research on the Internet is the immediate access to enormous amounts of information. But this access also harbors a keen disadvantage—determining the reliability of the information. Since so much material, often unjuried and unedited, is on the Net, your main challenge, perhaps more so than the actual searching process itself, is to determine what information from the Internet you can trust and therefore use. Sheer volume of information, biased writing, inaccuracy, and irrelevancy of material all require that you bring some solid critical skills to bear on your research procedure. You'll need to determine what information is backed by writers and institutions with authoritative reputations. For example, Usenet discussion groups, Listserv mailing lists and e-mail are resources vulnerable to unedited, biased, and inaccurate thoughts, but they are also excellent forums for contacting experts in the field. Your ability to contact the right people, to make time for research, to use critical examination skills when evaluating documents, and to work closely with your instructor will determine the quality of your research. Some guidelines for evaluating Internet sources can help you along.

Here is a Web site you can consult for very specific information:

"Evaluation of Information Sources," by Alastair Smith, at <http://www.vuw.ac.nz/~agsmith/evaln/evaln.htm>

Keep in mind four standard elements of critical thinking for evaluating Internet information:

1. *Authorship:* What do you know about the author's reputation, credentials, professional associations?

2 *Attribution:* On what sources and evidence does the author base his or her work? Is it opinion and hearsay or scientifically sound thinking, so far as you are able to tell?

3. *Disclosure:* Can you discern bias in the author's thinking? Does he or she have a political, religious, or personal ax to grind? Who supports his or her work?

4. *Timeliness:* Is the information current? When was it first issued and how often has it been revised?

One of the hidden advantages of traditional print resources—those you might find on the shelves of your local or university library—is the backing of the publishing industry itself. Many publishers have editorial boards of experts who examine material considered for publication. Readers are thus reasonably assured that reliable authorities have examined a work—book, article, printed interview, whatever. The Internet, however, has no such overall governing body to authorize material that appears on it. Anyone with the skills to get on the Net can "publish" his or her own words without objective evaluation. You'll need to exercise sound critical judgment, in consultation with your teacher, when considering Internet sources to support your paper.

EXERCISES

1. Regarding that long paper you turned in recently (see Exercise 1 on p. 432), did you outline it? Does the first paragraph state the paper's thesis clearly? Is the paper well organized and fully developed? How thoroughly did you evaluate the sources you used?

2. Find three sites on the Web that pertain to a topic that interests you. Evaluate these sources; then for each prepare a one-paragraph summary of what you have discovered and what you have concluded about the reliability of the source.

3. If you can do so (but haven't yet), use your e-mail capabilities to have at least two exchanges with your instructor about the progress of your research paper.

13

The Research Paper: Support and Documentation

So you are well launched on writing your research paper. Now, while you are writing, is the time to keep in mind the important distinction made in the previous chapter: Are you offering new information, or—the more likely possibility—are you developing a clear proposition about your subject? Make sure that you have formed a thesis, that you have stated it directly within the first couple of paragraphs, and that you are now organizing your paper around the defense of it. If you do not have to defend a proposition, at least be sure your paper has a purpose and that this purpose is readily apparent to every reader. Consider also whether your paper would be a better one with a controversial thesis, even though one is not required. For example, a paper that simply outlines the capital punishment controversy might be acceptable. But wouldn't you rather read an essay that took one side and gave a lively and vigorous defense of it?

You may find yourself rewriting more of the long paper than you did of the shorter ones. The larger the paper, the more unwieldy it becomes. Besides, you are still acquiring new information even as you write, and this information must find a place. Don't worry if the completed draft departs from the final outline—remember that outlines are servants, not masters.

After revising the prose of the draft, you are ready to print out the final version, which must include a "Works Cited" section, documenting only the sources you actually used in the paper. (Unless your instructor directs you otherwise, don't succumb to the temptation to show off by sneaking in works you did not use.) This chapter summarizes what you need to know about the proper ways to support the statements you have made and to document the sources you have used. It concludes with a sample paper that provides a helpful model.

A. DOCUMENTATION

In this section we'll examine what you have to document, how to document according to the MLA method, and how to document papers in the sciences.

A1. What to Document

Whenever your paper summarizes, restates, or makes use of the opinions or interpretations of someone else, you must document the source. Not to do so is a breach of honesty, since the ideas are not your own and should not be offered as if they were.

This basic principle is clear, but its application is more difficult. The delicacy comes in deciding what makes a legitimate summary or paraphrase. Here, for example, is a paragraph from the Charles L. Black, Jr., book discussed in Chapter 12:

> I think the answer has to be that, after all possible inquiry, including the probing of all possible methods of inquiry, we do not know, and for systematic and easily visible reasons cannot know, what the truth about this "deterrent" effect may be. We know that, on raw data, there has been somewhat more homicide in capital punishment states than in non-capital punishment states. But we cannot draw any valid conclusions from this, for factors other than the punishment system may easily explain the difference. The general problem that blocks knowledge here is that no adequately controlled experiment or observation is possible or (so far as we can see) ever will be possible. We have to use uncontrolled data from society itself, outside any laboratory.

A legitimate **summary** of that passage, condensing it to a single sentence and offering documentation (in the form of identifying the author and page number) would be:

Charles L. Black, Jr., on the other hand, contends that we will never know for sure whether capital punishment is an effective deterrent to crime (33).

Following is a legitimate paraphrase of the passage. **Paraphrases** restate the meaning of a passage, giving more details and coming closer to the original wording than a summary does. This paraphrase is proper because it offers a citation and avoids using Black's words:

Charles L. Black, Jr., contends that we do not know and will never know whether capital punishment can effectively deter people from crime. Current data are inconclusive, he says, because they may well be contaminated by other factors. Furthermore, it is impossible to draw up a satisfactory experiment when you cannot use a control group (33).

However, this paraphrase is not legitimate:

We do not know and will never know whether capital punishment can effectively deter people from crime. Current data are inconclusive, because they may well be contaminated by other factors. Furthermore, it is impossible to draw up a satisfactory experiment when you cannot use a control group.

The words may not be Black's but the *ideas* are clearly his. Yet the author never acknowledges this debt by means of a citation (the page number in parentheses). Paraphrases are very useful to a writer because they condense a larger body of material that would otherwise have to be given in direct quotation. Their usefulness, however, does not cancel the debt to the original author. Document just as fully when you borrow ideas as when you borrow words.

This paraphrase pays the debt of documentation, but it, too, is illegitimate, this time for a different reason:

The answer has to be that, after all possible inquiry, including the probing of all possible methods of inquiry, we do not know, and for obvious reasons cannot know, the truth about this "deterrent" effect. We have data showing there has been somewhat more homicide in capital punishment states than

in non-capital punishment states. But we cannot draw valid
conclusions from this, because other factors might explain
the difference. The problem is that no adequately controlled
experiment is possible or ever will be possible (Black 33).

This passage, because it lacks quotation marks, pretends to
be a paraphrase. But in reality it is a direct quotation, with
only a few words changed or left out. The reader deserves
to be told that the passage contains Black's *words* as well
as his ideas.

The only exception—and here is where the lines begin
to blur—is an idea in the public domain. Not all ideas in a
book or an article are unique to the author. Suppose, for
example, you had not heard of the 1972 Supreme Court decision on capital punishment before you started your paper. After all, you may not even have been alive in 1972.
Now you find several authors mentioning that decision and
saying that it caused intense public controversy. You want
to say the same thing in the first paragraph of your paper.
There is no need to document this statement just because
you had not heard of it before you began your research. The
idea is a common one, obvious, widely shared, and easily
proved; therefore, you can restate it without acknowledg-
ment. Of course, if you use somebody else's *words*, either
directly or in close paraphrase, then you must cite their
work. Otherwise, as long as the idea is put in your words,
documentation is unnecessary.

Let me give you another example. Almost every freshman writing handbook like this one has a chapter on the
research paper. And almost every chapter on the research
paper has a few paragraphs on paraphrasing. The ideas I
have been developing in the last few paragraphs are not presented for the first time here. But neither are they presented
for the first time in other handbooks. I do not need to ac-
knowledge any indebtedness to all those other handbooks
just because they have sections comparable to the one you
are now reading. These rules about paraphrases are in the
public domain, and as long as I offer them to you in my own
words I am being honest with you.

What happens when you cannot decide whether an idea is in the public domain? When in doubt, document. It won't hurt and it might help.

Some special problems arise with the use of Internet sources. When it comes to laws of copyright and "fair use" and the documentation of your research, the Internet is still pretty much uncharted territory. And while the electronic wilderness of the Net offers you the excitement of discovering new and unexplored lands, you may not realize you've trekked across property owned by someone else.

The philosophy of electronic copyright protection and the laws to express it are only in the early stages of debate and composition. Thus, you'll need to exercise caution as you accumulate information to support your research. Let's first take a look at some of the issues concerning ideas in the public domain of the Internet. Then, we'll consider some rules of thumb to help you deal with them.

Books, articles, software, photographs, tables, charts, graphs, and other images have copyright notices designed to protect them from unauthorized use. If you see the tag line "Copyright 2002 Jane Q. Public" beside an illustration or attached to a document, you know Ms. Public owns the material in question and deserves compensation for its use or reproduction. You should also assume someone else owns the right to information on the Internet even if there is no copyright notice. The law indicates that the creator of a work owns it by virtue of its creation and existence alone.

For the most part, you must obtain written permission from the copyright holder to use material found on the Internet. I say "for the most part" because the law does allow "fair use" of the material. In other words, you can take small portions (a few lines) of the document and use it as long as you put the portion in quotes or offset it from your text by indentation—and, of course, give the author proper credit. You should definitely seek written permission from the copyright holder if you plan to use extended passages— verbatim quotes or paraphrased ideas—in your paper.

Using Internet sources can make documenting your research precarious for several reasons: (1) laws are still being written to govern the Net (and you could be the unwitting victim of a retroactive application of a new law); (2) dishonest people are as free as honest people to use the Internet, so you may find yourself using stolen goods; and (3) different countries have different laws regarding intellectual property rights. That is, the laws of one country may not apply in another, especially in the global medium of the Internet.

You do have some recourse for deciding what information to use from the Internet. Rather than let fear get the better of you when considering laws of copyright and intellectual property, exercise good judgment and consider these suggestions:

1. Be honest with yourself. Don't use what's not yours without permission or without consideration for the dictates of "fair use."

2. Always assume that property belongs to someone if it doesn't belong to you. If the document or image says "copyright" or has the symbol © beside it, obtain permission to use it.

3. If you can't get permission—if it's not available or it's denied—you can summarize the source, include its URL number, and direct your readers to the site for supporting information. You may also choose to leave it out altogether and use some other available source.

4. If you're not sure what constitutes "fair use," check one of the many Web sites on copyright or intellectual property law. Here are a some Web sites I found just by typing in the keywords "copyright" and "intellectual property" in the search box:

   <http://www.benedict.com/>

   <http://lcweb.loc.gov/copyright/>

   <http://www.indiana.edu/copyright.html>

   <http://arl.cni.org/index.html>

   <http://galaxy.einet.net/galaxy/law/Intellectual-Property.html>

5. Be sure to consult with your instructor if you are in doubt about what information to use or how to use it.

A2. How to Document

There is no one way to document your sources. Which of the several available methods you use will depend on the purpose of your research paper and on the person for whom you are preparing it.

The MLA Method

Most instructors in humanities and business courses prefer the system recommended in the Modern Language Association's *Handbook for Writers of Research Papers*, 5th edition (1999). Papers for courses in the natural or social sciences may require a different style—see Section A4 for a discussion of citations for scientific papers.

The MLA documentation approach uses the author and page number of the cited work as a code to tell the reader which item in the Works Cited list is being referred to. Instead of using footnotes that give complete bibliographic information (an approach that some instructors and disciplines still prefer—see the next section), the author–page number method provides adequate information for the reader to locate the full citation in the alphabetized Works Cited at the end of the paper. No distinction is made at this stage among books, articles, and electronic sources.

To use the MLA method, place the author's name and the page number of the quoted or paraphrased material in parentheses following the material:

> Reinstating the death penalty seems to have no
> effect on the homicide rate (Lester 19).

Note that there is no comma between the name and the page number. If the author's name is introduced in the passage, it is unnecessary to repeat it in the citation; the page number will be sufficient:

> Ernest van den Haag cites another researcher's
> claim that every execution of a murderer deters
> 18 other potential murders (44).

If there are two or three authors, provide all their names:

> Even of those indicted for first-degree murder,
> only about 1 percent would actually be executed
> (Playfair and Sington 274).

If the work has more than three authors, use the first author's name plus "et al."

If your bibliography will contain more than one work by the same author, you will need to clarify your in-text citations by including the title (or a shortened version) of the particular work being cited:

> Professor Thorsten Sellin has been a tireless
> investigator of this subject, and he offers numer-
> ous examples. Colorado averaged 15.4 convic-
> tions per year for murder before it abolished the
> death penalty, 18 per year after abolition, and
> then 19 per year when the death penalty was
> restored. When Delaware dropped the death
> penalty in 1959, the murder rate actually
> shrank, from an average of 22.3 per year before
> abolition to 14.3 per year after (Capital Punish-
> ment 123). Professor Sellin also compares states
> with the death penalty to states without. "The
> conclusion is inevitable that the presence of the
> death penalty—in law or practice—does not
> influence homicide death rates" (138). Capital
> punishment, he says elsewhere, "has failed as a
> deterrent" ("Death and Imprisonment" 284).

When a work is not attributed to a specific author, use the title or a shortened form of it in place of the author's last name:

> Moreover, execution of a murderer is between four and eleven times more likely if the victim was white than if the victim was black ("Killers" 38).

If the reference is to the editor's portion of an edited work, simply treat the editor as the author; it is not necessary to include "ed." or some other indication of editorship in the citation, since that information will be readily available in the Works Cited section. If the reference is to Author A's contribution to a work compiled by Editor B, use A's name.

When you wish to refer to an entire volume within a multivolume set, give (and clearly label) the volume number in place of a page number. If you need to cite material from a work that has two or more volumes, give both volume and page number:

> Several key legal cases have contributed to the current confusion in this complex area (Pike vol. 7). Of particular interest are the precedent-setting Lee v. North Carolina and Morgan v. Indiana (Pike 2: 489).

If the material to which you refer was itself being quoted (in other words, if A's quote appears in B's book, and you want to use what A says), you need to indicate that you obtained the material secondhand by using the abbreviation "qtd. in" (quoted in), as thus:

> Anna Quindlen argues that what most people want from the death penalty—for "criminals to suffer as their victims did"—is exactly what they are least likely to get (qtd. in Miller 158).

And if you acquired the material in a personal interview or through attending a lecture, simply use the name of the person to whom you listened.

Since Internet sources often do not have numbered pages when printed out, you may have to refer readers to some point within the document's division. Use division indicators (e.g., subhead titles) provided by the document itself, not your software.

You will no doubt encounter a few sources that do not fit the examples provided here. If your documentation problems are unusually complex, you might ask your instructor for advice or consult a copy of the MLA Handbook.

I have been describing the methods for citing sources within the text of your paper. You must accompany the citations with a Works Cited list (described in further detail in Section A3).

Footnotes/Endnotes

Some instructors may prefer that you use the **footnote** method for documentation of your papers. With this method, you number the footnotes consecutively throughout the paper. At each point where you would otherwise place an author–page number citation, you type the footnote number, slightly above the line. Footnotes are placed at the bottom of the page, a quadruple space below the text. The lines in each item are single spaced, but the lines between items are double spaced.

When footnotes are placed together at the end of the paper they become **endnotes** and are double spaced throughout. The following endnotes style is based on MLA guidelines.

For **books and pamphlets,** the first time you refer to a work you must include its author, title, and publisher, the place and date of publication, and the page number of the material you are using. Type and punctuate the information like this:

[7]Michael Meltsner, Cruel and Unusual: The Supreme Court and Capital Punishment (New York: Random, 1975) 142.

Notice that this entry contains the following items, in order: (1) author's name in normal word order, followed by a comma;

(2) the full title, underlined to indicate italics; (3) a set of parentheses enclosing the city of publication, a colon, the publisher, a comma, and the year of publication; (4) one space and then the page number, followed by a period.

Any later references to the same book require only author and page number, plus a shortened title if you use more than one work by the same author:

[14]Black 71-73.

[15]Bedau, <u>Death Penalty</u> xi.

However, some books offer special difficulties. Here are the most common problems and how to solve them:

1. The book has more than one author.

[22]N. K. Teeters and J. Hedblom, <u>Hang by the Neck</u> (Springfield, Ill.: Thomas, 1966) 43.

Note that *Springfield* is followed by the abbreviation of its state, Illinois, for clarification—unlike such cities as Chicago, Boston, New York, or London, it is not obvious what state (or foreign country) it is in.

2. The book is an anthology or a collection and therefore has an editor rather than an author.

[23]Hugo Adam Bedau, ed., preface and introduction to <u>The Death Penalty in America: An Anthology</u> (Garden City, N.Y.: Doubleday, 1964) 6.

Bedau's remarks are found in the introductory material to the book, as cited here; if you cite one of the

articles included in an anthology, see item 1 on page
453.

3. The book is a translation.

[26]Fyodor Dostoyevsky, <u>Crime and Punishment,</u> trans. David Magarshack (Baltimore:
Penguin, 1951) 216.

4. The book has more than one volume.

[31]Luke O. Pike, <u>A History of Crime in England,</u> vol. 2 (London: Hodder and Stoughton,
1876) 2: 489.

This citation tells your reader that the page reference is
to the second volume of a multivolume work.

5. The book has more than one edition.

[34]Charles L. Black, Jr., <u>Capital Punishment:
The Inevitability of Caprice and Mistake,</u> 2nd ed.
(New York: Norton, 1981) 25.

6. The note refers to an encyclopedia entry.

[37]A. E. Woods, "Capital Punishment," <u>World
Book Encyclopedia,</u> 1958 edition.

The initials of the authors are printed at the end of the
entry; you can learn the author's full name by referring to
the list of contributors in the first volume. The edition/
year information is sufficient; you can dispense with page
numbers because the entries are found alphabetically.

7. The work was written by one author and then edited by
another.

[44]Clarence Darrow, <u>Attorney for the
Damned . . .</u> ed. Arthur Weinberg (New York:
Simon, 1957) 93.

If you encounter a special problem not covered by these
seven examples, check a style manual in the library or ask
your instructor for advice.

Articles are treated a little differently. The first reference includes author, title of the article, name of the jour-

nal, volume number, date, and page reference. Arrange and punctuate it like this:

⁵Jacques Barzun, "In Favor of Capital Punishment," The American Scholar 31 (1962): 185.

In front of excellence the immortal gods have put sweat, and long and steep is the way to it, and rough at first. But when you come to the top, then it is easy.
—Hesiod

The author's name is given in the normal word order, the article's title is capitalized and put within quotation marks, and the journal's title is underlined (italicized). There is no punctuation between the journal and the volume number—31—which is followed by the year within parentheses, and the page number is preceded by a colon. Later references to the same article require just the author's last name and the page number:

¹²Barzun 187-89.

Once more I should point to a few exceptions and ways to solve them.

1. If the essay or article is part of an anthology, there is no punctuation between the parentheses and the page number; if it is part of a journal, use a colon between the parentheses and the page number. In both cases allow one space before the page number.

    ¹⁶Ramsey Clark, "To Abolish Capital Punishment," in Capital Punishment, ed. James McCafferty (New York: Lieber-Atherton, 1974) 180.

2. The article is anonymous, from a popular magazine.

    ¹⁷"Closing Death Row," Time 10 July 1972: 37.

3. The note refers to a book review, with the reviewer's name first.

    ¹⁸J. J. Paris, rev. of Capital Punishment: The Inevitability of Caprice and Mistake, by Charles L. Black, Jr., America 8 Mar. 1975: 175.

4. The note refers to a newspaper article. (If the newspaper article has a byline, put the author's name before the title.)

[19]"Killers of Whites, Killers of Blacks," <u>New York Times</u> 17 Oct. 1986: 38.

5. The note refers to an electronic resource.

<u>Abolition Now</u>. "Death Penalty Racist? State Says Yes," 1995. 2 May 2002. <http//www.abolition-now.com/report/racist/html>.

These five examples can serve as models for treating the most common exceptions.

This whole array of customs and exceptions can be confusing, I know. Perhaps I can best simplify it by reducing these customs to a formula—one not unlike those you might have met in high school chemistry or biology. All you need do is plug in the proper data, and the formula guarantees an acceptable footnote or endnote. First, the formula for the first reference to the usual single-author, single-volume book:

author's name (first name first) + comma + title (underlined) + opening parenthesis + city of publication + colon + publisher + comma + year of publication + closing parenthesis + space + page number(s) + period

Second, the formula for a first reference to a standard journal article is this:

author's name (first name first) + comma + opening quotes + article's title + comma + closing quotes + journal's title (underlined) + space + volume number + space + opening parenthesis + date of issue + closing parenthesis + colon + page number(s) + period

Third, footnotes and endnotes for electronic documentation are modified from those for print. Detailed guidelines and examples for their use can be found in the fifth edition of the *MLA Handbook*. In many cases, electronic information can be documented according to this formula:

creator [person's last name + comma + first name] *or* sponsor [title of site/organization, underlined] + period + space + opening quotes + title of section being quoted [if available] + comma + closing quotes + space + date of site posting + period + space +date of your access to site + period +web address [within angle brackets] + period

Fourth, the formula for later references to all sources is simply this:

author's last name + space + page number(s) + period

Fifth, if you have cited at least two works by the same author, the formula for later references to books and articles is this:

author's last name + comma + space + abbreviated title + space + page number + period

These five formulas will cover perhaps 90 percent of the footnotes or endnotes in the usual long paper.

One final comment. If you have mentioned the name of the author or the title of the article in the text of your paper, you need not repeat that information in the note itself. For example, if in your paper you say, "Jacques Barzun makes an eloquent plea for the death penalty in his article 'In Favor of Capital Punishment,'" the note needs only the journal title and the information that follows it.

A3. List of Works Cited

After you have typed the rest of your paper, it is time for the List of Works Cited. (In the past these were often called *bibliographies*, but the new term more accurately reflects the fact that the list includes more than just books.) Ordinarily this list should include only the works cited in your paper. Label the list clearly: "List of Works Cited" (or simply "Works Cited"). "List of Works Consulted" would be appropriate if your instructor wants you to list all the works you read, even the ones you did not cite.

If you have used footnotes or the MLA documentation form described on pages 447–450, the list occurs at the end of the paper. If you have used endnotes, the Works Cited list follows them.

Such lists are arranged in alphabetical order by author. Enter books and pamphlets this way:

Meltsner, Michael. Cruel and Unusual: The
  Supreme Court and Capital Punishment. New
  York: Random, 1975.

(Comparing this entry to the footnote for the same book on page 451, you will note that the punctuation and indention are different and the page reference has been eliminated.)

Variations on the basic data would appear in a Works Cited list this way:

1. The book has more than one author.

   Teeters, N. K., and J. Hedblom. Hang by the
     Neck. Springfield, Ill.: Thomas, 1966.

2. The book is an anthology with an editor rather than an author.

   Draper, Thomas, ed. Capital Punishment. New
     York: Wilson, 1985.

3. The book is a translation; both author and translator are named.

   Gadamer, Hans George. Philosophical Apprentice-
     ships. Trans. Robert Collins. Cambridge: MIT,
     1985.

4. The book has more than one volume.

   Pike, Luke O. A History of Crime in England. 2
     vols. London: Hodder and Stoughton, 1876.

   Even if you cited from one volume only, list the complete multivolume work.

5. The book has more than one edition.

   Black, Charles L., Jr. Capital Punishment: The
     Inevitability of Caprice and Mistake. 2nd ed.
     New York: Norton, 1981.

6. The work was written by one author and then edited by another.

Darrow, Clarence. <u>Attorney for the Damned . . .</u>
Ed. Arthur Weinberg. New York: Simon, 1957.

7. The reference is to an encyclopedia entry.

Woods, A. E. "Capital Punishment." <u>World Book
Encyclopedia.</u> 1976 ed.

If the original reference is to the words of one author
being quoted in a book by another author, just give the full
citation for the "other" author (the book where you found
the quote) in the citation list.

Sometimes articles are listed separately. But for the average paper this separation is unnecessary—combine books
and articles, following the alphabetical order of authors' last
names. The form for the standard article is like this:

Lester, David. "The Deterrent Effect of Execution
on Homicide," <u>Psychological Reports</u> 64 (1989):
306-09.

In the text itself, you referred to a particular page number.
This time you note the inclusive pages; in other words, the
Lester article in question begins on page 306 and ends on
page 309.

Other kinds of articles or sources appear in the list in
these forms:

1. The article is part of an anthology.

Clark, Ramsey. "To Abolish Capital Punishment."
<u>Capital Punishment</u>. Ed. James McCafferty.
New York: Lieber-Atherton, 1972. 176-80.

2. The article is anonymous and appeared in a popular
magazine; it is alphabetized by the first word of the title.

"Closing Death Row." <u>Time</u> 10 July 1972: 37.

3. The entry refers to a book review (notice how all months
except May, June, and July are given in abbreviated form).

Paris, J. J. Rev. of <u>Capital Punishment: The
Inevitability of Caprice and Mistake,</u> by Charles
L. Black, Jr. <u>America</u> 8 Mar. 1975: 175.

4. The entry refers to a newspaper article; it is alphabetized by title.

"Bids to Witness Execution." <u>New York Times</u> 2
    Mar. 1986: 41.

5. The entry refers to an interview or lecture.

Underhill, Alexander. Personal interview. 8 May
    1990.

Citing sources from the Internet has its own rules. You can find guidelines and samples for MLA documentation on the Internet itself at <http://www.webcrawler.com/select/refbook50.html>. Since Web sites (unlike printed material) can change daily, I'm using generic "samples" rather than specific sites.

1. The entry refers to an online scholarly project, reference database, or professional or personal website. Here you will have to provide as much information as you can while recognizing that sometimes key elements cannot be determined.

<u>Complete Title</u>. Ed. Jane Q. Public Version 2.
    3 Jan. 2001. U of Virginia. 9 May 2002.
    <http://www.edu/home.html>.

2. The entry refers to an article in an online journal.

Public, Jane Q. "Title of Article." <u>Periodical's
    Name</u> 5 (Mar. 2001): 16 paragraphs. 9 May
    2002. <http://www.edu/home.html>.

3. The entry refers to information you gained from an e-mail exchange. The author is the sender of the message to you. The subject line from the e-mail is treated as the title and put in quotes, and the type of communication is included. Provide both the date the e-mail was sent to you and the date you accessed it, as well as the sender's e-mail address (be sure you have permission to use it).

Sample, John. "Subject line from posting." 12
   Feb. 2000. Personal mail. 14 Feb. 2000.
   <jsample@123456.1234.com>.

4. The entry refers to material gleaned from a Listserv or a
   Newslist. Here the "author" will be the person whose
   contribution to the list you are using, the dates will refer to when the contribution was posted and when you
   accessed it, and the URL will be the online address of
   the list.

Sample, John. "Subject line from posting." Online
   posting. 18 Nov. 2002. <spcoped@oped.stlu.
   edu>. 21 Nov. 2002.

5. The entry refers to a CD-Rom or diskette. In this case
   the information given will more closely resemble what
   you would find with a printed book.

Public, Jane Q., Ed. Title. CD-Rom. New York:
   Publisher/Producer, 1999.

A4. Scientific Papers

The MLA method of documentation and bibliography described in the previous sections is the most common one,
as noted before. It will serve you well in composition, business, history, literature, and philosophy courses—in fact, in
almost any course except those in the social and natural
sciences. Since it is quite likely you will be writing papers
for courses in these two areas, you should know how their
practices differ.

For example, suppose in the course of a paper you have
occasion to cite the following article in support of your
case:

White, Harrison. "Cause and Effect in Social
   Mobility Tables." Behavioral Science 8 (1983) :
   14-27. [MLA form]

In scientific writing there would be two common ways
to refer to this article. One way uses a coded expression

that includes the author's name and the year of publication;
the other uses a code number.

In the **author and date system,** such as the one used by
the American Psychological Association (APA), you insert
within parentheses the last name of the author you are citing and the year his or her study was published. For our
White example, suppose this is the sentence in your text
that you must support by a reference:

> This conclusion is further supported by a study
> undertaken by Harrison White.

Normally all you need do to complete the reference is include the year of publication within parentheses:

> This conclusion is further supported by a study
> undertaken by Harrison White (1983).

However, if the sentence in the text does not provide the
author's name, the author's last name must also be included
within the parentheses:

> An earlier study (White, 1983) also supports the
> conclusion I have been advancing.

If you must include a specific page number, as in the case of
a direct quotation, add a comma and the page number:

> This conclusion has been termed "most convinc-
> ing" by Harrison White (1983, p. 22).

If there is more than one author, give the last names of
both:

> Recent experiments (Hannan and Freeman,
> 1977) confirm this point.

More than one investigation by the same author or authors
would be listed chronologically:

> Cantril (1941, 1965) is the only expert who
> seems to disagree.

If more than one investigator arrived at the same conclusion, list all of them, in alphabetical order and separated by
semicolons:

Other researchers (Ryder, 1965; White, 1983) share this concern.

Your reader, should he or she wish to check your sources, would now turn to the list of references (called simply "References," not "Works Cited") at the end of your paper. That alphabetical list would include every source to which you gave an author-and-year citation in the text. A list based on the works mentioned above might look something like this:

Cantril, H. (1941). The psychology of social movements. New York: Wiley.

Cantril, H. (1965). The pattern of human concern. New Brunswick, N.J.: Rutgers University Press.

Hannan, H. & Freeman, J. (1977). The population ecology of organizations. American Journal of Sociology, 82, 929-964.

Ryder, N. (1965). The cohort as a concept in the study of social change. American Sociological Review, 30, 843-861.

White, H. (1983). Cause and effect in social mobility tables. Behavioral Science, 8, 14-27.

The reader finds the source by locating the author's name. Whenever necessary, as in the case of the Cantril references, the year will differentiate one work from another. If more than one work was published by an author in the same year, the works will still appear chronologically in the references (a March article, for example, before an August one); the textual citation will add small letters (White, 1983a; White, 1983b).

If you examine the above references, you will notice some other differences between the author-date and MLA formats, including (1) initials are often given instead of authors' first names; (2) the year of publication is in parentheses following the author's name and is followed by a period; (3) volume numbers for journals are underlined and followed by a comma and the page numbers (if the article is in a journal with continuous pagination) or by a comma plus *p.* or *pp.* with the page numbers (if the article is from a magazine that is renumbered for each issue); (4) only the first word of the title of the book or article is capitalized; (5) there are no quotation marks around article titles; (6) the publisher's name is given in full (such as "Oxford University Press").

So far we have discussed articles and books. For references to electronic information, apply the following guidelines; using them with (and comparing them to) the MLA guidelines on pp. 458–459.

1. The entry refers to an online scholarly project, reference database, or professional or personal website.

   Complete title (3 Jan. 2001). Ed. J. Public. Version 2. University of Virginia. 9 May 2002. <http://www.edu/home/html>.

2. The entry refers to an online journal.

   Public, J. (2001). Title of article. Periodical's Name, 5, 16 paragraphs. 9 May 2002. <http://www.edu/home.html>.

3. The entry refers to information you gained from an e-mail exchange.

   Sample, J. (14 Feb. 2000). "Subject line from posting." Peronal mail. 14 Feb. 2000. <jsample@123456.1234.com>.

4. The entry refers to material gleaned from a Listserv or a Newslist.

   Sample, J. (18 Nov. 2002). "Subject line from posting." Online posting. <spcoped@cped.stlu.edu>. 21 Nov. 2002.

5. The entry refers to a CD-Rom or diskette.

   Public, J., Ed. (1999). Title. CD-Rom. New York: Publisher/Producer.

The author-date style is less rigid than the MLA format and allows greater flexibility in handling of highly technical material. This format is not the only format used in scientific papers, but the reference lists above would be acceptable for the great majority of scientific papers.

The **number system** is a different way of providing the coded expression within the text. The reference list at the end is exactly the same, but each item on the list is numbered. Then, in the text itself, all you need do is put in parentheses the number of the reference item you wish to cite.

Using the earlier examples, you would first number every item in the list of references. The two Cantril books become numbers one and two, followed by the articles of Hannan and Freeman (3), Ryder (4), and White (5). Then in your text you simply refer to these books and articles by number:

These conclusions are supported by Ryder (4) and also by Cantril (1), (2).

Note how a separate set of parentheses is required for each of the two Cantril books. If the author's name is not mentioned in the text, it can be included inside the parentheses:

We now know (White, 5) the cause of this reaction.

If you must cite a particular page number, include it also within the parentheses:

But Hannan and Freeman disagree, claiming the earlier study "stretches the available evidence" (3, p. 931) and cannot be relied upon.

Cite electronic information much as you did with the author-date system.

No matter which you use, the author-year system or the number system, you may find that your instructor requires certain specific ways of preparing tables, graphs, and other data. He or she might also recommend ways to divide your material, such as cover page + abstract (a one-paragraph summary) + text (including introduction, method, results, conclusion, discussion) + references + tables. Obviously you

> *In science credit goes to the man who convinces the world, not to the man to whom the idea first occurs.*
> *—Sir Francis Darwin*

should conform to these suggestions, too.

Scientific writing may differ in format from writing submitted to teachers in other disciplines, but it has just as much need for clarity, just as much need for thoroughness, just as much need for persuasiveness as any other kind of writing. The skills we have been describing in this chapter and the preceding ones will be important to you in every kind of writing you undertake.

EXERCISES

1. Put the following information into proper MLA footnote form:

   A. A book written by Sidney Coulling titled *Matthew Arnold's Controversies* and published by the Ohio University Press, located in Athens, Ohio; the book was published in 1974 and you wish to cite from page 81.

   B. William Kane's article "Toward a New Aesthetic" appeared in the second volume of the *Tufts Review,* spring 1970 issue; you cite from page 22 of an article that occupied pages 21 through 27 of that issue.

   C. Katherine Ann Porter's short story "The Circus" was reprinted in an anthology edited by Edward M. White and titled *The Pop Culture Tradition;* this anthology was put out by W. W. Norton of New York in 1972; Ms. Porter's story occupies pages 118 to 123, and you quote a section on page 120.

   D. On August 7, 1890, the *New York Times* carried an account of the first electrocution under the headline "Far Worse Than Hanging"; this item appeared on page 1.

2. Take the four footnotes produced by the previous question and make them into a short "Works Cited" list in MLA style.

3. Then convert the four entries into "References" for the author-date citation system.

4. Study carefully the long paragraph beginning, "To make this difference clearer . . ." on page 410 in Chapter 12. Then prepare (1) a one- or two-sentence summary of the paragraph; (2) a legitimate paraphrase of sentences four, five, and six; (3) a direct quotation of sentence five. Include appropriate citations.

> *Example is always more efficacious than precept.*
> *—Samuel Johnson*

5. If you can, study a long paper you turned in recently. Did you outline it? Did you have a complete file of both bibliography and note entries? Are the in-text citations and Works Cited or References in proper form? If the answer to any of these questions is no, check the relevant sections of this chapter for guidance on how you might have improved it.

6. Compile a short preliminary list of sources for one of the following topics:

The NC-17 movie rating
Government aid for private schools
How language is acquired by young children
The Cuban missile crisis
Gandhi's theory of civil disobedience
How to acquire a fast-food franchise
Crop circles
Adaption of Phillip K. Dick works to film
Extinction of the dinosaurs

B. SAMPLE PAPER

It helps to have a concrete model from which you can work. Here is a research paper that illustrates the steps described in Chapter 12 and in Part A of this chapter. The paper has an arguable proposition, and it builds on the outline drawn up on page 434. Some comments in the margins call your attention to features worth noting. The paper follows MLA style, which does not include a title page. Your instructor may require a title page for your papers, however. If so, he or she will give you a preferred format.

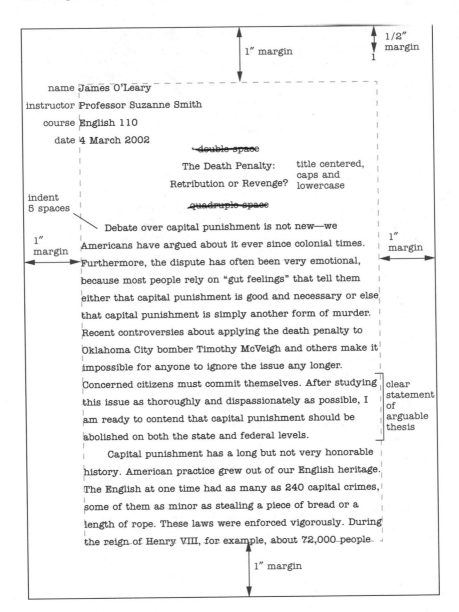

1″ margin

1/2″ margin

1

name James O'Leary

instructor Professor Suzanne Smith

course English 110

date 4 March 2002

~~double space~~

The Death Penalty:

Retribution or Revenge?

title centered, caps and lowercase

indent 5 spaces

~~quadruple space~~

1″ margin

Debate over capital punishment is not new—we Americans have argued about it ever since colonial times. Furthermore, the dispute has often been very emotional, because most people rely on "gut feelings" that tell them either that capital punishment is good and necessary or else that capital punishment is simply another form of murder. Recent controversies about applying the death penalty to Oklahoma City bomber Timothy McVeigh and others make it impossible for anyone to ignore the issue any longer. Concerned citizens must commit themselves. After studying this issue as thoroughly and dispassionately as possible, I am ready to contend that capital punishment should be abolished on both the state and federal levels.

1″ margin

clear statement of arguable thesis

Capital punishment has a long but not very honorable history. American practice grew out of our English heritage. The English at one time had as many as 240 capital crimes, some of them as minor as stealing a piece of bread or a length of rope. These laws were enforced vigorously. During the reign of Henry VIII, for example, about 72,000 people

1″ margin

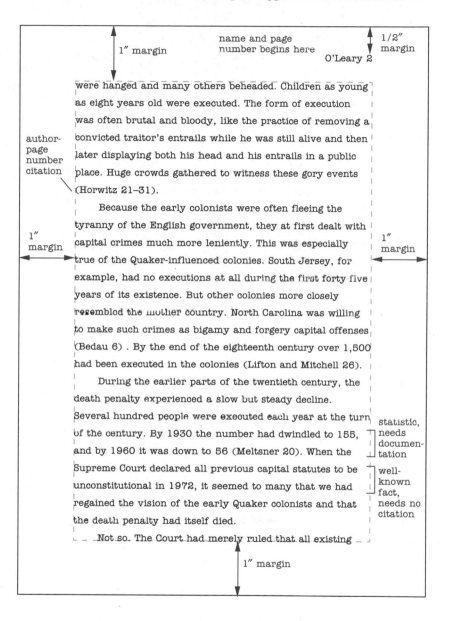

1″ margin

name and page
number begins here

1/2″
margin

O'Leary 2

author-
page
number
citation

were hanged and many others beheaded. Children as young
as eight years old were executed. The form of execution
was often brutal and bloody, like the practice of removing a
convicted traitor's entrails while he was still alive and then
later displaying both his head and his entrails in a public
place. Huge crowds gathered to witness these gory events
(Horwitz 21–31).

1″
margin

Because the early colonists were often fleeing the
tyranny of the English government, they at first dealt with
capital crimes much more leniently. This was especially
true of the Quaker-influenced colonies. South Jersey, for
example, had no executions at all during the first forty five
years of its existence. But other colonies more closely
resembled the mother country. North Carolina was willing
to make such crimes as bigamy and forgery capital offenses
(Bedau 6) . By the end of the eighteenth century over 1,500
had been executed in the colonies (Lifton and Mitchell 26).

1″
margin

During the earlier parts of the twentieth century, the
death penalty experienced a slow but steady decline.
Several hundred people were executed each year at the turn
of the century. By 1930 the number had dwindled to 155,
and by 1960 it was down to 56 (Meltsner 20). When the
Supreme Court declared all previous capital statutes to be
unconstitutional in 1972, it seemed to many that we had
regained the vision of the early Quaker colonists and that
the death penalty had itself died.

statistic,
needs
documen-
tation

well-
known
fact,
needs no
citation

Not so. The Court had merely ruled that all existing

1″ margin

O'Leary 3

another well-known fact

statutes were discriminatory, but it left room for legisla-
tures to redraw the statutes so that they met the new
guidelines specified by the Court. Many states hastened to
comply. In 1976 the Court affirmed its earlier decision by
approving some of the new laws, and in 1977 Gary Gilmore
became the first person to be executed under *one of* them. Since
then we have had hundreds of executions, with more
occurring almost every week. Because so many states are
grappling with the issue, and because so many people seem
to want to speed up the executions, we must examine the
relevant facts. Should any state reinstate the death penalty
or try to have more executions, it would have to ignore
five very important facts about capital punishment. These
facts also constitute my reasons for opposing the death
penalty.

author's late addition to manuscript

        Fact number one: The death penalty discriminates
against the poor and against minority groups, especially
blacks. In the United States, if you have money and
connections you will not get the death penalty, as the O. J.
Simpson case clearly showed. The rich can afford to hire
lawyers who will provide thorough pretrial investigation,
skilled representation in court, and—should the verdict still
be "guilty"—effective petitions for a reduced sentence or a
new trial. The poor must rely on overworked public
defenders. Since blacks make up a disproportionate share of
the poor in this country, they suffer doubly. Moreover,
execution of a murderer is between four and eleven times

use of statistics as support

O'Leary 4

more likely if the victim was white than if the victim was black ("Killers" 38). So disproportionate is the effect of the death penalty on African Americans that its imposition can be called racist ("Death Penalty Racist?").

A second fact: Imposition of the death penalty often results from public hysteria. American history affords numerous examples of groups of people dying because of a public clamoring for action against some real or imagined menace. During the Salem witchcraft trials of 1692, over twenty people were executed on the testimony of excited adolescent girls. The "red scare" that followed the First World War led directly to the Sacco-Vanzetti case, in which two Italian immigrants were electrocuted, not because their guilt had been proved beyond a reasonable doubt, but because local officials (including the judge) feared their political views and wanted to make an example of them. In these and other instances the social climate made it all but impossible for judges and juries to arrive at a fair and impartial verdict. Yet people paid with their lives for this irrationality, because the system of capital punishment makes no room for later changes of mind in a less heated atmosphere. Hysteria and thus barbarity are not impossible even in our more "civilized" modern times. In 1986 seven people bid $1,000 each for the right to watch a prisoner die in the electric chair ("Bids" 41). Equally unsettling is "the hypocrisy and callousness of the elected officials, judges, and prosecutors who [use] these cases for political advantage" (Wallace 2).

familiar history, no footnotes

to avoid an ugly "orphan" on the next page, finish the paragraph inside the bottom margin

O'Leary 5

Third, innocent people are sometimes executed. While such mistakes may not be too frequent, they do happen, and even one such mistake would be too many.

Even the most airtight case is not immune to error. In 1949 a man named Timothy Evans was accused of the murder of his wife and child in London, and he confessed to the crime. Later he rescinded his confession and said a man named Christie had killed them. Christie, a former policeman, denied it and testified for the prosecution. Evans was convicted and hanged. Three years later the authorities discovered that Christie had indeed killed Mrs. Evans, the child, and several prostitutes (Horwitz 170–171) .

[margin note: development by a single example—this paragraph summarizes four paragraphs in the original source]

In our own country the two most famous victims of mistaken identity are probably Bruno Hauptmann and Randall Dale Adams. Hauptmann was executed for the Lindbergh baby kidnap-murder. Recent evidence makes it much more likely that Hauptmann was as innocent as he insisted he was. A special irony of the case is that while Hauptmann was pleading his innocence, no less than 205 people were willing to confess their guilt (Ehrmann 21)! This fact, plus the fact that over a quarter of all "positive identifications" made in lineups are mistakes (Horwitz 168), should remind us of how shaky even the most "reliable" testimony can be. In the case of Adams, he came within seven days of execution before being spared. He was finally exonerated by the confession of the real murderer. Michael Radelet has shown that at least twenty-three

[margin note: Internet source; internal evidence shows author is reliable]

O'Leary 6

innocent people have been wrongly executed in the United
States in this century (1–5).

So frequent are the cases of condemning innocent
people to death that the governor of Illinois, George Ryan,
recently has declared a moratorium on capital punishment
in his state. His action was prompted by several instances
of DNA testing which revealed that certain prisoners on
death row could not have been guilty of the crimes for
which they were condemned. Since 1997 the American Bar
Association has also argued for a moratorium (Sarat 254).

The 205 would-be confessors to the Lindbergh murder
surely had twisted, perverted minds. Yet they point up still
another fact about murderers, the only class of criminals
who are now executed: All murderers are psychologically
sick, even if only temporarily. Charles Manson, Richard
Speck, and Sirhan Sirhan are alive today only because of
the 1972 Supreme Court decision. But now that the
immediate passions have cooled, can we seriously argue
that these men were sane when they committed their
crimes? What, then, can we say about Ted Bundy, another
sociopath but this time one who was executed? Or Jeffrey
Dahmer, the murderer turned cannibal? No one believes any
of them should have been freed to kill again. But neither
can we believe that they were normal, rational people who
could appreciate the enormity of their crimes.

Finally, these first four sets of facts lead me inevitably
to another: the fact that capital punishment as currently

O'Leary 7

used is unconstitutional. The primary reason for judging

author's correction of error caught in proof-reading

c**a**pital punishment unconstitutional is that it violates the
Eighth Amendment, the one that bars any "cruel or
unusual" punishment. The death penalty violates both
standards. It is cruel because it inflicts a very painful
death—many who have witnessed electrocutions, for
example, speak about the smell of burning flesh afterward,
and lethal injections can be just as traumatic (Goldman and
Fuller 39) . It is also cruel because it causes great psychological pain, as in the case of someone like Caryl Chessman,
who spent twelve years on death row before the postpone-
ments were exhausted and he went to the gas chamber.

The death penalty is "unusual" in the most literal
sense of that term. It does not happen often, at least at the
federal level, and it does not happen at all to those who are
rich and white. Even of those indicted for first-degree
murder, only about 1 percent would actually be executed
(Playfair and Sington 274). Any punishment applied so
infrequently and so randomly can have only a small impact
on the mind of a potential criminal, yet it will have terrible
consequences for those unfortunate few who become its
victims. Furthermore, any law, if it is to be constitutional
and worthy of our respect, must be applied without regard
to race, color, creed, or wealth. Yet we have seen how the
death penalty discriminates. The "unfortunate few" always
turn out to be poor and often black. Yet blacks are but the
latest victims. Before them the Irish, the Germans, the

O'Leary 8

Italians, and other immigrant groups suffered disproportionately because they were then poor and politically feeble.

Obviously it can be said that the Supreme Court has
declared capital punishment to be constitutional. The 1976
decision, however, should not be viewed as a legal decision
so much as a political one. Michael Meltsner, an authority
on the Court's debate over this issue, proves rather
conclusively that President Richard Nixon made his choices
for the Supreme Court partly on the basis of the candidate's
support for the death penalty. Justices Powell and
Rehnquist in particular were picked for this reason (258–
65). Former Attorney General Edwin Meese pulled political
tricks to get death penalty punishments approved by his
hand-picked U.S. Sentencing Commission (Cohodas 326).

Furthermore, Charles L. Black, Jr., Sterling Professor
of Law at Yale University and the nation's foremost
authority on constitutional law, argues that the death
penalty violates not only the Eighth but also the Fourteenth
Amendment: "There is not enough 'due process of law' in
our system to make it an acceptable instrument for the
'deprivation of life'" (105). Former Supreme Court justice
Harry Blackmun said in 1994 that the death penalty has
"inherent constitutional deficiencies" (qtd. in Sarat 253).

Many arguments have been made in favor of capital
punishment. Some of them are frivolous or even blood-
thirsty. But others have been offered by serious, reflective
people. I would like to examine these arguments more
closely, to show why I think they are inadequate.

Margin notes: these sentences summarize 8 pages in the original; lead-in identifies this authority; only page number is given; author is being fair to opponents

O'Leary 9

The first argument offered by supporters of capital
punishment is that the threat of death deters crime. They
claim that if the death penalty were eliminated entirely, the
murder rate would soar because people would not be afraid
to kill. Special attention is paid to the murderer sentenced
to life imprisonment: What sanction is left that can frighten
him or her, except death? Ernest van den Haag cites
another researcher's claim that every execution of a
murderer deters 18 other potential murders (44).

short —
direct
quotation

But van den Haag himself has to admit that "the
statistics are not conclusive" (44), a verdict also reached by
David Lester (306). In fact, some statistics suggest the
opposite conclusion. For example, a comparison of the
murder rates in a state before and after the temporary
abolition of capital punishment in 1972 shows that such
states experienced no appreciable rise in homicides.
Professor Thorsten Sellin, who has been a tireless investigator of this subject, offers numerous examples. Colorado
averaged 15.4 convictions per year for murder before it
abolished the death penalty, 18 per year after abolition, and
then 19 per year when the death penalty was restored.
When Delaware dropped the death penalty in 1959, the
murder rate actually shrank, from an average of 22.3 per
year before abolition to 14.3 per year after (Capital
Punishment 123). Professor Sellin also compares states
with the death penalty and states without. "The conclusion
is inevitable that the presence of the death penalty—in law

develop-
ment by
numer-
ous
examples

O'Leary 10

or practice—does not influence homicide death rates" (138).
Capital punishment, he says elsewhere, "has failed as a
deterrent" ("Death and Imprisonment" 284).

Still, many will dispute these facts. Reason, they say,
tells us clearly that at least *some* criminals, no matter how
few, will stop short of murder if they believe they might die
for it. Otherwise why would criminals fight so hard to avoid
the death penalty? If even one life is saved because of this
fear, capital punishment has served its purpose.

One cannot argue with such reasoning, because it rests
so much on guesses about how the criminal mind works.
Deterrence can probably never be proven or disproven
fully. The wisest words are Charles L. Black, Jr.'s:

double space

direct
quotations
of more
than four
lines are
indented

> I think the answer has to be that, after all
> possible inquiry, including the probing of all possible
> methods of inquiry, we do not know, and for system-
> atic and easily visible reasons cannot know, what the
> truth about this "deterrent" effect may be. We know
> that, on raw data, there has been somewhat more
> homicide in capital punishment states than in
> noncapital punishment states. But we cannot draw any
> valid conclusions from this. . . . The general problem
> that blocks knowledge here is that no adequately
> controlled experiment or observation is possible or (so
> far as we can see) ever will be possible. We have to use
> uncontrolled data from society itself, outside any
> laboratory. (33)

ellipses
to show
words
left out

double space

A second popular argument is that capital punishment is the one sure way to prevent a murderer from killing again. Put the criminal in jail, so the argument goes, and he or she will only serve a few years before being paroled and set free to murder someone else. Specific cases of repeat offenders are often mentioned. Execution represents a "final solution" for convicted murderers.

Again Thorsten Sellin has statistics that rebut this argument. Murderers are the group of criminals least likely to repeat their crimes. The state of Ohio, for example, paroled 273 first-degree murderers between 1945 and 1965. Not a single one of them was ever convicted of that crime again. The state of New York released some 514 murderers during the same period. Only one committed another murder, and that crime occurred when he killed two drinking companions in a brawl ("Death and Imprison-ment" 185–86).

One final argument remains to be treated—perhaps the most sophisticated argument of all. The death penalty is necessary, some proponents say, because it satisfies a very legitimate need for retribution. Society has been wounded by the murder, and only by repaying the crime with death can society express its horror and insist on the fundamen-tal value of human life. One of the most articulate defend-ers of this position is Walter Berns, whose book <u>For Capital Punishment</u> offers the opinion that anyone who has a true respect for the sanctity of human life must support the death penalty (153).

O'Leary 12

pronoun *I* is used sparingly; style of essay is formal

    I do not understand how we can show our value for life by taking away life. What we are really asking for is not justice but revenge. Revenge may be a very powerful motive, but it is not a very trustworthy one—in fact the Bible says that the Lord intends to keep that power to Himself rather than entrust it to humans. We can demonstrate more respect for life by refusing the opportunity for revenge. The advancement of any civilization can be measured by its respect for life. If the state takes away life, this cheapens life and gives some legitimacy to murder, or as John Conrad says, "the state is a teacher, and when it kills it teaches vengeance and hatred" (qtd. in Draper 176). Former Attorney General Ramsey Clark put it this way:

double space

no paragraph indent (long quote but not a separate paragraph in original)

    There is no justification for the death penalty. It cheapens life. Its injustice and inhumanities raise basic questions about our institutions and purpose as a people. Why must we kill? What do we fear? What do we accomplish besides our own embitterment? Why cannot we revere life and in so doing create in the hearts of our people a love for mankind that will finally still violence? (180)

double space

    Furthermore, Anna Quindlen argues that what people want most from the death penalty—for "criminals to suffer as their victims did"— is exactly what they are least likely to get (qtd. in Miller 158). And since those who support capital punishment have been shown to be the most authoritarian, dogmatic, and punitive among us (Harvey 673), we have every reason to resist their siren song.

last paragraph ties in with first page

The next few years will be crucial ones for determining the fate of the death penalty. Public support for the death penalty, which had been rising steadily, is now beginning to erode. At a time like this, when we seem to be poised between the tradition of the Salem witch trials and the

argument ends with call to action

tradition of the Quaker colonists, anyone who feels as I do— that the death penalty should be abolished—has a special obligation to make himself or herself heard.

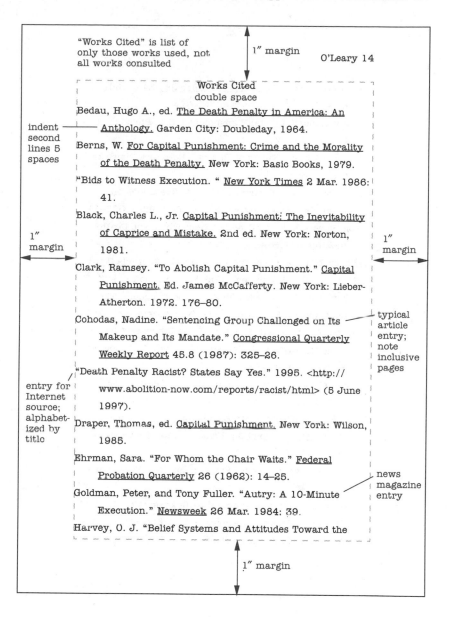

"Works Cited" is list of
only those works used, not
all works consulted

1″ margin

O'Leary 14

Works Cited
double space

Bedau, Hugo A., ed. <u>The Death Penalty in America: An</u>

indent ——— <u>Anthology.</u> Garden City: Doubleday, 1964.
second
lines 5   Berns, W. <u>For Capital Punishment: Crime and the Morality</u>
spaces
<u>of the Death Penalty.</u> New York: Basic Books, 1979.

"Bids to Witness Execution. " <u>New York Times</u> 2 Mar. 1986:

41.

Black, Charles L., Jr. <u>Capital Punishment: The Inevitability</u>

1″   <u>of Caprice and Mistake.</u> 2nd ed. New York: Norton,
margin
1981.   1″
margin

Clark, Ramsey. "To Abolish Capital Punishment." <u>Capital</u>

<u>Punishment.</u> Ed. James McCafferty. New York: Lieber-

Atherton. 1972. 176–80.

Cohodas, Nadine. "Sentencing Group Challenged on Its ——— typical
                                                            article
Makeup and Its Mandate." <u>Congressional Quarterly</u>   entry;
                                                            note
<u>Weekly Report</u> 45.8 (1987): 325–26.   inclusive
                                                            pages
"Death Penalty Racist? States Say Yes." 1995. <http://

entry for   www.abolition-now.com/reports/racist/html> (5 June
Internet
source;   1997).
alphabet-
ized by   Draper, Thomas, ed. <u>Capital Punishment.</u> New York: Wilson,
title
1985.

Ehrman, Sara. "For Whom the Chair Waits." <u>Federal</u>

<u>Probation Quarterly</u> 26 (1962): 14–25.   news
                                                            magazine
Goldman, Peter, and Tony Fuller. "Autry: A 10-Minute   entry

Execution." <u>Newsweek</u> 26 Mar. 1984: 39.

Harvey, O. J. "Belief Systems and Attitudes Toward the

1″ margin

Death Penalty." <u>Journal of Personality</u> 54 (1986):

659–75.

Horwitz, Elinor I. <u>Capital Punishment U.S.A.</u> Philadelphia: — typical book entry

Lippincott, 1973.

"Killers of Whites, Killers of Blacks." <u>New York Times</u> 17 — anonymous

Oct. 1986: 38.

Lester, David. "The Deterrent Effect of Executions on

Homicide." <u>Psychological Reports</u> 64 (1989): 306–09.

Lifton, Robert Jay, and Greg Mitchell. <u>Who Owns Death?</u>

New York: Morrow, 2000.

Meltsner, Michael. <u>Cruel and Unusual: The Supreme Court</u>

<u>and Capital Punishment.</u> New York: Random, 1973.

Playfair, Giles, and Derrick Sington. <u>The Offenders: The</u>

<u>Case Against Legal Vengeance.</u> New York: Simon, 1951.

Quindlen, Anna. "Death Penalty's False Promise." <u>The</u> —

<u>Informed Argument.</u> 2nd ed. Ed. Robert K. Miller. New

York: Harcourt, 1989.

Radelet, Michael. "Wrongful Executions." 1992. <http://

www.abolition-now.com/wrongful.html> (5 June 1997).

Sarat, Austin. <u>When the State Kills: Capital Punishment and</u>

<u>the American Condition</u>. Princeton, NJ: Princeton UP,

2001.

Sellin, Thorsten, ed. <u>Capital Punishment.</u> New York: Harper,

1967.

———. "Death and Imprisonment as Deterrents to Murder."

<u>The Death Penalty in America: An Anthology.</u> Ed. Hugo

A. Bedau. Garden City: Doubleday. 1964. 274–84.

Margin annotations:

- anonymous newspaper article, alphabetized by title
- two authors, only first has last name preceding first name
- selection from a collection
- this line is adequate if you have more than one entry by same person (alphabetize by title)

Van den Haag, Ernest. The Death Penalty: A Debate. New
    York: Plenum, 1983.
Wallace, Bill. "The Twisted Politics Behind the Death
    Penalty." San Francisco Chronicle. 1 Mar. 2002
    <http://www.cgi?RV23100.DTL:/chronicle/archive/
    1995/05/14/>.

The Glossaries

Glossaries, as you may know, are alphabetical lists of technical terms together with their explanations. They often provide convenience, an easy way to access and remind yourself of the material you explored earlier in greater detail. Here are three glossaries for your convenience: a glossary of grammatical terms, a glossary of Internet terms, and a glossary of usage.

A. GLOSSARY OF GRAMMATICAL TERMS

This glossary includes definitions of key grammatical terms that writers need to know or may want to know. Many of these definitions are condensations of longer discussions appearing elsewhere in this book. Sometimes you will have to go from one entry to another to get the fullest explanation—for example, to understand *noun* you may have to look up *complement* or *appositive* as well.

Active voice: see **Voice**

Adjective, adjectival An adjective is a word that modifies, defines, or specifies a noun, as in *thin* boy, *gorgeous* day, *this* dictionary, or *my* family. To say that it modifies a noun is to say that it changes—modifies—our idea of that noun (*thin* boy, not *fat* boy or *tall* boy or just plain *boy*). Adjectives therefore help a writer be more precise. The section on modifiers in Chapter 6 will help you here.

A good test of whether a word is an adjective is to ask yourself whether it can be compared by changing its form. A *thin* boy, for example, can be compared to another boy and

> *The greater part of this world's troubles are due to questions of grammar.*
> *—Montaigne*

thus be called the *thinner* boy. If still other boys are involved, he might be the *thinnest* boy. These comparative and superlative forms are often signaled by an *-er* and *-est* ending or by *more* and *most* when the adjective is three or more syllables (*more gorgeous, most gorgeous*). The comparative and superlative forms of a few adjectives are irregular, and you simply have to learn them individually: *good/better/best*, for example, or *bad/worse/worst*.

Sometimes we recognize adjectives because they occupy a position in the sentence that is typically an adjective position. Consider, for example, the sentence *The crowd seemed apathetic.* We recognize *apathetic* as an adjective because that position—the word following a linking verb—is usually filled by an adjective. (Try putting in a verb or a noun and see if the sentence makes sense.) Also, of course, we know that *apathetic* can be compared—*more apathetic, most apathetic.* See page 206 for more information. The same principle holds true for words that cannot be compared but that fill the same positions that other adjectives do. In the phrase *a brick wall*, for example, *brick* acts as an adjective modifying *wall* even though we cannot add an *-er* or an *-est* to it. Such words are called adjectivals.

There are many kinds of adjectives:

Demonstrative adjectives designate or point out a specific item (*this* notebook, *those* chairs).
Descriptive adjectives provide description (*busy* street).
Interrogative adjectives ask or question (*which* door?).
Possessive adjectives indicate possession (*our* house).
Predicate adjectives form part of a predicate and complement a verb or verb phrase (She was *ecstatic*).
Relative adjectives introduce subordinate clauses or phrases (the girl *whose* mother is a journalist).

Adjective clause An adjective clause is a dependent clause used as an adjective, modifying a noun:

They're looking for an employee *who can speak Japanese.*

The woman *who was sitting in front of me* was wearing a red hat.

Adverb, adverbial Just as adjectives modify nouns, adverbs usually modify verbs. Consider the sentence *She walked rapidly to the door. Rapidly* modifies the verb *walked;* it refines our idea of that verb (walks *rapidly*, not *slowly* or *sedately*). Adverbs usually have the ending *-ly*; the comparative is formed with *more*

(*more rapidly*), and the superlative is formed with *most* (*most rapidly*).

Adverbs can modify other parts of speech besides verbs. They sometimes modify adjectives: *He gave the poem an especially careful reading* (*especially* modifies *careful*, not *reading*). They can also modify other adverbs: *The reception room was decorated very tastefully* (the adverb *very* modifies the adverb *tastefully*, which in turn modifies the verb *was decorated*).

Occasionally other words not normally considered adverbs act as adverbs. Example: *Let's go Thursday.* Usually *Thursday* would be a noun, but here it tells when and modifies *go*. Words used in this way are called adverbials.

Adverb clause An adverb clause is a dependent clause used as an adverb—in other words, to tell time, place, manner, or whatever:

> Let me know *when you get there.*
>
> He left *without her seeing him.*
>
> I'll go with you *unless you decide to stay home.*

Agreement The term *agreement* is simply a way of expressing the relationship that ought to exist between one word or phrase and another closely connected word or phrase. Three kinds of agreement are important for our purposes: agreement of subject and verb, agreement of pronoun or possessive adjective and antecedent, and agreement of demonstrative adjectives with the nouns they modify. The first two are discussed in Chapter 6. Suffice it to say of the third category that a demonstrative adjective should be singular if the noun it modifies is singular (*this table, that painting*), and it should be plural if the noun it modifies is plural (*these tables, those paintings*).

Antecedent: see Reference

Appositive A word or phrase with the same function as another word or phrase and intended to further explain or describe it is called an appositive:

> My brother, the heavy metal freak, has his door closed and his CD player turned up to 9.

The phrase between the commas is the appositive. It has the same function as the subject noun it describes: *brother.* To determine

whether a word or phrase is an appositive, all you need do is eliminate the word being explained and its modifiers, then see whether
the appositive can take its place. If it can't, then it's not an appositive after all. Our example sentence still makes sense if the appositive fills in for the subject:

> The heavy metal freak has his door closed and his CD player turned
> up to 9.

Article Three familiar little words—*a, an, the*—are known collectively as articles. *The* is a definite article and *a* and *an* are indefinite articles. See **Determiner.**

Auxiliary verb Sometimes called a "helping verb," an auxiliary
verb is one that helps form a verb phrase expressing voice, mood,
and tense. Forms of the verb *to be, to do,* and *to have* are the most
common auxiliaries: for example, *she **is** buying, she **did** buy, or
she **has** bought.* Other common auxiliaries include *can, get, may,
might, must, need, ought, shall, should, used, will,* and *would.*
See **Verb, verbal.**

Case When we discuss the syntactical relationship of a noun, pronoun, or adjective to other words in a sentence (see **Syntax**), we
are discussing case. In English there are three cases: **subjective**
(or **nominative**), **objective,** and **possessive.** To find out which
one a certain word is, you must ask questions like "Is the word a
subject? a direct or indirect object? a possessive?" Most problems
of case occur with pronouns. When you have to choose among *I/
me/mine, he/him/his,* or *she/her/hers,* case is the chief factor in
deciding which form to use. See **Subject, Object,** and **Possessive** or Chapter 6, pages 188–194.

Clause A clause is a word group that contains a subject and a
predicate. Take this sentence:

> Even though we left at four, we still didn't get to LaGuardia until
> after the plane had landed on the runway.

This is a single sentence, but it contains three clauses, because
there are three subject-predicate combinations, *we + left, we +
didn't get,* and *plane + had landed.* Only one of those three clauses
could form a sentence by itself, however. You could convert *We
still didn't get to LaGuardia* into a separate sentence and it would
not seem strange. Therefore it is called the **main clause,** or the

independent clause. The other two clauses cannot stand by themselves in this way. They need a main clause to latch onto, and they are therefore said to be **dependent clauses.** Notice that length has nothing to do with determining which clauses are independent and which are not, since the second dependent clause here is longer than the independent clause. The crucial distinction is whether the clause can form a sentence on its own. (See Chapter 3, pages 79–80.)

Clauses are often confused with phrases. Just remember that a group of related words must have a subject and a predicate to be a clause. Thus, the words *on the runway* in the example sentence should be termed a phrase, not a clause. The words are clearly related, but they contain no subject or predicate.

Within a sentence clauses can take the place of nouns, adverbs, or adjectives. In this last case they are often known as **relative clauses,** because they relate to, or modify, nouns. Such clauses are often introduced by relative pronouns, such as *who, which, what,* and *that,* or by relative adverbs, such as *where, when,* and *why.*

Comparative: see Adjective, Adverb

Complement As the word implies, a complement is a word that fills out or completes something—in this case, a predicate. If your sentence contains a verb that usually has a direct object, that object is a complement to the verb. In the sentence *Mark threw the football,* the word *football* is a complement: It fills out the predicate, which in this case consists of the last three words. Similarly, if your sentence has a linking verb, the noun, pronoun, or adjective that completes the predicate can be termed a complement:

She is *a real professional.*

They appeared *foolish.*

Conjunction A conjunction is a word that joins: It can join words (*you **and** I*), phrases (*after the sunrise **but** before the rain*), clauses (*Sue was angry, **although** she kept her cool*), or sentences (*I left the party early. **Yet** I can't say I was really tired*). Some of the most common conjunctions are *and, but, or, nor, if, because, since, although, as, unless, before, after, when, for,* and *while.*

Contraction Contractions are words in which all or part of an unstressed syllable has been eliminated: *cannot* becomes *can't, did not* becomes *didn't, she is* becomes *she's.* An apostrophe replaces the eliminated letters. We use contractions quite often in conversation. Therefore, writing that reflects conversation or tends toward informality makes liberal use of contractions.

> Florence's hoteliers *aren't* as greedy as some of their Peninsular colleagues—but *they're* in there pitching. *Fielding's Guide to Europe*

More formal writing or speech, on the other hand, tends to avoid them. For instance, consider a sentence from Lincoln's Gettysburg Address:

> But in a larger sense we cannot dedicate, we cannot consecrate, we cannot hallow this ground.

How would this sentence have sounded if Lincoln had used *can't?* In your own writing, be careful about using contractions in research papers or other serious works; they tend to make writing sound informal.

Demonstrative Demonstrative adjectives or pronouns (*this, that, these, those*) point out or indicate *which* of a class of things is referred to (*this* camera, *that* one, *those* over there).

Determiner Determiners include articles (*a, an, the*); demonstrative, possessive, and indefinite adjectives (*those* cards, *her* cards, *some* cards); and words referring to number (*one, two, first, second*). Determiners occupy an adjective's position and do an adjective's work, but they do not have an adjective's form—for example, they cannot be compared.

Double negative Two negatives are not usually used in the same sentence. You write *I know **nothing** about it* (one negative) rather than *I **don't** know **nothing** about it* (two negatives). The idea behind the custom is that two negatives make a positive (affirmative), just as when you multiplied two negatives in seventh grade mathematics and got (or should have gotten!) a positive result. Taken literally, I *don't know nothing about it* would mean *I do know something about it.*

Ellipsis An ellipsis is the omission of certain words, usually from quoted material. Three spaced periods (. . .) mark the deletion.

Gender To ask about the gender of a word is simply to ask whether it is masculine, feminine, or neuter. English makes comparatively little use of distinctions of gender, except in things like the pronouns *he/she/it* and *his/hers/its*. The older custom of using alternative forms of a word to show sex, as in *blond* (m) / *blonde* (f), is disappearing. Similarly, few people would now distinguish between *mediator* (m) and *mediatrix* (f) or *poet* and *poetess*. On the other hand, most writers still use the alternative forms *actor* and *actress*. In between come the more complex decisions. Is it *chairman* or *chairwoman*, or *chairperson* or *chair* for both sexes? Does *congressman* describe just the job, with equal application to persons of both sexes holding that job, or should the title vary (*congresswoman, congressman*) with the sex of the incumbent? Tread carefully here (and see pages 289–292 for a discussion of sexist language).

Gerund The ancient Greeks believed in the existence of creatures called hermaphrodites—half man, half woman. A gerund is a hermaphroditic kind of word—half noun, half verb. In function it is a noun; it fills a noun's place. For example: *Overeating is my worst temptation.* The word *overeating* is quite clearly a noun subject. But in form it resembles a verb, because it has a verb ending (*-ing*), can take an object (*overeating pasta*), and can be modified by an adverb (*grossly overeating*).

Idiom An idiom is a phrase that has a certain agreed-upon meaning for users of the language but that cannot necessarily be understood from the individual words in the phrase; for example, *to rain cats and dogs, to be on Cloud 9, to paint the town red.* Other examples are:

His teammates *did the dirty work* that set up Harry's perfect shot. *Garry Wills* [In a basketball game, the "work," while difficult, doesn't usually soil the players' hands or clothes.]

A good union knows how to *drive a hard bargain.* [How do you *drive* a *bargain?*]

Idioms are used in very specific ways to mean specific things; instructors sometimes have to call a student's attention to phrases that are not idiomatically correct, as in this example from a student paper:

The U.S. should not ring its hands in despair.

If we take the words literally, it is probably as easy to *ring* your hands (like a bell) as to *wring* them (like a wet dishrag). But the proper idiom requires *wring*.

Infinitive Like gerunds, infinitives (*to* plus the present form of a verb, the stem of the infinitive) resemble verbs but often act as nouns. Greta Garbo's famous wish "I want to be alone" contains the infinitive *to be*. *To be* in this sentence takes a complement (*alone*) as a verb would. Yet by function it is a noun, in this case a noun that is the direct object of the verb *want*. Note that the distinction between gerund and infinitive is often one of form but not function: *I like to be alone* (infinitive); *I like being alone* (gerund). Incidentally, it is usually preferable not to split an infinitive (i.e., put a modifier between the *to* and the rest of the verb). Thus, *to examine closely* is preferable to *to closely examine*. However, splitting an infinitive is acceptable to avoid ambiguous or awkward constructions.

Interjection Interjections are words that express an emotion or give a command, such as a simple exclamation, but that are not related grammatically to the rest of the sentence in which they appear:

> She is in her grave
> And *oh!* the difference to me.
> *William Wordsworth*

Other examples: *Ouch! Ah! Alas! Ha!*

Intonation Intonation is a general term describing the sound qualities peculiar to a language: its patterns of pitch (tone—high or low frequency of sound) and of terminal juncture (e.g., the way we link *n* and *g* in a word like *ring*). Intonation determines whether a sentence is a statement or a question.

Intransitive: see **Verb**

Modifier A word or group of words that qualifies, or modifies, another word or group of words is said to be a modifier. Included in this general category are adjectives, adjectivals, adverbs, and adverbials. Also included are phrases or clauses that act as adjectives or adverbs. See the entry for **Clause,** and Chapter 6, pages 202–209, for more information.

Mood In English there are three moods, or forms, that a verb assumes in order to express the manner in which the action or state takes place: the **indicative,** the **subjunctive,** and the **impera-**

tive. Most sentences are in the indicative mood (which includes many tenses—present, past, future, and so forth—see **Tense**). Both questions and declarative sentences can be in the indicative mood. The subjunctive mood is used in dependent clauses to express (1) something hypothetical or contrary to fact (*If I were rich . . ., If only I could get up earlier . . .*), (2) necessity (*It's essential that he know the truth*), (3) wishing or willing (*I wish you were here, I insist that you be more attentive*). The imperative mood, finally, is used for commands: *Wash the dishes! Let's go! Be careful!*

Noun, nominal Like most other parts of speech, a noun can be identified two ways: by its form and by its function. In terms of form, nouns are words that can be made plural by adding *-s* or *-es: train, trains; crutch, crutches; box, boxes.* I imagine you are aware, too, of the many exceptions: words such as *barracks*, where singular and plural are the same, and words such as *man, ox,* or *memorandum*, which form plurals in unusual ways (*men, oxen, memoranda*). Another way to identify nouns is the use of an apostrophe and *-s* to show the possessive case. In a phrase such as *the dean's office*, the addition of *-'s* to *dean* shows that the office belongs to (is in the possession of) the person designated by the noun *dean*.

As for function, nouns fill several kinds of slots. They can be subjects (*The waves slammed against the dock*), direct objects of verbs (*She sent flowers*), or indirect objects of verbs, usually shown by their position before the direct object and by the implied presence of *to* or *for* after the verb (*Larry gave [to] his fiancée a ring*). Nouns can also be appositives (*His new toy, the Honda, is a dangerous one*), complements (*Their oldest appliance is a refrigerator*), or objects of prepositions (*Good luck on the exam*).

There are many categories of nouns. **Common nouns** are general, nonspecific (e.g., *constitutions*), whereas **proper nouns** are specific (e.g., the *U.S. Constitution*) and are capitalized. **Abstract nouns** are ideas or qualities (e.g., *socialism, mercy*), whereas **concrete nouns** are things (*window, mosquito*). Moreover certain words, phrases, or clauses can act as nouns and are therefore called nominals; gerunds and infinitives, for example, can be nominals.

Noun clause A noun clause is a dependent clause acting as a noun: *My only wish is that we arrive safely.*

Number This term, in the grammatical sense, merely indicates whether a noun, pronoun, or verb is singular or plural in form. See Chapter 6, pages 190–193 and 212–215.

Object Objects are nouns or nominals that are affected by the action of a verb, directly or indirectly, or that follow a preposition. Here is a sentence illustrating all three:

> The drunk gave the *cop* [noun as indirect object] a shaky *wave* [noun as direct object] of his *hand* [noun as object of preposition *of*].

Participle A participle is a verb form used as an adjective or adverb. It is also used to form certain tenses. A **present participle** ends in *-ing* (the form also used for gerunds) and is used in progressive tenses: *is **going**, has been **dancing**, will be **arriving**.* A **past participle** relates to the past or a perfect tense and takes the appropriate ending (*-d* or *-ed* for regular verbs): ***written** proof, **locked** door, had **finished**, will have **eaten**.* Past participles are also used in the passive voice (see **Voice**).

Parts of speech Grammarians have traditionally divided the English language into eight parts of speech: nouns, pronouns, verbs, adverbs, adjectives, prepositions, conjunctions, and interjections. For more information, see the entries for each.

Passive: see **Voice**

Person To describe the person of a pronoun means to show whether it refers to the speaker(s) (**first person:** *I, we*), to the person(s) spoken to (**second person:** *you*), or to some third party (**third person:** *he, she, it, they*). Verbs change depending on person only in some tenses—for instance, *I jog, you jog, she jogs* (present tense).

Phrase A phrase is a group of related words that, unlike a clause, lacks a subject-predicate combination. There are many types of phrases, defined by function: **noun, verb, adverb, prepositional, gerund, infinitive,** and **participial** (see the entries for these or related terms).

Possessive The possessive is a case, sometimes called the **genitive** case. Possessive pronouns and adjectives include *my, mine, his, her, hers, its, our, ours, your, yours, their, theirs,* and *whose.* Possession is also shown with an apostrophe or apostrophe and *-s* after a noun: *the owners' secretary, the dog's bone.*

Predicate A predicate consists of a verb plus all of its objects, modifiers, and complements. An easy way to identify the predicate of a sentence or clause is to first find the subject and all its modifiers; what remains is the predicate, since all simple sentences and clauses can be reduced to the formula S[ubject] + P[redicate].

Prefix A short, usually one-syllable form added at the beginning of a word changing the word's meaning is called a prefix. Familiar examples include *non-, un-, re-, con-, mis-,* and *ex-.* Prefixes are bound forms—that is, they must be attached directly to a word, sometimes with a hyphen.

Preposition One of the eight parts of speech, a preposition is a connective, **or** linking word; it usually has an object, as in the phrase *into* [preposition] *the garage* [object]. The most common prepositions are *in, into, from, of, with, to, by, for, on,* and *at*—there are many others. Sometimes two prepositions are used together as in *because of* or *due to.* Some words, such as *but, before, since, after,* and *for,* can be either prepositions or conjunctions, depending on how they are used. For example, in the sentence *We have not heard from him since Wednesday,* the word *since* is a preposition. But in the sentence *Of course I'm angry, since you won't listen to me,* the same word is a conjunction (see **Conjunction**). Incidentally, in formal writing you should avoid ending a sentence with a preposition unless rewording will create an awkward construction.

Pronoun A word that can be used in place of a noun or noun phrase is called a pronoun. Pronouns show case (*he,* subject; *him,* object; *his,* possessive) and number (*I,* singular; *we,* plural; *mine,* singular; *ours,* plural). They also show gender (*he, she, it*) and person (*I, you, he, she*). In general, pronouns perform the same functions as nouns: they can be subjects, indirect or direct objects, complements, or appositives. What makes pronouns different from nouns is that they need *antecedents,* nouns that they refer to and replace. (See **Reference**.)

Pronouns are sometimes categorized as **subject pronouns** (*Tom went, although **he** didn't want to*); **object pronouns** (*Give **it** to **her***); **reflexive pronouns** (*You shouldn't criticize **yourself** so harshly*); **indefinite pronouns** (***Anybody** can sing*);

relative pronouns (*The book **that** she chose is a bore*); **demon-strative pronouns** (***That** surprised me*); **reciprocal pronouns** (*Love **one another***); and **interrogative pronouns** (***Who** will be elected?*).

Proper names Proper names (nouns and adjectives) are specific names of people, places, institutions, and so forth: *President Bush, St. Louis, University of Colorado.*

Reference We noted in Chapter 6 (pages 194–197) that pronouns must agree with their antecedents. Reference is a term to describe this relationship: Each pronoun *refers* to an antecedent and there-fore must be the same as the antecedent in person (first, second, or third), in number (singular or plural), and in gender (mascu-line, feminine, or neuter).

Reference can also mean the naming of sources. If a statement in one of your papers has the word *Reference?* written next to it, and if there is no problem of pronoun reference, what your in-structor means is that you should have named the sources—the books, articles, or people—who gave you the information upon which your statement was based.

Relative clause, relative pronoun: see **Clause; Pronoun**

Sentence This topic is a large one—so large that Chapters 2 and 3 are devoted to it. If sentences are defined as grammatically com-plete expressions, they must have both a subject and a predicate. They must always be capable of standing alone; in other words, they cannot be dependent clauses (see pages 92–93), even though dependent clauses have both a subject and a predicate. The verb of a sentence predicate must also be complete in itself. Compare, for example, *I went home* and *I going home;* the former is satis-factory as a sentence, but the latter needs an additional word— *I **was** going home*—to be complete and acceptable.

There are many types of sentences. A **declarative sentence** states something and is followed by a period (such as the sen-tence you are reading). An **exclamatory sentence** shows force or emotion and is followed by an exclamation point: *Help! Go away! I can't believe it!* An **interrogative sentence** asks a ques-tion and is followed by a question mark: *What did you say?*

Sentences are also classified as **simple, compound, complex, or compound-complex.** A **simple sentence** contains only one subject and verb (that is, one main clause): *We are going.* A **com-**

pound sentence contains two main clauses (which have subjects and verbs and can each stand alone): *We are going, but they are staying home.* A **complex sentence** has a main clause and a dependent clause (the latter cannot stand alone): *We are going, unless it rains.* Finally, a **compound-complex sentence** has more than one main clause and at least one dependent clause: *We are going, but they are staying home in case John arrives.* Chapter 3 explains these distinctions in greater detail.

Subject A subject is usually a noun, nominal, or pronoun about which something is stated or asked. The complete subject is the simple subject plus all the modifiers associated with this noun, nominal, or pronoun—see Chapter 2, page 47. To put it another way, we can reverse what we said about predicates: since any simple sentence is S[ubject] + P[redicate], you need only subtract from a sentence all those words that form the predicate. What is left is the subject.

Suffix Just as prefixes are short forms that are attached at the beginning of a base word, so suffixes are forms that are attached at the *end* of a word. Examples: *-ing* (*going*), *-s* (*loves*), *-es* (*boxes*), *-ed* (*hoarded*), *-er* (*mixer*), *-ly* (*properly*), *-able* (*pardonable*), *-tion* (*consideration*).

Superlative: see Adjective; Adverb

Syntax Syntax is the study of the relationships among various words and/or phrases within a sentence. In other words, for the sentence *I am going to the post office,* we might note that the arrangement consists of subject (*I*) plus verb (*am going*) plus prepositional phrase (*to the post office*). We might further observe that this particular arrangement is required by our language. We cannot say *I to the post office am going,* or *Am going I to the post office,* even though these forms might be acceptable word order in other languages. To study this arrangement of the words within the sentence is to study aspects of syntax.

Tense Verbs can change form in order to enable us to specify when the action they describe is taking place (was taking place? will take place?). If we use the verb *to give* as an illustration, we think immediately of three tenses: present (*give*), past (*gave*), and future (*will give*). Further refinements of tense let us show less common tenses by using the past participle plus a form of the verb *to have:* thus present perfect (*has given*), past perfect (*had given*), future perfect (*will have given*), and conditional perfect (*would have given*). We might note also the progressive tenses, which require an *-ing* form of the verb plus another auxiliary verb: *has been giving, is giving, will be giving, would be giving.*

Transitive: see **Verb**

Verb, verbal Again we encounter a part of speech that can be identified by form or by function. In terms of form, verbs are words that show a distinction according to time, or tense. In the case of the verb *to run,* for example, the present-tense form is *run(s),* the past-tense form is *ran,* and the future-tense form is *will (shall) run.* When combined with auxiliaries, verbs can show many other time relationships, as in *has run* or *will have been running.* In one specific instance—third person, present tense—verbs also change their form according to number (*she runs,* singular; *they run,* plural). *Run,* by the way, is one of the many irregular verbs; regular verbs use the suffix *-ed* like *act, acted* (see Chapter 6, pages 211–213).

As to function, verbs are the essential parts of predicates. If there's no verb, there's no predicate; no predicate, no sentence. Predicates can of course include many other words, phrases, and clauses besides the verb, but the verb is essential—it makes the rest of the sentence work.

Verbs are often divided into **transitive verbs,** which can take a direct object (e.g., *throw, lift*), and **intransitive verbs,** which do not take an object (e.g., *exist, sit*). Some verbs can be used either transitively or intransitively.

Because verbs are often combined with other auxiliary verbs to show complex relationships, you might want to look at the entries for **Mood, Tense,** and **Voice,** and perhaps also at the verb-related sections dealing with **Complement, Predicate,** and **Sentence.** Chapter 6 is your best resource. Take special note also of **linking verbs** (pages 204–205).

Verbals are words derived from verbs that have verblike forms but act as another part of speech. See the separate entries for **Gerund, Infinitive,** and **Participle,** which collectively can be called verbals.

Voice The relationship in a sentence between the subject and the action of the verb is described by the term **voice.** That is, if the subject is performing the action, we say the sentence is in the

active voice: *He drives the car.* On the other hand, if the subject is being acted upon—*The car is driven by him*—the voice is said to be **passive.** (The active voice is preferable in most instances—see pages 105–106.)

B. GLOSSARY OF INTERNET TERMS

These terms are the ones you hear or see most frequently. They are explained more fully in Chapters 12 and 13.

Access (date)

Connecting to a database or an Internet site using a computer is to *access* it; the *access date* is the date you made the connection.

Angle brackets

Angle brackets are brackets like these, < and >, within which an e-mail address or URL number is enclosed to indicate that only the information within them is to be used as an address. (The angle brackets themselves are not part of the address.)

@

The "at" sign is used in an e-mail address to distinguish the username from the domain name.

Bookmark

Bookmarks are devices for recording and storing URL addresses for later use; they allow the user to return directly to a site without having to re-search for it.

Boolean logic/operator

Boolean logic is the systematic application of the terms AND, OR, and NOT in combination with keywords or parentheses to narrow a subject search.

Browser

A browser is a computer software application for exploring the Internet and web sites.

Cyberspace

This term is commonly used to indicate the Internet environment of interconnected computers; *cyber* means operation by an automatic control system.

Directory
> A collection of computer files can be summarized in a directory (just like a telephone directory).

Directory path
> A series of electronic addresses for accessing a collection of computer files forms a directory path.

Discussion group
> Also called a newsgroup, each discussion group is a forum on the Internet for exchange of information among individuals with similar interests.

Domain (name)
> A domain names the organization or group running a web site or an e-mail box, as indicated by its specific address. For example, the domain name in the address <http://www.yahoo.com> is *www.yahoo.com*.

Download
> To download information such as a computer file is to transfer it from one computer to another.

E-mail (electronic mail)
> Messages sent electronically via computer networks are termed e-mail for short.

FTP (file transfer protocol)
> The steps necessary to move and download computer files throughout the Internet are collectively referred to as the FTP.

Gopher
> Gopher is an Internet search process particularly useful for researching databases and catalogs.

html (hypertext mark-up language)
> This computer language is used especially for creating web pages; it commands a server to retrieve information and place it onto a page.

http (hypertext transfer protocol)
> The http process defines a series of steps taken to move to a web page.

Hyperlinks
> The highlighted icons, graphics, and text you click on to move from one web site to another are called hyperlinks.

Hypertext
> Web site documents, graphics, and text connected by hyperlinks are called hypertext.

Internet
> The Internet is a global network of interconnected servers and personal computers.

IRC (Internet Relay Chat)
> IRC is a system that allows individuals at various sites to communicate with each other in "real time" via the Internet.

Keyword
> Keywords are words used in the search box of a navigational program to locate information on a particular subject.

Mailing list
> An electronic database mailing list allows one to send copies of a message automatically to all subscribers on a particular topic.

Online
> To access and search the Internet is to "go online."

Posting
> To post a message is to send an online message to a person or a discussion group.

Search tool/engine
> A search tool or search engine is an Internet program for locating web sites by using keywords.

Server
> A server is any network computer, accessed by personal computers, that operates software and lets a user send and receive e-mail and access the Internet.

Telnet
> A telnet is an Internet program that uses a protocol to gain entry into a network computer from a personal computer.

Text index

If you access a list of web sites called up by typing keywords into the search box of Lycos or Alta Vista (programs for searching index), the search result will be a text index.

URL (uniform resource locator)

The address using *http* to find a page of information on the Internet is its URL.

Usenet

Usenet is a series of electronic discussion groups or newsgroups on the Internet.

Username

An Internet user's personal account-accessing information (the name that begins an e-mail address) is his or her username; the username often resembles (or is a shortened form of) the user's real name.

World Wide Web (the web)

The WWW is a network of Internet computer servers, operating via *http*, that lets a user move by hypertext links from one site to another and that allows for the use of graphics, sound, and video/animation.

Yahoo!

The joy of discovery is captured in the name of this common subject-oriented search tool.

C. GLOSSARY OF USAGE

This glossary deals with **usage:** the ways in which the English language is used by those educated people who speak and write it. The glossary of usage includes distinctions between words frequently confused, such as *farther* and *further* or *lie, lay,* and *lain.* The entries are arranged in alphabetical order.

Accept / except

To **accept** something means to receive it:

If you can accept our invitation, please reply by February 15th.

To **except** means to leave (something) out, to exclude:

Congress agreed to except small businesses from these provisions.

Except as a preposition means other than, or with the exclusion or exception of:

> *Those that will combat use and custom by the strict rules of grammar do but jest.*
> —*Montaigne*

No one was there except me.

Adapt / adept / adopt

Adapt and **adopt** are verbs. The first means to adjust something or make it suitable:

Like a chameleon, Sean can adapt himself to his surroundings.

Adopt means accept:

The resolution was adopted by the committee.

Adept, by contrast, is an adjective meaning "proficient":

My older brother is adept at getting the blame placed on my shoulders.

Advice / advise

Advice is the noun—what you do when you **advise** (verb) someone about something.

What did they advise? Was their advice reasonable?

Affect / effect

These two words are confused perhaps more often than any other pair in the English language, probably because their spelling, pronunciation, and meaning are so similar. To use them properly, remember that **affect** is normally a verb and **effect** is—usually—a noun.

To **affect** means to influence:

Nothing Hussein can do will affect the outcome.

Effect as a noun is simply a result or consequence:

The effect of inflation on the family budget is a matter of national concern.

Less frequently, **effect** is used as a verb, where it means to cause, accomplish, or bring about:

> The passage of the Red Sea was effected by a strong wind, which, we are told, drove back the waters. *Samuel Taylor Coleridge*

A lot / allot
A lot, meaning many, should always be written as two words. Perhaps because people sometimes confuse this term with **allot** (meaning "to apportion"), they write it as *alot.*

Already / all ready
Already means by this time or prior to a given time:

> The coffee was already brewing by the time I rolled up my sleeping bag.

All ready, on the other hand, consists of two separate words, each of which functions independently. **All** means everybody; **ready** shows the state of preparedness:

> We were all ready for the supreme test [we—all of us—were ready].

Among / between
The distinction here is that **between** is used with two items or people (*Divide the money between Glenda and Joan*) and **among** is used with more than two (*Divide the money among all the committee members*). Lately, though, **between** has become an acceptable alternative to **among** in the second instance; in other words, *Divide the money between all the committee members* is also acceptable to many readers, although not by any means to all.

An / a
Most writers know to put **an** before words beginning with a vowel (*an ambulance*) and **a** before words beginning with a consonant (*a colander*). The tricky part comes when a word begins with a vowel *sound* although the actual letter is a consonant; in such cases **an** is the appropriate article: *an hour* (but not *an hotel*), *an M* (but not *an C*).

And/or
While **and/or** is commonly seen in many kinds of writing, especially technical writing, most experts discourage its use in formal writing.

Anybody / any body / anyone / any one
Anybody and **anyone** each act as single nouns:

Is anybody home?

Anyone needing tickets for Tuesday's game, see Claire in Room 331.

Separate the words when **any** is used as a modifier:

Any body not claimed by relatives was immediately buried or cremated.

There are three clerks here, any one of whom can help you.

As / like

Everyone accepts the use of **as** (*as if, as though*) in clauses of comparison:

He leaned forward as if he were about to faint.

Many—most?—writers would accept the use of **like** in the same situation:

He leaned forward like he was about to faint.

But not everyone agrees, as the furor over Winston cigarette ads in the 1960s made clear ("Winston tastes good like a cigarette should"; "What do you want—good grammar or good taste?"). Still, you are probably safe in allowing **like** to encroach on the territory of **as** when they are conjunctions.

Awhile / a while / while

Awhile is an adverb meaning "for a while" and is written as one word: *Please stay awhile.* The noun **while** is often accompanied by the determiner **a**: *a while ago, for a while longer.* However, **while** is usually a conjunction expressing time: *Nero fiddled while Rome burned.*

Beside / besides

Beside is a preposition that usually means by the side of or next to:

Beside the tombstone was a small floral wreath.

Both **beside** and **besides** can mean aside from:

Can't you offer any other excuse beside(s) that one?

But **besides** can also act as an adverb, in which case it means moreover:

Besides, the price of meat has been going down recently.

Between: see **Among**

Breath / breathe
Breath is the noun (*take a breath*); **breathe** is the verb.

Can / may
In formal situations some writers restrict **can** to being able to do something (*I can press over 300 pounds*) and use **may** to show permission (*May I come in?*).

Center around
This phrase is confusing, since **center** implies the middle and **around** implies the circumference. The term *center on* is preferable.

Cite / sight / site
These three homonyms have quite different meanings. **Cite** is a verb meaning "refer to, quote":

> Be sure to cite all the information that relates to your case.

Sight and **site** are nouns. The first means a view, something seen (*a beautiful sight*); the second means a place or location (*a building site*).

Compliment / complement
As a noun, a **compliment** is the nice thing someone says about you, while a **complement** is something that completes, goes along with, or fulfills:

> Cabernet sauvignon is a good complement to beef dishes.

Both words can also function as verbs: *to compliment someone* or *to complement a dish*.

Compose / comprise
To **compose** is to fashion or create; to be **composed of** is to consist of, be made or constituted of.

> The book is composed of a series of essays.

To **comprise,** like to be **composed of,** means to include or contain. Avoid *is comprised of* when you mean *is composed of, consists of*:

> North America comprises [consists of, is composed of] Canada, the United States, and Mexico.

Council / counsel

A **council** (noun) is a group of persons called together to discuss or decide something, while **counsel** is a noun meaning "advice" or a verb meaning "to advise":

> She offers wise counsel.

> She counsels wisely.

Data

Although the noun **data** does have a singular form (*datum*), it almost always appears in the plural and therefore requires a plural verb: Data *are* [not *is*] available for the last several years. However, in computer-related works and publications, *data* is often treated as singular.

Different from

Although many people use *different than* in speech, the form to use in writing is **different from** (no one objects to the latter, but many people object to *different than*).

Due to

Many readers object to this phrase as a substitute for *because of:* The course was canceled *because of* [not *due to*] low enrollment.

Effect: see **Affect**

Either / neither / any / none

Use **either** to mean one of two, **any** to mean one of several:

> Either job [of two] sounds interesting.

> Any dated receipt [of several] will be sufficient.

Use **neither** to mean not one of two (neither = "not either"), **none** to mean not one of more than two:

> Neither your first nor your second proposal is satisfactory.

> None of us knows the answer.

Note that **either, neither, any,** and **none** normally take a singular verb.

Etc.

This abbreviation for the Latin *et cetera* ("and so forth") should be used only with lists and statistics, not as part of a normal prose sentence. If a sentence lists several items, mention them all. If you close a sentence with **etc.,** readers might think you are just too bored to finish. Write this:

> I packed some clothes, three books, and my tennis racket and headed home for the weekend.

Not this:

> I packed clothes etc. and headed home for the weekend.

By the way, since the *et* of *et cetera* means "and," don't use *and etc.* or *& etc.;* that's like saying "and and so forth."

Except: see Accept

Extra

Be reluctant to use **extra** to mean *very*, as in *Her tacos are extra good;* some people object to it in formal writing. Words such as *unusually*, *especially*, or *very* would be better choices.

Farther / further

Farther is generally preferred as the comparative of *far* (*Houston is farther than Dallas*). But **further** is gaining acceptance, too, in both writing and speaking. Of course, **further** is also used in reference to additional quantity or degree (*further information, to discuss further*).

Fewer / less

Fewer refers to nouns that can be counted: *fewer people, fewer cars.* **Less** applies to nouns that are not counted: *less energy, less bread, less attention.* In other words, **fewer** applies to number and **less** to quantity or degree.

Fine / good

Often used as adverbs in speech (*He talks good, She sings fine*), these words are really adjectives, and in most writing they should be used only in that capacity.

Good: see Fine; Well

Hopefully

As an adverb meaning "with hope," this word poses no problem:

We worked hopefully and earnestly.

But used to mean "let us hope" or "I hope" (*Hopefully, nothing will come up to prevent us from meeting the deadline tomorrow*), it is considered by many to be ungrammatical.

In / into

In primarily indicates position (*She was in the library*), while **into** shows the direction of an action (*The floppy disk goes into the slot on the computer*).

Irregardless

This nonword is sometimes used, mistakenly, in place of *regardless*.

its / it's

Its, without the apostrophe, is the possessive neuter pronoun (*everything in its place*). **It's,** apostrophe included, is the contraction of *it is*. A source of confusion is that *its* is a possessive and possessives normally have apostrophes. However, no possessive pronouns contain apostrophes (*yours, hers, whose*), to avoid confusion with contractions.

Kind / sort

Both of these words are singular in form and usually take singular demonstrative adjectives: *that kind of day, that sort of temptation*. The hitch comes when the noun associated with **kind** or **sort** happens to be plural. In such cases, the demonstrative adjectives are sometimes in the plural to agree with the noun (*these kinds of days, those sorts of temptations*), but they should not be plural unless **kinds** or **sorts** is used: *this kind of day* or *these kinds of days*.

Incidentally, the variants *kind of* and *sort of* as synonyms for *rather*—*it's kind of windy today*—are best restricted to informal writing.

Later / latter

Later can be used as an adverb meaning "subsequently" (*Later we stopped by the bowling alley*) or as an adjective (*a later appointment*). **Latter** means closer to the end of something (*the latter half of the book*) or refers to the second of two things that have been mentioned:

Of the two courses of action, resigning or fighting the case, I recommend the latter.

Avoid using **latter** when referring to the last of more than two items.

Lay / lie

The most troublesome usage problem of all? The only solution is memorizing the difference—or looking it up if you can't remember. First, decide which meaning you intend. Do you mean to recline (intransitive)? Then you *lie* down, or the bundle of wheat *lies* in the field. Yesterday the wheat *lay* in the field, and after thirty days we can say it *has lain* there for a month. But if you mean to place, with an object implied (i.e., transitive), then you *lay* down your umbrella. Perhaps yesterday you *laid* it down on the table, where you *have laid* it many times before.

In sum, the two verbs are **lie, lay, (have) lain,** and **lay, laid, (have) laid.** I think you can see why they are so often confused: The past tense of one and the present tense of the other are identical (*lay*); the meanings are similar (although you *have laid* your umbrella on the table, it may not *have lain* there long); and when followed by the word *down* the two are pronounced the same way (*lay down, laid down*). So the best approach is memorizing the distinction.

Lead / led

Since *read* (present tense) and *read* (past tense) are spelled alike but pronounced differently, some writers think they should use **lead** for the present tense and **lead** again for the past. But the correct past-tense form is **led.**

Less: see Fewer

Like: see As

Literally

This adverb means "in the strict sense of the term." Thus, to say that you have **literally** never heard of something means that you have in fact *never* heard of it before. Some writers mistakenly use **literally** as an intensifier: *That comedian literally kills me.* Someone who uses such a sentence would require the immediate services of an undertaker. Often the term that is meant is *figuratively.*

Loose / lose

Loose is the condition of being unrestricted, free, not tight: *a loose garment, a loose doorknob.* **Lose** is a verb meaning to no longer possess: *Did you lose your keys?*

May: see Can

Media

Like *data,* this word appears most frequently in its plural form and therefore needs a plural verb:

The media slander me but the American people know the truth.

Moral / morale

Moral is a lesson (*the moral of the story*); as an adjective, it means ethical, having to do with right or wrong conduct. **Morale** is a spiritual or psychological state (*their morale remained high*).

Neither: see Either

None: see Either

Off of

There is no need to push something **off of** the bed when pushing it *off* the bed does just as well.

Plus

This word is appropriate in place of *and* with numbers—two *plus* two—but in formal writing it is not appropriate as a conjunction beginning a main clause:

I like the shirt, and [not plus] it is on sale.

Principal / principle

A **principal** (noun) is a person who runs a school. This person will succeed only insofar as he or she is guided by certain clear **principles** (the noun meaning "code of conduct, fundamental truth or assumption"); absence of such principles could be a

principal (adjective meaning "main, primary") reason for later failure.

Quote / quotation

Quote is primarily a verb (*to quote from memory*) and is sometimes used as a noun or an adjective, but it should not be used in place of the noun *quotation:*

> Merrill buttressed his anthropology paper with several appropriate quotations [not quotes].

Raise / rise

The easiest way to know which of these verbs to choose is to see whether the verb will have an object. If it will—in other words, if the verb is transitive—the proper verb is **raise, raised, (have) raised,** which means to make something go up or appear:

> To decrease heat, raise handle to upper notch. [note *handle* as direct object of raise]

If the verb is intransitive—in other words, if it has no object and means simply to move upward—**rise, rose, (have) risen** is the right choice, as in these lines from the poet Samuel Taylor Coleridge:

> A sadder and a wiser man
> He rose the morrow morn.

Real / really

Real is an adjective meaning "genuine": *a real diamond.* In writing, **real** should not be used as a substitute for the adverb **really;** i.e., write *a really big prize*, not *a real big prize.* (Better yet, use *very* or perhaps no intensifier at all.)

Reason is because

This phrase is redundant (**reason** implies causation), so use *reason is that* or simply *reason is:*

> While voting percentages may be shrinking, the reason is a scarcity of good candidates, not voter apathy.

Shall / will

For both speech and writing the old distinctions between when to use **shall** and when to use **will** in the future tense are fast disappearing. At one time, **shall** was supposed to be used in the first person (I *shall go*). In practice the use of **will** to express all forms of the future tense is now just about universal.

Sight, site: see **Cite**

Someone / somebody: see **Anybody / anyone**

Sort: see **Kind**

Stationery / stationary
   Stationery is paper for writing letters; an object is **stationary** if it's not moving.

Their / they're / there
   Pronounced alike, these three words have quite different meanings: **their** is a possessive adjective (*their bicycles*), **they're** is the contraction for *they are* (*they're coming*), and **there** indicates place (*put it there*).

To / too / two
   To is the preposition (*go to bed*), **too** means also (*you come, too*) or excessively (*too heavy*), and **two** is the number (*two days*).

Try to / try and
   The expression *try and*, often used in speech (*Try and solve this equation*), should be replaced by **try to** in written English. The same goes for *take and* and *take up and*—they are colloquial and should not be used in formal writing.

-Type
   Avoid tacking this suffix onto a noun in an attempt to make an adjective out of it. In other words, avoid such constructions as *hardware-type merchandise* or *Nashville-type music*.

Used to
   Because the *d* and *t* sounds are so alike, we drop the *d* sound when we say these two words. But in writing always make sure the *d* is included; this applies especially to the past tense of *use*. Avoid a construction such as *We use to go to the movies more often.*

Weather / whether

Weather is what goes on outdoors: rain, sunshine, snow. Don't confuse it with the conjunction **whether** (*whether we win or lose*) despite the fact that the two words are pronounced the same.

Well

This adverb is often replaced by the adjective *good* in conversation: "How's your car running?" "Pretty good." In writing, **well** has the prerogative—*feeling well, sleeping well, painting well.*

Who's / whose

Who's is the proper contraction for *who is.* Keep **whose** as the possessive adjective—e.g., *the golfer whose clubs I carried.*

Will: see Shall

-Wise

Don't add this suffix to a noun in hope of converting it into an adverb; in other words, avoid a locution such as *contrariwise* or *studywise.* Check your dictionary for appropriate existing words with this suffix, such as *clockwise.*

Would've

Don't let the sound of this contraction when spoken seduce you into writing *would of.* This also holds true for *could've* and *should've* (*could of* and *should of* are incorrect).

Your / you're

Your is the possessive adjective (*your room*); **you're** is the contraction for *you are.*

Index